CW01429525

PHILOSOPHY AND INTERNATIONAL LAW

In *Philosophy and International Law*, David Lefkowitz examines core questions of legal and political philosophy through critical reflection on contemporary international law. Is international law really law? The answer depends on what makes law. Does the existence of law depend on coercive enforcement? Or on institutions such as courts? On fidelity to the requirements of the rule of law? Or is it conformity to moral standards? Answers to these questions are essential for determining the truth or falsity of international legal skepticism, and understanding why it matters. Is international law morally defensible? This book makes a start to answering that question by engaging with recent debates on the nature and grounds of human rights, the moral justifiability of the law of war, the concept of a crime against humanity, the moral basis of universal jurisdiction, the propriety of international law governing secession, and the justice of international trade law.

David Lefkowitz is Professor of Philosophy and Philosophy, Politics, Economics and Law (PPEL) at the University of Richmond. He is the founding coordinator of the PPEL Program and also has served as a Rockefeller Visiting Faculty Fellow at Princeton University, Class of 1958 Ethics Fellow at the US Naval Academy, and Isaac Manasseh Meyer Visiting Fellow at the National University of Singapore.

CAMBRIDGE INTRODUCTIONS TO PHILOSOPHY AND LAW

Series Editors

Brian H. Bix
University of Minnesota

William A. Edmundson
Georgia State University

This introductory series of books provides concise studies of the philosophical foundations of law, of perennial topics in the philosophy of law, and of important and opposing schools of thought. The series is aimed principally at students in philosophy, law, and political science.

Philosophy and International Law

A CRITICAL INTRODUCTION

DAVID LEFKOWITZ

University of Richmond

CAMBRIDGE
UNIVERSITY PRESS

CAMBRIDGE
UNIVERSITY PRESS

University Printing House, Cambridge CB2 8BS, United Kingdom

One Liberty Plaza, 20th Floor, New York, NY 10006, USA

477 Williamstown Road, Port Melbourne, VIC 3207, Australia

314–321, 3rd Floor, Plot 3, Splendor Forum, Jasola District Centre,
New Delhi – 110025, India

79 Anson Road, #06–04/06, Singapore 079906

Cambridge University Press is part of the University of Cambridge.

It furthers the University's mission by disseminating knowledge in the pursuit of
education, learning, and research at the highest international levels of excellence.

www.cambridge.org
Information on this title: www.cambridge.org/9781107138773
DOI: 10.1017/9781316481653

© David Lefkowitz 2020

This publication is in copyright. Subject to statutory exception
and to the provisions of relevant collective licensing agreements,
no reproduction of any part may take place without the written
permission of Cambridge University Press.

First published 2020

A catalogue record for this publication is available from the British Library.

ISBN 978-1-107-13877-3 Hardback
ISBN 978-1-316-50358-4 Paperback

Cambridge University Press has no responsibility for the persistence or accuracy of
URLs for external or third-party internet websites referred to in this publication
and does not guarantee that any content on such websites is, or will remain,
accurate or appropriate.

For Alli

Contents

1

Introduction

This book serves three purposes. The first is to introduce readers to certain core questions in the philosophy of law, including:

- What is law? What distinguishes law as a normative social practice from other types of normative social practice? What makes the statement "This society possesses a legal order" true or false? Does the existence of law depend on coercion? Or on certain types of institution, such as courts? Or on conformity to certain procedural or substantive rules, or to specific moral standards? If so, why, and what is the nature of this dependence?
- What is *the* law (in this particular community, or this particular case)? What are the truth conditions for statements such as "Your action is a violation of the law" or "You have no legal right to give away this book?" Are such claims warranted solely by certain social facts? If so, which ones? Or must moral considerations also figure in the proper identification of the law? Or indeed, are legal norms simply a subset of moral norms?
- Is there a moral duty to obey the law simply because it *is* the law? Under what conditions, if any, does the fact that a given act is illegal necessarily provide us with a moral reason not to perform that act?

These are some of the questions that comprise a philosophical investigation of the nature and normativity of law. In reflecting on the answers to them, we typically consider how well they cohere with the legal order most familiar to us, which is usually the domestic legal order of the state in which we are citizens.[1] While this approach has its virtues, it also suffers from certain limitations. Familiarity with a particular legal order can make it difficult to distinguish between features that are typical or essential properties of law in general and those that are only typical or essential features of a particular kind of legal order (or even just one example of a particular kind of legal order). Relatedly, it may make it harder to motivate certain

---

[1] Of course, philosophical reflection may lead us to revise our belief that our state possesses a genuine legal order.

types of question, or answers to them, particularly for those with a limited experience of the world and the many forms of social organization it contains. Considering the questions set out above in the context of international law serves to diminish these shortcomings. Furthermore, it tends to add a comparative dimension to the investigation of the nature and normativity of law. The differences between international and domestic law can deepen our understanding of the relationship between law and coercion, morality, specialization, and so on. It can also help us recognize why questions regarding the nature and normativity of law matter.

The second aim of this book is to acquaint readers with recent work by legal and political philosophers on conceptual and moral questions specific to particular domains of international law. For instance, in critically reflecting on international human rights law, how should we understand the concept of a human right? Similarly, a proper grasp of the concept of a crime against humanity seems to be a necessary condition for a sound moral assessment of the definition of that crime set out in international law (e.g., in the Rome Statute of the International Criminal Court). As for the justice of specific international legal rules and institutions, philosophers have recently questioned whether certain core features of the law of war are morally justifiable, whether international law ought to promote free or fair trade, whether the absence of an international legal right to unilateral secession is a moral defect in our practice of global governance, and much else besides. Critical moral reflection on the content of international legal norms and the design of international legal institutions is, or at least ought to be, central to international or global political philosophy.

The third goal that informs this book is the advancement of the debate on many of the topics discussed herein. Specifically, I defend a reading of H.L.A. Hart's views on international law at odds with the one defended by many contemporary legal philosophers and international legal theorists. I also offer a reading of Ronald Dworkin's philosophy of international law that largely renders it immune to the various criticisms that are leveled against it. The deeper challenge to Dworkin's characterization of international law as genuine law lies in the dubious quality of the international rule of law, or so I suggest.[2] How we ought to understand the concept of legitimacy, and the possible bases for a moral duty to obey international law, are two additional questions to which I offer original answers. Turning to the justice of specific international legal rules, I advance novel arguments in the debates over the proper understanding of a crime against humanity, the moral grounds of universal jurisdiction, the relationship between the morality and the law of war, and the moral justifiability of international law's current stance vis-à-vis unilateral secession.

---

[2]   This argument is developed in greater detail in David Lefkowitz, "A New Philosophy for International Legal Skepticism?" Draft on file with author.

The first half of this book is organized around the question "is international law really law?"[3] As H.L.A. Hart notes in the introduction to *The Concept of Law*, the person who poses this question does not intend to deny the existence of the social practice commonly labeled "international law." Rather, she wants to know whether that practice possesses some property or properties that warrant the claim that it is *law*, presumably because she thinks that something of explanatory or normative significance turns on the answer. Following Hart, then, we should delay giving any answer to the question "is international law really law?" until we have found out what it is that puzzles the person who poses it. "What more do they want to know, and why do they want to know it?"[4]

Let us answer these questions in reverse order. Those who question whether international law is really law, or simply assert that it is not, typically do so as part of a practical argument. That is, they advance a skeptical take on international law's status as genuine law to support a particular conclusion regarding what some agent, such as a state (official), should or should not do. Implicit in this skeptical challenge to international law is an assumption that law makes, or at least is capable of making, a distinctive contribution to human deliberation, and so to the production of social order. When a person argues that international law is not really law, she implies that international law does not, and perhaps cannot, matter in the way that law matters.[5]

Consider, now, the question of what more an international legal skeptic might wish to know. What assumptions regarding the nature or concept of law lead her to infer from certain observations that the label "international law" is a misnomer? One possibility is that the skeptic presumes an analytical connection between law and coercive enforcement. In Chapter 2, we consider two versions of this claim. The first is the legal philosopher John Austin's characterization of law as the command of a sovereign, or in Hart's apt phrase, as orders backed by threats. The second treats the mode of enforcement found in the modern state as a necessary condition for the existence of law. If true, each of these conceptual claims provides a sound basis for international legal skepticism. As we will see, however, there are compelling reasons to reject them both.

In Chapter 3, we investigate H.L.A. Hart's characterization of law as the union of primary and secondary rules, and its implications for international law's status as genuine law. While Hart is frequently identified as an international legal skeptic, that conclusion rests on a misreading of his analysis of international law, or in some cases, a misreading of his analysis of law. Hart does not deny that international law is law, only that it constitutes a *legal system*. Properly understood, this is a claim few of

---

[3] Most international lawyers and legal scholars, and a fair number of philosophers, will roll their eyes at this question, but that is likely because they misunderstand its import. See Carmen Pavel and David Lefkowitz, "Skeptical Challenges to International Law," *Philosophy Compass* 13, 8 (2018): 3.

[4] H.L.A. Hart, *The Concept of Law*, *3rd Edition* (Oxford: Oxford University Press, 2012), p. 5. [Originally published in 1961.]

[5] See Oona Hathaway and Scott Shapiro, "Outcasting: Enforcement in Domestic and International Law," *Yale L.J.* 121 (2011): 255–6.

his critics will deny. Whether it (fully) accounts for the persistence of international legal skepticism, as Hart seems to suggest, is a more contestable claim.

The arguments of Hart's most prominent critic, Ronald Dworkin, are the subject of Chapter 4. We begin by considering his criticisms of Hart and, more generally, of legal positivism; the view that the existence of law depends on certain social facts and not (necessarily) its moral merits. We then examine Dworkin's alternative analysis of the nature of law, and his argument, informed by that analysis, that international law is indeed a genuine legal order. As will become clear, the success of the latter argument depends on the international legal order exhibiting sufficient fidelity to the ideal of the rule of law. Indeed, the same condition holds if we accept a legal positivist account of the nature of law. In Chapter 5, therefore, we investigate the rule of law, including competing accounts of the elements that comprise it and the value of government in accordance with that ideal. We then briefly examine various grounds for questioning the existence of an international rule of law.

One reason to take seriously Hart's advice that we clarify the source of an individual's international legal skepticism before responding to it is that her choice of words may fail to accurately convey her concern. For example, a bit of probing may reveal that that the locus of her concern is not international law's status as law, but rather its legitimacy. Whether, and to what extent, that worry is warranted is the subject of Chapter 6. We begin with an examination of the concept of legitimacy and its relationship to a moral duty to obey the law. We then consider four possible grounds for international law's legitimacy: enhancing its subjects' ability to act as they have most reason to act, the consent of those it claims as subjects, considerations of fair play, and international law's democratic credentials. The chapter concludes with an examination of reasons why we should care about international law's legitimacy; indeed, why from a moral point of view increasing the international legal order's legitimacy might even take priority over making it more just.

In the second half of the book we shift our attention from international legal skepticism to contemporary philosophical investigations of specific international legal regimes. In Chapter 7, we engage with a recent debate among two schools of legal and political philosophers regarding the nature and grounds of human rights. Orthodox theorists argue that human rights are moral rights possessed by all human beings simply in virtue of their humanity. Political-practice theorists, in contrast, argue that human rights are constitutive elements of an ongoing attempt to reconceive state sovereignty and the international political order to which it is integral. This political undertaking, which includes the creation, application, and enforcement of international human rights law, provides the proper object of a philosophy of human rights. The bulk of this chapter is devoted to a critical examination of attempts by political-practice theorists to demonstrate the limited relevance of orthodox accounts of human rights to morally justifying international human rights practice (again, including international human rights law). It concludes with a brief consideration of the role that appeals to objective moral principles should play within that practice.

In Chapter 8, we assess four accounts of the relationship between the morality and the law of war and the implications that each has for the retention or replacement of two key features of the latter: the equality of combatants, and noncombatant or civilian immunity. Traditional just war theorists such as Michael Walzer defend these features of the law of war on the grounds that they mirror the content of the true morality of war. In contrast, revisionist just war theorists such as Jeff McMahan, Adil Haque, and David Rodin argue that in its commitment to the equality of combatants and noncombatant immunity, the law of war deviates from the content of the true morality of war. While Rodin argues that the law of war ought to be reformed so as to mirror the (revisionist) morality of war, McMahan and Haque both defend it on the grounds that combatants will generally do better at acting as morality requires if they follow the existing law of war than if they attempt to guide their conduct according to the (revisionist) morality of war. The last theorists we consider, Henry Shue and Janina Dill, reject the assumption shared by all of the aforementioned theorists that the law of war should aim to minimize the violation of individual rights. Instead, they argue that it should serve the humanitarian goal of reducing the harm war causes. The law of war's commitment to the equality of combatants and noncombatant immunity is morally justifiable, then, if it reflects the optimal balance between restrictions on how combatants may fight and their willingness to comply with those rules in their pursuit of self-preservation and victory in war.

Our exploration in Chapter 9 of philosophical contributions to international criminal law focuses on the concept of a crime against humanity and the justifiability of universal jurisdiction over those who commit such a crime. In what sense, if any, are crimes against humanity wrongs done to "humanity?" Does the label "crime against humanity" refer to a distinctive wrong committed by those who perform such acts? If not, what distinguishes crimes against humanity from other types of crime? In the first half of this chapter, we critically examine several competing analyses of the concept of a crime against humanity and the answers they provide to these questions. In the remainder of the chapter, we consider two approaches to justifying the international prosecution of crimes against humanity. The first grounds it in the dangers that such crimes pose to all human beings, while the second appeals to an (emerging) moral or political global community that makes perpetrators of crimes against humanity answerable to courts that act on behalf of all humanity.

Secession and the claims to territory it raises are the subject of Chapter 10. Following some preliminary remarks on the concept of secession and its status in international law, we examine competing answers to two questions that any theory of state secession must address. First, what sort of actor enjoys a prima facie moral right to secede, and in virtue of what features or considerations does that actor do so? Second, on what particular territory is an actor with a right to secede permitted to exercise that right? We then examine arguments for and against several international legal norms we might adopt to regulate unilateral secession, drawing on both moral theories of secession and empirically informed conjectures regarding the incentives those norms might create for various international and domestic actors.

Finally, in Chapter 11, we consider the moral justifiability of some of the international legal rules that govern international trade. Our primary focus is on the moral standards we ought to use to critically evaluate those rules or proposals for their reform. Thus we investigate several moral arguments for free trade, such as the claim that it provides an especially effective mechanism for alleviating poverty, and several arguments in defense of restrictions or conditions on trade, including the moral permissible of partiality to compatriots and the right of those whose cooperation makes international trade possible to a fair share of the benefits it yields. In the final section of this chapter, we explore the argument that by importing and consuming oil and other natural resources from countries ruled by tyrants, we violate existing international law and engage in trade in stolen goods.

Given the wide range of topics addressed in this text, the discussion herein can hardly do more than scratch the surface of what philosophers have had to say about them, let alone international legal theorists, political scientists, economists, sociologists, and historians. To this inevitable limitation must be added the cost of my decision to forgo a broader survey of schools, approaches, and positions in favor of a deeper exploration of the arguments advanced by a relatively small number of scholars. But as the title of this book makes clear, my primary goal is to offer the reader a useful *introduction* to some of the core questions in legal and political philosophy as they bear on the practice of global governance commonly referred to as international law. The reader should not infer from the absence of any discussion of a particular theorist, school of legal or political philosophy, or feature of international law that they are unimportant. Rather, my hope for this book is that those who read it will be inspired to dive deeper into the field and engage directly with the many questions and theorists it leaves out.

It is a pleasure to recognize and thank the many people who have assisted me in bringing this book to fruition. Brian Bix and William Edmundson offered me the opportunity to write it, and waited patiently while I took too long to do so. My colleagues in the Ethics Working Group at the University of Richmond have provided invaluable feedback on drafts of several chapters. I am particularly grateful to Richard Dagger, Jess Flanigan, Javier Hidalgo, Rob Phillips, Jeppe von Platz, Terry Price, and Steven Simon for conversations on secession, as well as the concept of a crime against humanity. Others who have provided helpful comments on one or more of the arguments advanced in this book include Edward Barrett, Samantha Besson, Adam Betz, Allen Buchanan, Alejandro Chehtman, Thomas Christiano, Win-chiat Lee, Matthew Lister, David Luban, Frank Garcia, Jose Luis Marti, Margaret Moore, Colleen Murphy, Terry Nardin, Carmen Pavel, Steven Ratner, Mitt Regan, Massimo Renzo, Nicole Roughan, Mortimer Sellers, Anna Stilz, John

Tasioulas, and George Tsai. A special thanks to Joshua Kassner and Bas van der Vossen for serving as sounding boards for the entire project. I also owe a debt of gratitude to the students enrolled in my Philosophy of Law and Normative Theory and International Law classes, as conversations with them have deepened my understanding of many of the topics discussed in this book.

Portions of this book were completed while I served as an Isaac Manasseh Meyer Visiting Research Fellow at the National University of Singapore, and as the Class of 1958 Rorer Ethical Leadership Visiting Fellow at the United States Naval Academy's Stockdale Center for Ethical Leadership. I am grateful to both institutions for their generosity; nevertheless, the views expressed herein are strictly my own.

I also wish to express my gratitude for the permission to reprint some earlier work. Chapter 3 includes material previously published in "What Makes a Social Order Primitive? In Defense of Hart's Take on International Law," *Legal Theory* 23, 4 (2017): 258–82, reprinted by permission of Cambridge University Press. Chapter 6 revises and expands the arguments first presented in "The Legitimacy of International Law," in *Global Political Theory*, eds. David Held and Pietro Maffettone (Cambridge: Polity Press, 2016), reprinted by permission of Polity Press. It also includes material previously published in "The Principle of Fairness and States' Duty to Obey International Law," *Canadian Journal of Law and Jurisprudence* 24, 2 (2011): 327–46, reprinted by permission of Cambridge University Press. A portion of the argument presented in Chapter 10 first appeared in "International Law, Institutional Moral Reasoning, and Secession," *Law and Philosophy* 37, 4 (2018): 385–413, reprinted by permission of Springer Nature.

Over the years I have had the good fortune to learn from a series of exceptional teachers and mentors, including Carl Wellman, Larry May, Judith Lichtenberg, William Galston, Samuel Kerstein, Christopher Morris, Terry McConnell, Michael Zimmerman, Andrew Altman, and Christopher Wellman. Any errors in this book are surely attributable to the student. I am deeply grateful to my in-laws, Mark and Marilyn Wetterhahn, for helping me to pursue my calling as a philosopher, and to my parents, Paul and Janice Lefkowitz, who have supported me in ways big and small for as long as I can remember. My appreciation for all they have done for me only grows as I raise my own children, Brie and JJ, who I thank for making me smile even on days when writing this book felt like a Sisyphean task. Finally, I am deeply grateful for the love and friendship of my wife, Alli, my best student and teacher.

2

John Austin: Enforcement and International Law

For those educated in the Anglo-Saxon tradition of legal philosophy, the character-ization of law defended by the nineteenth-century English legal theorist John Austin often serves as the entry point to discussions of both the concept of law and the status of international law as genuine law. This chapter begins with a brief description of Austin's analysis of law, often referred to as the command theory of law, and the international legal skepticism that follows from it. We then examine H.L.A. Hart's many criticisms of Austin's account of law. If successful, these criticisms undermine one basis for international legal skepticism. After all, if the command theory does not provide a compelling analysis of law, then the fact that international law lacks certain features the command theory treats as essential to law does not warrant the conclusion that it is not really law. Yet even if we reject Austin's analysis of law, we may remain sympathetic to the idea that the absence of any actor over and above individual states ready and able to coerce them to comply with the demands of international law undermines its claims to be law properly so-called. In the final section of this chapter, we consider a response to this skeptical challenge, namely, that it mistakenly assumes that the enforcement of the law must take the form it does in a modern state.

I AUSTIN AND THE COMMAND THEORY OF LAW

Austin maintains that positive law, or law properly so-called, consists in the com-mand of a sovereign.[1] As Austin understands the concept of a command, A commands B if and only if (1) A expresses a desire that B act or not act in a particular way, and (2) A is willing and able to impose a sanction on B, meaning a harm or an evil, in the event that B fails to act as A wishes.[2] By issuing a command to B, A places B under a duty or obligation; indeed, on Austin's account an actor has a duty or an obligation only if she is the target of a command. The duty or obligation

---

[1] John Austin, *The Province of Jurisprudence Determined*, ed. Wilfrid E. Rumble (Cambridge: Cambridge University Press, 1995), pp. 19, 165. [Originally published in 1832.]

[2] Ibid, p. 21.

counts as a legal one if and only if the actor who issues the command is a sovereign. A qualifies as a sovereign on Austin's account if and only if the bulk of a given society (B, C, D, etc.) habitually obeys A, and A does not habitually obey any other agent.[3]

Austin's analysis seems to capture certain features many people associate with law. For example, the claim that law properly so-called is created or posited by human beings, not an objective feature of the universe we discover, resonates with the common experience of the law as subject to regular revision by legislators and judges. Domestic criminal law may appear to consist of Austinian commands: that is, the government's expression of a desire that people not perform certain acts, together with a willingness and ability to impose a sanction on those who do. Finally, Austin's characterization of law provides a seemingly plausible explanation for the fact that the world consists of many distinct and independent legal orders; for example, the Canadian and US legal systems. People who live in Canada habitually act as the Canadian government commands them to act, while people who live in the United States habitually act as the US government commands them to act, and neither the Canadian government nor the US government habitually obeys any other agent.

As Austin observes, his analysis of the concept of law implies that international law is not really law:

> International law, or the law obtaining between nations, regards the conduct of sovereigns considered as related to one another. And hence it inevitably follows that the law obtaining between nations is not positive law: for every positive law is set by a given sovereign to a person or persons in a state of subjection to its author.[4]

Given the absence in international society of an actor habitually obeyed by the bulk of its members, but who is not in a habit of obedience to any other agent, so-called international law only qualifies as positive morality. Furthermore, Austin maintains that:

> [T]he law obtaining between nations is law (improperly so called) set by general opinion. The duties which it imposes are enforced by moral sanctions: by fear on the part of nations, or by fear on the part of sovereigns, of provoking general hostility, and incurring its probable evils, in case they shall violate maxims generally received and respected.[5]

In fact, it appears that on Austin's understanding of the concept of a duty, international legal norms do not even generate duties of positive morality unless and until one sovereign invokes them while issuing a command to another. Only in such cases is a general sentiment or feeling among nations that a certain (type of) act should or should not be performed transformed into a command.

---

[3] Ibid, p. 166.
[4] Ibid, p. 171.
[5] Ibid.

One might try to rebut Austin's international legal skepticism by contesting his descriptive claims. For example, one could argue that the enormous increase in treaty law since Austin wrote in the mid-nineteenth century significantly reduces the force of his complaint that (so-called) international law consists only of maxims generally received and respected, rather than determinate rules of conduct. Nevertheless, Austin's assertion that international society lacks a sovereign (as he understands that concept) remains true. Whether we think of international political society as composed of states or of all the individuals on the planet, there is no human agent – no ruler or government – to which the bulk of them are in the habit of obedience. A better strategy then, is to challenge Austin's account of the nature or concept of law.

II HART'S CRITICISMS OF THE COMMAND THEORY OF LAW

Austin's conclusion that international law is not law properly so-called follows only if he offers a compelling analysis of the nature or concept of law. That analysis has been subject to devastating criticism, however, most famously by H.L.A. Hart in his seminal book *The Concept of Law*.[6] Indeed, Hart's criticisms reveal even the aforementioned reasons for accepting Austin's analysis of law to be mistaken or confused. In elaborating the shortcomings of Austin's account of law, Hart draws on what he takes to be his audience's understanding or experience of municipal law, or the law of a moderately well-functioning modern state.[7] Like Austin and just about every other modern theorist of the nature or concept of law, Hart assumes that any satisfactory analysis of the concept of law must be able to render municipal law intelligible to those who practice or are subject to it. If Hart successfully demonstrates that Austin's analysis of law either fails to capture or misrepresents central features of municipal law, then we have a compelling reason to reject that analysis. This conclusion entails, in turn, that we ought to reject Austin's argument for international legal skepticism, since that argument presupposes the truth of his analysis of the nature or concept of law.

Hart levels three objections against the claim that law consists in Austinian commands, or as Hart puts it, orders backed by threats.[8] First, many commonplace laws do not demand the performance of particular acts; instead, they empower actors to make changes to their legal rights and duties with respect to people, inanimate objects, and other things. For example, legal rules governing the creation of a valid will do not require that individuals create a will; rather, they merely specify what an

---

[6] H.L.A. Hart, *The Concept of Law*, 3rd Edition (Oxford: Oxford University Press, 2012). [Originally published in 1961.]

[7] Even that description may be too generous, since Hart relies almost exclusively on English and US law. In his defense, however, the original intended audience for *The Concept of Law* was law students at the University of Oxford.

[8] Hart, *Concept*, pp. 26–44.

actor must do *if* she wishes to realize a specific allocation of legal rights to her property on her death.

In response, it might be argued that power conferring rules such as those involved in the making of a will should be understood as orders issued by a sovereign to subordinate legal officials, instructing them to enforce the terms of the will if and only if the manner of its creation satisfies certain conditions. Hart rejects this response on the grounds that it misrepresents the self-understanding of those who exercise power-conferring rules:

> Rules conferring private powers must, if they are to be understood, be looked at from the point of view of those who exercise them. Such power conferring rules are thought of, spoken of, and used in social life differently from rules which impose duties, and they are valued for different reasons. What other tests for difference in character could there be?[9]

While the theoretical virtue of simplicity should inform the attempt to characterize the concept of law, it must not do so at the price of distorting the object of theoretical inquiry. Moreover, Hart also contends that the above response ignores a crucial respect – perhaps *the* crucial respect – in which law contributes to the production of social order:

> The principal functions of the law as a means of social control are not to be seen in private litigation or prosecutions, which represent vital but still ancillary provisions for the failures of the system. It is to be seen in the diverse ways in which the law is used to control, to guide, and to plan life out of court.[10]

As we will see, this understanding of how law shapes human conduct figures centrally in Hart's own characterization of law as a system of rules. The key point to note here is that if we reflect on how law shapes our conduct *without assuming that it must do so by threatening the imposition of sanctions*, we will immediately recognize that it often does so by enhancing our ability to shape our own lives. As the example of law governing the creation of a valid will illustrates, law often serves to specify what counts as entering into a certain type of relationship with others, and renders more precise the content of the rights and duties possessed by those who do so.

Suppose, however, that a person fails to follow the procedures for the creation of a valid will. Does she not suffer a sanction as a result, and, if so, does this not lend some credence to the characterization of power-conferring rules as Austinian commands? Perhaps it would if noncompliance with the rules for creating a valid will resulted in a sanction, but it does not. As Hart points out, we do not describe a person who fails to comply with a power-conferring rule as acting illegally, or committing a legal wrong. Rather her act is merely legally invalid, an unsuccessful attempt to

---

[9]　Hart, *Concept*, p. 41.
[10]　Ibid, p. 40.

make some change to her own or others' legal rights or duties. While this person may suffer a harm or evil as a result of her failure to follow the law, that harm will not count as a sanction in Austin's sense. This is so because, on Austin's account, the purpose of a sanction, the reason why legal officials threaten to impose them on those who disobey the law, is to motivate individuals to act as the law directs. If Hart maintains correctly that the law does not care whether people create legally valid wills, then whatever evil may follow from a person's failure to do so cannot be properly described as the law's (or legislator's) attempt to motivate people to act as it desires. In sum, whereas Hart treats any harm that befalls a person who fails to comply with a power-conferring rule as incidental to that rule's status as law, Austin must depict it as necessary, a feat he can accomplish only by distorting the common understanding of such rules.

Hart's second objection to characterizing law as orders backed by threats is that it wrongly precludes the possibility of a legislator creating self-binding legal obligations. Given Austin's account of a command, the idea of commanding oneself is paradoxical. Yet as the case of promise making clearly demonstrates, a person can create obligations that bind him or her. Anticipating his own analysis of law, Hart observes that the legislator "like the giver of a promise . . . exercises powers conferred by rules: very often he may, as the promisor *must*, fall within their ambit."[11]

The third and final criticism Hart raises to Austin's characterization of law as composed of commands is that it misrepresents customary law. Austin maintains that customary rules become law only when judges use them to settle legal disputes and the sovereign to whom those judges are subordinate acquiesces in their doing so, for only then is obedience to the customary rule (implicitly) commanded, and so law. Once more Hart maintains that this description distorts the actual practice of law. Even on the first occasion she employs a customary rule to settle a legal dispute, a judge does not take herself to be making new law but rather to be applying existing law.

In light of the foregoing criticisms, one might concede that Austin errs in maintaining that *all* law consists of commands, yet still maintain that he offers the correct account of one crucial category of laws, namely those that impose duties or obligations. However, this conclusion rests on the assumption that Austin offers an accurate analysis of the concept of a duty or obligation, a position that Hart disputes. Recall that for Austin, one has a duty or obligation if and only if some agent stands ready to impose a sanction on you in the event you do not act as he or she wishes you to act. Yet Hart observes that there is no contradiction in asserting that a person has a legal obligation to perform some act even in a case where we can predict with total certainty that he or she will not be subject to any sanction for failing to do so.[12] In some cases, the fact that no sanction will be forthcoming may entail that the actor has no prudential reason to discharge his obligation. But it is one thing to deny that an agent has a prudential reason to fulfill his legal obligation, and quite another to hold that he has no legal obligation at all. We should not confuse claims regarding the existence of a legal obligation with claims regarding the existence of a reason to do that which one has a legal obligation to do. Hart admits that "at least in a municipal system it may well be true that unless *in general* sanctions were likely to be exacted from offenders, there would be little or no point in making particular statements about a person's [legal] obligations."[13] Yet Hart maintains it is a mistake to infer from (1) the need for some general level of enforcement if talk of legal obligations is to serve any practical purpose, that (2) in each and every case, the statement "A has a legal obligation to phi" is true if and only if there is some likelihood that A will suffer a legal sanction in the event he fails to phi. Put another way, the necessity of enforcement pertains to the legal system as a whole, not to every application of individual norms to individual actors.

More importantly, Hart points out that an analysis of obligation in terms of the likelihood that a person will suffer a sanction "obscures the fact that, where rules exist, deviations from them are not merely grounds for a prediction that hostile reactions will follow or that a court will apply sanctions to those who break them, but are also a reason or justification for such reaction and for applying sanctions."[14] Hart's insight here is that we do not use law only – or, for many of us, primarily – to calculate the likely prudential costs of engaging in a certain type of conduct. Rather, we use it to hold one another, and ourselves, accountable; for example, by invoking the law to criticize another's conduct, or to justify our own. For example, an individual's commission of a crime does not directly cause a court to punish him; rather, his illegal conduct figures centrally in the court's judgment that he *ought* to be punished, or that punishment is *appropriate*, and it is this judgment that explains why the court punishes him. The analysis of legal obligation simply in terms of a causal relationship between performing a certain type of conduct and some better than random likelihood of suffering a sanction appears compelling only if we adopt a standpoint external to the community whose law it is. However, it ignores the perspective of participants in that community, those who use the law "to guide, and to plan life out of court," which is to say, largely independent of prudential calculations regarding the law's enforcement. As we will see, Hart thinks this internal perspective crucial to understanding the nature or concept of law.

As part of an analysis of the concept of law, Austin's notion of a sovereign fares no better than does his notion of command.[15] A sovereign, recall, is an actor most members of a society habitually obey and who does not habitually obey any other actor. Hart points out that if we characterize sovereignty in terms of a habit of obedience, then we are unable to account for the apparent continuity of a legal

[13] Ibid.
[14] Ibid.
[15] Ibid, pp. 50–71.

system in the face of changes in those who govern. Canadian Federal Law, for example, certainly seems to continue to be in effect, that is, to exist as the very same legal system, through a complete turnover in the membership of its Parliament. If the existence of law depends on the existence of a habit of obedience to the lawmakers, however, then for some time after the new legislators take power there will be no law, for Canadians will not yet have developed a habit of obedience to them. Moreover, once they do so (or, indeed, *if* they do so), there will be a new Canadian Federal Law, quite similar in content to the one that preceded it, perhaps, but distinguishable from it by appeal to the identity of the person or persons to whom the bulk of Canadians are in a habit of obedience.

The foregoing example also highlights the difficulty Austin has in accounting for the persistence of law: the fact that judges, for example, regularly apply laws enacted by deceased lawmakers. It strains credulity to maintain that what explains the propriety of judges doing so is that the present population has a habit of obedience to a long-dead legislator. Austin employs the same strategy to circumvent this challenge as he does in his treatment of customary law: he argues that the present status as law of a rule enacted by some past sovereign is a function of a decision by the current sovereign, the actor or actors most members of society do habitually obey, not to overturn a judge's application of that rule. In response, Hart reiterates his criticism of Austin's account of customary law, namely, that it conflicts with the widespread view that in such cases judges are applying already existing law, not making new law. He also makes a second, telling, observation: Austin can offer no explanation for the fact that while courts frequently apply old laws that have not been repealed, they never apply laws that were repealed by a former sovereign. Were Austin's explanation for the persistence of law correct, we would expect that, at least occasionally, a judge would settle a case by appeal to a law that had been repealed by a former sovereign, in the belief that whatever the sovereign who repealed the law might have thought, the current sovereign would endorse the judge's use of the rule (and so tacitly command it). Yet we never observe this phenomenon, which gives us reason to suspect that Austin has not offered us a proper analysis of the persistence of law.

An Austinian sovereign necessarily enjoys unlimited legislative power. This conclusion follows from the claim that an actor counts as a sovereign only if he or she does not habitually obey another actor's commands. Yet there appear to be many examples of what are clearly legal systems in which no actor enjoys legally unlimited authority. The US Constitution, for example, restricts the power of all levels of government in the United States to limit speech, to require (a particular) religious practice, or to employ certain methods of punishment. Perhaps what this shows is only that it is not the US government that is sovereign, but the people. Americans, it might be thought, enjoy an unlimited power to make law, including any changes they might wish to make to the US Constitution. But how can the American people be in a habit of obedience to themselves? Austin is committed to such a claim, yet it seems not only descriptively false but also conceptually confused. Neither will it do to distinguish between Americans in their private capacity, who are subject to law, and Americans in their public capacity, who as citizens make law. For, as Hart points out, the concept of a citizen as it figures in this claim presupposes rules that specify who counts as a citizen (or who can and does occupy the office of citizen), the legislative powers enjoyed by those individuals, and what counts as the exercise of those powers. These rules cannot be the product of citizens' exercise of their legislative power, since they must already be in place in order for there to be citizens, as well as acts that count as the exercise of legislative power. In sum, either the US legal system is not law properly so-called, or Austin errs in claiming that a necessary condition for the existence of law is that it consists of commands issued by an actor with unlimited legislative power.

In light of Hart's detailed critique of Austin's analysis of law, we are now in a position to challenge the latter's claim that international law is not law properly so-called. Austin draws that conclusion on the grounds that international society lacks a sovereign (as he understands that concept) and that its content is akin to rules of etiquette, namely "maxims generally received and respected," rather than commands. We have compelling reasons to doubt that an Austinian sovereign is a necessary condition for the existence of a legal order, however, and therefore we should not take the absence of an international sovereign as a reason to deny international law's status as genuine law. Likewise, we ought to reject Austin's analysis of law as a species of command (or, more accurately, as orders backed by threats), partly because it ignores or distorts the nature of power-conferring laws, but perhaps more importantly in this context because it misconstrues what it is to have a legal obligation. Since we should not conceive of law as Austinian commands, the fact that international law rarely takes such a form gives us no reason to accept international legal skepticism. Of course, none of this proves that international law *is* really law, neither does it rule out the possibility that there may be other reasons for denying it that status. Still, it is no small thing to conclusively rebut what was once widely recognized as a good argument for international legal skepticism, and one that still strikes many newcomers to legal philosophy or international law as plausible, or even obviously true.

III INTERNATIONAL LAW AND THE MODERN STATE CONCEPTION OF ENFORCEMENT

Most contemporary legal philosophers agree that Hart advances a compelling rebuttal to the conceptual connection Austin draws between law and enforcement. Yet making a difference to what people do seems to be a necessary condition for the existence of law. After all, it is odd to describe as the law of some society S a system of norms that never has any effect on the conduct of S's members. And we might well think that as an *empirical* matter, law's ability to make a difference to what people do, to contribute to the production of social order, depends on the likelihood that it will be enforced.

Why might we draw that conclusion? For starters, many of us may have been tempted to break some law or other and refrained from doing so only because we feared having the law enforced against us. Other laws may prohibit acts that *we* would never consider doing, but that we (rightly) believe certain others would perform were the laws prohibiting them never enforced. In other cases, we stand ready to abide by the law, but only on the condition that (most) others will do so as well, and a certain probability of enforcement provides us with assurance that they will. At a minimum, this is true of laws that facilitate the production of public goods such as clean air, where individuals can receive the full benefits of others' compliance with the law without having to likewise limit their freedom. Finally, we may be aware of communities where enforcement of the law is so lax that the people in those communities feel the need to "take the law into their own hands," that is, to enforce it themselves, oftentimes with the consequence that the content of the actual rules that regulate interactions among people in those communities differs in various ways from the law "on the books." Although these anecdotal observations warrant more careful investigation, they suffice to justify a presumption that law's capacity to make a difference to how people live their lives depends on the likelihood that it will be enforced.

When we think about enforcement in the kinds of cases described above, many of us immediately picture police officers, agents of the FBI or Scotland Yard, correctional officers, or, in emergencies, soldiers. Indeed, with the exception of members of the last group, we often refer to these actors under the general label "law enforcement officers." Yet the international legal order has no police force, no correctional officers, and no army, no agents of its own who can affect people's behavior by using or threatening to use physical force against them. Indeed, the absence of such agents is one of the most salient differences between international law and the legal system of a modern state. It may seem quite reasonable, then, to conclude that because it lacks the mechanisms for enforcing the law characteristic of all moderately well-functioning municipal legal orders, international law is not really law.

This natural but mistaken argument for international legal skepticism rests on what Oona Hathaway and Scott Shapiro label the Modern State Conception (henceforth, the MSC) of law. According to the MSC:

> [A] regime counts as a legal one only if it seeks to affect behavior in the manner that modern states do: it must enjoy a monopoly over the use of physical force and employ this monopoly to enforce its rules. The Modern State Conception, in other words, requires legal systems to (1) possess *internal* enforcement mechanisms (2) that use the threat and exercise of *physical force*.[16]

---

[16] Oona A. Hathaway and Scott J. Shapiro, "Outcasting: Enforcement in Domestic and International Law," 121 *Yale L. Journal* 252 (2011): 268–9.

The MSC offers an unduly narrow characterization of enforcement, Hathaway and Shapiro argue, one that conflates the concept of law enforcement with one, contingent, form that law enforcement can take.

To support their claim, Hathaway and Shapiro describe in detail what they take to be two incontrovertible examples of legal systems that do not satisfy the MSC: Medieval Icelandic Law, and Classical Canon Law (that is, the law of the Catholic Church). Both of these legal systems largely relied on externalized outcasting rather than the internalized use of force to uphold the law. Enforcement is internal when it is undertaken by an agent of the legal regime, as in the case of a police officer who enforces a criminal statute by arresting the person who violates it. This example also illustrates the use of physical force to enforce the law. In contrast, enforcement is externalized when an agent of the legal regime authorizes or instructs other actors, who are not agents of the legal regime, to take certain actions against individuals found to have broken the law. Enforcement takes the form of outcasting when it involves denying someone "the benefits of social cooperation and membership," that is, when members of a cooperative scheme exclude a participant from some or all of their ongoing cooperation.[17] In Medieval Iceland, for instance, individuals found guilty of violating certain criminal prohibitions were declared outlaws.[18] In some cases, this entailed the complete withdrawal of any legal protections for the individual, the issuing of instructions to the victim who had brought the case to kill the criminal, and, in the form of a promise to revoke their own status as outlaws, an incentive to those who had received the same sentence to kill the criminal. In adopting this form of law enforcement, the Medieval Icelandic legal system externalized, or outsourced, the task of upholding certain legal rights to private actors, namely individual victims and the equivalent of modern day bounty hunters. Moreover, it provided its own incentive to comply with the law by promising to withhold from violators the benefit of being treated by other members of the community with respect for their legal rights to property, to bodily integrity, and to life. This difference in mode of enforcement aside, however, the Medieval Icelandic system mirrored quite closely the structure of a modern municipal legal order. For example, it possessed both a legislature and a court system. The same is true of Classical Canon Law. Although it relied to a considerable extent on outcasting and externalized uses of force to uphold its law, in other respects its institutional makeup matches quite closely that of a modern state's legal system.

Hathaway and Shapiro contend that international law provides a third example of a legal system that relies on externalized enforcement, or outcasting, or most often a combination of the two, to uphold subjects' legal rights and duties. As an example of law enforcement via the use of externalized physical force, they point to the UN Security Council's authorizing member states cooperating with the Kuwaiti

---

[17] Ibid, p. 258.
[18] Ibid, pp. 284–90.

government to use all necessary means, including military force, to restore Kuwait's independence following its invasion by Iraq in 1991.[19] The suspending of voting rights for member states who fail to pay their dues to the World Health Organization illustrates the use of internal outcasting to bring about compliance with international law. The WHO enforces member states' obligation to contribute financially to its operation by withhold some of the benefits that come from membership in the WHO.[20] Finally, the method of enforcement practiced by the World Trade Organization (WTO) provides an example of externalized outcasting.[21] Parties to the WTO agree to resolve disputes over compliance with their legal obligations under the treaty by submitting them to adjudication by the WTO's Dispute Settlement Body (DSB). If the DSB concludes that the party bringing the complaint is warranted in doing so, it may authorize that party to impose certain limited sanctions on the party found to be in the wrong. These limited sanctions take the form of tariffs and other forms of protectionism, and constitute a withholding of some of the benefits of more open trade to which the party found to have violated the WTO treaty would otherwise be legally entitled. The sanctions are not given effect by the WTO, however, but rather by the state that brought the complaint, which is to say, via the enactment and administration of domestic law or policy by that state's legislative and/or executive officials. In short, the WTO outsources enforcement of its legal decisions to actors who are not themselves agents of the WTO, and it attempts to induce compliance with its law by denying violators some of the benefits that flow from the cooperation of parties to the WTO, rather than through the threat or use of physical force.

Of course, someone might claim that Medieval Icelandic Law, Classical Canon Law, and international law are not *really* law, precisely because they did not or do not rely primarily on the internal use of physical force to enforce their (so-called) law. But why should we accept this claim? As a conceptual claim, it seems dubious, especially in comparison to the alternative of treating *some* form of enforcement as a necessary condition for the existence of law (at least in a human community of any size and complexity), while leaving it an open, and empirical, question as to what form enforcement might take. A dogmatic insistence that only those social orders that satisfy the MSC count as law may well be nothing more than an attempt to silence those who would employ international law to defend or criticize the actions of particular international or domestic actors.

Yet it may be that these skeptics simply fail to properly communicate the true basis for their skepticism, or perhaps even fail to recognize it themselves. The problem is not merely international law's reliance on external agents and/or outcasting to enforce its norms, but the fact that reliance on these methods renders international

---

[19]   Ibid, p. 304.
[20]   Ibid, pp. 305–6.
[21]   Ibid, pp. 266–7, 307. See also the discussion of the WTO's dispute settlement system in Chapter 11, section III, subsection C.

law unable to satisfy certain other conditions that are necessary for the existence of genuine law. These might include fidelity to the ideal of the rule of law, or satisfaction of certain basic demands of justice, or a certain autonomy from, and control over, politics, understood as agents' pursuit of their interests in light of their relative power. The use of external agents and/or outcasting to enforce international legal rights and obligations may not be the fundamental cause of international law's failure to satisfy one or more of these conditions. Rather, it may be a consequence of some other factors that also explain why those conditions are not met. These include the enormous power inequalities (and so enormous differences in vulnerability) between states, and the huge diversity of beliefs among the people of the Earth regarding the demands of justice and the nature of the good life. In short, some people's doubts about international law's status as genuine law may not stem merely from the fact that international law lacks internal mechanisms for using physical force to enforce its norms, but from the belief that there exists no international community willing or able to sustain such a practice of enforcement.

3

H.L.A. Hart: Social Rules, Officials, and International Law

H.L.A. Hart was the most influential legal philosopher of the twentieth century, at least in the English-speaking world. In this chapter, we consider his analysis of law and the light it sheds on the question "is international law really law?" We begin in section I with Hart's analysis of law as a union of primary and secondary rules, an explication of the contrast Hart draws between a legal order and a legal system, the grounds on which he distinguishes law from other types of rule-governed social practice, and his view on the relationship between morality and the existence and content of law. In section II, we consider Hart's responses to a variety of skeptical challenges to international law. Not surprisingly, he criticizes those who rely on an Austinian account of law. Yet Hart also rejects attempts to defend international law's status as law on the grounds that it exhibits all of the features we associate with the municipal legal order of a modern state. On the basis of these arguments, as well as his claim that international law lacks certain features necessary to fully address the skeptic, many readers have concluded that Hart denies that international law is really law. While some have identified this as a fatal flaw in Hart's analysis of law, others have argued that Hart simply errs in drawing out its implications for international law. As we will see, both arguments rest on a misreading of Hart, one we can explain and correct by drawing on the description of Hart's account of law set out in the first section of this chapter. Hart does not deny that international law is law, only that it constitutes a *legal system*. Properly understood, that is a claim that few of his critics will deny.

I HART'S ANALYSIS OF LAW

A *Primary and Secondary Rules*

In Hart's view, Austin's mistaken characterization of law owes principally to his failure to recognize the centrality of social rules to the concept of law.[1] To assert

---

[1]   Hart, *Concept*, p. 80.

a right to vote in a US election, for example, is to maintain that there is a general rule specifying the conditions under which actors enjoy such a right, and to claim that one satisfies those conditions. The same conclusion holds for other legal incidents, for example, a duty to pay one's taxes, or a power to will one's property to one's spouse. The concept of a social rule also accounts for other features of law Hart maintains Austin cannot satisfactorily explain. For instance, the existence of a social rule that instructs judges to apply a given law to settle cases unless and until it has been repealed both explains the persistence of that law as law even after the death of the actor who legislated it *and* the fact that judges never use laws that have been repealed to settle cases. Hart maintains that when we reflect on life under law from the point of view of those who live such lives, we see that law's primary contribution to the production of social order lies in its provision of standards or rules that actors use to guide their conduct. Each of the above examples illustrates this claim. Laws provide justifications, reasons to perform or not perform certain acts, and in the event of noncompliance with the law, a warrant for criticism.

Hart maintains that law consists of two types of rule. The first, which he labels primary rules, create obligations; for instance, duties not to murder or steal, or to pay one's taxes. The category of secondary rules, in contrast, comprises rules for identifying, changing, and applying rules. To make his case for the existence and importance of secondary rules, Hart invites his reader to imagine a society governed solely by primary rules, one he labels a primitive social order.[2] This description of a primitive social order is somewhat misleading, however, since in the ensuing discussion Hart actually draws *two* distinctions between a primitive society and a more advanced one. The first is the distinction just mentioned, namely, between a society that possesses only primary rules of obligation, and one that also possesses secondary rules for identifying and changing rules. The latter society possesses a hierarchy of rules or norms, while the former does not. The second distinction concerns the presence of specialization in the performance of governance tasks. A primitive society in this sense is one that lacks rules allocating the authority to make, apply, and enforce its rules to some subset of its members. In short, it has no (legal) officials. An advanced society, in contrast, is characterized by such specialization; it has a hierarchy of agents, the rulers and the ruled, as well as a hierarchy of rules. A society with a legislature (and so legislators), courts (and so judges), and a police force (and so law enforcement *officers*) is an example of an advanced society, in this sense of the distinction between a primitive and an advanced society. As we will see, keeping in mind the two distinctions Hart draws between a primitive and an advanced society is crucial if we are to properly understand his characterization of international law and its status as genuine law.

A primitive society, one that lacks both a hierarchy of rules and a hierarchy of agents, will likely suffer from three shortcomings.[3] The first is the problem of

---

[2] Ibid, p. 91.
[3] Hart, *Concept*, pp. 92–4. Hart notes that these defects might not arise in "a small community closely knit by ties of kinship, common sentiment, and belief, and placed in a stable environment."

uncertainty. In a primitive political society, there are no means for identifying the society's rules, and so its members' obligations, other than their actual use by members of that society to guide their conduct. Thus, a member of such a society who is unsure whether he has an obligation not to Ø may only be able to determine whether this is actually the case by observing how other members of the society react to his Ø-ing. If his conduct elicits criticisms such as "it is wrong to Ø," or "we (that is, the members of this community) do not permit Ø-ing here," or most clearly, "don't you know that Ø-ing is against the rules?" then he will know that a rule exists in his society that prohibits Ø-ing. Conversely, if his conduct goes unremarked on, or is praised, or is criticized as unwise but not wrong or forbidden in this community, then he will have good reason to conclude that his society has no rule prohibiting Ø-ing. However, what this individual cannot do is identify *in advance of his actually Ø-ing* whether or not such conduct is permissible.

A second problem that will plague a primitive political society is the static character of its primary norms. These rules exist and have the specific content they do simply in virtue of their use by the society's members; for example, to justify their own conduct or to criticize the conduct of others. Consequently, Hart maintains "the only mode of change in the rules known to such a society will be the slow process of growth, whereby courses of conduct once thought optional become first habitual or usual, and then obligatory, and the converse process of decay, when deviations, once severely dealt with, are first tolerated and then pass unnoticed."[4] In the most extreme variant of such a society, its members will lack not only a mechanism for making rapid and/or deliberate changes to its primary rules, but also to the obligations those rules create for particular individuals. For example, they will possess neither a means for making intentional changes to a general rule allocating property rights over land, nor a way to waive or otherwise alter the rights and duties that rule creates for particular individuals, by selling or gifting the items they own, for example.

Inefficiency in the application and enforcement of primary rules constitutes the third and final shortcoming Hart identifies with a primitive political society. Even in the absence of uncertainty as to the existence and content of the primary rules, Hart maintains that actors will constantly and interminably dispute whether particular actors have complied with them. Moreover, the fact that enforcement depends either on the efforts of the community as a whole or on self-help, meaning each actor's ability to enforce primary rules where their violation affects him or her, constitutes a poor use of scarce resources and an invitation to violence and instability.

Hart maintains that the adoption of secondary rules can mitigate each of these shortcomings.[5] For instance, rules of adjudication address inefficiency in the

---

[4] Ibid, p. 92.
[5] Ibid, pp. 94–9.

application of primary rules by assigning certain actors the task of authoritatively determining whether a rule violation has occurred. The costs of relying on either communal enforcement or self-help can also be reduced through the adoption of rules that both authorize and obligate specific individuals to enforce primary rules, and that specify (to some degree) the punishment or penalty these individuals may impose on an actor judged liable to such treatment in virtue of her failure to comply with a primary rule.

Members of a political society can enhance their responsiveness to changing circumstances or to revisions to their preferences by adopting rules of change. These include (1) rules that empower an individual to waive or modify his or her rights, and so in many cases others' duties, as well as (2) rules that empower certain individuals, typically a subset of that society's members, to create new primary rules binding on some or all of the society's members. Both an individual's right to transfer ownership of some of his property to another person, and a legislature's right to make changes to a general property rule, such as one forbidding the sale of human organs, are examples of rules of change. Note that a society might possess the first sort of rules of change – those that enable individual members to change the specific rights and duties that flow from society's general rules – without having any of the second sort of rules of change, namely, those that empower specific actors to deliberately modify general rules.

The solution to the problem of uncertainty also lies in the adoption of a rule regarding rules, in this case one that "specifies some feature or features possession of which by a suggested rule is taken as conclusive affirmative indication that it is a rule of the group."[6] Hart labels such a norm a rule of recognition. Where the social rules that (partially) structure the lives of members of a given society include a rule of recognition, individuals need not wait for others' reactions to their Ø-ing to determine whether doing so is permissible. Instead, they can answer that question ahead of time by employing a rule that specifies the source(s) of law in their society; for instance, one that identifies as law any norm that receives majority support in a unicameral legislature. A rule of recognition can also address uncertainty arising from (apparent) conflicts between rules, such as when one rule forbids conduct that another rule permits. For instance, a society may possess a rule that gives priority to rules made in one way, such as legislation, over rules made in another way, such as custom. In some cases of (apparently) conflicting directives, individuals will be able to use this rule to determine the legal status of a given type of conduct in advance of actually performing it. Rules of recognition, then, can be said to systematize the social rules of a given political society by picking out those rules that count as part of its law and by specifying certain relations that obtain between them, such as an order of priority.

---

[6] Ibid, p. 94.

A careful reader will note that Hart's solution to the problem of inefficiency consists entirely in the specialization of governance tasks; that is, in the adoption of rules that create positions such as judge and police officer, and the institutions in which those positions are embedded. In contrast, Hart's response to the defect of stasis involves the adoption of two different types of rule, each of which serves to ameliorate a distinct type of inflexibility. While the ability to modify rights and duties that flow from a society's primary rules of obligation does not require the existence of officials, a society's ability to quickly and deliberately modify those general rules does. Whether the solution to the problem of uncertainty, namely, the adoption of a rule of recognition, involves any specialization in the performance of governance tasks is less clear. As I will explain shortly, for Hart, there is a sense in which it is officials' use of a rule of recognition that distinguishes an advanced society, one with a legal *system*, from a primitive society that possesses only a legal *order*. The crucial point to note here, however, is the ambiguity that may attach to the description of a given social order as primitive. Does someone who makes such a claim mean to assert that the society in question lacks *any* rules for identifying and changing its norms? Or does he or she only mean to assert that such a society lacks those rules necessary for specialization in the making, and/or applying, and/or enforcing of rules, or what is the same, for legislative, adjudicative, and enforcement officials? As we will see, a failure to pay careful attention to this distinction accounts for certain misguided objections to Hart's characterization of international law.

B *The Idea of a Legal System*

Consider, once again, Hart's claim that a primitive society will suffer from the defect of uncertainty. The problem, he writes, is that when "doubts arise as to what the rules are or as to the precise scope of some given rule, there will be no procedure for settling this doubt, either by reference to an authoritative text or to an official whose declarations on this point are authoritative."[7] Reference to the existence of an official obviously implies specialization in the performance of governance tasks, or put another way, a division of labor between rulers and ruled. But so, too, does reference to an authoritative text, since such a text must have an author, someone whose judgment regarding the rules and their scope is taken as authoritative by other members of the community. Indeed, Hart says as much when he writes that the crucial first step from the pre-legal to the legal – or perhaps he ought to have said, from a primitive rule-guided social order to an advanced one – is not "the mere reduction to writing of hitherto unwritten rules" but "the acknowledgement of reference to the writing or inscription as *authoritative*, i.e. as the *proper* way of disposing of doubts as to the existence of the rule."[8]

---

7 Ibid, p. 92.
8 Ibid, p. 95.

Why does Hart describe this as the *first* but, by implication, not the final step from pre-legal to legal? Why does Hart describe a society's possession of even the simplest rule of recognition, such as one directing its members to a list or text viewed as authoritative, as providing "in *embryonic form* the idea of a legal system?"[9] Or once more, why is it that "in the simple operation of identifying a given rule as possessing the required feature of being an item on an authoritative list of rules we have *the germ* of the idea of legal validity?"[10] The answer to these questions, I believe, is that a society's possession of even a simple rule of recognition introduces more than the possibility of specialization in the identification of law. It also introduces the possibility of a *division of labor in the task of sustaining the law's existence*; that is, in making it the case that the society in question has law. That task is performed by the practice of holding accountable that Hart characterizes in terms of adopting the internal point of view to the social rules that regulate the affairs of members of a given society. For Hart, the presence of this particular division of labor, at least to some significant degree, is the defining feature of a legal *system*.

We must be careful here not to confuse the idea of a legal system with the idea of a system of laws (or rules) that Hart also invokes. A society possesses a system of rules, as opposed to a mere set, if it possesses a rule of recognition that addresses doubts over the scope of various rules by arranging them in an order of superiority; for example, on the basis of their source.[11] As we noted when we first introduced the idea of a rule of recognition, there is a straightforward sense in which such a rule serves to systematize (some of) the other rules that regulate the affairs of the society in question. Furthermore, when we speak of a rule of recognition in this context, we are referring to a genuine rule, one that actors can use to guide their conduct. Even a society that lacks any specialization in the performance of governance tasks can have a rule of recognition that serves the function of organizing its law.

Most of the passages in which Hart invokes the concept of a legal system, however, are best read as claims regarding the absence or presence of a division of labor in the task of sustaining the law by adopting the internal point of view to the rules that constitute it. Hart employs the phrase "rule of recognition" in these passages as well, but the phrase is a misnomer. What Hart refers to is not a rule that officials use to identify what the law is, but the social fact constituted by legal officials' practice of holding themselves and one another accountable for compliance with certain primary and secondary rules. Talk of a rule of recognition here is ontological, not practical, a description of *what makes it the case* that rules R1, R2 ... Rn are rules of the society in question.

Understood ontologically, the rule of recognition provides a legal system's foundation. The various rules that constitute it, including its rules of change and adjudication, count as law, or are *legally valid*, because they satisfy the criteria

9   Ibid, emphasis added.
10   Ibid, emphasis added.
11   Ibid, pp. 95, 101.

contained in the rule of recognition.[12] Thus, in a society that possesses a legal system, the status of a norm as law need not depend on actors using it to guide their own conduct or as a standard for appraising the conduct of others. The rule of recognition, in contrast, is a customary rule and as such its existence and content depends on the practice of legal officials, that is, in their use of the rule to identify what the laws of their legal system are, and as a standard for appraising others' claims to have identified the law. What counts as a source of law in this society, then, is a matter of what its legal officials treat as a source of law. Of course, some of those officials (or legal academics) may attempt to describe those sources in an attempt to provide guidelines for identifying the law, or what is the same, rules of recognition that serve an epistemic function. Nevertheless, it is what these officials *actually do*, and not any description of what they do, that determines what is law in this society.

The foregoing discussion helps illuminate Hart's assertion that there are "two minimum conditions necessary and sufficient for the existence of a legal system," namely, that "those rules of behaviour which are valid according to the system's criteria of validity must be generally obeyed," and that "its rules of recognition specifying the criteria of legal validity and its rules of change and adjudication must be effectively accepted as common public standards of official behaviour by its officials."[13] Why think satisfaction of both conditions is necessary and not merely sufficient for the existence of a legal system? The answer is that only when both conditions are satisfied (to some considerable degree) will a society have achieved a division of labor *in sustaining the practice of holding accountable that constitutes law* that marks the transition from a primitive to an advanced society. Hart continues:

> The assertion that a legal system exists is therefore a Janus-faced statement looking both towards obedience by ordinary citizens and to the acceptance by officials of secondary rules as critical common standards of official behaviour. [This] ... is merely the reflection of the composite character of a legal system as compared with a simpler decentralized pre-legal form of social structure which consists only of primary rules. In the simpler structure, since there are no officials, the rules must be widely accepted as setting critical standards for the behaviour of the group. If, there, the internal point of view is not widely disseminated there could not logically be any rules. But where there is a union of primary and secondary rules, which is, as we have argued, the most fruitful way of regarding a legal system, the acceptance of the rules as common standards for the group may be split off from the relatively passive matter of the ordinary individual acquiescing in the rules by obeying them for his part alone. In an extreme case the internal point of view with its characteristic normative use of legal language ("This is a valid rule") might be confined to the official world. In this more complex system, only officials might accept and use the system's criteria of legal validity.[14]

---

[12] Ibid, pp. 100–106.
[13] Ibid, p. 116.
[14] Id., p. 117.

To grasp the key point Hart makes in this passage, we must ignore certain infelicities in the language he uses to make it. First, by characterizing a "simpler decentralized" form of social structure as one consisting only of primary rules (of obligation), Hart conflates the two distinct senses in which a society can be simple, or primitive: either because it has no secondary rules at all, or because it has none of the secondary rules necessary for specialization in the performance of governance tasks. As the remainder of the passage makes clear, it is the second distinction he has in mind here, in which case his description of a simple social structure as one that consists only of primary rules is not an apt contrast. Second, while a simpler social structure, meaning one without officials, is on Hart's account a pre-*legal system*, it is not pre-*legal*. That is, for Hart such a social order still has law, or at least its lack of any division of labor in governing does not entail that it has no law. Finally, it is not the union of primary and secondary rules per se that provides the most fruitful way of modeling a legal system. Rather, it is the advent of specialization in sustaining a rule-guided social order, in making it the case that law contributes to the production of social order, that Hart thinks is the key to the idea of a legal system.

C Rule-Governed Practices, Law, and Morality

For Hart, the idea of a social rule provides the key to understanding how law contributes to the production of social order. However, not all rule-governed practices count as law. An annual neighborhood pot-luck dinner is a rule-governed activity, and so too are games such as baseball and chess, yet none is commonly described as examples of law. What, then, distinguishes legal orders from other types of rule-governed practice?

Hart's answer is that legal orders necessarily include "minimum forms of protection for persons, property, and promises" absent which it would be impossible for people to associate peacefully with one another.[15] Law is first and foremost a response to the threat that actors pose to one another's survival, although as the qualifier "first and foremost" indicates, it may and perhaps should serve other ends as well. The development or evolution of a legal order enables mutual cooperation that increases individuals' chances of survival by, for example, dramatically reducing (although not eliminating) uncertainty regarding what counts as a permissible use of

[15] Ibid., p. 199. To be precise, Hart makes this claim about municipal or domestic law, but as we will see he suggests that there are analogs in the case of international law. Hart also suggests that a general reliance on physical sanctions to motivate compliance with duty-imposing rules distinguishes law from other types of normative practice. By "physical sanctions," Hart means material costs, as opposed to psychological costs such as shame, remorse, and guilt. Hart emphasizes that the use of physical sanctions to induce compliance need be "neither closely defined nor administered by officials but . . . left to the community at large." Taken together with his observation that breaches of international law are held to justify reprisals (that is, coercion) and countermeasures (that is, a denial of the material benefits of cooperation), this claim evidences Hart's belief that international law exhibits the mode of "social pressure" for conformity to the rules typical of a legal order. See Hart, *Concept*, pp. 86, 220.

force against another actor, or who may use a certain object or resource. The rules governing pot-luck dinners also create rights to use a certain object, of course, but they do so only against a social background created and sustained by law. Legal orders, normative practices consisting at a minimum of general rules governing property, contract, and the use of force, are the sin qua non of human societies.

Peaceful association should not be confused with living together on just terms, however.[16] To defend his claim that law must provide minimum forms of protection for persons, Hart appeals to certain facts about human beings and the circumstances we inhabit, not a conceptual connection between law and morality.[17] It may be, then, that in any society there will be certain legal requirements that coincide with what justice requires. Nevertheless, neither their status as law nor their content depends on this coincidence. Rather, both are a function of the fact that any human society must possess *some* norms governing persons, property, and promises, and the fact that the members of this society, or at least the subset who govern it, have converged on *these particular norms* governing persons, property, and promises as standards of right conduct. The belief that the existence and content of law depends on social facts and not (necessarily) its moral merit is the defining feature of the legal positivist tradition of legal philosophy. It is a belief that Austin and Hart share, despite their conflicting accounts of the social facts that give rise to law, and how they do so.

II HART ON INTERNATIONAL LAW

Hart considers the question of whether international law is really law in the final chapter of his seminal book, *The Concept of Law*. There he writes:

> [T]he absence of an international legislature, courts with compulsory jurisdiction, and centrally organized sanctions have inspired misgivings, at any rate in the breast of legal theorists. The absence of these institutions means that the rules for states resemble the simple form of social structure, consisting only of primary rules of obligation, which, when we find it among societies of individuals, we are accustomed to contrast with a developed legal system. It is indeed arguable, as we shall show, that international law not only lacks the secondary rules of change and adjudication which provide for legislature and courts, but also a unifying rule of recognition specifying "sources" of law and providing general criteria for the identification of its rules. These differences are indeed striking and the question "is international law really law?" can hardly be put aside.[18]

Hart sets out to "inquire into the detailed character of the doubts which have been felt, and . . . ask whether the common wider usage that speaks of 'international law' is

[16]   Ibid, pp. 200–201.
[17]   Ibid, pp. 193–200.
[18]   Ibid, p. 214.

likely to obstruct any practical or theoretical aim."[19] Consequently, his discussion consists primarily of critical responses to various arguments offered in favor of international legal skepticism. However, he concludes by using his own analysis of the concept of law to identify one sense in which theorists (and others) are right to express misgivings regarding international law's status as law.

Once again, Hart traces certain confusions regarding the nature of law, and so international law's status as such, to an Austinian depiction of it. As we observed in Chapter 2, if we understand law to be the command of a sovereign then we ought to find paradoxical the very idea of states being subject to international law.[20] After all, it is states' sovereignty that accounts for the existence of domestic law, and to be sovereign they must not be in a habit of obedience to any other agent, including not only other states individually but the society of states collectively. Thus, as a conceptual matter there can be no such thing as international law properly so-called.

In response, Hart argues that Austin mistakenly treats sovereignty as prior to law when in fact the opposite is true. Law does not consist in the commands of an agent who pre-exists it, and who is necessarily legally unconstrained. Rather, law is constituted by social rules or norms, including in many cases rules that create specialization in the performance of governance tasks by constituting legal offices with specific rights and responsibilities. Thus, Hart writes that "there is no way of knowing what sovereignty states have till we know what the forms of international law are."[21] Since the state is itself a legal construct, it possesses only the autonomy the law accords it, or put another way, only those rights created or recognized in law. Therefore, there is no contradiction in the idea that sovereign states are bound by international law, or that international law serves to delimit their freedom, understood as the domain within which they may *rightly* engage in various forms of action.[22]

Hart also responds to Austin and others who challenge international law's status as law on the grounds that it does not provide for "enforcement by any central organ," or in other words, because international law does not satisfy the Modern State Conception (MSC) of enforcement.[23] This argument fails, he maintains, because it ignores the fact that the members of a society of individuals are roughly equal in physical strength and vulnerability, while members of the society of states are not. The rough equality of individuals makes the organized enforcement of law

[19] Ibid.
[20] Ibid, p. 220.
[21] Ibid, p. 224.
[22] Hart also points out that a conception of states as Austinian sovereigns is incompatible with a voluntarist account of international law, which holds that states are legally obligated to obey all and only those international legal norms to which they have consented. See Hart, *Concept*, pp. 224–6, for this and other criticisms of the voluntarist model of the international legal order. See also Chapter 6, section III.
[23] See the discussion in Chapter 2, section III.

necessary, since private enforcement is unlikely to deter would-be lawbreakers, and freeriding by such actors makes it irrational to limit one's freedom by submitting to the law. It also makes such enforcement possible, however, because the number of people prepared to obey the law as long as most others do will easily exceed the number of committed bad actors. Consequently, the former will be able to marshal sufficient power to deter the latter, at relatively little risk to themselves.[24] The same is not true for members of the society of states, where differences in power can make the enforcement of legal rights and duties quite risky. This fact does not preclude the possibility of a rule-governed society, however, since such an order may better enable states to live peaceably and to engage in mutually advantageous interactions.[25] Thus, we should expect states to speak of their own and other states' legal obligations, to hide or deny any violations of international law they commit, and to appeal to international legal rules to justify actions taken in response to purported violations of international law, for this is just what actors who employ shared social rules to govern their interactions with one another do. At least for a society of states, then, the absence of a centrally organized, coercive, mechanism for enforcement does not make the realization of a rule-governed social order impossible. Therefore, Hart concludes it does not provide a sound basis for international legal skepticism.

Hart acknowledges that the background facts that explain why states rarely resort to coercion to enforce their own or another state's legal rights may also entail that "rules [of international law] are efficacious only so far as they concern issues over which states are unwilling to fight."[26] His response, that "this may be so, and may reflect adversely on the importance of the system and its value to humanity" nicely illustrates Hart's commitment to legal positivism.[27] Again, this is the view that the existence of law does not depend on its moral merit, where that includes the justice of its content, the veracity of its claim to legitimacy, and its fidelity to a moral ideal of the rule of law. As we will see, other theorists argue that if international law merely serves to enhance states' pursuit of their national interests in light of their relative power, this reflects adversely not only on its value to humanity but also counts decisively against its claim to be a genuine legal order.

Interestingly, Hart also criticizes those who respond to international legal skepticism by arguing that it possesses mechanisms for making, applying, and enforcing law sufficiently analogous to those of a modern state to warrant characterizing it as genuinely legal. While he acknowledges some similarities, Hart maintains that the differences between the international and a municipal legal order are more important. For example, he observes that unlike courts in a state's domestic legal order, the International Court of Justice (ICJ) does not exercise compulsory jurisdiction.

[24] Ibid, pp. 193–8, 218–19.
[25] Ibid, pp. 219–220.
[26] Ibid, p. 220.
[27] Ibid.

Instead, it only has the authority to adjudicate disputes between parties if they voluntarily agree to its doing so.[28] Likewise, Hart thinks it unpersuasive, or perhaps better, unenlightening to describe a state's resort to war to uphold its international legal rights as an example of law enforcement. As he notes, "the law enforcement provisions of the [United Nations] Charter, admirable on paper, have been paralyzed by the veto and the ideological divisions and alliances of the great powers."[29] Hart's rejection of this argument by analogy for international law's status as law may seem to suggest that he embraces international legal skepticism. In fact, Hart is better understood as challenging those who *assume* that, to count as a genuine example of law, international law must include practices of legislation, adjudication, and enforcement similar to those of a modern state. This assumption is doubly problematic. First, it leads some defenders of international law to make claims on its behalf that only serve to deepen the intuition that international law is not really law. Second, it hinders a careful examination of the respects in which municipal and international law are and are not alike, and an appreciation of what these similarities and differences imply for law's ability to contribute to the production of social order.

In the very last paragraph of the last chapter of his book, Hart finally offers what many have taken to be his answer to the question "is international law really law?":

> What is the actual character of the rules as they function in the relations between states? . . . it is submitted that there is no basic rule providing general criteria of validity for the rules of international law, and that the rules which are in fact operative constitute not a system but a set of rules, among which are the rules providing for the binding force of treaties. It is true that, on many important matters, the relations between states are regulated by multilateral treaties, and it is sometimes argued that these may bind states that are not parties. If this were generally recognized, such treaties would in fact be legislative enactments and international law would have distinct criteria of validity for its rules. A basic rule of recognition could then be formulated which would represent an actual feature of the system and would be more than an empty restatement of the fact that a set of rules are in fact observed by states. Perhaps international law is at present in a stage of transition towards acceptance of this and other forms which would bring it nearer in structure to a municipal system. If, and when, this transition is completed the formal analogies, which at present seem thin and even delusive, would acquire substance, and the sceptic's last doubts about the legal "quality" of international law may then be laid to rest.[30]

Many readers of this passage conclude that Hart does not think international law is really law. The claim that international law must undergo a further evolution before

---

[28] Recent decades have seen the advent of international courts and dispute resolution bodies with a stronger claim to exercise compulsory jurisdiction, such as the International Criminal Court and the WTO's dispute settlement panels. Even in these cases, however, a tribunal's claim to jurisdiction generally depends on a state first choosing to join (and remain) a party to the treaty that created it.

[29] Ibid, p. 233.

[30] Ibid, p. 237.

the skeptic's last doubts may be laid to rest seems to imply that, at present, international legal skepticism has some merit. More importantly, in denying that international law possesses a rule of recognition, and therefore is not a legal system, Hart implicitly classifies it as a primitive social order, one that earlier in his book he describes as "pre-legal." Taken together with the apparent sympathy to international legal skepticism that Hart expresses at the beginning of his chapter on international law (quoted in the first paragraph of this section), it appears difficult to deny that Hart harbors serious doubts about international law's status as law.

To some, the belief that Hart endorses international legal skepticism provides a compelling reason to reject his analysis of law.[31] Others argue that the problem lies not with Hart's analysis of the concept of law, but with his use of it to assess international law's claim to be law properly so-called. Jeremy Waldron, for instance, maintains that Hart's arguments "become careless and their application thoughtless in regard to law in this area," and results in an embarrassingly inadequate account of the nature and status of international law.[32] Likewise, Jean d'Aspremont describes Hart's discussion as a "disappointing and unconvincing portrayal of international law as a very primitive set of rules."[33] Mehrdad Payandeh even asserts that Hart's "insistence that international law does not constitute a legal system seems almost as problematic as Austin's insistence that international law is not law."[34]

These criticisms all rest on a mistaken reading of Hart's discussion of international law, albeit one for which he bears considerable responsibility. As we saw in the previous section, Hart employs the contrast between a primitive and an advanced society to draw *two* distinctions: first, the absence or presence of a hierarchy of rules, and second, the absence or presence of a hierarchy of rulers, that is, of specialization in the performance of governance tasks. Hart's critics assume he has the first of these two distinctions in mind when he assesses international law's claim to be genuine law, and, admittedly, certain passages support such an interpretation. However, it is actually the contrast between a society that lacks specialization in the performance of governance tasks and one that possesses such specialization that informs Hart's reflections on international law.

Waldron develops his objections to Hart's views on international law by evaluating "Hart's claim that the international legal order is a primitive legal system,

---

[31] See, e.g., Jason A. Beckett, "The Hartian Tradition in International Law," *Journal Jurisprudence* 1 (2008): 56; Patrick Capps, "International Legal Positivism and Modern Natural Law," in *International Legal Positivism in a Post-Modern World*, eds. J. Kammerhofer and J. d'Aspremont (Cambridge: Cambridge University Press, 2014), p. 215; and Roger Cotterrell, "What Is Transnational Law?" *Law and Social Inquiry* 37, 2 (2012): 507.

[32] Jeremy Waldron, "International Law: 'A Relatively Small and Unimportant' Part of Jurisprudence?" in *Reading HLA Hart's The Concept of Law*, eds. d'Almeida et al. (2013), pp. 213, 211.

[33] Jean D'Aspremont, *Formalism and the Sources of International Law* (New York: Oxford University Press, 2011), p. 56.

[34] Mehrdad Payandeh, "The Concept of International Law in the Jurisprudence of H.L.A. Hart," *European Journal of International Law* 21, 4 (2011): 967, 978.

consisting of *nothing but primary rules*."[35] He begins by pointing out that international law includes secondary rules of adjudication, such as those set out in the statute creating the International Court of Justice, as well as secondary rules of change, such as those constitutive of the treaty-making process. Hart is clearly aware of these features of international law; as we noted earlier, he explicitly refers to both the ICJ and the United Nations Charter. Why, then, does he characterize international law as a relatively simple social order? Waldron postulates that he does so because the ICJ lacks compulsory jurisdiction, and because treaties only create obligations for those states that choose to become a party to them.[36] Although Waldron concedes that the absence of compulsory jurisdiction marks a significant disanalogy between a municipal or domestic legal system and international law, he points out that this does not warrant the inference that international law contains no rules of adjudication.[37] As for the fact that treaties do not apply to nonparties, Waldron writes: "[I]t is not clear why the point about 'binding states that are not parties' should be jurisprudentially so important," and in particular, why Hart should apparently treat it as a necessary condition for the existence of rules of change.[38]

Waldron assumes that it is the absence of a hierarchy of rules that makes a society primitive, and maintains that Hart has no good reason for denying that international law contains secondary rules. In fact, Hart does not deny the presence of secondary rules in international law; rather, he maintains only that international law "lacks the secondary rules of change and adjudication *which provide for legislature and courts*."[39] Take the point about legislation first. As we noted in the previous section, when Hart first introduces the idea of a simple society that lacks rules of change, he distinguishes between the absence of even an embryonic form of legislation, meaning rules that makes possible deliberate change to general rules and that introduce the germ of the idea of a distinction between ruler and ruled, and rules that make possible changes to "obligations which arise under the rules in particular cases."[40] The secondary rules that constitute treaty making are examples of this second type of rules of change; they alter obligations that obtain under the general rules of international law only for the particular states that sign (and, if necessary, ratify) them. As Hart notes, were international law to evolve so that multilateral treaties were generally recognized as binding states that were not parties to them, then the norms that comprise international law would include secondary rules that provide for legislation. That is, international law would possess a mechanism for making deliberate

[35] Waldron, "International Law," 216. See also Payandeh, "Concept of International Law"; Capps, "International Legal Positivism," 213; and Liam Murphy, *What Makes Law* (Cambridge: Cambridge University Press, 2014), pp. 147–50.

[36] Ibid, pp. 215, 217.

[37] Ibid, pp. 215–16.

[38] Ibid, p. 217.

[39] Hart, *Concept*, p. 214, emphasis added.

[40] Ibid, pp. 92–3.

changes to rules that apply generally, not only to those who agree to be subject to them, and that do so in advance of any actor using them to hold himself or others accountable. It would also include the distinct categories of rulers (or officials) and ruled (or subjects), and so no longer be aptly characterized as a horizontal political-legal order. Thus, we have an answer to Waldron's question regarding the jurisprudential significance of "binding states that are not parties" to a treaty: such a practice is sufficient for the existence of a division of labor in making changes to the general rules that regulate members of international society, and it is the development of specialization in this and other governance tasks that transforms a given society from primitive to advanced, in the sense that concerns Hart here.

Consider, now, Hart's remarks on international adjudication and enforcement. With respect to the latter, international law includes "secondary rules specifying or at least limiting the penalties for violation," which might make some contribution to reducing "the smouldering vendettas which may result from self-help."[41] But to the extent these vendettas occur primarily because of the "absence of an official monopoly on sanctions," with an emphasis on both monopoly and official(s), the fact that international law relies almost exclusively on self-help does indeed make it quite like a simple social order.[42] As for adjudication, international law clearly differs somewhat from a primitive society in that it contains secondary rules "empowering individuals to make authoritative determinations of the question whether, on a particular occasion, a primary rule has been broken."[43] Recall, however, that the defect that Hart believes courts and other adjudicatory bodies serve to mitigate is the fact that "disputes as to whether an admitted rule has or has not been violated will . . . continue interminably, if there is no agency specially empowered to ascertain finally, and authoritatively, the fact of violation."[44] Insofar as courts without compulsory jurisdiction lack this authority except in cases where parties to a dispute voluntarily place themselves under it, Hart likely concluded that their existence marks only a small advance in international law's contribution to the production of social order.

He may have been mistaken on this score. Arguably, a number of ICJ decisions have made significant contributions to how states understand their legal obligations, rights, etc., and in so doing shaped their conduct in ways that would not have occurred in the absence of a world court. Moreover, the proliferation within international law over the past few decades of adjudicatory bodies with compulsory jurisdiction, not to mention increasing engagement with international law by domestic courts, is surely the area of governance in which international law has moved furthest away from a simple social order. Nevertheless, if Hart's interest in the development of a division of labor in governance were motivated by the belief that it

---

[41]   Hart, *Concept*, pp. 93, 97.
[42]   Ibid, p. 93.
[43]   Ibid, p. 96.
[44]   Ibid, p. 93.

makes law a more effective tool for social control, then it was not implausible for him to conclude that a society that possesses only a court without compulsory jurisdiction was, in this respect, more like a social order that lacked any division of labor in adjudication than one equipped with compulsory courts of wide-ranging jurisdiction.

It is worth emphasizing here a point that both Hart and his critics make, although they then often ignore it: the property of being a primitive or advanced society is scalar, not bimodal.[45] While Hart does sometimes group primitive and international law together in a way that suggests they are equivalent, at other times, he offers a more nuanced characterization of international law. For example, in the introduction to his chapter on international law he writes: "[T]he absence of an international legislature, courts with compulsory jurisdiction, and centrally organized sanctions ... means that the rules for states *resemble* that simple form of social structure ... which when we find it among societies of individuals, we are accustomed to contrast with a developed legal system."[46] The argument in the preceding paragraphs takes this talk of resemblance seriously, not least because it discourages the tendency to fixate on classification for its own sake, and instead directs our attention toward the "more fruitful" and empirically informed study of how rules and institutions function to produce social order.

What should we make of Hart's assertion that "there is no basic rule providing general criteria of validity for the rules of international law, and that the rules which are in fact operative constitute not a system but a set of rules, among which are the rules providing for the binding force of treaties?"[47] In the previous section, we distinguished two functions that reference to a rule of recognition plays in Hart's analysis of law. The first is an epistemic function: a rule of recognition provides an epistemically authoritative description of what counts as law in a given legal order; that is, an account of the sources of law in that society, possibly including a description of which laws take priority over others in the event of (apparent) conflict between them. Understood in these terms, the claim that international law possesses no rule of recognition is obviously false. For example, as both Payandeh and Waldron point out, Article 38(1) of the ICJ Statute and the Vienna Convention on the Law of Treaties provide authoritative means for identifying international law.[48] As for systematizing international legal norms in the sense of identifying rules that regulate conflicts between them (or, perhaps better, specify

---

[45] See, for example, Waldron who shifts over the course of his discussion from describing Hart's view of international law as characterizing "international law as, in many respects, *more like* a system of 'primitive' law than like a municipal legal system" (Waldron, "International Law," 209, emphasis italics) to describing Hart as "claim[ing] that the international order *is* a primitive legal system" (Ibid, 216, emphasis added).

[46] Hart, *Concept*, p. 214, emphasis added.

[47] Ibid, p. 236.

[48] Waldron, "International Law," 219; Payandeh, "Concept of International Law," 989–90. See also Carmen Pavel, "Is International Law a Hartian Legal System?" *Ratio Juris* 31, 3 (2018): 317–19.

their scope so that they do *not* conflict), Payandeh identifies the existence of a number of international rules that serve this function (albeit not on the basis of a law's source).[49] Although these claims are correct, they fail to address Hart's assertion that international law lacks a rule of recognition and that therefore it does not count as a legal system. That is because in making this claim Hart invokes the ontological, not the epistemic, function that reference to the rule of recognition plays in his analysis of law.

Recall that for Hart a legal system exists when citizens or subjects generally obey the law and officials use it as a critical common standard of behavior.[50] This "composite character" is what distinguishes a legal system from "a simpler decentralized pre-legal form of social structure."[51] A legal system, then, is a social order characterized by a significant division of labor in sustaining the practice of holding accountable that constitutes a given society's law. Put another way, what makes law (that is, what accounts for its existence) in a society that possesses a legal system is the practice of secondary rules of change, adjudication, and enforcement by one set of actors (officials) who rule over another set of actors (subjects).[52] Given this characterization of what it is for a society to possess a legal system, Hart's assertion that the rules that comprise international law constitute not a system but only a set seems quite plausible. Only those international legal theorists who assume that international law's status as law depends on it possessing such a division of labor will deny it. As we have seen, Hart rejects this assumption. On his account, the claim that a given society lacks a legal *system* is neither equivalent to, nor does it necessarily entail, the claim that the society in question has no law.

Even if we restrict our interest to the ontological question of what accounts for the existence of law, Hart's claim that international law lacks a rule of recognition may seem false. After all, we can formulate the following "rule" of recognition for a primitive society, a description of the conditions under which rules regulate (some of) the conduct of its members: rule R_1, R_2, etc. are rules of primitive society P if and only if its members "*use* the rules as standards for the appraisal of their own and others' behaviour."[53] But, in fact, Hart does not deny that we can formulate such a rule, only the utility of doing so. Speaking of the "strange basic norm which has been suggested for international law: 'States should behave as they have customarily behaved'," Hart writes: "[W]e may be persuaded to treat as a basic rule, something which is an empty repetition of the mere fact that the society concerned (whether of individuals or states) observes certain standards of conduct

---

[49] Payandeh, "Concept of International Law," 992.
[50] Note that subjects may also use the law as a critical common standard of behavior, and Hart implies that one in which they do so will be morally superior to one in which they do not. He only denies that the adoption of the internal point of view to the law by the citizenry at large is a necessary condition for the existence of a legal system.
[51] Hart, *Concept*, 117.
[52] Particular individuals may be members of both sets, of course.
[53] Ibid., p. 98.

as obligatory rules."[54] In contrast, where a society is characterized by a division of labor in the performance of governance tasks, the formulation of a "rule" of recognition shines new light on how law contributes to the production of social order by calling our attention to the fact that it is the conduct of officials, actors occupying offices constituted by rules that empower them to make, apply, and enforce the law, that accounts for law's existence. Likewise, in a primitive society the claim that "this is a valid law" amounts to nothing more than the empty claim "this is a law of our society because it is a law of our society (in other words, because we treat it as such)," whereas once a division of labor in governance occurs the claim "this is a valid law" can be theoretically informative; for instance: "This is a valid law because it was enacted by Parliament." Thus, with some minor rephrasing, we can better convey the idea Hart meant to express in the passage quoted earlier: there is no *theoretically useful* basic rule in the international legal order of the sort that could provide *informative* general criteria of validity. This reflects the fact that there is relatively little division of labor in the performance of the governance tasks that constitute international law. It is, in this respect, not a legal system, and therefore bears a closer resemblance to a simple or primitive social order than to an advanced social order like the one realized in a well-functioning modern state.[55]

In the case of a primitive society, Hart maintains that positing a rule of recognition is not only theoretically pointless but also practically unnecessary, since we need not postulate the existence of such a rule in order to account for law's normativity:

> [I]t is surely conceivable (and perhaps has often been the case) that a society may live by rules imposing obligations on its members as "binding" ... [I]f rules are in fact accepted as standards of conduct, and supported with appropriate forms of social pressure distinctive of obligatory rules, nothing more is required to show that they are binding rules.[56]

It is true, Hart concedes, that in this:

> simpler case we cannot ask: "From what ultimate provision of the system do the separate rules derive their validity or 'binding force'?" For there is no such provision

---

54 Ibid, p. 236.
55 On this point, see also Richard Collins, *The Institutional Problem in Modern International Law* (Oxford: Hart Publishing, 2016), p. 83. As Hart notes, however, a legal system that exists in virtue of secondary rules that create the office of judge and the institution of a court "is necessarily also committed to a rule of recognition of an elementary and imperfect sort" (Id., at 97). One might point to the recent growth of adjudicatory panels and semi-autonomous administrative rule-making bodies in various domains of international law to make the case that it is now possible to formulate a theoretically useful ontological "rule" of recognition for international law. Doing so will require responding to skepticism regarding the genuine autonomy enjoyed by these administrative rule-making bodies, and rebutting the claim that the decisions of adjudicatory panels are merely epistemically authoritative claims regarding states' practice of holding accountable, but not themselves part of that practice (that is, part of what makes international law what it is). Whether one treats the European Union and the European Court of Human Rights as components of international law will likely also have a significant impact on the position one takes.
56 Hart, *Concept*, p. 234.

and need be none. It is, therefore, a mistake to suppose that a basic rule of recognition is a generally necessary condition of the existence of rules of obligation or "binding" rules. In the simpler form of society we must wait and see whether a rule gets accepted as a rule or not; in a system with a basic rule of recognition we can say before a rule is actually made, that it *will* be valid *if* it conforms to the requirements of the rule of recognition.[57]

Take this last sentence first. I suggest that it should be read as follows: in a legal system, that is, a social order characterized by specialization in the performance of governance tasks, observers and participants can state correctly that R1 is a rule of that society in advance of any actor using it to hold himself or another accountable. We can make this claim because there exists, and we can point to, a practice of legislation in virtue of which it is possible to make deliberate changes to the society's general rules. This is not possible in a simpler society, one that relies solely on a customary process of rule formation, in which successful rule change occurs only once most members of the society in question use, or acknowledge the propriety of others using, R1 to hold themselves and others accountable.[58] Of course, we can formulate a rule that tells us how to *identify* new customary rules in advance of their being practiced; for example, we ought to believe in the existence of a customary norm C if (a) actors generally conduct themselves in ways that comport with it (or try to hide the fact when they do not), and (b) we have reason to believe they do so out of a sense of obligation, or because they believe C is a norm that applies to them.[59] However, Hart's claim here is ontological, not epistemic, or so I contend.

Turning now to the other sentences in the above quotation, the existence of a rule-governed social order does not require a hierarchy of agents because the practice of holding accountable that constitutes such an order can be (and often has been) dispersed among all the members of the society in question. It is a mistake, therefore, to assume that there must be a basic norm or rule that makes it the case that R1, R2, etc., are valid or "binding" rules for every rule-guided social order. Rather, such a "rule" "is not a necessity, but a luxury, found in advanced social systems"; that is, in social systems characterized by a division of labor in the performance of governance tasks.[60]

Finally, recall Hart's claim that legal orders necessarily include rules governing property, agreements, and the use of violence against persons, absent which actors are unlikely to associate peaceably with one another. The oldest and most central

---

[57]   Ibid, p. 235.

[58]   See Gerald Postema, "Custom, Normative Practice, and the Law," *Duke Law Journal* 62, 3 (2012); David Lefkowitz, "Sources in Legal Positivist Theories: Law as Necessarily Posited and the Challenge of Customary Law Formation," in *The Oxford Handbook of the Sources of International Law*, eds. Samantha Besson and Jean d'Aspremont (Oxford: Oxford University Press, 2017), pp. 323–41.

[59]   Indeed, we can develop very sophisticated epistemic rules of this sort; see, among others, the International Law Commission's Draft Reports on the identification of customary international law, available at http://legal.un.org/ilc/guide/1_13.shtml.

[60]   Hart, *Concept*, p. 235.

elements of modern international law serve precisely these functions, and thereby make possible a political-legal society of states. International law's fundamental "property" rules specify the conditions under which states enjoy legal jurisdiction over particular territories and people. The maxim *pacta sunt servanda*, Latin for "agreements must be kept," is often described as a (or even the) basic rule of the international legal order. Moreover, in its modern incarnation, international law is often said to have originated, or at least to have reached a decisive stage in its development, in the *Treaties* of Westphalia. Through a combination of customary norms and treaties international law has long regulated the conduct of war. But perhaps the most compelling piece of evidence for the claim that international law serves the ends Hart maintains any legal order must serve can be found in the centerpiece of this stage in the evolution of a global political-legal order. Article 1 of the United Nations Charter identifies its purpose as the preservation of international peace and security and the peaceful resolution of international disputes, the development of friendly relations among nations based on respect for the equal rights and self-determination of peoples, and the achievement of international cooperation in solving international problems of an economic, social, cultural, or humanitarian character, and in promoting and encouraging respect for human rights and for fundamental freedoms for all without distinction as to race, sex, language, or religion.[61] It is in light of the foregoing characterization of international law that we should understand Hart's qualified endorsement of Bentham's claim that its similarities to municipal law warrant categorizing it as law. While "the analogy is one of content not of form [i.e. institutional structure] ... no other social rules are so close to municipal law as those of international law."[62]

---

[61] United Nations, *Charter of the United Nations*, 24 October 1945, 1 UNTS XVI.
[62] Hart, *Concept*, p. 237.

4

Ronald Dworkin: Interpretivism and International Law

Just as Hart develops his analysis of law in response to what he identifies as defects in Austin's characterization of it, so too Ronald Dworkin's alternative to legal positivism originates in what he perceives to be shortcomings in Hart's account of law. Indeed, Dworkin argues that Hart makes one of the errors that he repeatedly attributes to Austin, namely offering an analysis of law that is not true to how people, especially judges, experience it. These criticisms are the focus of this chapter's first section. In section II, we consider Dworkin's alternative account of law, before turning in section III to a consideration of several objections that have been leveled against it. Dworkin's reflections on international law are the subject of sections IV and V. In addition to being of interest in their own right, they usefully illustrate Dworkin's conception of law and the reason he thinks it superior to the conception defended by legal positivists. Yet the latter are not Dworkin's only opponents; rather, in his posthumously published essay on international law he also seeks to rebut those who challenge international law's status as genuine law. As will become clear, the success of this attempt depends on the existence of an international rule of law. How we should understand that ideal, and whether the existing globe-spanning practice of government exhibits a sufficient degree of fidelity to it, are questions we take up in Chapter 5.

I DWORKIN'S CRITICISMS OF LEGAL POSITIVISM

Dworkin's first objection challenges the legal positivist account of what makes law; for example, what makes it the case that an American citizen charged with a crime in the USA has a legal right to an attorney, or that all states have a legal duty to refrain from war except in the case of self-defense or when authorized by the UN Security Council to maintain or restore international peace and security. Legal positivists such as Hart maintain that the status of a norm as law depends on a social fact, namely, officials shared practice of recognizing the norm as law in virtue of its satisfying certain criteria. For example, the fact that a norm was enacted in accordance with the process set out in the US Constitution suffices to make it US law. Dworkin notes, however, that judges sometimes justify their decisions in particular cases by appeal to norms that lack a social source, such as the maxims "no one shall be permitted to profit from his own wrongdoing," or "a person is liable for all the foreseeable consequences of her actions."[1] Dworkin labels these norms legal principles, and argues that they have their status as law in virtue of their moral content. In the case of *Riggs v. Palmer*, for instance, the court treated the principle that no person should be permitted to profit from his own wrongdoing as a *legal* basis for denying a convicted murderer a right to inherit his victim's fortune, a position at that time stated neither in any statute nor in any previous judicial decision.[2] Crucially, in deciding cases on the basis of principles such as those mentioned above, many judges claim to be identifying and applying already existing law, not reforming or modifying the law on the basis of extra-legal moral standards of right conduct. Since legal positivism insists that the status of a norm as law is a matter of its social source and not its moral merits, it cannot account for judges (purported) self-understanding of what makes law. Therefore, Dworkin maintains, we ought to reject legal positivism's account of the truth conditions for propositions of law.

In response, legal positivists concede that judges (and other legal officials) sometimes reason on the basis of moral principles as well as social source-based rules, but they contend that it is possible to reconcile this practice with the positivist thesis that the existence of any law is solely a matter of social fact. Inclusive legal positivists argue that whether particular moral principles as such count as law depends on whether legal officials treat them that way.[3] Whether they do so is a contingent matter, however. While legal officials in a particular legal system *may* treat moral criteria as either necessary or sufficient for legal validity, it is also possible for a legal system to exist in which officials do not treat moral principles in either of these two ways. Exclusive legal positivists, in contrast, contend that moral principles cannot provide a criterion for legal validity in any legal system. Rather, whenever judges settle cases by appeal to moral principles they necessarily alter or reform the law; that is, they make new law. Crucially, both types of legal positivism deny what Dworkin seeks to defend, namely that moral principles *necessarily* figure in the grounds of law.

Whereas Dworkin's first objection to legal positivism challenges its account of what makes propositions of law true, his second objection challenges positivism's account of the nature of law. Legal positivists' mistaken view of the kind of thing law is, Dworkin contends, leaves them unable to account for what he calls theoretical

---

[1] Dworkin, "Model of Rules I," 23–31; Dworkin, *Law's Empire*, pp. 238–50.

[2] *Riggs v. Palmer*, 115 NY 506, 22 N.E. 188 (1889). Interestingly, the Permanent Court of International Justice also appealed to the maxim that "a party cannot take advantage of his own wrong" to justify its decision in the *Chorzow Factory* case. See *Factory at Chorzow (Germany v. Poland)*, 1927 P.C.I.J. (ser. A) No. 9 (July 26), 31.

[3] The modifier "as such" distinguishes moral principles from social rules, or posited norms, that have the same content as particular moral principles.

(legal) disagreement: disagreement among legal officials over what makes propositions of law true. Recall once again that for positivists like Hart what makes a norm
L a law of a particular legal order is the fact that officials in that order treat it as such.
Their doing so reflects a consensus on the properties that are necessary and/or
sufficient for a norm to count as law. Of course, legal officials sometimes draw
different conclusions as to what the law is. As long as they do so only because they
dispute whether the conditions for legal validity have been satisfied, such disagreements pose no challenge to the positivist account of what makes propositions of law
true or false. For example, disagreement over whether all of the steps in a legislative
process have been completed is fully compatible with the fact that legal officials
converge on treating any norms that emerge from the completion of all those steps as
law, and it is this convergence that positivists maintain provides the ground of law (or
more precisely, the ground of legislated law in a legal order that includes a legislative
mechanism). However, legal officials may also disagree over whether L is a norm of
their legal system because they do not converge on a common set of conditions for
legal validity. Here their disagreement is not an empirical one, a dispute over the
factual question of whether certain shared criteria for legal validity have been
satisfied. Rather, the dispute is theoretical; legal officials draw different conclusions
regarding what the law is because they disagree over what makes law and therefore
(sometimes) draw different conclusions from the same set of facts.

   Riggs v. Palmer also serves to illustrate this claim. As we noted earlier, the majority
on the Court of Appeals of New York held that Elmer Palmer had no legal right to
inherit any of his grandfather's estate. In reaching that conclusion, it took the
considerations relevant to determining the law to include not only the text of the
New York Statute of Wills, but also the principle "no one shall be permitted to profit
from his own wrongdoing," and a reasonable construction of the intentions of the
legislators who enacted that statute. Writing for the majority, Judge Earl wrote:

> [I]t could never have been their intention that a donee who murdered the testator to
> make the will operative should have any benefit under it. If such a case had been
> present to their minds, and it had been supposed necessary to make some provision
> of law to meet it, it cannot be doubted that they would have provided for it. It is
> a familiar canon of construction that a thing which is within the intention of the
> makers of a statute is as much within the statute as if it were within the letter; and
> a thing which is within the letter of the statute is not within the statute, unless it be
> within the intention of the makers The writers of laws do not always express their
> intention perfectly, but either exceed it or fall short of it, so that judges are to collect
> it from probable or rational conjectures only.[4]

Note that Judge Earl's concern is not with the actual intentions of the legislators with
respect to cases like *Riggs*; as he notes, they may never have considered such a case.
Rather, Judge Earl maintains that we can identify the law in this case by considering

---

[4]   *Riggs v. Palmer*, 509.

what an "upright and reasonable" legislator would have included in the Statute of Wills had he or she contemplated the possibility of a murderer seeking to inherit the estate of his or her victim.

In a dissenting opinion, Judge Gray challenged not only the majority's conclusion that Elmer had no legal right to inherit his grandfather's estate but also the reasons Judge Earl offered to support that conclusion. The Statute of Wills, he maintained, exhaustively identifies the conditions under which individuals enjoy a right to inherit (at that time, in the State of New York): "The capacity and the power of the individual to dispose of his property after death, and the mode by which that power can be exercised, are matters of which the legislature has assumed the entire control, and has undertaken to regulate with comprehensive particularity."[5] While the Court might believe that an "upright and reasonable" legislator concerned to regulate wills "with comprehensive regularity" would include in the Statute of Wills a prohibition on murderers inheriting from their victims, the court is not free to act on its conscience but is instead "bound by the rigid rules of law, which have been established by the legislature."[6] Likewise, with regard to the principle that no person should benefit from his or her own wrongdoing, Judge Gray concedes that principles of "equity and natural justice" may justify a law that "annul[s] testamentary provision made for the benefit of those who have become unworthy of them."[7] However, he maintains that "these principles only suggest sufficient reasons for the enactment of laws to meet such cases."[8] In other words, while they may provide a justification for legislation, they do not provide the Court with a justification for denying Elmer a legal right to inherit absent the actual enactment of legislation barring murderers (or others who have become unworthy) from inheriting the estates of their victims.

Judges Earl and Gray draw different conclusions regarding Elmer's legal right to inherit because they work with different understandings of what makes propositions of law true. They do not agree on the criteria for legal validity, and so they employ different tests to answer the question of whether Elmer is legally entitled to inherit his grandfather's estate. Moreover, Dworkin maintains that the sort of disagreement we see in *Riggs* regarding the grounds of law is both common and pervasive. Given their account of what makes law, legal positivists must treat disputes that originate in officials' conflicting conceptions of the criteria for legal validity as disagreements over what officials ought to treat as the grounds of law in their legal system, and so what the law of that legal system ought to be, rather than disputes over what the law is. Dworkin argues once again that this description is not true to legal officials' experience. Moreover, if theoretical legal disputes are pervasive, as Dworkin maintains they are, legal positivism entails that there is either far less or far more law than it seems. The former conclusion follows from the positivist's claim that L_1, L_2, and so

---

[5] Ibid, p. 516.
[6] Ibid, p. 515.
[7] Ibid, p. 517.
[8] Ibid.

on, exist as norms of a particular legal system only if they satisfy certain criteria on which officials of that system converge when identifying law; little or no convergence entails little or no law. Conversely, the positivist account of law entails that there is more law, or more legal systems, than it seems, if different sets of legal officials employ two or more bodies of law, grounded in two or more understandings of what makes law shared by some but not all officials, to determine actors' legal rights, duties, powers, and immunities. Either conclusion radically distorts the phenomenon it seeks to describe, Dworkin claims, and therefore offers a compelling reason to reject legal positivism's analysis of the nature of law.

II DWORKIN'S ACCOUNT OF LAW

Dworkin advances his own approach to theorizing law, frequently referred to as interpretivism, as a response to the inadequacies of legal positivism. Once again, these are its inability to account for the pervasiveness of disagreement among legal officials regarding the truth conditions for propositions of law, and the fact (as he sees it) that moral principles necessarily figure among the grounds of law, meaning that moral principles necessarily figure in any complete argument for the truth or falsity of a proposition of law.

Dworkin maintains that we should understand legal practice not as a system of rules but instead as a semi-structured argumentative practice oriented to the goal of guiding and constraining the exercise of coercive government. Law is a dynamic process whereby over time, through repeated challenge and response, members of a political community pursue just and fair terms for living together. Understood in very abstract terms, the political ideal of the rule of law provides the overarching structure for the argumentative practice that is law. The rule of law, Dworkin writes, "insists that force not be used or withheld, no matter how useful that would be to the ends in view, no matter how beneficial or noble these ends, except as licensed or required by individual rights and responsibilities flowing from past political decisions about when collective force is justified."[9] The law of a particular political community, then, "is the scheme of rights and responsibilities that meet that complex standard: they license coercion because they flow from past decisions of the right sort."[10] However, Dworkin notes that this concept of the rule of law "is compatible with a great many competing claims about exactly which rights and responsibilities, beyond the paradigms of the day, do follow from past political decisions of the right sort and for that reason do license or require coercive enforcement."[11]

The dispute between Judge Earl and Judge Gray in *Riggs v. Palmer* nicely illustrates this conclusion. While the judges agree that Elmer has a legal right to

---

[9]   Dworkin, *Law's Empire*, p. 93.
[10]   Ibid.
[11]   Ibid.

inherit his grandfather's estate only if past political decisions warrant such a conclusion, they disagree on what counts as the best understanding of their community's political history, and so what follows from that history for the case before them. Judge Earl maintains that the historical record of the community's past political practice points to a strong presumption against allowing individuals to claim legal benefits as a result of their own wrongdoing, and to a practice of reading into legal texts what their authors would have included in them had they considered the case at hand and were "upright and reasonable" agents. Judge Gray maintains instead that a proper reading of the community's past practice requires the court to base its decision solely on the text of the Statute of Wills, which he contends communicates an exhaustive list of the conditions under which the community has determined that a will may be altered or revoked. Each maintains that the other draws the wrong conclusion as to what the law is because each thinks the other has a mistaken understanding of the grounds of law. That misunderstanding reflects an erroneous view of the value(s) served by the rule of law, and so what counts as an exercise of government in accordance with that ideal.[12]

This last point comes into clearer focus once we recognize that, from Judge Gray's standpoint, the Court in *Riggs* does not apply already existing law but instead substitutes its own moral judgment for the political community's, as expressed in the Statute of Wills. In doing so, Judge Earl and the other members of the Court fail to govern in accordance with the rule of law, and instead subject Elmer to the arbitrary rule of their personal moral judgment. Note that this conclusion is not specific to Judge Gray's conception of what it is to govern in accordance with the rule of law. Had the other judges on the Court sided with Judge Gray instead of Judge Earl, then from the latter's standpoint the Court would have acted contrary to the rule of law. In each case, the dissenting judge might have accused the other judges on the court of making new law (that is, legislating), rather than applying existing law. Crucially, the object of this complaint is not merely the performance of a task reserved for a different set of officials; rather, it is the failure to satisfy the core requirement of the rule of law, which is that government exercise coercive force – in *Riggs*, to uphold the property rights of particular individuals – only "in accordance with standards established in the right way before that exercise."[13]

As *Riggs* illustrates, one common way for members of a given community to engage in the argumentative practice that is law is to advance claims regarding what the law is; for example, to assert the existence of a particular legal right, or to assert that some type of conduct falls within the scope of a specific legal right. Positivists err

---

[12]   The error here may involve either the values served by government in accordance with the rule of law, or the bearing those values have on the case at hand. The latter may reflect disputes over the nature of a particular value, such as individual liberty, as well as disagreements over the proper resolution of (apparent) conflicts between values served by government in accordance with the rule of law, such as liberty and security.

[13]   Dworkin, *Justice in Robes*, p. 169.

in thinking that these claims are purely descriptive, statements of fact regarding a consensus among legal officials (at least) that A has a right to Ø, or that A's right to Ø encompasses X but not Y. Rather, they are normative claims regarding the legitimate (in other words, morally justifiable) exercise of coercive government sanctioned by a particular conception of the rule of law. Judge Earl's finding that Elmer has no legal right to inherit his grandfather's estate, and Judge Gray's finding that Elmer does enjoy such a right, are both the product of a constructive interpretation of a particular community's past practice of coercive government in accordance with the ideal of the rule of law. Analytically, this process of constructive interpretation involves comparing different answers to the legal question at issue along two dimensions, which Dworkin labels fit and justification, with the aim of identifying the answer that shows the law in its best light.[14]

The dimension of fit characterizes the extent to which a candidate answer coheres with the community's past practices of coercive government, its findings of law as contained in legislation and judicial and administrative decisions. Fit plays two roles in the evaluation of candidate answers to the question "what is the law?" First, it provides a threshold that any answer must cross to count as a plausible *interpretation* of past political practice. The law, recall, consists of the scheme of individual rights and responsibilities that flow from past political decisions about when collective force is justified, and any response to the question "what is the law" that coheres with few or none of those past political decisions clearly fails to satisfy this understanding of what law is. Second, fit reflects a community's fidelity to its principles, the values it aspires to honor or advance through government in accordance with the rule of law. The failure of a candidate answer to cohere with some part of a political community's historical rule implies that in making and acting on those past political decisions, the community failed to live up to its principles. All else equal, in comparing two constructive interpretations of the community's past political practices we ought to choose whichever one shows the community to have done better at living up to its moral commitments. The dimension of justification characterizes the responsiveness of a claim regarding what the law is to the value or values served by government in accordance with the rule of law, the principles of political morality that serve to justify the community's use of force. Theories of justice such as those defended by John Rawls, Robert Nozick, G.A. Cohen, and Dworkin himself provide examples of rival attempts to spell out these principles of political morality.[15] Competing conceptions of justice will sometimes warrant different constructive

[14] "Analytically" because Dworkin maintains that those immersed in the practice of law will likely not experience the process of constructive interpretation as proceeding in the stepwise fashion his description suggests.

[15] John Rawls, A *Theory of Justice* (Cambridge, MA: Harvard University Press, 1971); Robert Nozick, *Anarchy, State, and Utopia* (New York: Basic Books, 1974); G.A. Cohen, *Self-Ownership, Freedom, and Equality* (Cambridge: Cambridge University Press, 1995); Ronald Dworkin, "What Is Equality? Part 1: Equality of Welfare," *Philosophy and Public Affairs* 10, 3 (1981): 185–246, and "What Is Equality? Part 2: Equality of Resources," *Philosophy and Public Affairs* 10, 4 (1981): 283–345.

interpretations of a community's past political practices, say with respect to the existence or scope of private property rights or the content of a constitutionally protected right to free speech.

A specific answer to the question "what is the law (in this case)" shows the law in its best light if it better satisfies the criteria of fit and justification than do rival answers. There is no algorithm that specifies how much importance to assign to fit and how much to justification when determining what the law is. In some cases, it may be that an answer that does worse on the dimension of fit but better on the dimension of justification than do other contemplated answers best represents the political community's attempt to govern itself in accordance with a proper understanding of the value of the rule of law. In other cases, the opposite will be true. Moreover, regular disagreement on these matters is to be expected; even the question of whether a candidate answer to the question "what is the law" crosses the threshold of fit is one that members of a political community may sometimes reasonably dispute. This does not necessarily imply that there is no right answer to disagreements over the content of the law; indeed, Dworkin maintains the opposite. But because the right answer depends on concepts that are inherently contestable, like justice, freedom, equality, and the rule of law, it is almost inevitable that even when some identify the right answer others will mistakenly conclude that it is the wrong one.[16]

As Dworkin notes, an understanding of law as an argumentative practice concerned with morally justifying the exercise of coercive government does not rule out the possibility that the law ought to be identified solely on the basis of social facts. Rather, the best constructive interpretation of the past political practice of coercive government in a particular community may support just such a test for legal validity. Even if successful, however, this is a *moral* argument for (exclusive) legal positivism, since it is a conclusion that follows from a particular conception of the value(s) served by government in accordance with the rule of law.[17] Indeed, Dworkin contends that the utilitarian philosopher Jeremy Bentham offers precisely such an argument in defense of legal positivism.[18] Bentham viewed law as a tool for the promotion of social welfare, a means for advancing social coordination by providing

---

[16] The argumentative nature of legal practice comes out clearly in contexts where members of a given political community dispute the legality of an actor's actual or mooted conduct. However, it is latent in every circumstance where the law bears on the justifiability of an agent's conduct. In practice, at any given point in time in the history of a particular political community the legality of many act types will not be a matter of dispute. No one will disagree, for instance, that a particular manner of taking possession of another's property counts as theft. Yet in principle, all claims regarding the legality of a particular type of conduct are contestable. In particular, changes in how members of a political community understand the values served by government in accordance with the rule of law can result in legal challenges that, a few generations earlier, would have appeared so outlandish as to barely merit a response.

[17] In contrast, Hart is generally understood as defending legal positivism on descriptive grounds, though he also maintains that positivism offers certain moral advantages over non-positivist accounts of law.

[18] Dworkin, *Justice in Robes*, p. 174.

certainty in the form of clear, identifiable, statements of its members' rights, duties, powers, and immunities.[19] Law best serves this goal if those it addresses identify the law solely on the basis of social facts, namely, the past decisions made by legal institutions. Although many subsequent defenders of legal positivism rejected Bentham's utilitarianism, they continue to give pride of place to law's (alleged) capacity to provide its subjects with certainty in their accounts of the nature of law.

Dworkin rejects this instrumental account of the value of the rule of law. In a complex social world like the one(s) we inhabit, a positivist conception of what makes law will frequently entail the presence of gaps in the law; that is, cases where no consensus exists among legal officials (or subjects) regarding the (content of) the rights and responsibilities that flow from past political decisions. In these cases, positivists argue, legal officials should (and must) exercise discretion. But discretionary rule ignores the value of political integrity, which Dworkin maintains is integral to legal practice. Political integrity, he writes, "requires government to speak with one voice, to act in a principled and coherent manner toward all its citizens, to extend to everyone the substantive standards of justice or fairness it uses for some."[20] Like the other values that serve to justify government in accordance with the rule of law, political integrity partly characterizes the basic demand to which all moral agents are subject, namely that they treat others with equal concern and respect. It comes into play when members of a political community of principle disagree as to what justice or fairness requires; that is, whether a particular exercise of government conforms to one or more of these ideals. In such circumstances, fidelity to the basic moral demand for equal concern and respect entails that those who exercise political power on behalf of the community do so only in ways that the community can be shown to have sanctioned. Legal officials who do so exhibit the virtue of political integrity:

> Integrity becomes a political ideal ... when we insist that the state act on a single, coherent set of principles even when its citizens are divided about what the right principles of justice and fairness really are. We assume ... that we can recognize other people's acts as expressing a conception of fairness or justice or decency even when we do not endorse that conception ourselves. This ability is an important part of our more general ability to treat others with respect.[21]

Clearly, states can disrespect their subjects by governing in ways that treat some of them unjustly or unfairly, and, in that regard, deny their fundamental status as moral equals. But even government officials who are genuinely committed to the moral equality of all members of their political community disrespect those they rule when they act on their own, personal, judgment as to when and how the community

---

[19]   Ibid, p. 174.
[20]   Dworkin, *Law's Empire*, p. 165. For Dworkin, fairness concerns the design of political procedures that distribute political power, while justice concerns the ends at which we ought to aim in our exercise of political power.
[21]   Ibid, p. 166.

should use force to uphold its members right and responsibilities. The judge who exercises discretion in pursuit of maximizing aggregate welfare may count gains and losses to individuals' welfare equally, and likewise for one who exercises discretion to advance or honor fundamental human interests that ground (moral) human rights. Nevertheless, by privileging their personal moral judgment, these individuals arrogate to themselves an authority over other members of the community at odds with respect for its members status as moral equals.

Law as integrity, Dworkin's own account of government in accordance with a proper understanding of the value of the rule of law, directs officials and subjects alike to constrain their moral judgment regarding the justifiable exercise of coercive government by satisfying a demand for coherence with other elements of the law; that is, with their political community's past practice of coercive government. When they do so, any claim regarding what the law is will be characterizable as the *community's* understanding of what justice and fairness require, rather than an expression of the legal official's or subject's personal moral judgment. Consequently, in a community of principle that governs itself in accordance with law as integrity, the apparent tension between the hierarchy characteristic of the relationship between ruler and ruled and the fundamentally equal status of all moral agents is dissolved, as no individual is subject to the arbitrary rule of another. Where legal officials govern with integrity, all subjects enjoy equality before the law, and that is what respect for moral equality requires in communities united in their commitment to abstract principles of justice and fairness, but divided on what precisely counts as fidelity to those principles.

One final feature of Dworkin's philosophy of law warrants attention, before we turn to his account of international law. On Dworkin's account, a community possesses law only to the extent that its practice of coercive government manifests a commitment to a particular conception of the rule of law as a political ideal. On that conception, the exercise of political power is legitimate in virtue of its being responsive to considerations of justice, fairness, and integrity. Legal skepticism, then, consists in the judgment that an exercise of coercive government cannot be justified on the grounds that it flows from this conception of the rule of law as a political ideal. Thus understood, legal skepticism comes in degrees. It may be quite local, as in the case of an individual who concludes that her state's past and current practice of upholding property rights displays fidelity to law as integrity except in the case of murderers who stand to inherit from their victims. But legal skepticism may be broader, as in the case of a person who concludes that the best constructive interpretation of her community's legal regulation of property shows it to be deeply compromised, premised on a mistaken moral view of what gives a person a property right in something, or a morally dubious shielding of property rights from democratic control. Nevertheless, there may be some elements of the community's practice of coercive government that do not address or have significant implications for property rights, and that do not suffer from any defects that call into question their status as law. In this case, the community will be one that sometimes governs legally, meaning in accordance with a proper conception of the rule of law, but that sometimes does not. Finally, it may be that no aspect of the practice of coercive government in a particular community reflects an attempt to realize law as integrity. Perhaps those who exercise political power in the community in question exhibit no concern for fairness and justice. Or while they do sometimes act from a concern for one or the other of these values, they do not take it to be a condition on their exercise of political power that it be "in accordance with standards established in the right way before that exercise."[22] In other words, they display no commitment to political integrity. In the former case, rules may facilitate the effective and efficient exercise of power, but only in the interest of some form of private aggrandizement and not for the ends that legitimate coercive government, namely, the treatment of all members of the community with equal concern and respect. In the latter case, while those who govern may sometimes benefit or respect the governed, the governed will always be vulnerable to the whims of the governors. Of course, the most common form of absolutism or despotism combines both of these elements: a disregard for the rule of law as well as the values that government in accordance with that ideal serves to honor or advance.

We began this section with Dworkin's characterization of law as a semi-structured argumentative practice concerned with the justification of coercive government and informed by a fundamental commitment to the rule of law as a political ideal. We then briefly explored a central aspect of this practice, namely, the use of the method of constructive interpretation to identify legal rights and duties, or to contest others' findings of law. Together, these accounts of the nature of law and the truth conditions for specific propositions of law explain the pervasiveness of theoretical legal disagreement as well as the essential, if not always explicit, role that principles of political morality play in legal argument. Next, we juxtaposed two accounts of the moral value of government in accordance with the rule of law. The first was an instrumental *moral* argument for legal positivism that emphasized the rule of law's utility for producing morally desirable outcomes. The second, defended by Dworkin, emphasized the constitutive contribution the rule of law makes to the community's treatment of all its members with equal concern and respect. Finally, we noted the possibility of employing Dworkin's account of law as integrity to justify a skeptical conclusion regarding the legality of (some aspect of) a practice of coercive government.

A grasp of each of these points will prove useful in understanding Dworkin's reflections on international law, as well as certain challenges to them. First, however, we should note a few of the criticisms that philosophers have leveled against Dworkin's general account of law.

---

[22]   Dworkin, *Justice in Robes*, p. 169.

III OBJECTIONS TO DWORKIN'S ACCOUNT OF LAW

Some philosophers dispute certain empirical claims central to Dworkin's argument for interpretivism. For example, Dworkin defends the claim that law is an interpretive concept on the grounds that only such an understanding of law can make sense of the theoretical legal disagreements he maintains are pervasive in any legal order. Brian Leiter contests the pervasiveness of such disagreements; by and large, he argues, legal officials and subjects concur in their understanding of the social facts that determine what the law is (in any particular case). If so, then contra Dworkin's assertion the salient feature of legal practice that any theory of law must explain is this consensus, and Leiter maintains that legal positivism fares much better on this measure than does interpretivism.[23]

Consider, too, Dworkin's claim that interpretivism best accords with the experience of those who specialize in identifying the law, especially judges and lawyers, because it justifies their sense that, even in hard cases, they are attempting to determine what the law is rather than making new law through the exercise of discretion. As Andrei Marmor points out, some judges do describe their decisions in such cases as legislation, the product of a moral judgment regarding the best way to proceed that fills a gap in existing law.[24] Dworkin maintains that these judges misunderstand the nature of the practice in which they participate. Either they mischaracterize what they have done when they correctly identify the legal rights or duties that flow from the best constructive interpretation of their community's past practice of coercive government, or they draw a mistaken conclusion vis-à-vis what the law is, abetted perhaps by their erroneous understanding of their responsibilities as law appliers, not lawmakers.[25] Yet if a match with the self-understanding of judges and lawyers is meant to serve as a reason for accepting interpretivism, Dworkin cannot assume its truth in order to dismiss the self-reports of legal officials that do not support his philosophy of law.

Marmor also maintains that judges are well aware that they sometimes exercise discretion to fill gaps in the law:

> I am not claiming that it is a secret that judges often make new law – far from it. But it has the status of an inconvenient truth, so to speak, widely recognized as it is. And this inconvenience puts judges under considerable pressure to coat the making of new law in the rhetoric of law application.[26]

---

[23] Brian Leiter, "Explaining Theoretical Disagreement," 76 *U. Chi. L. Rev.* 1215 (2009): 1226–32.
[24] Andrei Marmor, *Philosophy of Law* (2011), p. 90.
[25] Note that in the latter case they do not make new law, even if the parties to the dispute they settle treat their decision as law. Over time, however, that mistaken finding may become embedded in the community's legal practice, and so influence the content of its law. As a regulatory ideal, however, Dworkin takes the aim of a legal practice to be the elimination over time of all mistaken conclusions regarding the community's justifiable use of political power.
[26] Ibid.

Given that we have a ready explanation for why judges might present their law-making as merely discovering already existing law, it is questionable how much credence we ought to give to Dworkin's philosophy of law simply because it fits with judges' description of their decisions in hard cases.

Positivist critics also argue that Dworkin's philosophy of law has troubling implications, ones that do not follow from their own analysis of law. Consider, for example, law's utility as a tool subjects can use to predict how the political community will respond to their performing a certain act, and one that officials can use to predict how other officials will react to their exercise of political power. The greater the consensus on what the law is, the greater its utility in this regard. Interpretivism, however, seems to invite dissensus and disagreement, and so weakens people's ability to use the law to identify the rights and duties the community will enforce on demand. Dworkin concludes his most influential book in legal philosophy by describing law as, "a protestant attitude that makes each citizen responsible for imagining what his society's public commitments to principle are, and what these commitments require in new circumstances."[27] In other words, each member of the political community has a moral right and a moral responsibility to engage in a constructive interpretation of the community's past practice of coercive government in order to determine what the law is. If theoretical legal disagreement is pervasive, as Dworkin maintains, the result will be constant debate rather than a settled set of standards agents can use to help plan their lives. In response, Dworkin might maintain that in any healthy community of principle, members are likely to agree on a fair number of propositions of law that flow from their political history, as well as permissible procedures for contesting allegedly mistaken findings of law.[28] By the same token, Dworkin may also double down on his description of law as a semi-structured argumentative practice. Law does not displace moral disagreement over our political rights but instead channels it in such a way that it meshes effective government with ongoing contestation of the demands of justice and legitimacy.

Finally, if Dworkin's analysis of law is correct, then it may well be that much of what is treated as law in a given community is not really law. That is because past courts may have made wide-ranging and systematic errors in their constructive interpretation of the rights and duties that flow from the community's past political practices. Of course, any plausible account of law must allow for the possibility that courts sometimes err in their identification of the law. Yet it surely counts against an

---

[27] Dworkin, *Law's Empire*, p. 413.

[28] This is particularly true if those who specialize in the task of identifying the law are educated in a similar manner, and have other commonalities of culture, economic class, and so on. Note, too, that individuals might become adept at predicting the conclusions officials will draw even though they do not think those propositions flow from the best constructive interpretation of the community's past practice of coercive government.

analysis of law if it entails that much of what generations of legal officials and subjects have treated as their community's law turns out not to have been law at all.

On reflection, however, this implication may come to be seen as a virtue of Dworkin's jurisprudence. Reflecting on the history of coercive government in a particular state, we might well conclude that it was not an example of rule in accordance with a proper conception of the rule of law but the legally unconstrained and therefore illegitimate use of power by some to oppress or subjugate others. Or perhaps we will view it as having once been a highly defective legal order, extending the full benefits of the rule of law to some (for example, white male property owners), a more limited set of benefits to others (say, white females), and no benefits to a third group (for instance, black slaves). We might then conclude that while this state's present practice of coercive government is less defective than it once was, in some domains, such as its criminal justice system, the state's rule continues to more closely resemble a practice of oppression or subjugation than one committed to the treatment of all of its citizens with equal concern and respect. Members of this community may express that judgment by saying things such as "the law is unjust," or "the law is unconstitutional." But Dworkin maintains that the labels or phrases individuals use in this context tell us nothing interesting.[29] Rather, what matters to the members of this community, and also, therefore, provides the focal point for a worthwhile philosophy of law, is the moral justifiability of the state's exercise of political power.

For Dworkin, when we consider the legality of some act we normally treat the rest of our community's existing practice of coercive government as legal. That assumption is provisional, however, and over time the community may revisit that judgment as it pertains to other aspects of its overall practice of government. In some cases, the community may find that the provisional finding of legality cannot be sustained, in which case, it will likely revise its characterization of the rights and duties its members may demand without any further legislation. If the process goes on long enough, we may be able to look back and judge that much of what was once treated as law was not really law. All judgments of law are provisional, subject to change in light of an improved understanding of the principles of political morality imminent in our political community, the recalibration of judgments of fit in light of unanticipated cases, and the recognition of places in which the law falls short of integrity. We cannot change them all at once, however. This is partly a practical matter; just as it is not possible for sailors at sea to replace too many planks on the boat at once without sinking, so, too, it is not possible to simultaneously revise too much of what a community treats as its law without causing a serious breakdown in social order. But it is also partly a consequence of limits on our ability to discern what justice requires of us. Only by engaging in the semi-structured argumentative practice of

---

[29] "The ancient jurisprudential problem of evil law is sadly close to a verbal dispute." Dworkin, *Justice for Hedgehogs*, p. 412.

government in accordance with the rule of law can we work our way toward a better understanding of what treatment with equal concern and respect requires.

IV DWORKIN'S PHILOSOPHY OF INTERNATIONAL LAW

Dworkin develops his account of international law as an alternative to orthodox international legal positivism (OILP), which holds that states are legally bound only by those standards to which they have explicitly or tacitly consented.[30] On this account of what makes international law, a state's exercise of will accounts for both the content of its legal obligations and their normativity. If we wish to know a state's international legal obligations when it comes to, say, the conduct of war, we simply need to identify the standards for waging war to which it has agreed. Likewise, if anyone asks why the state must comply with those standards, the answer will be that the state chose to subject itself to them; for instance, by signing (and, where necessary, ratifying) the Geneva Conventions, or by failing to persistently object to evolving customary legal rules governing the conduct of war.

Unsurprisingly, Dworkin finds in OILP's account of the grounds of international law the same defects he finds in legal positivism's account of the grounds of law in any legal order. First, as a constructive interpretation of the state system of coercive government, OILP entails the existence of "gaps" in international law, meaning circumstances in which international legal actors cannot guide their conduct in accordance with the law but instead must exercise discretion. For example, Dworkin maintains that OILP identifies no priority among the different sources of law it identifies. If so, then in any case where a treaty-based international legal norm conflicts with a rule of customary international law, any resolution of the conflict will necessarily reflect the private moral judgment of an individual state, ICJ judge, and so on, not the public moral judgment of the international community. If there is no answer to the question "do States have a legal right to Ø" prior to a particular state or an international judge asserting that there is, then at least the first exercise of political power premised on that assertion will not satisfy the requirement that "power be exercised only in accordance with standards established in the right way before that exercise."[31]

Second, Dworkin argues that OILP offers an unworkable strategy for identifying the content of states' international legal obligations: "If a constraint is part of international law for particular nations only because they have consented to it . . . then the master interpretive question must be: what is it most reasonable to assume that these nations, whose consent made the principle law, understood that they were consenting to?"[32] Even the ability to consult a written text, as in the case of international legal conventions, may not provide an answer to this question. To illustrate,

[30]   Dworkin, "A New Philosophy for International Law," *Philosophy and Public Affairs* 41, 1 (2013): 3–10.
[31]   Dworkin, *Justice in Robes*, p. 169.
[32]   Dworkin, "New Philosophy," 7.

Dworkin asks his reader to consider what sort of constraints on the use of force flow from Article 2(4) of the UN Charter's provision that "all members shall refrain in their international relations from the threat or use of force against the territorial integrity or political independence of any state, or in any other manner inconsistent with the Purposes of the United Nations."[33] Does an armed humanitarian intervention that aims only to halt a genocide or crimes against humanity, and not to make any changes to the targeted state's boundaries or constitution, violate this international legal prohibition? What about the use of drones to carry out targeted attacks on non-state actors (terrorist groups, say) residing in the territory of another state? If a state's government has for some time failed to exert effective control over large parts of the territory that nominally belongs to it, can it still justifiably invoke a right to territorial integrity to contest other states' armed intervention in those places? Dworkin maintains that we cannot answer these questions by appeal to a consensus among states (and other international legal officials) that comprehensively addresses when the use of force is permissible, and what forms it may take. There is little reason to believe that states agreed on the answer to these questions when they created the United Nations, or that any consensus has developed since then. Indeed, Dworkin asserts that it is "unclear whose opinion, among the different officers or citizens of these states, counts as manifesting a state opinion," and so what would even count as a consensus among states regarding the legally permissible use of force.[34]

A third criticism Dworkin levels against OILP is its inability to account for features of existing international legal practice that stretch beyond the breaking point the idea that each states' legal obligations are a product of it agreeing to limit its freedom in the ways specified by various international legal standards. For example, the peremptory status of certain international legal norms, such as the prohibitions on genocide and slavery, entails that individual states lack the power to alter some of their rights and duties under international law. The problem, as Dworkin sees it, is not simply that OILP's account of the grounds of law does not fit the practice. Rather, the problem is that OILP fundamentally conflicts with the advancement of the moral aims that legitimate international law; that is, that morally justify the enforcement of international legal rights and duties. As we will see, Dworkin holds that a genuine international legal order necessarily constrains the scope of state

[33] United Nations, *Charter of the United Nations*, 24 October 1945, 1 UNTS XVI.
[34] Dworkin, "New Philosophy," 8. As we will see, Dworkin acknowledges that a "general endorsement" by states often figures among the truth conditions for propositions of international law. However, it does so as a premise in a *moral* argument for the superiority of one candidate finding of law over another. Thus, international lawyers may have good reason to assert or deny the existence of a (near) consensus among states vis-à-vis the legality of some act type, as they often do. But it is a mistake to treat these assertions or denials as a complete statement of the conditions in virtue of which they are true, a complete presentation of the reasons why others ought to view the conduct in question as legally permissible or impermissible. Rather, the full argument for the truth of any proposition of international law also includes those principles of political morality that warrant the enforcement of international legal subjects' rights and responsibilities.

sovereignty, including a state's liberty to determine for itself the extent of its international legal obligations. A conception of international law as the product of state-by-state consent cannot account for the necessity of such constraints on state sovereignty, and so cannot provide the "jurisprudential foundation" for a genuine, legitimate, international legal order.[35]

Dworkin develops his alternative to OILP on the basis of two claims, one descriptive and the other normative. Descriptively, Dworkin characterizes International law as "very young . . . effectively reborn in 1945."[36] It is slowly evolving out of the nonlegal global political order that preceded it, namely the Westphalian one that began to take shape in the seventeenth century and reached its zenith in the late-nineteenth and early-twentieth centuries. This description of international law explains why Dworkin frames international jurisprudence, or the construction of a philosophy of international law, as a matter of *how far* we can treat the existing practice of global coercive government as an example of genuine law. As we will see, it also sheds light on the relatively limited moral aim Dworkin ascribes to contemporary international law, namely mitigating the worst injustices states can perform or enable when their rule is unconstrained by the rule of law and a proper understanding of its value.

Normatively, Dworkin asserts that all who exercise coercive government have a standing duty to enhance their legitimacy, to continuously improve on their community's past attempts to exercise political power only in ways that are properly responsive to the ideals of justice, fairness, and integrity within the framework imposed by a commitment to the ideal of the rule of law. This duty has implications for both legislation and adjudication. In the first case, it calls for reforms to existing norms that fall short of fidelity to one or another of the aforementioned ideals. An example would be the replacement of a deeply unfair norm allocating voting rights on new legislation with one that better satisfies the claims of all those with a right to participate in the legislative process.[37] In the case of adjudication, the identification of legal subjects' rights and duties under existing law, the duty to enhance the legitimacy of coercive government requires officials to correct for mistaken constructive interpretations of the community's past political practices. These mistakes involve either finding that certain legal subjects have rights or duties when the best constructive interpretation of the community's past political practice warrants the opposite conclusion, or vice versa.

The duty to enhance the legitimacy of coercive government, Dworkin writes:

---

[35]   Ibid, 7.

[36]   Ibid, 29. Elsewhere Dworkin describes international law as "fragile, still nascent and in critical condition." Ibid, 23.

[37]   See, for example, Dworkin's claim that were the UN General Assembly to take on a legislative function the standing duty to enhance the legitimacy of coercive government would require changes to its existing allocation of voting rights. Ibid, 27–8.

arises not just *within* each of the sovereign states who are members of the Westphalian system but also *about* the system itself: that is, about each state's decision to respect the principles of that system. For those principles are not independent of but are actually part of the coercive system each of those states imposes on its citizens. It follows that the general obligation of each state to improve its political legitimacy includes an obligation to try to improve the overall international system. If a state can help to facilitate an international order in a way that would improve the legitimacy of its own coercive government, then it has a political obligation to do what it can in that direction.[38]

Dworkin identifies four respects in which states fail to enhance the legitimacy of their rule over their own citizens when they adopt or sustain a Westphalian conception of state sovereignty.

First, each state owes its citizens protection from their own government's violation of their basic human rights, and, therefore, each state stands to improve its legitimacy by promoting an effective international order that will weaken the hold on power of current tyrannical governments and prevent the (re-)emergence of tyrannical government in the future. If, instead, states attempt to preserve the Westphalian view that they enjoy total freedom in their domestic affairs as long as their rule does not threaten international peace and stability, then they act contrary to their duty to enhance their legitimacy. Second, each state owes its citizens protection from the threat that other states (and non-state actors) may pose to their human rights: "Any state therefore has a reason to work hard toward an international order which guarantees that the community of nations would help it resist invasion or other pressures."[39] A Westphalian order, in contrast, treats international conflicts as of concern only to the parties and those states that choose to ally themselves with one of the parties. Security from external threats in such an order largely depends on state's interests and relative power, rather than a commitment by all states – the community of nations – to enforce each of its members' rights not to be attacked. Third, when governments act on the basis of a Westphalian conception of state sovereignty, they make it difficult or even impossible to achieve the international cooperation needed to address certain threats to their citizens, such as those arising from climate change, pandemics, and the flow of illegal money and goods across international borders. In part, the problem is one of agreeing on the terms for international cooperation, such as the cost each state must bear as part of the collective effort to address climate change. If states are legally bound only by those standards to which they consent, then each has an incentive to hold out in the hopes that other states will agree to its optimal terms for cooperation. But the Westphalian conception of sovereignty also raises a barrier to the exercise of effective monitoring and enforcement, which can be necessary to get cooperative schemes off the ground, and to sustain them once they exist. The result may be no cooperation, or at best

[38] Ibid, 17.
[39] Ibid.

suboptimal forms of cooperation that leave many states doing less to protect their citizens from these threats than they might have done had they embraced a less robust conception of state sovereignty. Finally: "[T]he legitimacy of coercive government requires, fourth, that people play some genuine, even if minimal and indirect, role in their own government."[40] For many people, domestic laws and policies enacted in other states increasingly shape their life prospects. If their own state adopts a Westphalian conception of state sovereignty, it commits itself to the position that these individuals have no right to a say on laws and policies that deeply affect them. In doing so, it helps to sustain a practice of coercive government that fails to treat many people fairly (in Dworkin's sense). The duty to enhance its legitimacy requires instead that this state, indeed every state, work to revamp the contours of state sovereignty so that "people everywhere be permitted to participate in some way – even if only in some minimal way – in the enactment and administration of at least those policies that threaten the greatest impact on them."[41]

Each state's duty to enhance the legitimacy of its rule requires not only that it take steps to craft an international order that will better protect its citizens' basic human rights but also one that will better enable them to fulfill their moral duties, including those they owe to noncitizens. Dworkin observes that:

> [P]eople around the world believe they have – and they do have – a moral responsibility to help protect people in other nations from war crimes, genocide, and other violations of human rights. Their government falls short of its duty to help them acquit their moral responsibilities when it accedes to definitions of sovereignty that prevent it from intervening to prevent such crimes or to ameliorate their disastrous effects.[42]

As with any exercise of political power, a state that chooses not to intervene to protect noncitizens from evils such as genocide owes its citizens a justification for the actions it takes in their name; that is, on behalf of the political community whose government it is. Appeal to a Westphalian conception of state sovereignty cannot establish the legitimacy of the government's decision because it falsely denies that the members of the community have a right to intervene when in fact they have a duty to do so. Instead, each state's government has a duty to work toward an international order in which the Westphalian system's absolute ban on interference in another state's domestic affairs is replaced with one that identifies and facilities morally justifiable interventions.

Dworkin maintains that at least at this early stage in its development, international law has only a limited moral aim, namely, mitigating the dangers and injustices of a global political order premised on the Westphalian conception of state sovereignty. The duty of mitigation, he writes, "provides the most general structural principle and

---

interpretive background of international law."[43] Dworkin notes, however, that the duty of mitigation is too abstract to provide an account of the grounds of international law; and so, of international legal subjects' rights and duties. Therefore, he introduces a second fundamental structural principle, the principle of salience, which states that: "[I]f a significant number of states, encompassing a significant population, has developed an agreed code of practice, either by treaty or by other form of coordination, then other states have at least a prima facie [moral] duty to subscribe to that practice as well, with the important proviso that this duty holds only if a more general practice to that effect, expanded in that way, would improve the legitimacy of the subscribing state and the international order as a whole."[44] To fully grasp the role played by salience, it may be helpful to recall that Dworkin conceives of law as a semi-structured argumentative practice. The structure is provided by a rough and often evolving consensus on (a) abstract principles of political morality, the ideals that participants in the practice invoke in debates over the justifiability of (specific examples of) coercive government; (b) a language for advancing constructive interpretations of these principles, a way of talking about the legitimacy of coercive government that all can understand; and (c) examples of coercive government that the practice does, and does not, warrant, or in other words, paradigmatic cases of legal and illegal conduct. This rough consensus provides a focal point without which the argumentative practice that is law cannot exist.

As Dworkin notes, when international law first emerged among European states, Christian doctrine and the Roman idea of *ius gentium*, legal principles common to all (European) states, provided a salient set of principles of political morality, a common language for arguing about them, and a set of paradigmatic cases (for instance, drawn from the Bible, or the history of the Roman Republic). The growth of secularism in the West, the emergence of a powerful block of Communist countries, including the USSR and China, and the emergence of dozens of new states in Africa and Asia following the demise of colonialism left these traditions unable to provide a focal point for an international community. Instead, the necessary salience was provided by the charter and institutions of the United Nations, as well as the Universal Declaration of Human Rights (UDHR). Over the ensuing decades, this germ of a new world order took root, as states and other actors invoked the principles set out in these documents and the practices of the institutions they created to defend or contest the legality of their own or others' conduct. Central to this attempt to forge a new semi-structured practice of argumentation on the basis of the principles described in the UN Charter and the UDHR was an alternative to the Westphalian conception of sovereignty, one that placed new limits on state's legal exercise of political power in the interest of preserving international peace and promoting respect for individual human rights. This attempt to fulfill the

[43] Ibid, 19.
[44] Ibid.

duty of mitigation would have been impossible, however, without the nearly global embrace of the principles set out in the Charter, the language of human rights as it emerged from the UDHR and subsequent Human Rights Conventions, and an evolving consensus on paradigms of legal and illegal conduct under this new regime. The salience of this ideology, this way of conceiving of the relationship between states, and between states and individuals, makes it possible to pursue the task of rendering the duty to mitigate determinate.

Recall that for the orthodox international legal positivist, state consent provides the grounds of international law, the consideration in virtue of which propositions of international law are true or false. In contrast, at least with respect to the rights and duties that constitute state sovereignty, Dworkin maintains that we identify the law by constructively interpreting the practice of international coercive government since the UN Charter came into force in 1945 as an attempt to mitigate the risks and failures of the Westphalian state system. Moreover, the combination of a duty to mitigate and salience also offer an alternative basis for international law's normativity. As Dworkin writes:

> The charter and institutions of the United Nations are best understood ... as an order all nations now have a moral obligation to treat as law. The obligation is created not by consent but by the moral force of salience as a route to a satisfactory international order. Indeed – more generally – multilateral agreements setting out conceptions of such an order, like the Charter, the Geneva Conventions, the genocide agreement, and the Treaty of Rome establishing the International Criminal Court, are made international law for all, not just their initial signatories, through that principle.[45]

Since all coercive governments have a standing moral duty to enhance their legitimacy, there is no need to show that states have agreed to the limits on how they may exercise political power described (perhaps imperfectly) in the UN Charter, the Geneva Conventions, and other legislative efforts that serve to mitigate the risks and failures of the Westphalian state system. Rather, we only need to show that specific legal obligations that flow from those past practices of international government serve the goal of enhancing the legitimacy of a state's rule over its citizens.[46] Put another way, where international law serves to strengthen the moral justifiability of a state's rule, its government is not free to decide whether it wishes to be bound by that law. Instead, the state is automatically subject to the international legal norm or regime in question in virtue of the fact that being so bound, that is, acknowledging those limits on its sovereignty, constitutes a partial fulfillment of its standing moral duty to enhance its legitimacy.

---

[45]　Ibid, 20.
[46]　Or, as we will discuss in the next section, serve the goal of enhancing the legitimacy of the state system as a whole.

Suppose, however, that a state concludes that particular "agreed code[s] of practice" developed by "a significant number of states, encompassing a significant population," fall woefully short of the goal of enhancing the legitimacy of coercive government. Perhaps the duties these codes impose on states to take action to address climate change, or to aid refugees, or to reduce the risk of nuclear war, are far too undemanding, and consequently sanction practices of coercive government that, at best, only weakly enhance states' legitimacy. Why should the state in question adhere to the legal norms set out in these agreed codes of practice? Why should it not instead act on its own judgment regarding the specific, enforceable, duties that all states have to address climate change, the plight of refugees, and the dangers of nuclear annihilation, ones it believes derive from the more general duty to mitigate the risks and failures of the Westphalian state system? Dworkin briefly gestures at two answers to this question, one moral and one practical. The moral argument is that collective coercive government is essential to our dignity.[47] If a state acts on its own conception of the rights and duties constitutive of sovereignty, the result will either be anarchy or, if it is powerful enough to impose its judgment on other states, tyranny. In either case, power alone will determine whatever order exists in international affairs, an outcome clearly at odds with the moral imperative on all coercive governments to enhance their legitimacy. The practical argument concerns the inability of any state to realize the moral aims international law serves through unilateral action. This is clearest where each state can effectively respond to a threat to its citizens' basic human rights only by collaborating with other states, as in the case of climate change or, perhaps, the proliferation of weapons of mass destruction. It may also be true in the case of reducing the dangers of international conflict and domestic tyranny, however. A common understanding of the conditions under which war is permissible may reduce its incidence, especially if it leads to collective efforts to enforce that understanding against those who flout it. Likewise, a shared commitment to standards for legitimate domestic rule, such as respect for human rights and democracy, may contribute in various ways to improving the legitimacy of each state's government. In short, despite its shortcomings, states will almost always do better at enhancing the legitimacy of coercive government by conforming to a consensus on states' rights and obligations as spelled out in an "agreed code of practice" than they will if they act on a conception of state sovereignty that better fulfills the duty to mitigate but is not widely accepted by other states.

Dworkin briefly lists several advantages his characterization of the grounds and normativity of international law has over OILP.[48] For example, the peremptory status of certain legal norms, such as those prohibiting genocide or slavery, follows from the fact that coordination on norms permitting such conduct could never serve to enhance the legitimacy of the states subject to them. This explains why states lack

---

[47] Dworkin, *Justice for Hedgehogs*, p. 320.
[48] Dworkin, "New Philosophy," 21–2.

the right (that is, normative power) to modify their duty not to permit slavery by, say, entering into bilateral agreements that create an international market for the purchase and sale of human beings. However, he emphasizes that the primary value of his philosophy of international law is not its ability to provide a rationale for various features of the international legal order. Rather:

> [T]he major yield of any theory about the grounds of international law is an interpretive strategy for international law. We should interpret the documents and practices picked out by the principle of salience so as to advance the imputed purpose of mitigating the flaws and dangers of the Westphalian system. The correct interpretation of an international document, like the UN Charter, is the interpretation that makes the best sense of the text, given the underlying aim of international law, which is taken to be the creation of an international order that protects political communities from external aggression, protects citizens of those communities from domestic barbarism, facilitates coordination when this is essential, and provide some measure of participation by people in their own governance across the world.[49]

The legal rights and obligations constitutive of state sovereignty are those that flow from a constructive interpretation of the UN Charter and subsequent efforts to develop its vision of a genuine, global, community of legitimate states that portrays these past practices of government in their morally best light. In virtue of their salience, the UN Charter, the Geneva Conventions, the UDHR and various Human Rights Conventions, and the Rome Statute are central elements of the practice – the Charter Project – that any finding of law must fit in order to count as the identification of an existing legal right or obligation. Candidate constructive interpretations must also be assessed along the dimension of justification, however, and the principle of mitigation provides the requisite principle of political morality for carrying out such an assessment.

To illustrate his account of how we ought to identify the legal rights and duties constitutive of state sovereignty, Dworkin considers the legality of unilateral humanitarian intervention (UHI). UHI consists of armed intervention by one or more states in the territory of another state, undertaken without authorization by the UN Security Council, for the purpose of alleviating a grave human rights situation, paradigmatically that constituted by crimes against humanity or genocide. NATO's intervention in Kosovo is widely viewed as an instance of UHI, and almost universally judged to have been illegal on the grounds that it violated Article 2(4) of the UN Charter. Dworkin questions whether this conclusion rests on a mistaken constructive interpretation of Article 2(4), and suggests that "perhaps we should understand its prohibitions to be limited to the use of military force aimed at territorial change or political dominion."[50] On the dimension of justification, this conclusion

---

[49] Ibid.
[50] Ibid, 23.

might follow from reading the "purposes of the United Nations" cited in Article 2(4) as "those that flow from the moral responsibility nations had to create that institution: the responsibility to protect people from the dangers of the insulated sovereignty of the Westphalian system."[51] On the dimension of fit, Dworkin points to several texts in which, he maintains, states have endorsed this conception of the United Nation's purposes, including the UN General Assembly's United for Peace Resolution and the outcome document of a 2005 World Summit in which nearly all states endorsed the Responsibility to Protect. Dworkin acknowledges that the text describing the Responsibility to Protect requires Security Council authorization of any armed humanitarian intervention.[52] Nevertheless, he maintains that its true importance lies in the fact that it treats states' rights to territorial integrity as conditional on their protecting their citizens (or, more broadly, residents) from genocide, war crimes, crimes against humanity, and ethnic cleansing. Perhaps, then, the best constructive interpretation of the past practices of government relevant to identifying the legal rights and duties created by Article 2(4) will yield a finding of law that fits the description of states' right to territorial integrity in the Responsibility to Protect, but not its description of the conditions under which other states are authorized to intervene.

In fact, Dworkin concludes that UHI is illegal.[53] His reason for doing so has less to do with considerations of fit than with the belief that such a finding of law scores better along the dimension of justification than does a finding that international law permits UHI. A legal norm permitting states to engage in UHI might well enable states to engage in aggressive war under cover of carrying out a unilateral humanitarian intervention. If so, then a legal right to engage in UHI would actually decrease the legitimacy of coercive government in two ways. First, it would effectively enable individual states to exercise political power in ways they cannot morally justify either to their own citizens or to the citizens of the states they invade. Second, the dangers of abuse would likely make almost any state's invocation of the right to justify its armed intervention in the territory "massively divisive," and so weaken the prospects for collaboration on the further development of the Charter Project.

Ultimately, Dworkin is less interested in defending a specific conclusion regarding the legality of UHI than he is in suggesting how the principles of mitigation and salience at the root of the Charter Project ought to inform its continued development. Since international law is still nascent, only just emerging from the Westphalian political order that preceded it, he notes that arguments regarding its content will often have a "freewheeling character."[54] This means they will rely far more on principles of political morality than on fit with past political practice (which, even following the creation of the UN order, may often still be distorted

---

[51] Ibid.
[52] 2005 World Summit Outcome, A/RES/60/1, paras. 138–40.
[53] Ibid, 25.
[54] Ibid, 29.

by a Westphalian residue). Those who associate law with the practices of a mature legal order, one with a well-developed doctrinal structure that is the product of centuries of legislation and adjudication, may look askance at such arguments. Indeed, given how prominently considerations of justification will figure in them, many may be tempted to describe these arguments as attempts to create new law, rather than as the identification of existing legal rights and duties. But Dworkin contends that if we look back to the early days of these mature legal orders we will find similarly "freewheeling" arguments; that is, cases in which specific legal conclusions rested far more on judgments regarding law's moral aims than on coherence with past practice. If law, or government in accordance with a proper conception of the rule of law:

> serves its community well, its doctrines will crystallize over time. Its roots in political morality will grow less prominent – though will be available when needed – in ordinary legal argument. That progress from principle to doctrine will signal its success.[55]

The development of a genuinely legal international order has only just begun, however. Therefore, as we argue over the rights and duties of sovereign states as one part of our efforts to enhance the legitimacy of coercive government, we should pay less attention to concrete doctrinal conclusions and more to the abstract moral principles at the core of the Charter Project. As Dworkin puts it, "we need, now, to nourish the roots, not the twigs, of international law."[56]

V CRITICISMS OF DWORKIN'S PHILOSOPHY OF INTERNATIONAL LAW

Although only recently published, Dworkin's philosophy of international law has already attracted criticism.[57] We will focus here on three objections advanced by Thomas Christiano, since a consideration of how Dworkin might respond to them will help shed light on his international jurisprudence.[58] Briefly, those three criticisms are as follows. First, Dworkin errs in limiting his analysis of the legitimacy of international law to the contribution it makes to justifying each state's rule over its own citizens. This leads him to neglect the critical role that the idea of a cosmopolitan political community must play in any such analysis. Second,

---

[55] Ibid, 30.
[56] Ibid.
[57] Of course, if Dworkin's general account of the nature of law is mistaken, then his analysis of international law will be as well, since the latter is simply Dworkin's application of his general theory of law to the specific case of the existing practice of global coercive government. The discussion in this section assumes *arguendo* the truth of Dworkin's general account of the nature of law.
[58] Thomas Christiano, "Ronald Dworkin, State Consent, and Progressive Cosmopolitanism," in *The Legacy of Ronald Dworkin*, eds. Wil Waluchow and Stefan Sciaraffa (New York: Oxford University Press, 2016).

Christiano thinks it impossible to reconcile Dworkin's arguments in favor of reducing states' freedom to make law and policy unilaterally with the moral aim of enhancing the legitimacy of each state's domestic government. Finally, Dworkin offers an impoverished conception of contemporary international law's moral aims.

Christiano's first and second criticisms both target what he labels Dworkin's non-cosmopolitan associativism. Dworkin's international jurisprudence is non-cosmopolitan because it takes the moral aim of international law to be enhancing the legitimacy of each state's rule over its own citizens. It is associative because the legitimacy of each state's government is a function of the quality of the association its citizens enjoy, meaning the extent to which its "laws and policies can . . . reasonably be interpreted as recognizing that the fate of each citizen is of equal importance and that each has responsibility to create his own life."[59] Christiano acknowledges that states may enhance their legitimacy by signing on to international human rights treaties, insofar as doing so mitigates the risk that their governments will violate the human rights of their citizens. However, he notes that regional human rights conventions such as the European Convention on Human Rights may better serve this end, in which case mitigation and salience might not generate any obligations under international human rights conventions. More importantly, Dworkin's non-cosmopolitan associativism "does not get at the main impulse behind these human rights laws for states that are fairly stable human rights protectors," namely "that people have duties to help others avoid invasion and severe human rights violations everywhere."[60] International law, Christiano maintains, is not simply an adjunct to the domestic constitutional law of each state but is, instead, part of the constitutional law of a global political community. Institutionally, the practice of government in this cosmopolitan political community is distributed among states. Nevertheless, the legitimacy of that government is a matter of how it treats all people, and not simply the contribution it makes to each state's rule over its own citizens.

As we noted earlier in this chapter, Dworkin includes among the defects of the Westphalian conception of sovereignty the fact that it largely prohibits citizens from discharging their moral responsibility to help protect people in other nations from egregious violations of their basic human rights. He implies that mitigating this defect constitutes one of the Charter Project's moral aims. Might we conclude, then, that Dworkin can and does accommodate the "main impulse" behind human rights respecting states' decision to undertake international human rights obligations? Christiano offers two reasons to think the answer is no. First, he does not see why the state's role in facilitating or inhibiting its citizens' fulfillment of their cosmopolitan moral duties should have any effect on the quality of their association with one another. If a state's political legitimacy depends solely on the quality of the association it realizes among its citizens, and if international law's legitimacy depends

---

[59] Dworkin, *Justice for Hedgehogs*, pp. 321–2.
[60] Christiano, "Ronald Dworkin," 58.

entirely on its contribution to that end, then it is far from clear that Dworkin can incorporate a concern with protecting the basic human rights of people living in other states into his account of international law's moral aims. Second, Christiano asks "if there are duties that are sufficient to ground the state's duties to participate in international law advancing the basic human rights, why not see the normative underpinnings of international law as directly grounded in these duties?"[61] In other words, once we acknowledge cosmopolitan moral responsibilities, as Dworkin explicitly does, there is no reason to adopt the non-cosmopolitan approach to theorizing international law's legitimacy. These same objections apply to Dworkin's claim that legitimate international law serves to mitigate the injustice individuals suffer when they have no legally recognized role in the crafting of law and policy that deeply shapes their life prospects. As Christiano observes, "the idea that people ought to be able to participate in the making of international law does not seem to involve enhancing the legitimacy of domestic societies at all."[62]

How might Dworkin respond to these objections? Consider, first, the associative dimension of political legitimacy. For Dworkin, a legitimate government is one that facilitates its legal subjects' enjoyment of their political rights and the fulfillment of their political responsibilities. It does so by enforcing their legal rights and duties in the community's name, or on behalf of the community conceived of as a community of principle. In practically every discussion of legitimacy during his lifetime, Dworkin's concern was with the legitimacy of domestic law (indeed, even more narrowly, with the legitimacy of US and English law), and especially the community's treatment of its own members. Perhaps this explains why, when he characterizes the legitimacy of these laws, Dworkin focuses on the quality of the association they instantiate among members of a single political community. Yet Dworkin appears to believe that individuals have political responsibilities to individuals who are not members of their community; at a minimum, a duty to "help protect people in other nations from war crimes, genocide, and other violations of human rights."[63] If so, then a state's legitimacy must also depend on the contribution it makes to its citizens fulfillment of this political responsibility. With respect to this particular facet of a state's exercise of political power, what matters is not simply the quality of association it realizes among its citizens but also the quality of their collective association with nonmembers. In other words, if individuals have cosmopolitan political duties, such as duties to act collectively via their community's political institutions to help protect members of other political communities from egregious assaults on their dignity, then the legitimacy of their state's government depends in part on whether it enables or inhibits their fulfillment of those duties. This observation, it seems to me, offers a promising starting point for responding to

[61]   Ibid, 60.
[62]   Ibid, 59.
[63]   Dworkin, "New Philosophy," 18.

Christiano's objection that facilitating the performance of cosmopolitan duties may contribute little or nothing to enhancing each state's domestic legitimacy.

It might be thought that if the political communities constituted by modern states have cosmopolitan political duties, then the moral point of international law cannot simply be to enhance each state's rule over its own subjects. Rather, it must also include protecting the basic human rights of all people, as well as their right to participate in some way in the creation and administration of law and policy that deeply affects them. Christiano offers the following sketch of a cosmopolitan conception of international law:

> [S]tates represent collections of persons who have these duties [correlative to basic human rights] and thus possess a kind of duty to help to attempt to fulfill the duties of their members in the making of international law. States are uniquely capable of carrying out this function in light of the fact that they are the main institutions in the modern international system that are capable of making power accountable to persons.[64]

Perhaps Dworkin could seize on this last point to defend his non-cosmopolitan account of international law. States are accountable to their citizens because they act in the name of, or on behalf of, the members of that particular political community. This is true not only for their exercise of political power within the community, but also outside it. While states may sometimes act to advance the interests of members of other political communities, as in the case of disaster relief or, perhaps, armed humanitarian interventions, they do so in their capacity as the agents of specific non-cosmopolitan political communities, not on behalf of a global one, or in the name of all humanity. When as a matter of law or policy a state uses the resources of the political community it governs to aid nonmembers, it owes its members a justification for doing so. That justification may invoke cosmopolitan principles of political morality, such as the community's responsibility to protect people in other nations from "war crimes, genocide, and other violation of human rights." Nevertheless, the best constructive interpretation of the Charter Project is one that takes its aim to be reconceiving sovereignty in ways that make states better serve their citizens, rather than as instruments for advancing the interest of all humanity conceived of as members of a cosmopolitan political community.

In fact, Christiano's criticism of Dworkin for defending a non-cosmopolitan account of international law's legitimacy reflects an incomplete description of Dworkin's position. At the close of his discussion of the defects that characterize the Westphalian state system, Dworkin writes:

> These are all ways in which the unchecked state sovereignty system impairs or threatens the legitimacy of the individual states that make up the system. But since each of those states derives its moral title to govern a particular territory from the

---

[64] Christiano, "Ronald Dworkin," 60.

arrangements that make up that international system, it therefore has the further, independent reason, different from those I just listed, for concern that the system on which its legitimacy depends in that more fundamental way is not itself illegitimate.[65]

The legitimacy of each and every state's rule depends in part on the legitimacy of the state system, the globe-spanning political order that distributes the right to rule discrete portions of the Earth, and the people who live there, to different states. Therefore, each state has a standing moral duty to enhance the legitimacy of the international political order, as well as the legitimacy of its own rule. A plausible case can be made that the moral aims of the Charter Project include revisions to state sovereignty that, when realized, add to the moral case in favor of this system's allocation of political power. For example, the Responsibility to Protect enhances the legitimacy of the state system by making any state's right to noninterference in its rule over a particular part of the Earth conditional on its government fulfilling its "responsibility to protect its populations from genocide, war crimes, ethnic cleansing and crimes against humanity."[66] Along the same lines, the legal permissibility of UN Security Council authorized uses of force to end intrastate campaigns of crimes against humanity arguably serve to enhance the legitimacy of the state system as a whole, at least by comparison to the absolute ban on such interventions that existed in the Westphalian order. The 1951 Convention Relating to the Status of Refugees, together with the 1967 Protocol, provide another example of reforms to state sovereignty that serve to enhance the legitimacy of the state system. By limiting the right of sovereign states to turn away refugees and asylum seekers, this treaty strengthens states' moral claim to control entry into, and settlement within, the particular territory it governs.[67] Finally, although Dworkin makes no mention of it, the Charter Project's commitment to the self-determination of peoples also marks a major improvement to the legitimacy of the international political order. A practice of international government that rejects colonial rule clearly has a greater claim to legitimacy than does one that permits it, or indeed, that exists largely to further the colonial project. Furthermore, as a principle of political morality the self-determination of peoples may figure in a constructive interpretation of the Charter Project that takes its aim to be preserving a society of states, rather than as a first step toward the creation of a world state.

Characterizing the Charter Project to include the moral aim of enhancing the legitimacy of the state system adds a cosmopolitan dimension to Dworkin's international jurisprudence. Note, however, that the legal rights and duties all states have to

[65] Dworkin, "New Philosophy," 19.
[66] The Responsibility to Protect, Paragraph 138 of the 2005 World Summit Outcome Document.
[67] See David Owens, "In Loco Civitatis: On the Normative Basis of the Institution of Refugeehood and Responsibilities for Refugees," in *Migration in Political Theory: The Ethics of Movement and Membership*, eds. Sarah Fine and Lea Ypi (New York: Oxford University Press, 2016), pp. 269–90. The argument in the text suggests that when states fail to fulfill their responsibilities under the Refugee Convention, and perhaps also when they pursue policies intended to prevent the triggering of those responsibilities, they forfeit their moral right to closed borders.

advance noncitizens' secure enjoyment of their basic human rights are largely limited to rescue efforts, as in the case of an armed intervention to halt a genocide, or the granting of asylum to individuals outside their country of nationality or habitual residence who are unable or unwilling to return due to a well-founded fear of persecution based on race, religion, nationality, political opinion, or membership in a particular social group.[68] A duty to temporarily shelter members of another political community at risk of brutal violations to their basic human rights coheres nicely with the limited moral aim of enhancing the legitimacy of a state system, an international order constituted by an association of political communities whose individuals relate to one another as citizens of different, non-cosmopolitan, communities. Such a restricted set of enforceable rights and duties to noncitizens seems to fit less well with the cosmopolitan conception of international law Christiano sketches, one that construes certain core elements as the law of "a cosmopolitan community of people who are divided into states," and whose cosmo-politan duties to one another presumably include more than a duty of rescue. If so, then considerations of fit provide some reason to favor Dworkin's constructive interpretation of the Charter Project as an effort to mitigate the risks and failures of the Westphalian system over the more morally ambitious constructive interpreta-tion Christiano suggests.

It may be helpful here to recall Dworkin's characterization of the law of a given community as those political rights its members can demand its institutions enforce without the need for any further collective political decision.[69] At any point in the political community's history, the law may not (indeed, likely will not) exhaust their moral-political rights. Put another way, there will be a gap between what the law is and what it ought to be. When this is the case, members of the community will still have valid moral claims to their political community enacting legislation granting them new rights, revising existing duties, and so on. In the case of international law, then, it may be that Dworkin offers us the most compelling account of what the law is, while Christiano points to what it ought to be. Dworkin clearly believes there is a considerable gap between what international law is and what it ought to be, or what is the same, that considerable work remains to be done to improve the legitimacy of coercive government at the international or global level. Indeed, he appears open to the possibility that in light of increasing economic interdependence, and perhaps other features of globalization, closing that gap may require the creation of a single, global, political community constituted by and governed via the institutions of a world state.

---

[68] UN General Assembly, *Convention Relating to the Status of Refugees*, July 28, 1951, United Nations Treaty Series, vol. 189, p. 137, and UN General Assembly, Protocol Relating to the Status of Refugees, January 31, 1967, United Nations Treaty Series, vol. 606, p. 267.

[69] Dworkin understands political rights as a subset of people's moral rights, namely, those rights that individuals have against a political community, or against individuals acting collectively via political or governmental institutions.

The hybrid nature of Dworkin's essay on international law, concerned as it is with both how we ought to identify existing international law and what sort of legislative reforms are needed to enhance its legitimacy, sheds some useful light on his discussion of international law's democratic deficit. While the Charter Project has made modest progress in mitigating the risks states pose to people's secure enjoyment of their basic human rights, Dworkin seems to believe it has made no progress in giving people a morally appropriate say in crafting international law. This is because states have refused to pursue the necessary reforms to the rights and duties constitutive of sovereignty. A comparison of Dworkin's discussion of UHI with his discussion of international law's democratic deficit illustrates this point. Given the advances we have made in mitigating the gravest dangers that states pose to their own subjects, he thinks we can treat the question "do states enjoy a legal right to engage in UHI?" as a question about what the law *is*. In contrast, when Dworkin considers international law's role in mitigating the obstacle Westphalian sovereignty poses to genuine self-government in an increasingly globalized world, he advances a proposal for what the law *ought to be*.[70]

Recall that Christiano struggles to see how such legislation would enhance the legitimacy of each state's rule over its own subjects. Dworkin does not maintain that it will. Instead, he argues that reforms to international lawmaking that increase opportunities for those affected to participate in its enactment will enhance the legitimacy of the state system as a whole. Each nation, he writes, "has a general responsibility to do what it can to improve the legitimacy of its own coercive government, and therefore a responsibility to improve the organization of states in which it functions as a government."[71] Apparently, Dworkin believes that a system for allocating legislative authority that gives all states an equal say in the crafting of new law despite their vastly different populations conflicts with the fundamental requirement that coercive government, including the state system, treat all individuals with equal concern and respect. If so, then reforms that take into account each state's population, while also ensuring that countries with small populations continue to exercise a meaningful voice, would strengthen the moral case in favor of the state system's allocation of the power to enact, modify, repeal or replace international legal norms. Or as Dworkin puts it, such a reform would "improve the legitimacy of the international arrangement."[72]

Christiano's last objection to Dworkin's philosophy of international law targets the meager moral aims he ascribes to the Charter Project. Specifically, he maintains Dworkin errs in "excluding the increase in wealth or the alleviation of global poverty from considerations grounding the moral basis of international law."[73] The problem is partly one of fit. The purpose of the WTO treaty is to make the parties to it richer,

---

[70] Dworkin, "New Philosophy," 27–9.
[71] Ibid, 27.
[72] Ibid.
[73] Christiano, "Ronald Dworkin," 59.

with a special focus on fostering growth in developing and least developed countries, while the UN Millennium Declarations evince states' commitment to meeting the needs of the world's poorest people. Yet Christiano also maintains that these examples challenge Dworkin's constructive interpretation of the Charter Project along the dimension of substance, since it is not obvious how their pursuit serves to enhance the quality of the association among the members of each state.

As should be abundantly clear by now, this second criticism rests on an overly narrow view of the role international law plays in enhancing the legitimacy of coercive government. Once we include morally justifying the state system as a whole, as well as each state's exercise of political power within that system, there is a clear path to defending increases in aggregate wealth and the alleviation of global poverty as among international law's moral purposes. That said, Dworkin might resist such an argument. It is far from clear that the Charter Project accords all states as such a legal *obligation* to contribute to increasing global wealth, or indeed, to increasing its domestic wealth. Moreover, while all states enjoy a legal right to enter into trade agreements, some argue that existing practices are designed neither to achieve a fair distribution of any gains from trade nor a reduction in global poverty.[74] It may be true, then, that increasing aggregate wealth is one of the goals of the existing practice of international system, or perhaps more accurately, a consequence of each state's attempts to increase its own wealth. But this is a *prudential goal*, not a *moral* one, and so it cannot figure in a constructive interpretation of the WTO treaty that treats it as law, or that characterizes countermeasures undertaken in accordance with the WTO treaty as morally justifiable in virtue of that fact.[75]

Likewise, it is debatable whether the Charter Project accords all states as such a duty to alleviate global poverty.[76] Since the Millennium Development Goals are the product of a UN General Assembly Resolution (the Millennium Declaration), they do not describe legal obligations incumbent on all states, only aspirations states have publicly pledged to pursue. Consider, too, that the text of the Refugee Convention does not warrant the conclusion that states are legally obligated to aid desperately poor noncitizens – unless they have a well-founded fear of persecution, of course, in which case it is that fact and not their poverty that provides the basis for the legal obligation. Once again, we must keep in mind the distinction between what the law is and what it ought to be. Currently, states may have no enforceable obligation to alleviate global poverty, and yet the principles of political morality

---

[74]   See the discussion of the WTO Dispute Settlement System in Chapter 11.

[75]   Countermeasures often involve a complainant state raising tariffs on goods imported from the state found to have violated the terms of the WTO treaty. The question is whether we should treat the imposition of such tariffs as a morally justifiable attempt to enforce a legal obligation, or as a bargaining tool one state can deploy against another as each seeks to advance its own interests in light of its relative power. On Dworkin's account of what makes law, the latter constructive interpretation entails that the WTO treaty is not really law.

[76]   Note that this duty is distinct from a duty to alleviate the poverty of their own citizens, one that correlates to a combination of several international legal human rights.

immanent in the Charter Project may justify the claim that they ought to be legally required to do so. Supposing that is true, the creation of legal obligations on all states to take specific steps to reduce global poverty would enhance the legitimacy of the state system.

***

Our exposition of Dworkin's philosophy of international law in section IV focused on his account of the grounds and normativity of international law, and more briefly, on his argument for its superiority to the account orthodox international legal positivists provide. Yet Dworkin does not begin his reflections on international law with this dispute. Instead, skepticism provides his point of departure, as it does for Austin and Hart. As we noted earlier, Dworkin maintains that true propositions of law provide a moral justification for the political community's exercise of coercion to enforce a right or duty. A system of coercive government qualifies as a genuinely legal one if and only if those who participate in it exhibit fidelity to a conception of the rule of law as valuable for the constitutive contribution it makes to the treatment of all its individual human subjects with equal concern and respect. Thus, to question whether international law is really law is to challenge the claim (or the assumption) that the existing global practice of coercive government meets this standard. Can we constructively interpret (so-called) international law as a practice of coercive government whose participants exhibit fidelity to the ideal of the rule of law, and who broadly share a conception of what makes government in accordance with the rule of law valuable? Does (so-called) international law satisfy the conditions that are individually necessary and jointly sufficient to morally justify the coercion it sanctions? Dworkin maintains that the advent of the Charter Project allows us to answer this question in the affirmative, while also recognizing that the international legal order is young and, in many respects, still nascent. Yet the discussion of an international rule of law in Chapter 5 suggests that Dworkin may be overly optimistic about the progress we have made in realizing a genuinely legal international order. If skepticism regarding an international rule of law is warranted, and if Dworkin rightly identifies law with the practice of government in accordance with the rule of law, then we ought to accept international legal skepticism.[77]

---

[77] I develop this argument and its implications for how international officials ought to exercise the powers that attach to their offices at length in David Lefkowitz, "A New Philosophy for International Legal Skepticism?"

5

An International Rule of Law?

Is the (so-called) international legal order an example of government in accordance with the rule of law? Legal philosophers largely agree that if the answer is "no" then international law is not really law. However, they disagree over how we ought to understand the ideal of the rule of law; that is, what this ideal consists in, and what makes government in accordance with it desirable, or indeed, a necessary and perhaps sufficient condition for the existence of law. These disagreements raise the possibility that international law may exhibit sufficient fidelity to the rule of law on one understanding of that ideal but not on another. Thus, our response to the international legal skeptic may well depend on which understanding of the rule of law we ought to adopt. Of course, it is also possible that despite their differences competing conceptions of the rule of law yield the same answer to the question "is the international legal order an example of government in accordance with the rule of law?" Even if this is so, however, they may differ in the implications they have for preserving an international rule of law, if it exists, or in (some of) the reforms that are necessary to create it, if it does not.

We begin our examination of the ideal of the rule of law in sections I and II with a discussion of its elements, the characteristics exhibited by the practice of government in accordance with the rule of law. In section III, we consider various accounts of the value of the rule of law, explanations of what makes government according to the rule of law superior to government without (enough of) it, or to other forms of rule. Following a brief consideration of some challenges to the ideal of the rule of law in section IV, we turn in section V to the question with which we began, namely is the global political-legal order characterized by fidelity to the international rule of law? Although the discussion leans toward a pessimistic conclusion, the international legal order does display some features of the rule of law, and there may be some reason to hope that it will improve on this score.

I ELEMENTS OF THE RULE OF LAW

What does it mean to characterize a society as one that possesses the rule of law, or conversely, as one that *lacks* that quality? The most common route to answering that question, which I adopt here, begins with an attempt to characterize the elements of the rule of law. These are the features a practice of government must manifest, at least to an adequate degree, in order to qualify as an example of government in accordance with the rule of law. They include government through law, the supremacy of law, equality before the law, independent adjudicatory institutions, and a culture of respect for the rule of law among both officials and subjects. I describe each of these in this section.

As an expository approach, this route has its virtues. Most importantly, it offers a person new to the study of the rule of law a relatively clear depiction of its object. This approach also has certain limitations, however, two of which I mention here. First, the question "what is the rule of law?" may not be one we can answer in isolation from the answer we give to the question "what makes the rule of law valuable?" Different answers to this second question may lead, in turn, to different answers to the first one; that is, to different albeit somewhat overlapping accounts of the conditions a practice of government must satisfy in order to qualify as government in accordance with the rule of law. Arguably, this explains disputes over the inclusion or exclusion of respect for basic human rights and democracy among the elements that make up the rule of law. Moreover, even when competing accounts of the value of the rule of law both endorse a certain feature as constitutive of government in accordance with that ideal, they may offer different explanations for why that is so. Second, while some theorists construe the rule of law as a virtue of government, one that contributes to its efficiency, efficacy, or legitimacy, others use the label "rule of law" to refer to a particular form of association or social order. Although they intersect in various ways, these two ways of framing reflection on the rule of law can sometimes cause confusion, even if they also generate deeper insight into its nature and importance. As with many of the topics addressed in this book, where you start can influence or even fully determine where you end up, and therefore it is important to recognize the possibility of different starting points.

One point on which all theorists of the rule of law agree is that it requires that government be exercised through the medium of law. To satisfy that standard, legal subjects and officials alike must be able to use the law to guide their conduct; for example, to identify their own legal rights and obligations. This requires in turn that legal norms meet certain formal criteria; "formal" because they describe the form laws must take, whatever their content may be. Specifically, legal rules or standards must be clear, prospective, public, stable, and general, and they must not make contradictory or impossible demands of those they address.[1] In addition, laws must be administered in a manner congruent with their enactment. To see why this is so, imagine you live in a society in which government officials systematically disregard these requirements. You may find the wording of certain laws incomprehensible or

---

[1] See, for example, Lon L. Fuller, *The Morality of Law*, rev. ed. (New Haven: Yale University Press, 1969), pp. 33–41; Joseph Raz, *The Authority of Law* (Oxford: Clarendon Press, 1979), pp. 214–18.

exceedingly vague, so that you can make no sense of the rights or duties they purport to recognize or create, or for whom they do so. Or you may find yourself lacking rights you thought you enjoyed as a result of secret laws, ones you become aware of only when they are applied to you in a criminal or civil court or enforced against you by the police. Or you may be made liable to criminal prosecution or civil liability for conduct that was legal when you performed it. Or you may be unable to avoid acting illegally because the law requires you to both perform and not perform the same act. Or you may find that the police and the courts regularly disregard enacted law, and so, in practice, you do not enjoy certain rights that, on paper at least, you do possess. In such a society, you cannot rely on the law to plan your affairs; for example, to identify the conduct you can engage in without fear of criminal prosecution, or the forms of transfer or exchange the government will uphold. Therefore, you have no reason to take the law into account when deciding what to do.

In short, a necessary condition for the rule of law is that the law rules. But the law can only rule if, in general, it is rational for officials and subjects to use it when deliberating. This requires that the conditions set out above be satisfied to an adequate degree if a society is to enjoy the rule of law at all. It also provides a basis for evaluating government in societies that surpass this threshold, insofar as they can and should seek to improve their conformity to the formal standards that comprise government through law.

The rule of law also requires the supremacy of law, or as it has sometimes been put, a government of law and not a government of men (or women). The law governs when, or to the extent that, officials exercise power only in legally authorized ways. Those who govern are not free to use their office and the powers that attach to it to pursue whatever aims they want, and however they think best. Rather, they may only pursue those aims the law authorizes them to pursue, and only in the ways the law authorizes. For example, in their pursuit of legally authorized aims officials may not transgress any standing legal prohibitions or restrictions, even if doing so would make their efforts more efficient or effective. In short, supremacy of law ensures that those who rule are not outside the law in two ways. First, it requires that they identify a legal authorization for any specific attempt to govern; that is, any act of lawmaking, law application, or law enforcement. Those who rule do so as legally constituted agents, not as natural persons. Second, supremacy of law locates every exercise of governmental power within a web of existing legal rights and duties, thereby ensuring that it will not unduly threaten others' ability to rely on the law as a whole when deciding what to do, both immediately and in the more distant future.

Some theorists also include respect for "higher law" in their characterization of law's supremacy. One form this may take involves constraints on the normal law-making process, as in the case of constitutionally protected rights. While it may be possible to modify these rights via a constitutional amendment, the process for doing so is typically more demanding and involves greater participation from the political community than is true for ordinary legislation. A second form of "higher law" treats certain constraints on government as irrevocable and unalterable. In some cases, these limits are the product of a political community's constitution, which either provides no mechanism for amending certain constitutional norms or explicitly excludes the possibility of doing so. In other cases, the irrevocable and unalterable nature of certain limits on the exercise of political power follows from a conception of legitimate and/or just rule. Not surprisingly, theorists who maintain that supremacy of law requires deference to objective moral norms that limit the scope of permissible governmental action typically treat respect for basic moral rights as among the elements that constitute the rule of law.

Equality before the law is another standard for the exercise of political power frequently included in descriptions of the rule of law. The equality in question here is formal, not substantive. It requires that like cases be treated alike, or put another way, that officials not unjustly discriminate in their application of the law. However, equality before the law does not require that the law itself treat people equally, in the sense that it not rely on morally dubious distinctions when it specifies the rights and duties subjects enjoy. Thus, the content of a law may be discriminatory, say because it accords a certain legal right only to white property-owning men, while also being applied in a nondiscriminatory way, if all white property-owning men have that right upheld by a court and enforced by the police. Arguably, equality before the law is simply a consequence of government through law, namely the combination of generality and congruence between the law on the books and the law in action. Still, treating it separately may serve to highlight the respect in which the rule of law constitutes a certain type of fair treatment, a feature that is obscured when the features of government through law are explained in terms of law's capacity to guide conduct.

The ideal of the rule of law includes not only the aforementioned standards to which government ought to conform – government through law, supremacy of law, and equality before the law – but also certain institutional and social arrangements. These include an impartial and independent judiciary and a robust culture of fidelity to the ideal of government in accordance with the rule of law, especially among legal professionals. These arrangements constitute elements of the ideal itself because apparently ineradicable and pervasive features of human nature make it impossible for any political society to create or sustain the rule of law in their absence. That said, the design or character of the institutional and social arrangements essential to the realization of the rule of law admits some variation. Therefore, we should be careful not to confuse those features of a political community's adjudicatory institutions and legal culture that are the product of its specific history with ones that are necessary for the realization of the rule of law in any society.

Effective recourse to an independent and impartial agent charged with determining the legality of conduct undertaken by public or private actors is crucial for government through law. As Grant Lamond notes: "[F]or the law to govern, there must be processes to resolve disputed questions of *law* in a principled way, as well as processes for determining whether the conditions for the application of the law have been satisfied."[2] The resolution of a legal dispute often has significant implications for the parties to it. Consequently, their judgment regarding the content of the law and whether they or the other party has violated it may be biased in their own favor, or at least perceived as such by the other party to the dispute. Thus, if individuals are to interact with one another according to law, it cannot be solely on the basis of their own understandings of what that involves. Rather, in cases of disagreement the question of what the law is, as well as the question of whether a particular agent has violated it, should be determined by a neutral third party.

An independent and impartial judiciary is also necessary to realize and sustain the supremacy of law. As with private actors, public officials will often be tempted to interpret the law in ways that permit them to do what they wish, whether for the common good or for their own private benefit. For law to effectively constrain the exercise of political power, and, in particular, the use or threat of force, a distinction must be drawn between those agents empowered to administer the law and those charged with determining what the law requires, forbids, or permits the government to do. While judges play the central role here, Brian Tamanaha notes that certain executive officials also make a crucial contribution, as in the case of public prosecutors whose duties include holding government officials to the law.[3] Supremacy of law, and so the rule of law, requires that they enjoy a level of independence as well.

In addition to mandating independent judicial institutions, the ideal of the rule of law imposes certain requirements on the adjudicatory process. Agents must be informed of the violation(s) of the law they are alleged to have performed. Furthermore, they must be permitted to be present when their case is heard and given an opportunity "to confront and question any witnesses, and to make legal argument about the bearing of the evidence and the various legal norms relevant to the case."[4] In making their case before the court, agents must be permitted legal representation. Finally, some theorists maintain that the rule of law entitles at least the parties to the dispute, and perhaps all members of the political community in question, "to hear reasons from the tribunal when it reaches its decision, which are responsive to the evidence and arguments presented before it."[5] Collectively, these procedures serve the goal of government through law by facilitating the identification of the law, including the content of specific legal norms, and what it entails for the particular case at hand. They also serve the goal of supremacy of law by making

---

[2] Grant Lamond, "The Rule of Law," in *The Routledge Companion to Philosophy of Law*, ed. Andrei Marmor (New York: Routledge, 2012), p. 502.

[3] Brian Tamanaha, "The History and Elements of the Rule of Law," *Singapore Journal of Legal Studies* (December 2012): 239.

[4] Jeremy Waldron, "The Rule of Law," in *The Stanford Encyclopedia of Philosophy* (Fall 2016 ed.), ed. Edward N. Zalta, https://plato.stanford.edu/archives/fall2016/entries/rule-of-law/, last accessed October 24, 2019.

[5] Ibid.

the identification and application of the law to particular agents a public exercise. This is particularly true when judges explicitly state the legal reasoning behind their decision. Even when they do not, however, we may be able to draw some conclusions about how they identified the law from the fact that they were not convinced by certain arguments regarding its content, namely, those advanced by the party whose legal claim they denied.

But who upholds the supremacy of law vis-à-vis judges, or at least those whose decisions are not reversible by judges sitting on a superior court? How do we ensure that they decide cases on the basis of law, and not their personal preferences or moral judgment? Institutional design plays a role here, as it does in checking the temptation of those who execute the law to place themselves above it. For example, judges may be required to stand for election, or they may be vulnerable to impeachment by the legislature. Furthermore, courts famously have no army or police, no way of making their decisions effective if those charged with enforcing the law choose to ignore their decisions. But defenders of the rule of law also identify a distinctive ethos or culture among lawyers, including judges, as essential for government in accordance with the rule of law: "Without a body of lawyers committed to the law and to the Rule of Law, there can be no Rule of Law, for the knowledge, activities, and orientations of lawyers as a group are the social carriers of the law – they are the group whose collective activities directly constitute the law."[6] To be a lawyer in the sense at issue here is not simply a matter of one's job or occupation. Rather, it is to be a member of a profession, a community of practitioners called to serve something that is normally of great value to human beings. In the case of medical professionals, for example, that thing is physical and mental health. In the case of legal professionals, that thing is government in accordance with the rule of law.

Indeed, David Luban maintains that when Lon Fuller describes government through law as the internal *morality* of law, he has in mind the professional ethic or virtue of individuals who take their purpose to be the reduction of relations among people to a reasoned harmony via subjecting human conduct to the governance of rules.[7] This morality is internal in two respects. First, it is internalized by the legal professional, in the sense that it frames how she approaches the task of ordering relations among human beings. Second, fidelity to the ideal of the rule of law provides her with an intrinsic motive, a reason for action that she has simply because she is a legal professional. Put another way, her reason for conforming to the demands of the rule of law – government through law, supremacy of law, and so on – is simply that doing so is what virtuous lawyers do. In contrast, institutional checks such as periodic elections for judges provide an *external* reason for fidelity to the rule of law; in this case, the fear of being replaced on the bench.

---

[6] Brian Tamanaha, "A Concise Guide to the Rule of Law," in *Relocating the Rule of Law*, eds. Gianluigi Palombella and Neil Walker (Portland, OR: Hart Publishing, 2009), p. 12.

[7] David Luban, "Natural Law as Professional Ethics: A Reading of Fuller," *Social Philosophy and Policy* 18, 1 (Winter 2001); Fuller, *Morality of Law*.

Of course, some lawyers may fail to live up to the professional standards that apply to them. That is why realizing and sustaining the rule of law requires robust and independent mechanisms for legal education and professional development. Yet as with every other element of the rule of law discussed thus far, the influence of a professional legal culture on those who govern in any particular society may wax and wane. Crucially, where that culture becomes fully corrupted, or where it has never existed in the first place, institutional elements like the separation of powers, fair procedures in the courts, and techniques for holding judges accountable will fail to maintain or realize the rule of law. Conversely, in the absence of these and perhaps other institutional features it may prove quite difficult to sustain a culture of fidelity to the rule of law, and the influence that culture has on the practice of government will likely be muted.

II ARE HUMAN RIGHTS OR DEMOCRACY ELEMENTS OF THE RULE OF LAW?

One point of disagreement regarding the ideal of the rule of law concerns the question of whether to include respect for human rights or democracy among its elements. Descriptions of the rule of law issued by political bodies sometimes do so. For example, in a 2005 Report of the UN Secretary General, the rule of law was characterized as:

> a principle of governance in which all persons, institutions, and entities, public and private, including the State itself, are accountable to laws that are publicly promulgated, equally enforced and independently adjudicated, and which are consistent with international human rights norms and standards. It requires, as well, measures to ensure adherence to the principles of supremacy of law, equality before the law, accountability to the law, fairness in the application of the law, separation of powers, participation in decision-making, legal certainty, avoidance of arbitrariness and procedural and legal transparency.[8]

Likewise, a commission charged by the Council of Europe with investigating the rule of law concluded that its elements include not only equality before the law and access to justice before independent and impartial courts, but also "a transparent, accountable, and democratic process for enacting law" and "respect for human rights."[9] Among theorists of the rule of law, Ronald Dworkin is perhaps the best-known

---

[8]   UN Security Council, *The Rule of Law and Transitional Justice in Conflict and Post-Conflict Societies: Report of the Secretary-General*, August 23, 2004, UN Doc. S/2004/616: 4. In 2012, the UN General Assembly adopted a Resolution regarding the rule of law at the national and international levels in which it affirmed "that human rights, the Rule of Law and democracy are interlinked and mutually reinforcing and that they belong to the universal and indivisible core values and principles of the United Nations." UN General Assembly resolution 67/97, *The Rule of Law at the National and International Levels*, A/RES/67/97 (December 14, 2012), available from undocs.org/en/A/RES/67/97. This suggests that human rights and democracy are not themselves elements of the rule of law.

[9]   European Commission for Democracy through Law (Venice Commission), Report on the Rule of Law, adopted at its 86th plenary session (Venice, March 2011), http://www.evnice.coe.int/webforms/

advocate of the view that it includes respect for individual moral rights. Indeed, for Dworkin, the rule of law just is "the ideal of rule by an accurate public conception of individual rights."[10] The eminent jurist Tom Bingham has also recently asserted that respect for human rights ought to be treated as an element of the rule of law. "A state which savagely represses or persecutes sections of its people cannot in my view be regarded as observing the Rule of Law, even if the transport of the persecuted minority to the concentration camp or the compulsory exposure of female children on the mountainside is the subject of detailed laws duly enacted and scrupulously observed."[11]

The more common view, however, holds that we should not treat respect for human rights or democracy as elements of the rule of law. In principle, and perhaps also in practice, a society can enjoy the rule of law even if it neither acknowledges the existence of human rights nor embraces a democratic form of government. Before we examine the arguments offered for this conclusion, some clarification is in order. Certain rights described in various international human rights declarations and treaties, as well as state constitutions, simply specify features of the rule of law that we have already discussed. These include a right to a fair trial, a right not to be arbitrarily detained, and a right to nondiscrimination as it pertains to the application and enforcement of the law. Therefore, any real disagreement over the place of human rights in the characterization of the rule of law must concern rights to forms of treatment other than those constitutive of government through law, the supremacy of law, equality before the law, and the various institutional features that serve first and foremost to advance these aims. The issue might be best put as follows. Does the rule of law concern only how government power is exercised? Or does it also require that government power be exercised for certain substantive ends (for instance, protecting human rights), and/or that the law be made and perhaps also administered by certain agents (for instance, the *demos*)?

One argument offered in favor of the first of these options, often referred to as a "thin" conception of the rule of law, is its analytical utility. Joseph Raz maintains that "if the Rule of Law is the rule of good law then to explain its nature is to propound a complete social philosophy. But if so, the term lacks any useful function."[12] By implication, a narrower construal of the rule of law does serve a useful function. Useful for what, we might ask? One possibility is that a thin characterization of the rule of law offers descriptive or explanatory advantages over a thicker one. Tamanaha, for instance, defends the former in part because "it hews to common ground and it applies to the broadest range of systems."[13] More

documents/?pdf=CDL-AD(2011)003rev-e. The Council of Europe is composed of forty-seven states from across that continent.
[10] Ronald Dworkin, *A Matter of Principle* (Cambridge, MA: Harvard University Press, 1985), pp. 11–12.
[11] Tom Bingham, *The Rule of Law* (London: Penguin UK, 2010), pp. 66–7.
[12] Raz, *Authority*, p. 211.
[13] Tamanaha, "Concise Guide," 14.

importantly, however, Raz and Tamanaha both argue that the thin conception of the rule of law has *moral* advantages over a thicker one: "It is necessary to maintain a sharp analytical separation between the Rule of Law, democracy, and human rights, as well as other good things we might want, like health and security, because mixing all of these together tends to obscure the essential reality that a society and government may comply with the Rule of Law, yet still be seriously flawed or wanting in various respects."[14] Excluding substantive standards of justice from our conception of the rule of law may also reduce the frequency with which theorists talk past one another, and perhaps also generate deeper insights into the actual and possible relations between different aspects of legitimate or just government.

A second, related, reason to accept the thin conception of the rule of law is that it guards against the danger of parochialism masquerading as universalism. The worry is that a widely accepted desideratum for government, namely the rule of law, will be used as a Trojan horse to impose more contested (and perhaps contestable) demands on communities that do not accept them.[15] Interestingly, the worry may also run in the opposite direction: actors who reject human rights or democracy as foreign to their own societies may also be led to reject the elements that comprise the thin conception of the rule of law. If so, then we have a weighty reason not to associate the ideal of the rule of law so tightly with human rights or democracy, at least if the following two conditions are met: first, that it really is possible to realize the rule of law in a society that is not committed to human rights or democracy, and second, that the barriers to unjust government that the rule of law raises exceed the contributions it makes to the effective or efficient performance of injustice.

Ultimately, the question of whether the rule of law includes respect for human rights or democracy may depend on the concept of law a person adopts. For example, Raz maintains that law necessarily claims legitimate authority.[16] Roughly, that claim is sustained whenever a legal subject will do better at acting on the reasons that apply to her by following the law than by acting on her own judgment. While particular laws may not be legitimate, the fact that they necessarily *claim* legitimate authority entails that they must be capable of guiding the conduct of those they address. The rule of law, then, should be understood to consist of all and only those conditions that must be satisfied to an adequate degree for law to be capable of guiding its subjects' conduct.[17] This clearly requires government through law. Moreover, it provides a rationale for the supremacy of law, equality before the law, an independent judiciary, and a robust legal profession, insofar as they "ensure that the legal machinery of enforcing the law should not deprive it [i.e. the law] of its ability to guide through distorted enforcement" and that it "be capable of supervising

---

[14]   Tamanaha, "History and Elements," 236.
[15]   Ibid, p. 234.
[16]   See the discussion in Chapter 6, section II.
[17]   Raz, *Authority*, pp. 225–6.

conformity to the Rule of Law."[18] Law's capacity to guide human conduct does not depend on respect for human rights or democracy, however. This is true even if respect for human rights and/or democracy are necessary or sufficient conditions for law's legitimate authority, since Raz does not maintain that law necessarily *enjoys* legitimate authority, only that it necessarily *claims* legitimate authority. In sum, Raz's account of the rule of law follows from his conception of law.

The same is true for Ronald Dworkin's description of the rule of law as "the ideal of rule by an accurate public conception of individual rights."[19] According to Dworkin, law's essential function is to legitimate the exercise of coercive government. Put another way, where it exists law necessarily provides a (normally undefeated) moral justification for a government's use or threat of force to uphold legal subjects' moral rights. If we adopt this understanding of law, it would be rather odd to think a government could exhibit fidelity to the idea of the rule of law and yet fail to regard its subjects as bearers of individual rights, possibly including a right to some form of participation in their own governance. Perhaps this explains why Bingham so strenuously objects to Raz's claim that "a non-democratic legal system, based on the denial of human rights, on extensive poverty, on racial segregation, sexual inequalities, and religious persecution may, in principle, conform to the requirements of the Rule of Law better than any of the legal systems" of political communities that do not suffer these defects.[20] Still, Raz is surely right to caution against equating the ideal of the rule of law with a complete social philosophy. Theorists such as Dworkin and Bingham may be able to satisfy that requirement by offering an account of what makes law legitimate that does not require that it be fully just.

A third option allows that as a *conceptual* matter neither respect for basic human rights nor democracy is an element of the rule of law, while also defending a tight association between them that reflects their common root. That common root is respect for individual autonomy, a conception of human beings as responsible agents capable of serving as the authors of their own lives.[21] As I explain in greater detail in the next section, some theorists locate the essential value of government in accordance with the rule of law in the fact that it recognizes legal subjects as autonomous agents. Many human rights can be defended on the same grounds; that is, they serve to protect the exercise of responsible agency, or the conditions necessary for its development and meaningful exercise. Likewise, insofar as acting as the author of his or her own life includes living with others in a political community, respect for a person's autonomy entails that the community provide him or her with genuine opportunities to participate in the crafting of its laws and policies, and

---

[18]   Ibid, p. 218.
[19]   Dworkin, *Matter of Principle*, pp. 11–12.
[20]   Bingham, *Rule of Law*, pp. 66–7, responding to Raz, *Authority*, p. 211.
[21]   Attributing this capacity to human beings does not presume that individuals can, do, or should create themselves from scratch, as if our identities and our lives are not deeply shaped by the social and natural environments we inhabit.

perhaps also in their administration. Analytically, then, we may be able to distinguish the rule of law from respect for human rights or democracy. In practice, however, any government that fails to recognize its subjects' status as autonomous agents is extremely unlikely to constrain its rule over them in accordance with the demands of the rule of law. These are the grounds on which Fuller rejects the claim by Raz and others that a government may be deeply evil in myriad ways and yet exhibit fidelity to the rule of law. As Luban notes, Fuller thinks this view "bizarre, and even perverse" because it "assume[s] that an evildoer would for some mysterious reason choose as an instrument of evil a relatively ineffective tool – a tool, moreover, that is relatively ineffective because it displays precisely the kind of moral regard for its victim than an evildoer lacks."[22]

III THE VALUE OF THE RULE OF LAW

In explicating the value of the rule of law, many theorists emphasize the contribution it makes to instrumentally rational choice. As F.A. Hayek writes, the rule of law "makes it possible to foresee with fair certainty how the authority will use its coercive powers in given circumstances and to plan one's individual affairs on the basis of this knowledge."[23] The more individuals can predict when and how a government will use force, whether against them or on their behalf, the greater their ability to control how their lives unfold. Of course, the law may also place significant substantive constraints on the choices they may make. For example, it may deny them rights to free speech, or to freedom of religion, or to political participation. Nevertheless, freedom from the fear that at any moment their lives may be turned upside-down, and that if this happens they will have no recourse to an effective remedy, is both valuable in itself and for its contribution to the ability to lead whatever ways of life the law permits.

The certainty and predictability provided by the rule of law also facilitate efficient markets. Absent secure property rights and the effective enforcement of contracts, people have far less reason to engage in production or exchange. Again, the property and contract regimes may be severely unjust in various ways. Yet holding all else equal, if a society's property and contract law generally satisfies the conditions for the (thin) rule of law, its members will generally be better off than they would be if it did not.

While reliable knowledge of when and how a government will exercise coercion is valuable regardless of the content of the law, it is even more so when the law is legitimate. For example, suppose Raz offers the correct analysis of what makes law legitimate, namely, that those it addresses will do better at acting on the reasons that apply to them by following the law than they will if they act on their own judgment.

---

[22] Luban, "Natural Law as Professional Ethic," 189. See also John Finnis, *Natural Law and Natural Rights* (Oxford: Clarendon Press, 1980), pp. 273–4.
[23] Tamanaha, "History and Elements," 240.

It follows that in any society that possesses at least some legitimate laws, the rule of law contributes to an increase in at least some people's conformity to the reasons that apply to them, in comparison to what would likely occur were the society not governed in accordance with the rule of law.

Note that where the law is legitimate it creates a genuine obligation, a moral duty to obey the law. Even where the law is illegitimate, however, it may still be a useful means for predicting how political power will be exercised. Some theorists use the phrase "rule *by* law" to describe a practice of government in which law serves only to attach costs or benefits to engaging in particular types of conduct, and to clarify what counts as performing an act of a particular type. The rule *of* law, in contrast, refers to a social or political order in which law identifies, constitutes, or creates genuine rights and duties, either because the law itself is a component of morality or because there is (in some cases, for some actors) a moral duty to obey the law. Certainty and predictability are virtues of both rule by law and the rule of law, but their value takes on an added dimension in the latter case.

Grant Lamond maintains that we ought to distinguish between the basic rationale or justification for the rule of law and the values served by its observance. While he acknowledges that the rule of law respects people's capacity for rational agency and autonomous choice, he questions whether this provides its basic rationale. First, he notes the now familiar point that in principle a government may adhere to the (thin) rule of law while disrespecting its subjects' agency and autonomy in myriad other ways. Second, given this fact about the rule of law, Lamond maintains that its importance has less to do with guiding subjects' or officials' conduct than it does with putting processes in place that can be used to hold officials accountable, and to ensure that they do not misuse their position.[24] This conclusion is reinforced by the fact that the rule of law is consistent with governments using a variety of methods other than issuing laws to shape the conduct of their subjects. These include persuasion (perhaps through public education campaigns and propaganda), providing services and resources (such as roads and flood insurance), or by changing the circumstances of choice (for instance, through expanding or contracting the money supply and deploying more police on the streets).[25] Lamond concludes that "what matters from the perspective of the Rule of Law is not that non-officials always be guided by standards, but that the measures taken to influence behavior are authorized by the law, i.e. that the actions of officials are subject to the law."[26]

For Hayek and Raz, government through law is the essence of the rule of law, and the supremacy of law is justified on the grounds that it enhances the effectiveness of government through law. The value of the rule of law, therefore, is linked to the value of government through law, namely, the way it respects human agency by facilitating planning and mediating between actors and the reasons that apply to

[24]   Lamond, "Rule of Law," 503.
[25]   Ibid, 498.
[26]   Ibid, 504.

them. Lamond takes the opposite view: the essence of the rule of law is supremacy of law, the requirement that specific exercises of political power be authorized by law, and that they not transgress any standing legal restriction. The importance of government through law as an element of the rule of law lies in its contribution to realizing the supremacy of law. The rule of law's core rationale or justification is constraining the arbitrary exercise of political power, or what is the same, mitigating the vulnerability of the ruled to the capricious whims of those who rule. While the rule of law may serve to enhance instrumentally rational choice and responsiveness to right reason, its essential value lies not in these services but in the protection it provides against "a standing risk of corrupt and self-interested actions" by government officials.[27]

In their accounts of the value of the rule of law, both Raz and Lamond appear to presuppose a hierarchical relation between rulers and ruled. Either the rule of law serves to protect the latter from the former, or it identifies conditions that must be met for political rule to be legitimate. Lon Fuller's depiction of the rule of law suggests a somewhat different picture, one in which the rule of law realizes relationships of reciprocity, whether between private parties or between governors and the governed. Fuller contrasts the rule of law with both the rule of terror and managerial rule. All three orders treat human beings as capable of acting for reasons, but only law treats every person as "a responsible agent, capable of understanding and following rules, and answerable for his [or her] defaults."[28] Rule by terror disregards people's capacity to act on the basis of rules or norms, and instead relies on threats (and sometimes rewards). The Nazi regime provides an apt example, relying as it did on fear and greed to perpetuate its rule.[29] Managerial rule treats individuals as capable of acting on the basis of rules or norms, but unlike law, it conceives of those individuals solely as resources rulers can use to advance whatever goals they set. Moreover, managerial rulers rely on rules to govern only to the extent that doing so is the most efficient or effective means for achieving their aims. Where it is not, they readily violate the conditions constitutive of the "enterprise of subjecting human conduct to the governance of rules" by, for example, abandoning congruity between the rules on the books and the rules in action. In contrast, Fuller maintains that the rule of law is not "like management, a matter of directing other persons how to accomplish tasks set by a superior, but is basically a matter of providing the citizenry with a sound and stable framework for their interactions with one another."[30] To be a responsible agent, then, is not simply to be capable of acting for reasons or guiding one's conduct according to rules. Rather, it consists in a power to choose for oneself how to live one's life, including both the ability to participate in

---

[27]   Ibid, 505.
[28]   Fuller, *Morality of Law*, p. 162.
[29]   Lon L. Fuller, "Positivism and Fidelity to Law: A Reply to Professor Hart," *Harvard Law Review* 71, 4 (1958): 648–55.
[30]   Fuller, *Morality of Law*, p. 210.

setting the terms on which one will interact with others and the capacity to conform to those terms once set, that is, to be answerable for one's defaults. Unlike in the case of managerial rule, when individuals are governed by the rule of law they are treated as creatures capable of setting their own goals or ends, as well as choosing the means to them. Where the rule of law obtains, "the law does not tell a man what he should do to accomplish specific ends set by the lawgiver; [instead] it furnishes him with baselines against which to organize his life with his fellows ... [and] provides a framework with which to live his own life."[31]

For Fuller, the value of the rule of law is not instrumental, its utility as a means for predicting government officials' exercise of coercion, or for better conforming to right reason, or for constraining arbitrary rule. Rather, its value lies in the fact that when people associate with one another in accordance with the rule of law, they treat one another as responsible and autonomous agents. This is true of the relationship between governors and governed, as well as between individuals considered as private actors (for instance, as parties to a contract). Government in accordance with the rule of law depends on reciprocity between ruler and ruled, with each treating the other as a responsible agent. The governed must trust that the governors will "act upon the citizens" only in those ways "previously declared as those to be followed by the citizen and as being determinative of his rights and duties."[32] After all, "if the citizen knew in advance that in dealing with him government would pay no attention to its own declared rules, he would have little incentive to abide by them."[33] However, "the rule-maker will lack any incentive to accept for himself the restraints of the Rule of Law if he knows that his subjects have no disposition, or lack the capacity, to abide by his rules."[34] In short, the virtues of fidelity to the rule of law on the part of those who govern, and law abidingness on the part of those who are governed, are mutually dependent and reinforcing. Or as Fuller puts the point, "the functioning of a legal system depends upon a cooperative effort – an effective and responsible interaction – between lawgiver and subject."[35]

Jeremy Waldron also emphasizes respect for individual autonomy in his explanation of why the rule of law requires that institutions charged with applying the law accord the parties who appear before them certain procedural rights:

> Courts, hearings and arguments – those aspects of law are not optional extras; they are integral parts of how law works; and they are indispensable to the package of law's respect for human agency. To say that we should value aspects of governance that promote the clarity and determinacy of rules for the sake of individual freedom, but not the opportunities for argumentation that a free and self-possessed individual

---

[31] Lon L. Fuller, *The Principles of Social Order: Selected Essays of Lon L. Fuller*, ed. Kenneth I. Winston (Durham, NC: Duke University Press, 1981), p. 234. See the discussion in Luban, "Natural Law," 187.

[32] Fuller, *Morality of Law*, p. 210.

[33] Ibid, p. 217.

[34] Ibid, p. 219.

[35] Ibid.

is likely to demand, is to slice in half, to truncate, what the Rule of Law rests upon: respect for the freedom and dignity of each person as an active intelligence.[36]

Government in accordance with the rule of law does not treat legal subjects as passive recipients of instruction, as managerial rule does. Rather, it accords them an active role in realizing associations premised on the rule of law, including the one that obtains between all citizens as such. This includes not only adhering to the law but also forming a view regarding its content, the details of the rights and duties it accords various actors, and what follows from it in a particular case.[37] Although always present, these latter aspects of the law's self-application often come to the fore when the legality of an agent's conduct is a matter of dispute. The reciprocity between ruler and ruled that Fuller emphasizes figures here as well. Legal subjects take the law seriously by invoking it to defend their conduct; other considerations, such as the conduct's advantageousness for the actor or for the community at large, will not serve. In return, legal officials provide subjects with a fair opportunity to make their case, which may include advancing a particular understanding of what the law is as well as what it implies in their circumstances. And, of course, the verdict they reach in the case before them must be grounded in the law. In a community that approximates this ideal, government officials empowered to uphold the law fulfill their role as "guardian[s] of the integrity of the system."[38]

To reiterate a point made earlier in this chapter, reflection on the value of the rule of law serves not only to clarify the reasons we have to pursue it but also to improve our understanding of what fidelity to that ideal requires. For example, it may help us identify allegedly essential elements of the rule of law that are, in fact, parochial, specific to a particular community's history of coercive government but not necessary for the existence of the rule of law in any society. Likewise, an improved grasp of its value may open our eyes to novel mechanisms for instantiating the rule of law, whether they already exist in other societies or have yet to be dreamed up by theorists or practitioners. Finally, it may facilitate critical reflection on how well a practice or institution that serves the rule of law in one society performs that function in another one. We may find, for example, that similarities of outward form mask crucial differences in operation, as in the case of courts populated by officials uncommitted to the ideal of the rule of law.

IV CHALLENGES TO THE RULE OF LAW

Although widely praised, the political ideal of government in accordance with the rule of law is not without its critics. For instance, it is sometimes condemned as

---

[36] Jeremy Waldron, "The Concept and the Rule of Law," *Georgia Law Review* 43, 1 (Fall 2008): 60.
[37] Dworkin develops a similar point under the heading of the protestant attitude toward law. See Dworkin, *Law's Empire*, pp. 190, 413. See also the exposition of this point in Win-Chiat Lee, "The Judgeship of All Citizens: Dworkin's Protestantism About Law," *Law and Philosophy* 34, 1 (January 2015): 23–53.
[38] Fuller, *Morality of Law*, p. 210.

antidemocratic. Among theorists, the principle complaint targets "higher law" restrictions on the scope of a democratically elected legislature's right to make law, oftentimes in conjunction with an objection to the application of that "higher law" by judges who are less democratically accountable than legislators. These arguments are sometimes extended, and distorted, by political leaders who maintain that their electoral mandate justifies conduct that violates the supremacy of even normal law. While the latter arguments constitute a wholesale rejection of the rule of law, those that concern the supremacy of "higher law" or the authority accorded to the judiciary need not do so. To take one example, it may be that a practice of strong judicial review, in which courts have the authority to make statutes inapplicable by deeming them in violation of "higher law," detracts from the rule of law by encouraging the rule of judges and the politicization of the judiciary.[39]

Some theorists of the rule of law maintain that fidelity to that ideal requires the rejection of the modern welfare state, one that acts purposefully to ensure that its subjects enjoy certain benefits or entitlements. A rule of law state, they maintain, is one that conforms to the classically liberal or libertarian conception of legitimate government. It is no surprise, then, that the debate over the moral purpose of government sometimes takes the form of a dispute over the desirability of the rule of law. This occurrence may buttress the argument of those who argue for the adoption of a thin conception of the rule of law on the basis of its analytical utility.[40]

Certain risks and limitations are inherent to the rule of law. Foremost among these is the danger that it becomes the rule of judges: "The inevitability of human participation in the application and interpretation of rules provides the opening for the reintroduction of the very weaknesses sought to be avoided by resorting to law in the first place."[41] Institutional design and the acquisition of a professional ethic centered on fidelity to the rule of law provide some defense against this possibility. Nevertheless, supremacy of law may sometimes require judges to thwart initiatives undertaken by the executive or the legislature, some of which may be supported by a significant proportion of the political community's members. This may lead, in turn, to various attempts to undermine the judiciary's independence, including politicizing the process of elevating individuals to the bench and delegitimizing specific courts or even the judiciary as a whole. Both responses weaken the rule of law. The first does so by increasing the likelihood that judges will exercise the powers that attach to their office to advance a political program instead of upholding the law. The second effectively removes a key institutional mechanism for holding the executive and the legislature legally accountable, and so reduces the barrier the rule of law raises to their abuse of political power. Of course, to describe this scenario as *a risk* to the rule of law is already to reject the more skeptical view that the rule of law

---

[39]   See, among others, Jeremy Waldron, "The Core of the Case Against Judicial Review," *Yale Law Journal* 115, 6 (April 2006): 1346–406; Tamanaha, "Concise Guide," 15.

[40]   Waldron, "Rule of Law."

[41]   Tamanaha, "History and Elements," 244.

is simply an illusion, with every exercise of political power really nothing more than an example of agents pursuing their perceived interests.

Government through general and prospective rules or standards inevitably leads to some degree of conflict between fidelity to the rule of law and the achievement of just outcomes. Generality entails that rules or standards will typically be over- or under-inclusive, or, oftentimes, both. In the former case, conformity to a legal norm will sometimes fail to advance or honor the value(s) that norm serves. In the latter case, the law will not extend to every case in which it could do so. Generality does not preclude either complex norms or a system of norms that specify exceptions and special conditions. Yet while this may serve to reduce the occurrence of over- and under-inclusivity, it cannot eliminate it altogether. Moreover, given the limits on our ability to anticipate all the circumstances to which a law might apply, including those produced by unforeseen social, technological, or environmental change, the requirement that government officials act only in accordance with existing law will unavoidably produce suboptimal outcomes on some occasions. All things considered, the benefits of certainty and predictability may often warrant upholding the law even when doing so produces an inefficient or in some respect unjust result. The same may be true if fidelity to the rule of law constitutes a form of respect for individual autonomy. Nevertheless, we should be cognizant of the tradeoff in such cases, and we should not assume that these particular benefits of fidelity to the rule of law will always exceed the costs. Where the content of the law is deeply unjust, the ideal of the rule of law may provide only a weak reason to uphold it, one that may be outweighed by the moral duty to combat the injustice the law facilitates.[42]

Tamanaha notes that, in some circumstances, the attempt to regulate agents' interactions on the basis of law may prove problematic. Standing on one's legal rights may erode bonds of care and connection, particularly within more intimate communities. Perhaps more importantly given this book's focus, the attempt to address disputes within a rule of law framework may not be suitable for "situations that threaten an eruption of violence within or between communities – peace might better be achieved through political efforts. When responding to disputes of this sort, the primary concern often is to come to a solution that everyone can live with . . . [and] coming to a compromise may better achieve this goal than strict rule application."[43] Tamanaha is surely right that in some circumstances actors should aim only at peace or the avoidance of conflict, and that a process of continual negotiation and balancing rather than rule making and application provides the best means for doing so. Nevertheless, as we will discuss in Chapter 9, it may be that

---

[42] Hart, *Concept*, pp. 211–12. This conclusion holds even for those who defend conceptions of the rule of law that incorporate substantive requirements such as respect for individual rights. Again, as long as the theorists who defend such a view can distinguish between legitimacy and (perfect) justice, they will be able to acknowledge the possibility and perhaps inevitability of conflicts between fidelity to the rule of law and just outcomes in particular cases.

[43] Tamanaha, "History and Elements," 242.

government in accordance with the rule of law can play a crucial role in the creation of a community premised on shared or overlapping conceptions of justice, and not just a principle of live and let live.

V INTERNATIONAL LAW AND FIDELITY TO THE IDEAL OF THE RULE OF LAW

With a relatively clear understanding of several competing (but also partly congruent) conceptions of the nature and value of the rule of law, we can now consider the extent to which the international legal order satisfies that ideal. We will limit our investigation here to the elements that comprise the thin conception of the rule of law: government through law, supremacy of law, equality before the law, independent adjudicatory institutions, and a culture of fidelity to the rule of law as a political ideal on the part of officials and subjects.[44] First, however, it may be useful to emphasize the object of our investigation, since international legal theorists sometimes have something else in mind when they speak of an international rule of law. Our interest is the extent to which the international legal order, or the practice of public international law, satisfies the elements of government in accordance with the rule of law. This is a descriptive question concerning the degree to which a particular normative ideal informs the exercise of political power at the international level. It is distinct from, although not entirely unrelated to, another question sometimes formulated in terms of an international rule of law but that might be better put as: "does international law rule?" At issue here is whether and how international law causally contributes to the production of social order, both internationally and domestically. Depending on how we understand the concepts of law and the rule of law, it may be possible for international law to rule despite the fact that it suffers certain serious defects from the standpoint of the rule of law as a political ideal. In other words, while a necessary condition for the international rule of law is that international law rules, the converse may not be true (again, depending on what we take to be essential for the rule of law).

The international rule of law should also be distinguished from the rule of international law. The latter phrase is best construed as referring to normative concerns regarding the constraints that international law places on the self-determination of the political communities over whom it claims jurisdiction. Skepticism regarding the compatibility of constitutional democracy at the state level with the authority of international organizations constituted by international law, such as the World Trade Organization, is one example of a challenge to the rule of international law. As with international law's rule, the extent to which questions

---

[44] If the rule of law requires democracy then there is clearly no international rule of law, since international legal norms are neither the product of a global, democratically elected parliament nor fair negotiations between democratic states. See the discussion of democracy and international law's legitimate authority in Chapter 6, section V.

concerning the rule of international law are relevant to the conclusion we should draw regarding the international rule of law will depend on how we characterize the latter. Still, I believe some progress can be made in assessing how well the international legal order measures up to the ideal of government in accordance with the rule of law even if we set aside concerns with the morally justifiable scope of the rule of international law.[45]

How well does the existing international political order measure up against the ideal of the rule of law? Consider, first, government through law. Arguably the existing international political order satisfies the demand that coercive government be exercised only in accordance with prospective, general, and publicly promulgated standards fairly well, especially given the explosion of treaties in recent decades and the continuing efforts at codification undertaken by actors such as the International Law Commission. Still, the increasing tendency of the United Nations Security Council to legislate in secret (when acting under Chapter VII of the UN Charter), and, as in the case of targeted sanctions, to generate legal regimes that are far from transparent, are cause for concern.[46] How well international law satisfies the requirement of clarity will likely be a bone of contention, particularly where the absence of an adjudicatory body that enjoys compulsory jurisdiction and a de facto practice of reliance on precedent results in a paucity of case law. International law's satisfaction of the noncontradiction condition is threatened by its increasing fragmentation, the proliferation of multiple legal regimes and/or tribunals that claim jurisdiction over the same actors and conduct but apply different bodies of law, with no hierarchical arrangement or conflict rules to settle disputes between them. This development increases the likelihood that actors will be subject to two (or more) contradictory legal rules or judgments, with the resolution of conflicts dependent on political negotiations rather than the application of prospective, publicly promulgated standards.

Formal equality before the law also seems problematic, with powerful states enjoying greater latitude in their international undertakings than do weaker states. As Rosalyn Higgins observed while serving as the President of the International Court of Justice:

> The realities of power, coupled with the promotion of their own interests and the protection of other favoured states, means that the decisions of the Security Council, while striving for a principled application based on Charter requirements, are subject to "the achievement of the possible." That in turn means that Security

---

[45] For a useful survey of recent debates regarding the rule of international law, see Allen Buchanan and Russell Powell, "Constitutional Democracy and the Rule of International Law: Are they Compatible?" *Journal of Political Philosophy* 16, 3 (2008): 326–49.

[46] Rosalyn Higgins, "The ICJ and the Rule of Law," speech delivered at the United Nations University, April 11, 2007, available at http://archive.unu.edu/events/files/2007/20070411_Higgins_speech.pdf (accessed March 14, 2018): 13; Simon Chesterman, "I'll Take Manhattan: The International Rule of Law and the UNSC," *Hague Journal on the Rule of Law* 1 (2009): 70–3.

Council decision-making is not always regarded as "applicable equally to all." Arguments about consistency in the application of sanctions to different states said to be violating the Charter illustrate the point.[47]

The UN Human Rights Council's continually one-sided condemnations of Israel offer further grounds for doubting that the practice of international law rests on a commitment to formal equality before the law.[48] The same is true for the ICC's activities to this point, which have focused exclusively on the conduct of officials in relatively weak states, mostly located in Africa.

From the standpoint of realizing the rule of law, the greatest shortcoming of the existing international order surely concerns the supremacy of law. Resistance to this aspect of the rule of law is both cause and effect of the dearth of independent tribunals recognized by all international legal subjects as enjoying standing authority to determine what the law is, and whether they have conformed to it. Sir Arthur Watts is one of many commentators on the International Court of Justice who note this shortcoming:

> [Since] jurisdiction in all cases requires the consent of the States whose dispute is to go before the Court ... a reluctant defendant State can prevent a dispute being referred to the Court – or indeed to any other form of judicial or arbitral settlement, for example by an ad hoc tribunal, since any such reference is similarly subject to the defendant State's consent. Such a purely consensual basis for the judicial settlement of legal disputes cannot be satisfactory in terms of the Rule of Law.[49]

Consider, too, ICJ Judge James Crawford's observation that "it may be that decisions of the Security Council are subject to the authority of the Charter, but the fact is that there is no regular institutional means for bringing Charter constraints to bear on the Security Council."[50]

The fact that the enforcement of international law is generally left to the injured party also likely weakens government according to the rule of law, insofar as it makes the correlation between law in the books and law in action dependent on states' relative power. For example, a weak state's attempt to use countermeasures authorized by the WTO's Dispute Settlement Body to enforce its rights under that treaty against a much stronger state may well prove ineffective, and perhaps even counterproductive.[51] Consider, too, recent examples of states refusing to implement

---

[47]   Higgins, "Rule of Law," 3–4.
[48]   Note that the claim here concerns only equality before the law, not the justifiability of the charges leveled against Israel. See also the discussion of the ICJ's advisory opinion regarding the legal consequences of the construction of a wall in the occupied Palestinian territories in Joshua Kleinfeld, "Skeptical Internationalism: A Study of Whether International Law is Law," *Fordham Law Review* 78, 5 (2010): 2452–530.
[49]   Sir Arthur Watts, "The International Rule of Law," *German Yearbook of International Law* 36 (1993): 37.
[50]   James Crawford, "International Law and the Rule of Law," *Adelaide Law Review* 24, 1 (2003): 10.
[51]   See the discussion in Chapter 11, section III.

the findings of international courts or arbitral panels, including member states' refusal to act on the International Criminal Court's order to surrender Sudanese President Al Bashr, and China's refusal to acknowledge as legally binding the International Tribunal for the Law of the Sea's judgment regarding its claim to sovereignty in the South China Sea.[52] Moreover, international law makes no provision for the enforcement of many of the norms to which states are subject, apart from whatever persuasive force attaches to being publicly held to account for their violation. Arguably, these examples evidence a weak or non-existent culture of fidelity to the rule of law in many states' conduct of international affairs.

Finally, the actions of some state officials reflect a mistaken understanding of the purpose of the rule of law. Broadly speaking, that purpose is to constrain and guide the exercise of government for the benefit of the individual human beings who are subject to it. Whereas individuals are free to act as they will unless the law proscribes doing so, the reverse is true for government. Absent a legal authorization to do so, government officials are not free to act. As Jeremy Waldron argues, this distinction has important implications for the approach lawyers ought to take when advising their clients.[53] In the case of private actors, lawyers are permitted to interpret any lack of clarity in the law in ways that favor their clients' freedom to act as they wish. Lawyers who advise government officials, in contrast, ought to be quite cautious in concluding that the law accords their clients discretion to act as they think best. After all, the more discretion government officials enjoy, the less the law will serve to provide subjects with certainty and predictability, or protection from the arbitrary exercise of force, or a form of government that respects their status as responsible agents.

State officials and the lawyers who advise them sometimes approach international law as if the state occupies the same position vis-à-vis international law that individuals do with respect to domestic law. This leads them to interpret international law so as to limit as much as possible the constraints it places on the state's freedom to act. In doing so, however, they ignore several crucial disanalogies between individuals and the state. Most importantly, "states are not themselves bearers of ultimate value ... [rather] they exist for the sake of human individuals."[54] Whereas an individual's liberty is valuable in itself (conditional, perhaps, on how it is exercised), the state's liberty is only instrumentally valuable, good in virtue of whatever contribution it makes to advancing the well-being of individuals. Consider, too, that states are not only subjects of international law but also legislators and administrators of it. Once we foreground this disanalogy with individual subjects of a domestic legal

---

[52] See Andreas Zimmermann, "Times are Changing – and What About the International Rule of Law Then?," www.ejiltalk.org/times-are-changing-and-what-about-the-international-rule-of-law-then/ (published March 5, 2018; accessed October 25, 2019).

[53] Jeremy Waldron, "The Rule of International Law," *Harvard Journal of Law and Public Policy* 30, 1 (Fall 2006): 15–30.

[54] Ibid, 24.

order, we should recognize that "advising a government in the realm of international law ... is much more like advising an executive official in the municipal arena than like advising a private individual or business."[55] If international lawyers do not recognize this fact, then they will fail to honor one of their profession's core ideals, namely the supremacy of law. Since the existence of an international rule of law depends fundamentally on a commitment to that ideal on the part of international lawyers, especially those who advise or who are public officials, the more pervasive this mistaken understanding of its purpose the less that ideal will be realized.

Perhaps the foregoing description of the international legal order is unduly pessimistic. After all, many international lawyers rightly note that states and other subjects of international law typically conform to its demands.[56] Moreover, the past few decades have seen a marked increase in the judicialization of specific domains of international law. Some of these adjudicatory bodies exercise compulsory jurisdiction, at least vis-à-vis the states that are party to the Convention that created a specific legal regime, such as the WTO Treaty, the UN Convention on the Law of the Sea, and the Rome Statute of the International Criminal Court.[57] Finally, we should not forget that many international legal disputes are adjudicated by domestic courts. Insofar as the institutional design and culture of these courts exhibit fidelity to the rule of law, we might expect that ideal to inform their engagement with international law.

Those skeptical of an international rule of law are unlikely to find these rejoinders compelling. First, they will point out that insofar as a state's international legal obligations are largely a product of its voluntarily agreeing to be bound by specific international legal norms, it would be incredibly surprising if states did not largely conform to them. Moreover, many international legal regimes facilitate mutually beneficial coordination and cooperation among states (or at least certain interest groups that are able to shape the conduct of particular states). When this is so, pursuit of the national interest will suffice to motivate conformity to international law. That possibility undermines any straightforward inference from general compliance with international law to states commitment to the international rule of law. Finally, as we noted earlier, states' willingness to accept international legal norms as binding is often not matched by a willingness to submit to third-party adjudication, let alone third-party enforcement. States often have much to gain by defending their conduct as legal, especially with regard to perceptions of their domestic legitimacy, and little to lose by doing so when those who disagree can do nothing more than

---

[55] Ibid.
[56] As Louis Henkin famously wrote "almost all nations observe almost all principles of international law and almost all of their obligations almost all of the time." Louis Henkin, *How Nations Behave: Law and Foreign Policy*, 2nd Edition (New York: Columbia University Press, 1979), p. 47.
[57] The ICC may also exercise jurisdiction in the absence of state consent if the United Nations Security Council authorizes the Prosecutor to conduct an investigation.

publicly object to those claims.[58] In such circumstances, states purported compliance with their legal obligations may offer little evidence of their fidelity to the ideal of the rule of law.

We must also be careful not to assume that the increased judicialization of the international legal order has brought with it a strengthening of the rule of law. Most of these new tribunals have quite limited resources for carrying out their function, which likely limits access to them as a means for resolving disputes. More importantly, some international tribunals may not be designed to govern in accordance with the rule of law, but only to enhance the efficiency of rule by law.[59] Finally, the design of some dispute resolution bodies may be in tension with the ideal of the rule of law. For example, a party to a dispute before the ICJ has a right to the appointment of an ad hoc judge who is a citizen of that state, in the event that no sitting judge meets that condition. While these judges do not automatically find in favor of their own state, empirical studies indicate that they do side with them at a fairly high rate.[60] The appointment of judges to international tribunals are also subject to formal or informal norms that allocate seats on the bench to different "civilizations" or regions that share certain political, cultural, religious, and legal traditions. On the one hand, this might advance impartiality by combating deliberate or unwitting parochialism. On the other hand, it may also create or reinforce a practice in which judges represent the interests of the group that nominates them.

Neither should we exaggerate the extent to which the application of international law by domestic courts serves to advance the international rule of law. To begin with the obvious, some states display little fidelity to the rule of law even in their domestic affairs. Where courts are systematically corrupt or politicized, an arm of the executive rather than a check on it, there is no reason to think they will suddenly conform to the demands of the rule of law when presented with a case that turns on a question of international law. Even in rule of law states, domestic courts have a mixed record of contributing to the international rule of law. While they frequently apply international law to settle disputes between private actors, the same is not true for cases that involve the state. When domestic courts perceive a case as one that is regulated by international legal norms governing relations between states, they generally treat it as political matter rather than a legal one.[61] Consequently, domestic courts use various techniques to avoid reaching any decision on the legal merits of the case,

---

[58] Of course, other states may invoke their own view of the law to justify imposing some type of cost on the state whose conduct they wish to change. The key point here is that the dispute will not be settled on the basis of government in accordance with the rule of law, but instead through the exercise of power (such as use of tariffs, economic sanctions, armed attack, and so on).

[59] See the discussion of the WTO's dispute settlement system in Chapter 11, section III.

[60] See Xuechan Ma and Shaui Guo, "An Empirical Study of the Voting Patterns of Judges of the International Court of Justice (2005–2016)," *Erasmus Law Review* 10, 3 (2017): 163–74; Eric A. Posner and John C. Yoo, "Judicial Independence in International Tribunals," *California Law Review* 93, 1 (January 2005): 3–74.

[61] See David L. Sloss and Michael P. Van Alstine, "International Law in Domestic Courts," in *Research Handbook on the Politics of International Law*, eds. Wayne Sandholtz and Christopher A. Whytock

including denying their jurisdiction over it, adopting a narrow understanding of who has the standing to bring a case, and explicitly identifying the issue as a political question that lies outside the court's purview. In cases of this type, then, domestic courts refuse to serve as mechanisms for realizing the supremacy of international law.

The situation is more complicated, and somewhat more positive, when it comes to international legal norms that govern relations between states and their subjects. International law sometimes figures centrally in the design of domestic constitutional and statutory norms, so that when a court invokes the latter to conclude that the state has acted illegally it might be said to be "silently applying" international rule of law.[62] In their interpretation of domestic legal standards, state courts sometimes rely on a presumption that these standards should be understood to be consistent or compatible with their state's international legal obligations. The application of this presumption seems to be inconsistent, however.[63] In part, this may be due to broader disagreements over the approach to legal interpretation that judges ought to adopt. Yet there is also some evidence that judges more often invoke the presumption when doing so supports the conclusion they favor than when it does not. If so, this fact weakens the claim that domestic courts contribute to the supremacy of international law.[64] Domestic courts appear most willing to uphold state's international legal obligations to their subjects when the states in question acknowledge the authority of a regional court to do so as well.[65] These include European countries subject to the European Court of Human Rights and Latin American countries that recognize the jurisdiction of the Inter-American Court of Human Rights. From the standpoint of assessing the existence of an international rule of law, however, this observation provides a double-edged sword. It suggests that national court's effectiveness at upholding the international rule of law depends to a considerable extent on the existence of a supra-state tribunal. Yet it is precisely the absence of such tribunals with compulsory jurisdiction in many areas of international law that figures prominently in skeptical challenges to an international rule of law.

* * *

Although some will disagree, it seems plausible to conclude that the ideal of the rule of law is at best only weakly realized in the contemporary international legal order. If law exists only where government is exercised in accordance with the rule of law, then it follows that international law is not really law. As with many of the other

---

(Northampton, MA: Edward Elgar Publishers, 2017), pp. 89–92. See also André Nollkaemper, *National Courts and the International Rule of Law* (Oxford: Oxford University Press, 2011), pp. 47–109.

[62] Sloss and Van Alstine, "International Law," 104–5.

[63] Ibid, 107.

[64] It may also be invoked to support a more radical skeptical challenge to the rule of law in general, of course.

[65] Ibid, 108–13.

skeptical challenges to international law discussed in this book, however, this summative judgment is less important than the story that lies behind it. In this case, that story consists in a nuanced assessment that pays careful attention to the specific ways in which the international order does and does not exhibit fidelity to the ideal of the rule of law and explanations for why that is so. This assessment provides the starting point for arguments over what can and should be done to rectify the international legal order's rule of law shortcomings, and what conclusions we should draw in the meantime regarding international law's normativity, legitimacy, and justice.

6

The Legitimacy of International Law

Hart maintains that doubts regarding international law's status as law originate in the observation that it deviates in certain respects from the "standard case" of municipal law; that is, the legal system of a modern state. For some, the deviation that motivates their skepticism may be the one Hart identifies, namely international law's horizontal structure, the relative paucity of specialization in the performance of governance tasks that characterizes the international legal order. For others, the deviation that grounds their skepticism may lie elsewhere. In the previous chapter, we identified it as the perception that the global political order manifests insufficient fidelity to the ideal of the rule of law. In this chapter, we locate it in the suspicion that international law lacks legitimacy, a moral claim to authority over international legal subjects correlative to their moral duty to obey the law.

   We begin in section I with an analysis of the concept of legitimacy, or perhaps, more precisely, the concept of legitimate authority. In sections II–V we consider four possible grounds for international law's legitimacy: enhancing its subjects' ability to act as they have most reason to act, the consent of those it claims as subjects, considerations of fair play, and international law's democratic credentials. Our focus in each case is twofold: first with arguments for thinking that a particular ground is either necessary or sufficient for international law's legitimacy, and second with the implications the account in question has for international law's present claim to legitimacy. As will become clear, none of the grounds for international law's legitimacy considered herein, either separately or in combination, shows the existing international legal order to be fully legitimate; indeed, it likely falls well short of that (perhaps ideal) standard. Still, just as the failure of any existing social order to realize a conception of justice does not by itself provide a reason to reject that conception, so too the failure of the international legal order to qualify as legitimate according to some standard of legitimacy does not by itself provide a reason to reject that standard. We conclude in section VI by examining a number of reasons why we should care about international law's legitimacy; indeed, why from a moral point of view increasing the international legal order's legitimacy might even take priority over making it more just.

I THE CONCEPT OF LEGITIMACY

A *Legitimacy as a Right to Rule*

Judgments of political legitimacy concern attempts to rule or govern. A attempts to rule or govern B with respect to some domain of conduct if and only if A maintains that B ought to defer to A's judgment regarding what B may, must, or must not do; that is, if and only if A claims practical authority over B. When A does so, she maintains that her directives provide B with content-independent and exclusionary reasons for action. So, if A claims authority over B and she directs B not to Φ, then she maintains that B has a reason not to Φ simply because A instructed him not do so, a reason that makes no reference to the content of A's direction to B (that is, what Φ-ing is). Moreover, she maintains that B ought to treat A's instruction not to Φ as a reason to exclude from his deliberation some or all of the reasons he might have to Φ. From B's perspective, to treat A's directive as a content-independent and exclusionary reason just is to defer to A's judgment, or in other words, to recognize her as having practical authority over him.

An illustration may be helpful. Suppose Ali promises to meet Betty for dinner this evening at a restaurant of Betty's choosing. Her promise gives Betty a right to rule Ali with respect to one very circumscribed aspect of her life, namely, where Ali will dine tonight. Betty chooses McDonald's, thereby giving Ali a content-independent and exclusionary reason to join her for dinner there. The reason is content-independent because it is the fact that Betty chose McDonald's, and not any facts about McDonald's such as its low prices or fast service that account for Ali's obligation to dine there. Had Betty chosen a different restaurant, then Ali would have been obligated to join Betty there. Ali's promise to Betty also excludes certain reasons for not dining at McDonald's that she would otherwise be permitted to act on. For example, Ali may not particularly like the type of food McDonald's serves, or she may prefer to stay home. Her promise precludes her from acting on those reasons (although not from forming the belief that she would be better off if she did *not* join Betty for dinner). In contrast, suppose Ali had not made this promise to Betty, and that, instead, Betty had simply proposed to Ali that they go to McDonald's for dinner. In this case, Ali would be justified in acting on her dislike for the food McDonald's serves or her preference for staying home, since Betty would have no claim against Ali that precludes her acting for those reasons.

A's attempt to rule over B is *legitimate* if and only if A has a right to rule B, a right that correlates to B's duty to obey A. Strictly speaking, what the subject of a legitimate authority owes her is not conduct but a certain form of deliberation or practical reasoning, one that treats the authority's directives as content-independent and exclusionary reasons for action. Put another way, the duty to obey correlative to another's right to rule is best understood in terms of deference to the ruler's judgment. Particular conduct may also be owed to the ruler, but it need not be.

For example, B may have a duty not to damage C's property, one correlative to C's property right, and a duty to defer to A's judgment regarding what counts as damage to C's property (that is, what counts as a violation of C's property right). The latter duty may correlate to A's moral right to direct B's conduct (vis-à-vis C's property), or to C's moral right to B reasoning in whatever manner will make him most likely to respect C's property right, or both. Getting clear on this conceptual point is important if we are to avoid the common but mistaken assumption that a successful theory of legitimacy must explain how those subject to a putative authority can owe *it* conduct in accordance with its directives.

To claim the right to rule is not to have it. If A's attempt to rule over B is illegitimate, then while A may claim that B ought to treat her instruction not to Φ as a content-independent and exclusionary reason, B has no duty to do so. Note, however, that B may still have prudential or moral reasons not to Φ, perhaps even conclusive ones; the denial of a putative authority's legitimacy is neither equivalent to nor does it entail the claim that an agent should not act as the putative authority would have him act. Moreover, A's attempt to rule over B may correctly be judged to be good, or at least better than the likely alternatives, even if A has no right to rule B. Both of these points bear emphasis since many accounts of what makes law legitimate entail that international law often lacks the authority it claims, or in other words, that it is illegitimate.

If states and other international legal subjects can still have a conclusive or all things considered moral reason to act as international law or an international legal institution directs, even though it is illegitimate, then why should we care about its legitimacy? In the next subsection, we will consider whether this question points to the need to revisit the characterization of legitimacy as a right to rule. Here, however, I want to review several responses advanced by legal philosophers who accept that characterization.

We can begin by noting that it does not follow from the fact that an agent *can* have an all-things-considered moral reason to act as an illegitimate law or legal institution would have her act that she will always, or even often, have such a reason. In practice, the legitimacy of law or legal institutions may make a significant difference to what agents have a moral reason to do. But more importantly, legal rights and obligations are frequently treated as conclusive reasons for action in both private deliberation and public justification or criticism. That is, the assertion that a given act is legal or illegal is often taken to suffice as a justification for performing an act, or for holding an agent accountable for performing it by, say, criticizing her or withholding some benefit to which she is normally entitled. Therefore, it is worth investigating the conditions under which these attempts at justifying conduct actually succeed, which is to say the conditions law must satisfy to be legitimate.

John Tasioulas maintains that "the law's distinctive contribution to a community's realization of valuable goals consists precisely in successfully laying down authoritative standards of conduct."[1] Some might argue that this entails only that we can have a weighty moral reason to encourage people *to believe* the law is legitimate, but not necessarily a reason to be concerned with whether the law *truly is* legitimate.[2] Respect for individuals as autonomous moral agents militates against such a conclusion, however. Rather, if we maintain that in general people ought to defer to the law, then we owe them an argument demonstrating that the law is legitimate. Indeed, as we will discuss later in this chapter, it may be that justice can only be fully realized among agents who interact with one another on terms set out in legitimate law. If so, then we have a very compelling reason to be concerned with what makes law, including international law, legitimate.

B *Against Legitimacy as a Right to Rule*

Recently, several philosophers have criticized the traditional characterization of legitimacy as a right to rule.[3] One impetus for this challenge comes from the observation that we can (and should, and arguably do) assess the legitimacy of international institutions that neither claim authority over others nor exercise any ability to coerce them. Therefore, we need a broader notion of legitimacy, one that satisfies two desiderata. First, it must be one we can employ to judge the legitimacy of institutions that rule as well as those that do not. Second, those judgments must play the same role in our deliberation, since otherwise they will not constitute the use of the same concept. In other words, concluding that an institution is legitimate must have the same significance for our practical reasoning regardless of whether that institution is one that attempts to rule.[4]

Allen Buchanan's Meta-Coordination View of the concept of legitimacy meets both of these requirements. Judgements of legitimacy, he maintains, serve a specific practical function, namely, facilitating:

> [T]he achievement of a consensus on whether an institution is worthy of our moral reason-based support. The assertion that an institution is legitimate represents an all-things-considered judgment regarding the moral reasons to support it, namely that those reasons weigh in favor of supporting the institution, in spite of the risks that such support entails.[5]

[1] John Tasioulas, "The Legitimacy of International Law," in *The Philosophy of International Law*, eds. Samantha Besson and John Tasioulas (New York: Oxford University Press, 2010), p. 100.

[2] Of course, where legal norms and institutions facilitate injustice, the loss of de facto legitimacy that renders them less able to contribute to the production of social order may be morally desirable.

[3] See, for instance, Allen Buchanan, *The Heart of Human Rights* (Oxford: Oxford University Press, 2013); Allen Buchanan, "Institutional Legitimacy," in *Oxford Studies in Political Philosophy, Volume 4*, eds. David Sobel et al. (Oxford: Oxford University Press, 2018); Eva Erman, "Global Political Legitimacy Beyond Justice and Democracy," *International Theory* 8, 1 (2016): 29–62; N.P. Adams, "Institutional Legitimacy," *Journal of Political Philosophy* 26, 1 (2018): 84–102.

[4] As will become clear, the claim that a judgment of legitimacy must have the same significance for our deliberation does not entail that we must engage with or relate to all institutions in exactly the same way.

[5] Buchanan, "Institutional Legitimacy," 54–5.

Elsewhere, Buchanan states that to claim that an institution is legitimate is to claim that it satisfies certain criteria in virtue of which agents have moral reason to accord that institution the respect necessary for it to function well.[6] The form respect for an institution must take, or what counts as exhibiting the proper respect, varies depending on both the nature of the institution and the relationship an agent stands in to that institution: "For those to whom the institution addresses its rules, it involves a presumption of compliance that operates independently of an assessment of the content of any particular directive."[7] Those not addressed by such an institution but able to impact its operation should "at the very least, not interfere with its efforts to promulgate and promote compliance with its directives."[8] Presumably, respect for legitimate institutions that do not rule likewise requires that agents not interfere with their functioning well. For example, in the case of treaty bodies that monitor states' compliance with the Human Rights Conventions they have signed (and, if necessary, ratified), this might include refraining from conduct that makes it difficult or impossible to collect the information needed to conduct its assessment. Finally, if an institution is legitimate then the means agents may adopt to respond to its failings are generally more morally constrained than in the case of an illegitimate institution.[9] Legitimate institutions merit reform, whereas illegitimate ones warrant revolution and replacement.

Should we replace a description of legitimacy as a right to rule with Buchanan's more abstract concept of legitimacy as "having a standing that commands certain forms of respect?" or being "morally worthy of our support?"[10] We can, but I will offer two reasons why we need not do so. First, the dispute between Buchanan and theorists of legitimacy as a right to rule may rest entirely on different uses of the term "legitimacy" rather than any substantive disagreement. Second, even if we accept *arguendo* Buchanan's concept of legitimacy, any assessment of *international law's* legitimacy will pay special attention to those international institutions that enact, apply, and enforce international law. That is, it will offer criteria for the legitimacy of institutions that rule. This account of what makes international law or international legal institutions legitimate will either be identical to one of the accounts offered by a theorist who conceives of legitimacy as a right to rule, or a rival to it. In either case, we can proceed with the normative question of interest in this chapter without having to resolve the debate over how best to understand the concept of legitimacy.

Consider, first, the claim that the dispute between Buchanan and proponents of the narrower concept of legitimacy that equates it with a right to rule is merely verbal, a difference in the use of the term "legitimate" that does not track or shine light on any substantive disagreement. For example, A. John Simmons defines a state's legitimacy as "its exclusive right to impose new duties on subjects by

---

[6]   Buchanan, *Heart of Human Rights*, p. 179.
[7]   Buchanan, "Institutional Legitimacy," 56; see also *Heart of Human Rights*, p. 184.
[8]   Buchanan, *Heart of Human Rights*, p. 184.
[9]   Ibid, p. 185.
[10] Ibid, p. 180; Buchanan, "Institutional Legitimacy," 55.

initiating legally binding directives, to have those directives obeyed, and to coerce noncompliers."[11] In short, a legitimate state is one that has a right to rule.[12] However, Simmons also maintains that states may be justified or unjustified, by which he means prudentially rational, morally acceptable, or both. Justifications of the state, or any other institution, involve "rebutting certain kinds of possible objections to it: either comparative objections – that other acts or institutions (etc.) are preferable to the one in question – or noncomparative objections – that the act in question is unacceptable or wrong or that the institution practices or sanctions wrongdoing or vice."[13] What follows if an institution such as the state is justified? On Simmons' preferred account, this fact "gives us moral reasons to refrain from undermining it and will typically give us moral reason to positively support that state (or perhaps even to promote the existence of similar states ...)."[14] This looks very similar to Buchanan's claim that an institution's legitimacy gives us reason to support it, to act in ways that contribute to that institution functioning well and to refrain from acting in ways that interfere with it doing so. Moreover, Simmons' acknowledgment that the justifiability of an institution will sometimes be comparative entails that it will rest on precisely the sort of balancing of costs and benefits that Buchanan defends as appropriate for carrying out assessments of legitimacy (in his broad sense of that term). It appears that Buchanan simply uses the term "legitimate" to refer what

[11] A. John Simmons, *Justification and Legitimacy: Essays on Rights and Obligations* (New York: Cambridge University Press, 2001), p. 137.

[12] A *state's* right to rule includes a right to coerce noncompliers because states necessarily claim "a monopoly of the legitimate use of physical force within a given territory" (Max Weber, "Politics as Vocation," in *Max Weber: Essays in Sociology*, eds. H. H. Gerth and C. Wright Mills (New York: Oxford University Press, 1946), p. 4). On one reading, this claim describes a legal-political order in which the coercive enforcement of the law is normally undertaken by state officials (understood broadly to include both state employees and contractors), with self-help exercised only rarely, in self-defense against an imminent threat, for example. As we have seen, international law lacks specialists in law enforcement. This difference in the nature of the two types of legal-political order explains why the defense of a state's right to rule must include a justification of its exclusive right to coerce noncompliers while a defense of the international legal order's right to rule does not.

Alternatively, we might read the above quote from Weber with an emphasis on the idea of legitimacy. What distinguishes the modern state is not the fact that it monopolizes the use of physical force within a given territory, or its claim to do so. Rather, it is the state's assertion that it enjoys the sole authority to determine what counts as the *legitimate*, meaning rightful or permissible, use of force within a given territory that distinguishes it from the form of political society that preceded its emergence in Europe. International law has long made a similar claim with respect to the use of force between states (and in the form of prohibitions on genocide and crimes against humanity, as well as UN Security Council authorized armed humanitarian interventions, it has begun to circumscribe states' right to coercively enforce law on their own territory). This reading implies that we should treat (coercive) enforcement of the law as simply another form of conduct over which authority may be exercised but not conduct in which an agent must engage in order to qualify as an authority. If so, then we ought to characterize the *concept* of ruling solely in terms of the exercise of authority, and so conceive of a right to rule as the exercise of legitimate authority. This is so even if the *justifiability* of a putative authority's claim to legitimacy depends on its ability to reliably impose costs on the disobedient and grant benefits to the obedient.

[13] Ibid, p. 125.

[14] Ibid, p. 137.

Simmons' describes using the term "justified," or perhaps to refer to both of the features that Simmons picks out using the terms "justified" and "legitimate."[15]

Are there any reasons to prefer one characterization of legitimacy over the other? Fit with the use of that term in ordinary public discourse might provide one, but as Buchanan and others rightly note there is no single, unified, practice regarding the use of the term "legitimate." Some speakers treat it as synonymous with "legal," others with "justified," and still others with "just"; indeed, the same speaker may mean different things by "legitimate" in different contexts. Buchanan emphasizes that one virtue of his account of the concept of legitimacy is that it distinguishes judgments of legitimacy from assessments of an institution's justice or its prudential value.[16] Yet theorists such as Simmons can make the same claim on behalf of their characterization of legitimacy, insofar as the moral basis of an institution's right to rule is not reducible to its being just, prudentially optimal, or for that matter, justifiable in Simmons' sense of that term. Arguably, political philosophers have converged on an understanding of legitimacy as a right to rule (even while disagreeing over the nature of that right), but perhaps we should not put too much weight on that fact. In using a term such as "legitimacy" for theoretical purposes, what matters most is the insight provided by a particular use of that term in combination with the use of other terms that figure in the overall theory. Simmons worries that certain uses of the term "legitimacy" by contemporary political philosophers pose a risk of conflating the two dimensions of institutional evaluation he distinguishes using the terms "legitimacy" and "justification." At times Buchanan appears to do just that.[17] Still, I suspect that we can use either Simmons' or Buchanan's approach to framing the substantive moral assessments of institutions, as long as we pay careful attention to the moral questions we are asking and precisely what follows from the answers we give.

Ultimately, Buchanan's objection to traditional accounts of legitimacy as a right to rule rest on three related criticisms of the theorists who use it to evaluate political and legal institutions. First, from a practical standpoint the question of whether we have moral reason to support an institution – whether it is legitimate in Buchanan's broad sense, or what Simmons calls justifiable – is currently a far more pressing matter than whether we have the specific sort of moral reasons to support it that concern theorists of legitimacy as a right to rule. Second, a focus on legitimacy as a right to rule leads theorists to ignore the need to develop and apply criteria for morally assessing the exercise of (political) power by institutions that make no claim to rule. Third, theorists

---

[15] Adams argues that Simmons' does not go far enough when he distinguishes justification and legitimacy because the latter concept still refers to a number of dimensions along which we can morally assess an institution, or at least the state. See Adams, "Institutional Legitimacy," 17.

[16] Buchanan, "Institutional Legitimacy," 54.

[17] For instance, Buchanan offers as an objection to Simmons' understanding of legitimacy the fact that we can have moral reasons to support an institution even when we have no duty to obey it ("Institutional Legitimacy," 68–9). Simmons will reply that this argument conflates two dimensions along which we can morally evaluate an institution.

of legitimacy as a right to rule tend to engage in ideal theory, with a focus on developing arguments from first moral principles with little attention to empirical realities. Yet in a decidedly nonideal world such theories are of little or no practical value. To put the point using Simmons' terminology, if we live in a world where no international political or legal institution comes close to satisfying the criteria for legitimacy, then the question on which we ought to focus is whether any of these institutions are justifiable. Likewise, if reforms that would make these institutions legitimate are far less feasible than those that would make them justifiable, then that gives us a weighty moral reason to focus our efforts on the latter rather than the former. Therefore, at least those political and legal philosophers with an interest in shaping contemporary practice ought to devote far more effort to developing theories of international institutions' justifiability than to theories of their legitimacy.

Although not without merit, I suspect these criticisms of many theorists of legitimacy as a right to rule are overdrawn. More importantly for our purposes, however, is that none of Buchanan's arguments precludes the need to assess the moral authority of international law, and so to develop and defend criteria for carrying out such an assessment. That is because on Buchanan's account an institution's legitimacy (in his broad sense of that term) gives us a moral reason to support it by according it the form of respect it needs from us in order to function well. In the case of legislative and adjudicative institutions, that means treating the directives they issue as authoritative, that is, as providing content-independent and exclusionary reasons for action. Therefore, whatever the upshot of the debate over the best way to characterize the concept of legitimacy, we need a normative theory of international law's *legitimate authority*, an account of the conditions it must satisfy if the legal status of an agent's conduct per se is to provide him or her with a moral reason for action. In the remainder of this chapter, we consider several attempts to provide one.

II THE INSTRUMENTAL ARGUMENT FOR INTERNATIONAL LAW'S LEGITIMACY

A *Law in the Service of Right Reason*

Justifications of authority fall into one of two categories: those in which deference to authority is instrumental to the just treatment of others, and, more broadly, to acting as one has reason to act, and those in which deference to authority is (also) constitutive of the just treatment of others. In contemporary debates, the first of these approaches is most closely associated with the philosopher Joseph Raz, with Samantha Besson and John Tasioulas among those who have drawn on Raz's work to offer an analysis of international law's legitimacy.[18] According to Raz, law is

---

[18] Joseph Raz, *The Authority of Law* (Oxford: Clarendon Press, 1979); Joseph Raz, "The Problem of Authority: Revisiting the Service Conception," *Minnesota Law Review* 90, 4 (2006): 1003–44;

legitimate, or has a justified claim to authority vis-à-vis its subjects, when the following two conditions are met:

(1) The Normal Justification Condition (NJC): The subject would better conform to reasons that apply to him anyway (that is, to reasons other than the directives of the authority) if he intends to be guided by the authority's directives than if he does not.

(2) The Independence Condition (IC): The matters regarding which the first condition is met are such that with respect to them it is better to conform to reason than to decide for oneself, unaided by authority.[19]

A's claim to authority over B is justified, then, if B is more likely to act as he has most reason to act by deferring to A's judgment regarding what he should or should not do than by acting on his own judgment, except in cases where it is more important that B decide for himself what to do than that he decide correctly, or in other words, than that he do what he has most reason to do. In such cases, A enjoys a right to rule B, and B has a duty to obey A's directives.

Some theorists contend that the NJC does not suffice to justify one agent's claim to authority over another. They argue that the mere fact that B will do better at acting as he has most reason to act if he defers to A's judgment does not entail that A has a right to rule B.[20] Raz concedes this point in some cases, namely, those where it is more important that an agent act on his own judgment than that he act in accordance with right reason. When and why this is the case is a point over which theorists may disagree without disputing Raz's general account of when one agent's claim to authority over another is justified. Moreover, it is not merely the fact that an agent will do better at acting on the reasons that apply to him by deferring to the law that renders the law legitimate, or what is the same, that generates a duty to obey the law. Rather, it is that fact in conjunction with the nature of the reasons that apply to the agent independently of the law that does so. If B has a moral duty to treat C justly, a reason for action that exists independently of the law, and if B is more likely to fulfill that duty by obeying the law than by acting on his own judgment, then those two facts suffice to establish the law's legitimate authority over B. If, in fact, B is more likely to treat C justly if she defers to A's judgment regarding what that requires than if she acts on her own judgment, then it is hard to see why that does not suffice to establish B's duty to obey A.[21]

Samantha Besson, "The Authority of International Law: Lifting the State Veil," *Sydney Law Review* 31, 3 (2009): 343–80; Tasioulas, "Legitimacy of International Law."

[19] Raz, "Problem of Authority," 1014.

[20] See, among others, Allen Buchanan, "The Legitimacy of International Law," in *The Philosophy of International Law*, eds. Samantha Besson and John Tasioulas (New York: Oxford University Press), p. 85.

[21] The worry is likely that the foregoing argument does not establish that B owes her duty of obedience to A. But as we noted in the previous section, it is a mistake to build that into the concept of legitimacy (or

Some argue that satisfaction of the NJC cannot suffice to establish the law's authority over an agent because if it did then even a deeply unjust state could be legitimate.[22] The fact that state officials or some of its subjects stand ready to perpetrate even greater injustices if an individual does not act as the law directs may give the individual a reason to treat the law as authoritative, but surely it does not entail that the state has a *right* to rule the individual, that is, that it enjoys *legitimate* authority. In response, it is important to keep in mind that on Raz's instrumental account, the duty to obey the law of a deeply unjust state may rarely be owed to the state. Rather, it is owed to those individuals a person is more likely to treat justly by obeying the law than by acting on his or her own judgment. But, second, we should distinguish between the NJC's being satisfied and an agent having good reason to believe that it is. Subjects of a deeply unjust state will often have little reason to believe that either its law or its legal institutions aim to improve their conformity to the independent (moral) reasons that apply to them, or, in other words, that the law reflects a good faith effort to satisfy the NJC. Therefore, they will have little or no reason to treat it as authoritative; that is, as providing them with content-independent and exclusionary reasons for action. This is likely to be so even where, as a matter of fact, the law of a deeply unjust state does satisfy the NJC, at least vis-à-vis some of its subjects. In such cases, while the individuals in question ought to defer to the law rather than act on their own judgment, they will likely not be blameworthy for their failure to recognize that this is the case.

Suppose, *arguendo*, that the independence condition is met. How might international law help those over whom it claims jurisdiction improve their conformity to right reason; that is, to act as they have most or undefeated reason to act? One way it may do so is by correcting for ignorance or mistaken beliefs. Tasioulas offers as an example international legal rules created via the enactment of multilateral treaties.[23] The process whereby such rules are crafted makes it likely that they reflect information that any single party to the convention would fail to acquire on its own, and so fail to take into account when deciding what sort of foreign policy or domestic legal regime to adopt. Moreover, negotiations over multilateral treaties can serve as a useful corrective to biases that undergird parties' mistaken beliefs, once again facilitating practical reasoning that is better informed and so likely to more closely approximate or conform to right reason than would unilateral decision making. In some cases, international law may also provide some of its subjects with access to expertise they cannot produce domestically.

---

legitimate authority). Whether an agent owes her obedience to law to those who govern depends on the independent moral reasons that apply to her, and to which she better conforms by obeying the law than by acting on her own judgment. That is, the question of who enjoys the right correlative to an agent's duty to defer to the law is a substantive one, not a conceptual one.

[22] See, for example, Thomas Christiano, *The Constitution of Equality: Democratic Authority and Its Limits* (New York: Oxford University Press, 2008), p. 234.

[23] Tasiouals, "Legitimacy of International Law," 101.

International law can also protect its subjects against what Tasioulas labels volitional defects. For example, state officials may come under great pressure from more powerful states, representatives of multinational corporations, or domestic interest groups to engage in conduct that promotes those actors' perceived interests or vision of justice but that is contrary to right reason. International law provides a mechanism for resisting such pressure.[24] International law's ability to steel its subjects against temptation is particularly important given the general human disposition to impatience, the tendency to treat oneself or one's circumstances as exceptional, and the fact that the interests of legal officials in remaining in power may diverge from both the prudential interests of the state's present and future members and the demands of justice.

Finally, and perhaps most importantly, international law can enhance its subjects' conformity to right reason by facilitating coordination on common standards of right conduct.[25] In some cases, it may do so by rendering more determinate a shared but vague standard, where the parties are rightly indifferent between any of a number of possible ways in which the abstract standard may be made more concrete. Far more common, however, are disputes over what the standard of right conduct is. Examples include disagreements regarding the moral principles that govern the use of force, international migration, trade, financial transactions, and the use of and control over the oceans or the Earth's atmosphere. In all of these cases, international actors are generally likely to do better at approximating justice by conforming to common standards set out in international law than by acting on their own judgment. In some instances, such as addressing climate change, this may be because justice can only be achieved via the cooperation of (nearly) all states. In others, the attempt by a state or international organization to act on its own understanding of what justice requires, even when it is accurate, may well result in an overall increase in international (and perhaps domestic) injustice. That is partly because one state's genuinely just war or trade policy may appear to another to be an act of aggression or beggar-thy-neighbor protectionism. But in addition, state officials acting in bad faith may offer the example of another state's just but illegal conduct as cover for their own unjust conduct. Both of these observations provide reasons to conclude that injustices are likely to follow when states and other international legal subjects deviate from the common standards of right conduct set out in international law. Indeed, Besson speaks for many political and legal theorists when she writes that: "[I]n conditions of pervasive and persistent reasonable disagreement about justice, the creation of a legal order as a means of general co-ordination over matters of justice is actually in itself a requirement of justice."[26]

---

[24]   See the discussion of international trade agreements in Chapter 11, section I.
[25]   Besson, "Authority of International Law," 352–7; Tasioulas, "Legitimacy of International Law," 102; Allen Buchanan and Robert Keohane, "The Legitimacy of Global Governance Institutions," *Ethics and International Affairs* 20, 4 (2006): 407–8.
[26]   Besson, "Authority of International Law," 353.

Where international law's legitimacy is a function of its facilitating coordination on common standards of right conduct, international law's de facto legitimacy is a necessary condition for its de jure authority.[27] It follows, Tasioulas notes, that "in order to maintain this source of legitimacy . . . public international law must not stray too far from implementing values that resonate widely with its would-be subjects."[28] As a consequence, at a given point in time the content of international law may diverge considerably from what justice truly requires. Yet, as long as international legal subjects are more likely to act justly (or, perhaps better, less unjustly) by obeying international law than by acting on their own judgment, they have a duty to do so.

The instrumental account entails that international law's legitimacy may be piecemeal. For any particular international legal norm or legal regime, the NJC may fail to establish its authority over some or even all of the actors whose conduct it purports to direct. Some argue that existing international law only serves the interests of powerful states (or elites within those states), or that it frequently prioritizes peace and stability at the expense of justice. Even those who maintain that international law is not merely the product of power and interest acknowledge that those two factors play a considerable role in determining its content. Consequently, international law's dictates may often diverge from what right reason requires precisely because it is the result of legislative activities that are not undertaken on the basis of a good faith effort to identify it. Perhaps the argument from coordination on common standards of right conduct still serves to justify the legitimacy of many international legal norms even when they are not the product of an effort to identify just terms of interaction. Yet that fact (if it is one) may also warrant a fair bit of skepticism regarding the extent of international law's legitimacy.

B Identifying Law that Satisfies the Normal Justification Thesis

Thus far we have focused on the various ways in which international law can satisfy the NJC. Yet a theory of the legitimacy of international law should do more than explain the normative basis of international law's legitimacy, in other words, what *makes* it authoritative. It should also offer guidance on how to *identify* legitimate international law, reasons to believe that international law, or international legislators and adjudicators, meet the normal justification condition. The complex standard of legitimacy for global governance institutions advocated by Allen Buchanan and Robert Keohane provides an excellent starting point for developing such an account.[29]

---

[27] Raz, "Problem of Authority," 1036. See also Besson, "Authority of International Law," 356.
[28] Tasioulas, "Legitimacy of International Law," 102.
[29] Buchanan and Keohane, "Legitimacy of Global Governance." The authors characterize global governance institutions broadly to include "multilateral entities" such as the WTO, the UN Security Council, and the climate change regime built around the Kyoto Protocol (or, now, the Paris Climate Agreement).

The complex standard consists of a set of substantive and procedural requirements that, when met, provide compelling evidence for the legitimacy of a global governance institution's attempt to rule.[30] The former include not persistently violating the least controversial human rights, not foregoing institutional changes that would provide greater benefits than existing ones and that are both feasible and accessible without excessive transition costs, and not intentionally or knowingly engaging in conduct at odds with the global governance institutions' purported aims and commitments. The latter include mechanisms for holding global governance institutions accountable for meeting the aforementioned substantive requirements as well as mechanisms for contesting the terms of accountability; that is, the ends that global governance institutions ought to pursue and the means they should employ in doing so. To be effective, mechanisms for holding officials accountable must be broadly transparent. This includes making information about how the institution works not only available but accessible to both internal and external actors (including inspectors general and nongovernmental organizations), as well as the provision of public justifications for the most consequential efforts at governance.

What unifies the various elements of the complex standard is that they all provide the legal subjects of global governance institutions with reason to believe that officials in these institutions are making a good faith effort to determine what justice requires. The point may be clearer if we consider the converse: the absence of one or more elements of the complex standard of legitimacy gives subjects of an attempt at global governance reason to doubt that the putative rulers aspire to enhance their conformity to right reason. Instead, subjects may suspect, and perhaps rightly so, that governance is being exercised in pursuit of other goals, such as the national interest of powerful states or the private interests of businesses or religious groups, that partly deviate from or even conflict with the demands of justice. Consider, for example, the substantive elements of the complex standard: no attempt at international governance by either global governance institutions or by states that persistently violated "the least controversial human rights" or that systematically discriminated in the application and enforcement of international legal norms could plausibly claim to be making a good faith effort to enhance its subjects' conformity to right reason. The procedural elements that compose the complex standard evidence a good faith effort to determine what right reason requires partly because they militate against efforts to deploy international law for private interest rather than the public or common good, and partly because they improve the quantity and quality of the information on the basis of which global governance is conducted. As the first of these claims implies, the complex standard's procedural elements are desirable not only for their

---

[30] These two categories correspond closely to the categories of output and input legitimacy employed by many international relations or IR-influenced scholars. See Daniel Bodansky, "Legitimacy in International Law and International Relations," in *Interdisciplinary Perspectives on International Law and International Relations: The State of the Art*, eds. Jeffrey L. Dunoff and Mark A. Pollack (New York: Cambridge University Press, 2013), pp. 321–41.

evidentiary value but because they are likely to facilitate efforts at governance that actually succeed in being legitimate; that is, that actually meet the normal justification for authority. As an example of the second claim, the requirement that global governance institutions facilitate effective engagement with external epistemic agents such as Human Rights Watch and the International Committee of the Red Cross likely leads to more informed and less biased rules and decisions than either these institutions' officials or those they directly or indirectly govern would achieve on their own.

International law's value as a means for enhancing its subjects' conformity to right reason is not the only ground theorists have offered for its legitimacy. Many have sought instead, or at least in addition, to defend noninstrumental accounts according to which obedience to legitimate international law constitutes the just treatment of others. At least since the nineteenth century, the most prominent such account used to justify international law's claim to authority has been state consent. More recently theorists have identified considerations of fair play as a basis for international law's legitimacy, or maintained that the justifiability of international law's claim to authority requires that it be democratically enacted. We will consider each of these approaches in turn.

III CONSENT AS A BASIS FOR INTERNATIONAL LAW'S LEGITIMACY

Consent involves a minimum of two parties: an agent who grants another a claim right or power and thereby acquires a correlative duty or liability, and an agent who acquires the right. For example, in signing and ratifying a treaty setting out the terms that will govern their use of a river that runs through or along both of their territories, two states may be said to grant one another rights to conduct that conforms to those terms, and to acquire obligations to act as the treaty directs. Similarly, in joining the WTO states consent to its Dispute Resolution Body's authority to resolve their disputes regarding compliance with their obligations under that treaty. In conforming to the terms of a treaty to which they have consented, states uphold their duties to one another, which is to say that, in at least one respect, they treat one another justly. They may also treat one another justly because the content of the treaty reflects or determines what justice truly requires vis-à-vis the use of a common resource, trade, the use of force, and so on. This need not be the case, however; a state that has consented to govern its conduct according to certain terms may not unilaterally disregard them simply because it believes that justice or its national interest require contrary conduct.[31] Rather, the state owes its obedience to the other party or parties to the agreement, or, in other words, the state's consent makes the norms that comprise the agreement authoritative.

---

[31] Note that the claim here concerns whose *judgment regarding what justice requires* ought to control. As I discuss below, an agent's consent to perform some act cannot render permissible what it would otherwise be unjust for him to do.

Consent's attraction as a basis for a duty to obey the law rests on its ability to reconcile a conception of agents as morally free and equal with their submission to authority. If an agent chooses to place himself under a duty to another then those duties are the product of the agent's control over his life, not requirements imposed on him or a facet of his subjugation to the will of another agent. If consent is to manifest this kind of control it must be free and informed. Agreements that are made involuntarily or as a result of fraud generate neither moral duties nor moral rights. Moreover, one agent may consent on another's behalf only if the latter authorizes him to do so, since only then will the resulting obligations be properly characterized as a product of the obligated agent's control over his life. Finally, the moral freedom and equality of all agents places limits on the obligations any can acquire via consent; even when free and informed, agreements to commit murder, theft, fraud, and other crimes are null and void.

Each of the foregoing conditions on the generation of moral obligations via consent provides a basis for challenging consent-based arguments for international law's legitimacy. In light of the costs their citizens are likely to suffer if they refuse, the consent of economically and militarily weak states to bilateral or multilateral treaties frequently fails to qualify as voluntary.[32] Even where the costs of nonparticipation do not rise to the level necessary to render agreement nonvoluntary, if the distribution of benefits and burdens set out in the agreement reflect unrectified past injustices committed by one party against another, then the agreement may still be at odds with the commitment to the treatment of all as free and equal that underpins consent-based accounts of legitimacy. Put another way, where the terms of an agreement reflect unrectified exploitation, consent may not be morally binding even if it is not coerced.

States increasingly consent to general frameworks that are then filled in by treaty-based but partly autonomous bodies that exercise quasi-legislative and/or quasi-judicial powers.[33] As a consequence, states may find themselves subject to obligations they did not anticipate or intend to acquire when they consented to the original framework. Generally speaking, while an agent need not know the precise details of the obligation she is acquiring via consent, the greater her ignorance of these matters the less compelling it will be to describe the agent's consent as the exercise of control over her life rather than as abdication of control to another. Insofar as a treaty permits signatories to withdraw their consent to its terms, as many do, it might be argued that a state's decision not to do so constitutes its tacit or ongoing consent to specification of its terms by semi-autonomous international organizations such as the WTO or the

---

[32]   See, for instance, the critical discussion of the Central American Free Trade Agreement in Frank J. Garcia, *Global Justice and International Economic Law: Three Takes* (New York: Cambridge University Press, 2013), pp. 240–62.

[33]   Mattias Kumm, "The Legitimacy of International Law: A Constitutionalist Framework of Analysis," *European Journal of International Law* 15, 5 (2004): 914.

ICC. Of course, this argument succeeds only if the costs of withdrawal from the treaty are not so high as to render continued submission to it nonvoluntary.

The current governments of some and perhaps even many states lack the legitimate authority to consent to obligations on behalf of the political communities they claim to represent. Clearly this is true if a necessary condition for state officials having the standing to morally obligate their citizens under international law is that the state be sufficiently democratic and respectful of some core set of its subjects' rights.[34] It may still be true of a fair number of states even if we should employ a somewhat broader understanding of what it is for state officials to adequately represent their citizens. Whether democratic or not, states may consistently fail to represent the interests of certain domestic minorities, such as indigenous peoples. The existence of persistent minorities challenges any state's claim to the standing to acquire obligations on behalf of all its subjects. Finally, some theorists point to the fact that much international lawmaking is carried out not by states' legislators but by members of their executive branches as a reason to doubt that those who purport to acquire international legal obligations on their citizens' behalf have the moral standing to do so. In some cases, such as legislative ratification of treaties negotiated by a state's executive branch, those who are empowered by a state's constitution to make law have some say in its acquisition of international legal obligations. Where that amounts to little more than an up or down vote on terms negotiated entirely, and perhaps secretively, by the executive, there may be reason to doubt that legislative consent suffices to render the resulting duties consistent with the treatment of the state's citizens as free and equal.

If any international legal norm or regime requires conduct that treats people in a manner incompatible with a proper understanding of their moral status as free and equal, then no state's consent to abide by those norms generates a genuine moral duty to do so. Thus, if Thomas Pogge is right to maintain that the WTO, the IMF, and the World Bank systematically contribute to the persistence of severe global poverty, and if, in doing so, they fail to treat the global poor as a proper understanding of their moral status as free and equal requires, then no state's consent to rule by these organizations gives rise to a moral obligation to act as they direct.[35] Much depends on the proper understanding of people's moral status as free and equal, of course. However defined, if consent matters because and to the extent that it enables agents to control or shape their lives by altering their rights, duties, powers, and immunities vis-à-vis others, then it cannot render permissible let alone

[34] Note that what is at issue here is a government's *moral* standing to create a *moral* obligation on the part of the state and its citizens to conform to certain international legal norms, such as those set out in a particular treaty the government signs (and, where necessary, ratifies). This is distinct from the government's *international legal* standing to sign the treaty, in virtue of which it can generate *legal* obligations for the state's citizens and officials. Or so a legal positivist will maintain. Since Dworkin argues that legal obligations are simply a species of moral obligation, any practice of government that has no claim to legitimacy does not count as a genuinely legal one.

[35] Thomas Pogge, *World Poverty and Human Rights* (Malden, MA: Polity Press, 2002).

obligatory conduct at odds with a proper appreciation for any agent's moral freedom and equality.

The foregoing arguments suggest that even where consent seems most likely to justify international law's claim to legitimacy, namely with respect to treaty-based law that applies to states, its success is likely to be piecemeal at best.[36] This conclusion is only strengthened when we consider customary international law (CIL). Where CIL is a product of longstanding state practice, then those states that voluntarily and knowingly engage in the practice, or that at least do not persistently object to it, might be said to tacitly consent to the norms that structure that practice.[37] Once again, however, this conclusion does not follow for those states whose participation or failure to object is nonvoluntary; for instance, postcolonial states subject to customary international legal norms developed largely by European powers prior to or during the colonial era. Consent also appears to be an inadequate basis for the legitimacy of international legal norms that apply directly to individuals. These observations are typically offered to support the conclusion that, at best, consent offers an incomplete ground for international law's legitimacy. It is worth noting the possibility of drawing the opposite conclusion, however. If consent provides the only possible basis for a moral duty to obey the law, because only consent reconciles a conception of agents as free and equal with their submission to authority, then significant portions of international law may simply be illegitimate.

IV   FAIR PLAY AS A BASIS FOR INTERNATIONAL LAW'S LEGITIMACY

A number of contemporary theorists argue that the principle of fair play provides a compelling alternative to consent as a basis for the moral duty to obey domestic law.[38] That alone warrants investigating whether fair play (also) grounds a moral duty on the part of states' and perhaps other international actors to obey international law. But in addition, the principle of fair play may provide an account of a moral duty to obey international law in cases where an appeal to consent requires contorting that concept almost beyond recognition. For instance, the claim that states have a moral duty to obey customary international legal norms because they accept the benefits that follow from others' compliance may better cohere with the practice of customary international law than does the claim that states consent to these norms. Similarly, even if many states have signed on to treaties or acquiesced to evolving norms of customary international law in circumstances that rendered their actions

---

[36]   See Matthew Lister, "The Legitimating Role of Consent in International Law," *Chicago Journal of International Law* 11, 2 (2011): 664–91.

[37]   Our concern here is with the ability of consent to account for the *legitimacy* of customary international legal norms, not with the role it (allegedly) plays in the emergence or existence of such norms.

[38]   See, for example, George Klosko, *The Principle of Fairness and Political Obligation* (Lanham, MD: Rowman & Littlefield, 1992); Richard Dagger, *Civic Virtues: Rights, Citizenship, and Republican Liberalism* (New York: Oxford University Press, 1997), pp. 68–78; and *Playing Fair: Political Obligation and the Problems of Punishment* (New York: Oxford University Press, 2018).

involuntary, at some later date they may come to accept the benefits that follow from the other signatories' compliance with the resulting legal norms, and thereby acquire a duty of fair play to likewise abide by those norms. Together, these considerations suggest that conceiving of deference to international law as a matter of fair cooperation is worth exploring.

In H.L.A. Hart's words, the principle of fair play holds that "when a number of persons conduct any joint enterprise according to rules and thus restrict their liberty, those who have submitted to these restrictions have a right to similar submissions from those who benefited by their submission."[39] In these conditions, a beneficiary who chooses not to limit her liberty takes unfair advantage of those who do so. She is a free rider who takes the benefits provided by others' participation in a cooperative scheme that requires them to limit their liberty in some way without bearing the cost of likewise limiting her own liberty.

While Hart's formulation of the principle of fair play makes sense of the widely shared intuition that free riders treat participants in a cooperative scheme unfairly, Robert Nozick maintains that it sweeps too widely.[40] Specifically, it seems to allow those who organize a joint enterprise to simply impose the benefits of the scheme on anyone, and then demand that those persons contribute their fair share to the operation of the scheme in return for the benefits they have received. To many, such an exercise of arbitrary control over others' lives and liberty is incompatible with respect for their status as free and equal, or as autonomous agents. If we are to honor a person's status as a creature capable of acting as the author of her own life, we cannot restrict her liberty to exercise that capacity simply by imposing benefits on her and then demanding that she limit her liberty in certain ways so as to contribute to the production of those benefits.

Simmons argues that we can avoid this implication by taking an agent's obligation to do her fair share in maintaining a cooperative scheme to be conditional on her acceptance of the benefit it provides her.[41] To accept the benefit produced by others' cooperation an agent must either try to get it, or, if she cannot avoid receiving the benefit, then she must do so knowingly and willingly. The latter conditions require that the person know she is receiving a benefit; know that the benefit is produced by others' participation in the cooperative scheme; believe the benefits are worth the cost of restricting her liberty in the ways participation in the scheme demands, and not have the benefits forced on her against her will. Note that on Simmons's interpretation, fair play obligations are voluntary, or acquired, ones. A person comes to have an obligation to contribute her fair share to the operation of a cooperative scheme that provides her with a nonexcludable benefit only as a result of her free and informed formation of a preference order that ranks the

---

[39]   H.L.A. Hart, "Are There Any Natural Rights?" *Philosophical Review* 64, 2 (1955): 185.
[40]   Robert Nozick, *Anarchy, State, and Utopia* (New York: Basic Books, 1974), pp. 93–5.
[41]   A. John Simmons, *Moral Principles and Political Obligation* (Princeton, NJ: Princeton University Press, 1979), pp. 123–36.

receipt of benefits, at the cost of doing her share to maintain the scheme, over freedom from contributing to the scheme at the cost of going without the benefits it provides.

Many (although not all) of the benefits provided by the international legal order are nonexcludable. These include relatively secure borders and peaceful relations between states in most parts of the world, various sorts of environmental benefit (such as protection against the ill effects of a hole in the ozone layer or, hopefully one day, protection against dangerous climate change) and health benefits (such as protection from global pandemics), common rules governing air travel, shipping lanes, and so on. Individual states benefit not only through their own actions under these rules – some of which they might be denied – but, more importantly, from other states' compliance with them. Insofar as these are benefits states necessarily receive, rather than ones they enjoy only if they try to get them, it follows that they can acquire a fair play obligation to contribute to their provision only if they receive them knowingly and willingly. But what would it be for states to knowingly and willingly receive the benefits provided by the international legal order? Can any sense be made of this idea? And does it even matter whether they do so, or might mere receipt of the benefits that result from other states' submission to international law suffice to generate a fair play obligation on a state to do likewise.

The initial case for claiming that only states that accept the benefits provided by the international legal order have a fair play obligation to obey it rests on intuitions regarding the importance of political self-determination. As Christopher Heath Wellman points out, without postulating a deontological right to political self-determination it is impossible to account for the judgment that the United States would act wrongly were it to annex Canada (or vice versa), even if doing so were to result in improvements to the welfare of both countries' citizens.[42] This example suggests that a certain kind of group enjoys a right to self-determination consisting, at least, of a claim right against others that they not interfere with that group's attempt to live a particular way of life.[43] In this respect, a group's right to political self-determination mirrors an individual's right to self-determination.[44]

As we noted earlier, in the absence of the acceptance of benefits condition the principle of fair play conflicts with individual autonomy because it entails that an individual is subject to the arbitrary will of other agents. They can restrict an individual's self-determination simply by bestowing benefits on her, since her receipt of benefits produced by their cooperative scheme will generate an obligation to do her fair share in maintaining it. Likewise, in the case of political self-

---

[42]   Christopher Heath Wellman, *A Theory of Secession* (Cambridge: Cambridge University Press, 2005), pp. 47, 50–1.

[43]   As in the case of individuals, a group's moral claim to noninterference in its pursuit of a particular way of life is limited by certain natural (that is, nonvoluntary) duties it has to other groups and individuals.

[44]   See Chapter 10 for an extended discussion of the moral basis of a group's right to political self-determination.

determination, without the acceptance of benefits clause the principle of fair play will leave those states inhabited by a group with a right to political self-determination vulnerable to the arbitrary will of other states. Those other states will enjoy a moral power to restrict the political autonomy (or liberty) of the state in question simply by bestowing certain benefits on it. As long as the benefits the state receives outweigh the costs to it of contributing to the scheme that produces them, the state will have a moral obligation to do its fair share in maintaining the scheme, *even if it would prefer not to do so and go without the benefits the scheme provides*. But just as it is wrong to deny an individual the liberty to choose to go without a particular benefit, so, too, it is wrong to deny a group the liberty to choose to go without a particular benefit. The upshot is that a state (or perhaps more accurately, a group that exercises a moral right to political self-determination via the institutions of a state) has a fair play duty to obey international law, or at least those legal norms constitutive of a particular international legal regime, only if it accepts the benefits it provides.

States do not have mental states, and, so it might seem, cannot knowingly and willingly receive the benefits provided by the international legal order. Nevertheless, we frequently speak of a state's agency; for example, we say that states launch wars, sign treaties, and disregard norms of international law. State's act, we believe, when individual persons occupying offices in them act, in their capacity as legal officials. Moreover, we frequently speak of state's mental states, saying that states *intend* to launch wars, *decide* to sign treaties, and *choose* to disregard norms of international law. Here too, we mean to refer to legal officials, although in this case their mental states, rather than their actions. There is nothing mysterious in this statement: "China believes that even limited economic sanctions against Iran will threaten its access to Iranian oil, and will therefore choose to veto any proposal that the United Nations Security Council implement such sanctions." Such a statement is not merely a prediction of future behavior, but also a description of what the speaker takes to be the beliefs and intentions of those Chinese government officials legally empowered to take such an action. I suggest, therefore, that we understand a state's acceptance of benefits in terms of the mental states had by certain legal officials in that state. Specifically, a state accepts the benefits provided by the international legal order if and only if the following two conditions are met: (a) the state officials legally empowered to negotiate the terms on which it will participate with other states in (the cooperative scheme that is) the international legal order knowingly and willingly accept the benefits provided by international law; and (b) these officials have the moral standing necessary to place their subjects under a moral obligation, or put another way, to acquire a moral obligation that is binding on the political community in whose name they act.[45]

---

[45] For discussion of several challenges to this characterization of a state's acceptance of benefits, see Lefkowitz, "The Principle of Fairness and States' Duty to Obey International Law," *Canadian Journal of Law and Jurisprudence* 24, 2 (2011): 335–8.

Suppose we grant that the principle of fair play could justify the claim that states have a moral duty to obey international law. Does it actually do so? A fully satisfactory response to that question requires a detailed empirical investigation that lies beyond the scope of this book. As a starting point, however, it may be worth considering whether Simmons' concerns with the use of the principle of fair play to justify a moral duty to obey domestic law apply equally to its use to justify a moral duty to obey international law.

Simmons poses two challenges to those who attempt to ground a duty to obey domestic law in the principle of fair play.[46] First, he argues that genuine cooperation requires that each cooperator know that the others share the goal to be achieved by working together, and understands his or her contribution as part of a joint effort to achieve that goal. The small-scale cooperative schemes from which Simmons claims we draw our intuitions regarding obligations of fair play are characterized by face-to-face interaction, horizontal structures of power and authority, and a conscious and willing sacrifice of individual liberty for the sake of the common good. Modern states, in contrast, are massively impersonal, built around hierarchical structures of power and authority, and populated mainly by agents who comply with the law's demands largely from habit and fear of punishment. If Simmons is right to deny that states constitute genuine cooperative schemes, and that fair play obligations arise only in the case of such schemes, then it follows that the duty to obey domestic law cannot be justified by appeal to the principle of fair play.

Second, even if Simmons is wrong about either of these two claims, he also contends that few citizens of modern states accept the benefits their state provides them: "Many citizens barely notice (and seem disinclined to think about) the benefits they receive" from their domestic legal system, to which it might be added that even in cases where they are aware of the benefits, subjects of modern states often fail to recognize that their provision results from others' obedience to law.[47] If correct, it follows from these claims that few people meet the knowledge condition for the acceptance of benefits. Simmons also suggests that many citizens of modern states do not believe that the benefits they receive from government are worth the price they are forced to pay for them in taxes, service, and restrictions on their liberty. Even if that conclusion is false, those who believe it will still not accept the benefits in the sense necessary to generate a fair play obligation to obey the law. Third, Simmons questions whether most people regard the payment of taxes to the state as a contribution to the operation of a cooperative scheme. Instead, they may well regard the government as something like a company from which they purchase certain goods, albeit one that in many cases exercises monopoly power and the use of coercion to compel people to buy its products. If people do not recognize the benefits they receive from government as the product of a cooperative scheme,

[46] Simmons, *Moral Principles*, pp. 136–41. See also Simmons, *Justification and Legitimacy*.
[47] Simmons, *Moral Principles*, p. 139.

then they will not accept those benefits in the requisite sense, and so once again they will have no duty to obey the law grounded in the principle of fair play.

These reasons for doubting that citizens accept the benefits their state provides them are less plausible when we turn to states' acceptance of the benefits they receive from the international legal order. For example, even if individuals are unaware of the benefits of public health, or that they are the product (in part) of a cooperative scheme realized in law and public policy, the same is unlikely to be true for legal officials in most states. To the contrary, many states include institutions devoted partially or entirely to pursuing public health via legal and political coop-eration with other states and with international bodies such as the World Health Organization. Indeed, in general, states are far likelier to meet the knowledge condition for acceptance of benefits, since they do not face the same limitations on time, energy, and ability that individuals do. Moreover, officials in a state institution concerned with issues of public health are often directly involved in negotiations over the aims, scope, content, and implementation of international legal norms that impact public health. Even when they do not participate in such activities themselves, they often influence these decisions indirectly by informing and shaping the views of those officials who do exercise the authority to form international legal agreements and regimes. Thus, the existence of such institutions, and the conduct of officeholders in them, provides evidence both that states are aware of the benefits they receive from the participation of other states in the international legal order, and that the benefits they receive are the result of such participation.

Now consider Simmons' claim that the principle of fairness only applies to a genuine cooperative scheme – one that, as Donald Regan writes, "involves a real (and successful) attempt to achieve a jointly valued outcome by coordinated behavior."[48] The interna-tional legal order may well satisfy this condition. States do share certain broad goals they hope to achieve via participation in the international legal order, peace and prosperity foremost among them. In addition, states are often more self-conscious about their obedience to international law than is the case with individuals and their obedience to domestic law. This may make states more likely to view obedience to law as their contribution to the joint achievement of a stable, peaceful, and prosperous society of states. Additionally, several of the features Simmons identifies as distinguishing genuine cooperative schemes from a modern domestic legal order do not apply equally to the international legal order. These include the number of participants in the scheme and a horizontal structure of enforcement and authority. Collectively, the observations set out in this paragraph and the preceding one suggest that Simmons' reasons for skepti-cism regarding the existence of a fair play duty to obey domestic law do not apply equally, or perhaps at all, to the argument for a fair play duty to obey international law.

---

[48] Donald Regan, *Utilitarianism and Cooperation* (Oxford: Oxford University Press, 1980), p. 127. Quoted in Simmons, *Justification and Legitimacy*, pp. 39–40.

Nevertheless, the attempt to justify a moral duty to obey international law by appeal to the principle of fair play encounters many of the same challenges as the argument from consent. For instance, the acceptance condition on the acquisition of duties of fair play reflects the moral importance of autonomy or self-determination. Fair play obligations follow only where actors voluntarily participate in a cooperative scheme. This condition is not met where the terms of a treaty reflect past, present, or the threat of future unjust coercion or exploitation. The same is true for customary legal norms whose content reflects unjust power differentials. Indeed, it may be inaccurate to describe the collective action these treaty and customary legal norms facilitate as examples of cooperation. Moreover, the officials of states with illegitimate governments lack the moral standing necessary to acquire fair play obligations on behalf of the political community they rule. Their acceptance of the benefits provided by other states' compliance with (particular) international legal norms generates no moral duty on the state or its subjects to likewise comply with the law. Consequently, when a state's illegitimate government is replaced by a legitimate one, the new government may rightly reject the claim that it has a fair play duty to comply with (particular) international legal norms, at least until it has determined whether the benefits of participation in the scheme constituted by those norms warrants the limits on liberty they impose. While they do not rule out the possibility that some states currently have fair play obligations to obey certain international legal norms, the two arguments canvased here offer plausible reasons to think this will often not be the case.

V DEMOCRACY AND INTERNATIONAL LAW'S LEGITIMACY

Is a voluntary act, whether in the form of consent or the acceptance of benefits, a necessary condition for international law's legitimacy? Perhaps not. As we noted earlier in this chapter, some philosophers maintain that in circumstances character-ized by disagreement over what counts as rightful conduct, agents have a moral duty to subject themselves to a common juridical order, that is, one in which all are governed by common standards. Obedience to law itself constitutes a form of respect for others' moral status as free and equal, distinct from the respect exhibited by complying with laws that correctly track what counts as treating others morally independently of the law requiring it. But what conditions must law satisfy if it is to constitute just relations between agents? One popular answer is that it must be democratic.

At the domestic level, some form of democratic decision making understood in individual-majoritarian terms is widely viewed as at least a necessary condition for legitimacy, so much so that few rulers feel able to go without at least the facade of democratic rule. It may seem natural, therefore, to conclude that the legitimacy of global governance institutions and international law more generally requires that they become more democratic. Whether this is so depends, however, on the manner in which democracy contributes to law's legitimacy. Like legitimacy, democratic governance may be defended on both instrumental and noninstrumental grounds. As an example of the former, individual-majoritarian decision making may have epistemic advantages over the feasible alternatives.[49] Depending on how substantive a conception of democratic decision making we employ, it may result in greater collective deliberation than would otherwise take place. Two important points follow from this observation. First, democracy's instrumental value contributes to its legitimacy only insofar as it increases the probability that democratically enacted law meets the NJC, or in other words, improves its subjects' conformity to right reason. Second, if democracy is valuable only because its output satisfies the NJC, then there is little reason to think democracy is a *necessary* condition for law's legitimacy. In some cases, nondemocratic decision-making procedures may perform equally well or better at producing legitimate law; for example, where democratic decision-making procedures systematically lead to unjustifiable discrepancies in the weight or importance given to the interests of some over others, as state level democratic governance may do vis-à-vis the interests of citizens and noncitizens.[50] Indeed, even if democratically enacted law best satisfies the NJC, nondemocratically enacted law will still be legitimate if no democratic decision-making procedure exists and those over whom the law claims authority do better by deferring to it than by acting on their own judgment. In short, if democracy's value is entirely instrumental, then international law's democratic deficit need not preclude its legitimacy.

Many of those who defend democratic decision making as a necessary condition for the legitimacy of domestic law do so on noninstrumental grounds, however. For example, Thomas Christiano argues that in circumstances characterized by both the moral necessity of coordination on common standards of right conduct and disagreement as to what those standards should be, justice requires that people organize their lives together on the basis of rules that publicly treat them as equals.[51] In the case of a modern state, this entails that law must be made democratically. To defend these claims, Christiano introduces three concepts: fundamental interests, the facts of judgment, and the fundamental interests in judgment. An agent's fundamental interests are those that figure centrally in a person's well-being, and in the absence of which an agent is very unlikely to enjoy any well-being at all. Justice requires the equal advancement of fundamental interests, Christiano maintains. The facts of judgment include diversity in people's natural talents and cultural surroundings; cognitive biases in the interpretation of their own and others' interests (including what counts as their advancement), as well as the value of their own interests in comparison to the interests of others; and fallibility in both moral and nonmoral judgment. The facts of judgment explain why disagreement as to what justice truly

---

[49] Robert Goodin, *Reflective Democracy* (New York: Oxford University Press, 2003); David Estlund, *Democratic Authority* (Princeton, NJ: Princeton University Press, 2008).
[50] Buchanan and Keohane, "Legitimacy of Global Governance," 415–16.
[51] Christiano, *Constitution of Equality*, pp. 75–130, 231–59.

requires will be rife, even among those committed to the equal advancement of interests. Finally, the fundamental interests in judgment consist of the interest in correcting for others' cognitive biases, the interest in being at home in the world, and the interest in being treated as a person with equal moral standing. Each of these interests provides a moral basis for a claim against others that one's judgment regarding matters of justice be given equal weight in the collective task of determining how the shared aspects of social life ought to be arranged. Should agents be denied the proper recognition of their interests in judgment, they are extremely unlikely to be successful in the pursuit of whatever other interests they may have; hence their inclusion on the list of *fundamental* human interests.

Given the facts of judgment, the fundamental interests in judgment generate a moral demand that government publicly treat people as equals. Against a background constituted by diversity, cognitive bias, and fallibility, and the pervasive disagreement to which they give rise, agents will have compelling reason to believe that their fundamental interests in judgment, and so their other fundamental interests, are not being unjustifiably set back only if political power is exercised within institutions that publicly realize equality. Democratic decision making satisfies this criterion, since it "enables us all to see that we are being treated as equals despite disagreements [regarding the true demands of justice] as long as we take into account the facts of judgment and the interests that accompany them."[52]

Our interest in correcting for others' cognitive biases appears to be instrumental in nature, insofar as its value lies in mitigating the setbacks to other interests that frequently follow when people act on mistaken understandings of what others' interests are or what counts as advancing them. To this extent, Christiano's argument for the legitimacy of democratic lawmaking might be characterized as an instrumental one; obedience to law is a means whereby actors can better approximate the aim of honoring or promoting the interests of all equally than if they act on their own judgment of what that requires.[53] In contrast, obedience to democratically enacted laws that determine how various shared aspects of social life ought to be arranged just is to acknowledge others' interest in being treated as moral equals, as well as their interest in being at home in the world. To deny someone a say in how the shared aspects of social life ought to be arranged, or to disregard an answer to that question reached via a democratic decision procedure, is to assert one's moral superiority over others. Hence the only way to honor others' fundamental interest in being treated as a moral equal is to obey democratically enacted law. In the same vein, if individuals are to feel at home in an egalitarian social world, one premised

[52] Ibid, 76.
[53] Christiano contends that, as a matter of fact, any process that fails to accord people an equal say in determining the form that the shared aspects of social life ought to take will inevitably result in a set back to their interests. Although this is an empirical, and so contingent, claim, Christiano maintains that it rests on extremely deep features of human nature and human society, so deep that political philosophers need not be very concerned with counterarguments that rest on worlds in which these features are absent.

on an understanding of moral equality as the equal advancement of interests, then they must be able to see that world as one that they help to create and sustain, rather than one that others impose on them.

Although Christiano maintains that domestic law ought to be made democratically, he does not draw the same conclusion vis-à-vis international law. To the contrary, he argues that, at present and for the foreseeable future, a global parliament that created international law through a process of majoritarian decision making would almost certainly fail to govern in a manner that publicly treated all of the individuals it ruled as equals.[54] In part, Christiano worries that a global parliament would fail to be sufficiently democratic. For example, it might too readily produce persistent minorities, discrete and insular groups that never succeed in making legislation. Were this to occur, the law enacted by the global parliament would likely fail to advance the interests of the minority, or at least fail to do so in a manner that treated those interests as equal in their moral importance to the interests of the majority. From the standpoint of legitimacy rather than justice, however, the more important shortcoming would be the global parliament's failure to publicly treat the members of the permanent minority as equals. After all, what reason would they (or we) have to believe that the legislative process respected their fundamental interests in correcting for cognitive biases, being at home in the world, and being treated as a person with equal moral standing if the law never reflected their view of the terms on which the shared aspects of the global social world should be arranged? Christiano also argues that the weakness of international civil society warrants skepticism regarding the prospects for a global parliament satisfying the principle of public equality, and so generating legitimate international law. As he remarks, "political parties, interest groups, and diverse media outlets ... are absolutely necessary to democracy because citizens can only devote a small amount of time to political questions, so there must be intermediate institutions that enable citizens to acquire a grasp of the key political issues and alternatives."[55] In the absence of a robust civil society, government is likely to become the preserve of a largely unaccountable ruling elite, and thereby lay the seeds for a populist backlash that, under the leadership of a demagogue, can easily become antidemocratic and illiberal.

Even if a global democracy were to function flawlessly, producing neither persistent minorities nor government by a largely unaccountable elite, Christiano maintains it would *still* fail to produce legitimate law. That is because democratically enacted law publicly treats all those it addresses as equals only if there is a great deal of interdependence among their interests and each has a roughly equal stake in the normative social order the law creates. Consider the latter point first. If a system of

[54] Thomas Christiano, "Democratic Legitimacy and International Institutions," in *The Philosophy of International Law*, eds. Samantha Besson and John Tasioulas (New York: Oxford University Press, 2010), pp. 129–36.
[55] Ibid, 135.

rules will affect two parties to very different degrees, with one party's life barely impacted while the other's plans and prospects are deeply dependent on the content of these rules, then it would be unfair to give them an equal say in settling what those rules should be. To do so would give the first party too much control over the second one, with the second party unable to view the process as one that publicly treats all parties as moral equals. But why does the public equality argument for democratic rule apply only when there is a great deal of interdependence among agents' interests? Why not treat each interest or issue separately? Christiano replies that "since democratic decision-making must be taken by majority rule, it is important that there be many issues so that those who come up losers on some issues be winners on others."[56] In the absence of recurring decision making on a bundle of issues, losers in a majority-rule process have little reason to view it as publicly treating them as equals. Like permanent minorities, they have no procedural evidence, namely victories in the decision-making process, that they can point to as reason to believe that the governing institution is truly committed to the equal treatment of all those it rules.

Christiano acknowledges a few instances of interdependence among the interests of all individuals around the world, such as the danger posed by climate change. However, he maintains that international legal institutions governing trade and the environment typically impact individuals' interests far less than domestic legal orders do, and at least by implication not enough to meet the first of the two conditions for the existence of a common world. Moreover, even when international legal norms do impact the lives of individuals around the world they do so to very different degrees. The life plans and prospects of some individuals may depend a great deal on international trade, while for others the impact may be quite small. Were all to exercise an equal say in determining the international rules that ought to govern cross-border trade then those whose lives depend heavily on those rules could rightly complain that the procedure for governing global trade did not publicly treat them as moral equals.

If a global parliament will not produce legitimate international law, that is, law that publicly treats all those it addresses as equals, then what legislative process could do so? Christiano's answer is the consent of democratic states to rules that are the product of fair negotiations. Rather than pursuing global democracy, our efforts to reform the international legal order should aim at its evolution into a fair democratic association. In principle, at least, state-level democratic procedures offer individuals a voice in the shaping of international legal norms, and, in practice, they might better serve this end than would a global parliament, even if they fell well short of the ideal. For example, a fair democratic association can help protect against one scenario in which a group finds itself a permanent minority, namely, where the populations of small states find themselves consistently outvoted by the populations

---

[56]   Ibid, 131.

of large states. Democratic societies can also protect indigenous peoples and other insular minorities against the danger of never exercising an effective voice in the crafting of international law by granting them special consultative rights or representative bodies domestically. Properly designed, these mechanisms could enable such groups to leverage their state's influence over international legislation to better ensure that their interests are considered. Moreover, many democratic societies have thriving civil societies that pressure their political and legal institutions to accommodate and represent the interests and concerns of all their citizens.

Christiano also maintains that a fair democratic association offers a better institutional response to the limited interdependence that characterizes relations between citizens of different states, as well as the fact that they often have quite different stakes in specific international legal regimes: "Democratic association allows states to pick and choose what terms they enter into and so allows them to determine how important issues are to their peoples and to sub-populations within their societies."[57] For example, some democratic states may choose to enter into regional associations that largely eliminate barriers to the movement of goods and people across their borders, and that pool some of their resources for the pursuit of shared or common ends. The European Union provides the clearest example of such an association. Other states may choose to associate on terms that broadly preserve their political-legal independence from one another. However, Christiano argues that certain morally mandatory aims limit states' freedom to choose whether to become a party to an international agreement, or to persistently object to an evolving customary international legal norm. These include the protection of persons against serious and widespread violations of their human rights, the avoidance of global environmental catastrophe, the alleviation of severe global poverty, and the establishment of a fair system of international trade.[58] To illustrate, while democratic states need not consent to international legal norms that completely eliminate their right to restrict immigration, they have no right to withhold consent to international legal norms mandating that they grant refuge or asylum to noncitizens who face an existential threat that their own state is either unable or unwilling to address. Yet a system of global government that incorporates an element of state consent may be advantageous even where it addresses morally mandatory aims; for instance, if it encourages regional associations of states to design and test alternative legal norms or regimes that serve this end.[59]

While state consent plays a prominent role in the Fair Democratic Association model of global government, that role is not the one it has traditionally been thought to play in explaining international law's legitimacy, or states' duty to obey it. Rather, consent is a feature of a process for creating international law that publicly treats as

---

[57] Ibid, 136.
[58] Thomas Christiano, "Legitimacy and the International Trade Regime," *San Diego Law Review* 52, 5 (2015): 987–8.
[59] Ibid, 989.

moral equals all of the individuals over whom it claims jurisdiction, either directly or as citizens of a particular state. Put another way, were the international legal order to evolve into a Fair Democratic Association, the "normative force" of states' moral duty to obey the law would not be grounded in their agreement to abide by the law. Instead, its justification would lie in the fact that by obeying international law produced by a legislative process that assigns state consent a central role (albeit with certain limitations), actors would publicly treat the citizens of other democratic states as moral equals.[60] In circumstances characterized by the moral necessity of adherence to common rules and pervasive disagreement regarding what those rules ought to be, deference to law that publicly treats all of its subjects as equals is itself a requirement of justice.

Yet the Fair Democratic Association model of global governance confronts serious challenges. To state the obvious, many states are currently either nondemocratic or democratic in name only. Furthermore, economic and military inequalities enable some states to exercise far more power in international negotiations than do others, which they frequently use to press for their own advantage (even if they occasionally make concessions they need not offer to gain other states' cooperation). Indeed, Christiano says as much, describing the fair democratic association as an ideal of global government whose realization is at best quite far off. More worrisome, however, is the possibility that a free democratic association may fail to provide even a principled basis for the legitimacy of international law. Voluntary agreements will publicly treat the parties to them as equals only if they are negotiated and entered into in free and fair conditions. Securing such conditions, however, requires a public law whose legitimacy cannot itself depend on voluntary agreement. Put another way, in order to ensure that negotiations between democratic states take place on a level playing field we need an institution that can effectively settle what counts as fair and unfair bargaining by issuing and enforcing rules to that effect. Clearly that institution's legitimacy cannot be the product of fair negotiations among democratic states since the existence of such an institution is itself a condition for the fairness of any negotiations. As Christiano himself recognizes, realizing the conditions for a free democratic association "seems to drive us in the direction of global institutions, which in turn must be evaluated in terms of democratic principles."[61] This appears to leave us at an impasse, unable to ground international law's legitimacy in either its enactment by a global democratic legislature or in a voluntary association of democratic states.

---

[60] See Samantha Besson, "State Consent and Disagreement in International Law-Making: Dissolving the Paradox," *Leiden Journal of International Law* 29, 2 (2016): 305–15.

[61] Thomas Christiano, "Is Democratic Legitimacy Possible for International Institutions?" in *Global Democracy: Normative and Empirical Perspectives*, eds. Daniele Archibugi et al. (New York: Cambridge University Press, 2011), p. 92.

VI WHY CARE ABOUT LEGITIMACY?

In this chapter, we have construed the skeptical challenge to international law as a concern with its legitimacy. In light of our survey of several justifications for law's legitimate authority and a correlative moral duty to obey the law, some degree of misgiving appears warranted. How much depends partly on which of these accounts accurately describes the grounds of a moral duty to obey the law, and partly on empirical questions regarding the extent to which the conditions they set out are currently met.

Does international law's legitimacy deficit matter? Yes and no. As we noted earlier, we should be careful not to infer from the illegitimacy of international legal norms or global governance institutions that agents have no moral reasons to support them (including, in some cases, acting as they require) or to work for their reform rather than their replacement. Crucially, however, the sort of arguments that can be offered in support of complying with illegitimate rules and institutions differ from the one available when rules and institutions are legitimate, namely, that one has a moral duty to obey those rules and institutions. Moreover, where international law's illegitimacy owes largely to its being an instrument for the unjust advancement of national or special interests by the relatively powerful, the less powerful may have little choice but to play by the existing legal rules. Doing so may be the right thing to do not only prudentially but also morally if conduct that violates those rules is either unlikely to bring about a more just world or, possibly, if there are limits on the setbacks to their own interests that agents must bear in order to combat injustice.

Nevertheless, there are compelling reasons to pursue the goal of a more legitimate international legal order. First, greater legitimacy entails an increase in justice. This conclusion follows necessarily from the instrumental account of what makes law legitimate; holding compliance with the law constant, a world with more legitimate law is one in which actors more often conform to right reason than they do in a world with less legitimate law. Empirically, we have compelling evidence that mechanisms of accountability, transparency, and participation in the crafting of law and in governance more generally typically lead to outcomes widely viewed as just, or at least as more just than those produced by governance in the absence of such mechanisms.

Second, it seems plausible to maintain that an increase in the actual legitimacy of international law will lead to an increase in belief in its legitimacy, which will, in turn, increase international law's actual legitimacy by making it more effective at guiding its subjects conduct. The converse point may be even more powerful; the failure to pursue greater legitimacy for the international legal order may lead to more injustice as cynicism erodes some of the advances in, for example, managing conflicts, promoting human rights, and protecting the environment to which inter-national law has been a significant contributor.

Third, it may be possible to reach greater agreement on international law's legitimacy than on its justice. Recall in this regard Christiano's argument that democratic governance allows individuals to see the political institution that rules them as committed to the equal advancement of all its subjects' interests even when the substance of some of its law offer reason to doubt it. Legitimacy also requires less than justice, both in terms of what it takes for an agent to enjoy legitimate authority and in terms of the duty it imposes on agents. In particular, an agent may concede the law's legitimacy while working to change it, perhaps even by acts of civil disobedience.

Finally, it may be that we should be at least as concerned with the legitimacy of international law as with its justice. The aforementioned possibility that we are more likely to achieve widespread agreement on legitimacy than on justice provides a pragmatic reason to draw this conclusion. However, as we have noted there may also be a principled argument for doing so, namely, if just relations between agents can only be realized within a legitimate legal order. If true, this claim entails that the pursuit of global justice requires the realization of a legitimate international legal order.

***

Time, now, to take stock of the progress we have made in responding to international legal skepticism. In this chapter and the preceding ones, we have pursued the strategy Hart urges on those who wish to address legal skeptics, namely identifying "what they want to know and why they want to know it."[62] We now have a much clearer understanding of the different theoretical assumptions and practical concerns that may lie behind the question "is international law really law?" This understanding can help us avoid talking past one another when we debate international law's status as genuine law, while also highlighting what follows from the position we take on this issue given a particular conception of law and its relationship to concepts such as the rule of law and legitimacy. If, as Hart maintains, the purpose of legal philosophy is to clarify and advance both theoretical inquiry and moral deliberation, then ours is a job well done.[63]

---

[62] Hart, *Concept*, p. 5.
[63] Ibid, 214.

7

International Human Rights Law: Concepts and Grounds of Human Rights

As we saw in the first part of this book, before responding to an international legal skeptic we must first identify the source of our interlocutor's doubt. What assumptions regarding the concept or the nature of law lead her to infer from certain empirical observations that what we commonly refer to as international law is not really a genuine example of law? Is her concept of law a sound one, or does her skepticism rest instead on a misunderstanding? We noted as well that international legal skepticism rarely expresses a concern with classification for its own sake. Rather, individuals advance it as a premise in a normative argument; for instance, to justify the claim that the reasons for action provided by so-called international law differ in kind from those provided by genuine law (or, perhaps, by legitimate law).

Our philosophical investigation of human rights in this chapter proceeds along the same lines. Skepticism provides its impetus. Is there really a human right to social security, to the highest attainable standard of physical and mental health, or to periodic holidays with pay?[1] Does every person have a right not to marry unless he or she freely and fully consents to do so?[2] If so, how should we reconcile such a right with a human right to freedom of religion if a particular religion confers on fathers the right to select their daughter's spouse?[3] Do people have a human right to engage in sexual intercourse with someone of the same sex?[4] Are all people entitled to

---

[1] Articles 9, 12, and 7, *International Covenant on Economic, Social and Cultural Rights*, December 16, 1966, United Nations, Treaty Series, vol. 993, p. 3, available at https://treaties.un.org/doc/Publication/UNTS/Volume%20993/v993.pdf.

[2] Article 16, *Universal Declaration of Human Rights*, December 10, 1948, 217 A (III), available at www.un.org/en/universal-declaration-human-rights/.

[3] Article 18, *International Covenant on Civil and Political Rights*, December 16, 1966, United Nations, Treaty Series, vol. 999, p. 171, available at https://treaties.un.org/doc/publication/unts/volume%20999/volume-999-i-14668-english.pdf.

[4] UN Office of the High Commissioner for Human Rights (OHCHR), *Born Free and Equal: Sexual Orientation and Gender Identity in International Human Rights Law*, September 2012, HR/PUB/12/06, available at www.ohchr.org/Documents/Publications/BornFreeAndEqualLowRes.pdf; UN Human Rights Council, *Protection against Violence and Discrimination Based on Sexual Orientation and Gender Identity: Resolution/Adopted by the Human Rights Council*, July 15, 2016, A/HRC/RES/32/2, available at https://digitallibrary.un.org/record/845552?ln=en.

public treatment on the basis of the gender with which they self-identify?[5] These are all examples of local human rights skepticism; they express doubts regarding the existence of a specific human right either recognized in international law, or that some argue *should* be recognized in international law. In contrast, global human rights skepticism challenges the existence of any human rights whatsoever. For global human rights skeptics, international human rights law is either a form of Western imperialism or merely empty words.

Just as an assessment of international legal skepticism requires that we first identify the concept of law on which it relies, and determine whether we should accept it, so too an assessment of human rights skepticism requires that we identify the concept of a human right it presupposes and evaluate the reasons offered in its defense. This is particularly true if different concepts of a human right provide different criteria for the existence of a human right; that is, competing accounts of the conditions that must be satisfied in order to justify the claim "A has a human right to X." In this chapter, we will investigate the conceptual question "what is a human right?" and the normative question "in virtue of what considerations does A enjoy a human right to X?" by examining the recent debate between two schools of legal and political philosophers.

Orthodox theorists argue that human rights are a moral right possessed by all human beings simply in virtue of their humanity. In contrast, political-practice theorists argue that human rights are constitutive elements of an ongoing attempt to reconceive state sovereignty and the international political order to which it is integral. This political undertaking, which includes the creation, application, and enforcement of international human rights law, provides the proper object of a philosophy of human rights. These descriptions may suggest that the debate between orthodox and political-practice theorists concerns how we ought to understand a single concept – *the* concept of a human right. There is some truth to that claim. However, I maintain that the dispute is more productively understood as a disagreement regarding the relevance of orthodox theories of human rights, or what I will sometimes refer to as moral human rights, to the justification of political human rights, by which I mean the human rights norms constitutive of the recently emerged international human rights practice, including international human rights law. By and large, political-practice theorists accept the existence of some moral rights possessed by all human beings simply in virtue of their humanity. However, they maintain that a theory of such rights, in other words, an orthodox account of human rights, is quite different from the sort of theory that interests them, namely, one that takes the international human rights practice as its object. Moreover, some of them argue that we need not, or even that we cannot, appeal to moral human rights in order to justify many of the norms constitutive of this practice. If so, then an

---

[5]   Neela Ghoshal and Kyle Knight, "Rights in Transition: Making Legal Recognition for Transgender People a Global Priority," last modified 2016, available at www.hrw.org/world-report/2016/rights-in-transition.

orthodox theory of human rights is far less useful for those interested in justifying or criticizing international human rights law, or the international political practice of which it is a part, than we might first assume.

Our exploration of the debate between orthodox and political-practice theorists of human rights begins in section I with a description of the answers each offers to the conceptual question, "what is a human right?" We then turn in section II to several attempts by political-practice theorists to demonstrate the limited relevance of orthodox accounts of human rights to morally justifying the norms that constitute (or that should constitute) the international human rights practice; again, including international human rights law. We also consider a number of objections to these arguments advanced by orthodox theorists, as well as some rejoinders to those objections put forward by political-practice theorists. In section III, we briefly consider the role that appeal to objective moral principles should play in the international human rights practice.

We should note at the outset that the discussion in this chapter will not yield a response to any of the skeptical challenges to human rights just canvassed. What it will do, however, is clarify the fundamental conceptual and justificatory matters on which any answer to those challenges ultimately depends.

I THE CONCEPT OF A HUMAN RIGHT

A *The Orthodox Concept of a Human Right*

The orthodox account characterizes human rights as "moral rights possessed by all human beings simply in virtue of their humanity."[6] Each element of this analysis requires explanation, beginning with the idea that human rights are rights. Many human rights are (or at least include) claim rights; the rightholder has a claim against at least one other agent, the duty bearer, that he or she perform or refrain from performing some act. The duties correlative to a right determine its content. Put another way, to answer the question "what does the right to religious freedom, or to free-speech, or to health include?" we need to determine the specific duties that correlate to it, and who bears them. Barring a justification, nonperformance of a duty correlative to a right constitutes a distinctive wrong done to the rightholder. It does not simply harm her; indeed, it may not make her any worse off than she would have been otherwise. Neither does it merely manifest a disregard for the impact that nonperformance has on the rightholder's interests (in bodily integrity, religious practice, and so on). Rather, it involves a failure to *respond*

---

[6] John Tasioulas, "On the Nature of Human Rights," in *The Philosophy of Human Rights: Contemporary Controversies*, edited by Gerhard Ernst and Jan-Christoph Heilinger (Berlin: Walter de Gruyter, 2011), p. 26.

appropriately to her title or claim to the duty bearer performing or refraining from performing some act.[7]

Rights, or the duties to which they correlate, provide categorical reasons for action. This means that the duty bearer's reason to perform or refrain from performing some action does not depend on any particular goal or preference she may have. My property right in my computer generates a duty on my neighbor not to use, take, damage, or transfer it to another person without my permission, a reason for action that does not depend on her having the goal of remaining my friend, avoiding jail, or any other consideration she takes to be constitutive of a good life. One way to understand rights (or the duties to which they correlate) is as exclusionary reasons for action; my property right provides my neighbor with a reason not to act on certain reasons, such as the fact that she would finish her work more quickly if she used my computer.

Next, consider the claim that human rights are essentially *moral* rights. While individual human rights may be recognized in international human rights law or the constitutional law of a particular state, orthodox theorists argue that human rights exist independently of any body of law, or for that matter, any social or customary rule.[8] Moreover, orthodox theorists offer two objections to depicting human rights as moral rights that ought to be recognized in law. The first is that law is necessarily ill-suited to protecting or promoting certain moral rights that all human beings possess simply in virtue of their humanity, for example, the right not to suffer personal betrayal. The second is that even where it is possible to use law to protect or promote a human right, there may be other mechanisms that are more effective, less costly, or both. In sum, orthodox theorists caution against too close an association between the concept of a human right and legal practice.

Orthodox theorists divide over how to properly characterize the universality expressed in the claim that human rights are possessed by all human beings. Some maintain that this includes human beings at every point in the past, present, and future, while others argue that human *rights*, as opposed to the interests that ground them, are indexed to modernity. For example, John Tasioulas argues that human rights are those possessed by all human beings who live in circumstances characterized by "significant levels of scientific and technological expertise and capacity; heavy reliance on industrialized modes of production; the existence of a market-based economy of global reach; a developed legal system that is both efficacious and broad-ranging; [and] the pervasive influence of individualism and secularism in shaping forms of life."[9] Which of these two interpretations a theorist adopts often has

---

[7] Note that nonperformance of a duty exhibits this wrong-making feature only where performance is owed to a specific actor, the rightholder. We will revisit this point later in the chapter.

[8] "Independently" may not mean antecedent to law, or not conditional on the existence of law. Rather, it may mean only that moral human rights provide a reason for action distinct from the reason for action provided by a legal human right. See the discussion in section II.

[9] Ibid, 36.

implications for the list of specific moral human rights he or she recognizes, or at the limit, his or her willingness to acknowledge the existence of any moral human rights at all.

The qualifier "simply in virtue of their humanity" indicates that the possession of certain moral rights depends on neither membership in a particular community or relationship nor any particular type of interaction.[10] Thus, human rights differ from the moral (and legal) rights individuals possess in virtue of their citizenship in a particular state, or membership in a sporting club, or marital relationship. They also differ from moral (and legal) rights that individuals acquire when they enter a contract or suffer harm as a result of another agent's failure to exercise due care. Human rights are grounded in certain features or interests possessed by all human beings as such, although the duties correlative to those rights may depend on other considerations, including membership in a particular political community. Orthodox theorists agree on this *conceptual* claim even though there is some dispute among them as to which interests ground human rights, and why they do so.

There are many questions we can pose regarding human rights, understood as orthodox theorists do. In this chapter, however, we will largely focus on the concept of a human right as political-practice theorists understand it, or what is the same, the concept of a human right as it figures within the international human rights practice that emerged following the Second World War. In general, proponents of the latter view do not deny the existence of moral rights possessed by all human beings simply in virtue of their humanity; indeed, many explicitly acknowledge their existence.[11] Nevertheless, they challenge the relevance of orthodox theories of human rights to the project of understanding or modeling the international human rights practice, or to morally justifying the norms that constitute it, or both. The main question, then, is not which of these two accounts of the concept of a human right is correct, but whether political-practice theorists are right to insist that theorizing the international human rights practice requires a break from orthodoxy.

B *Political-Practice Conceptions of a Human Right*

Political-practice theorists take the international human rights practice that began to emerge following the Second World War to be the proper object of a philosophy of

---

[10] Reference to "the human family" in certain human rights documents suggests one reading of "in virtue of their humanity" that does reference membership in a particular community. Even if we set aside suspicions regarding the extent to which all human beings comprise a family in the morally relevant sense (as opposed to the biological notion of descent from a common ancestor), I suspect orthodox theorists of human rights would reject this reading. It is nonrelational features or interests possessed by all human beings that ground human rights.

[11] See, for instance, Allen Buchanan, *The Heart of Human Rights* (Oxford: Oxford University Press, 2013), pp. 10–14; Joseph Raz, "Human Rights Without Foundations," in *The Philosophy of International Law*, eds. Samantha Besson and John Tasioulas (Oxford: Oxford University Press, 2010), pp. 334–7.

human rights. In order to grasp the concept of a human right, they maintain, we must understand the role that concept plays within this political practice. Put another way, to know what human rights are we need to identify the ways in which participants in the international human rights practice use human rights as action-guiding norms.[12] As we will see, international human rights law figures centrally in political-practice theorists' description of the international human rights practice.

Political-practice theorists occasionally suggest that their approach offers the only defensible analysis of the concept of a human right. For example, Joseph Raz maintains that there is not enough commonality in the use of the phrase "human rights" across the various contexts in which people use it to sustain a project of identifying the elements of a single concept employed by all those who speak the language of human rights.[13] Setting that concern aside, Raz also expresses skepticism regarding the idea of a moral right that all human beings possess simply in virtue of their humanity. As he observes, few of the rights recognized in the UDHR or the Human Rights Conventions are ones we can plausibly attribute to cave dwellers in the Stone Age.[14] Orthodox theorists of human rights offer a variety of responses to this challenge.[15] Yet the success of these arguments may not matter much to the dispute between orthodox and political-practice theorists of human rights. That is because the latter's primary concern is not with the question of whether there are any moral rights that all human beings possess simply in virtue of their humanity. Rather, they emphasize the following two points. First, an orthodox theory of human rights is not a theory of the international human rights practice. Second, some political-practice theorists contend that we should not assume that the norms constitutive of either the existing or the morally best international human rights practice must be justified by appeal to moral human rights. Rather, our analysis of the concept of a human right should treat as an open question what sort of (moral) considerations serve, or can serve, to justify those norms. If we do so, then when we turn to the task of justifying specific norms constitutive of the emerging international human rights practice, or the morally best version of it, we may find that while some can be justified by appeal to moral human rights many others need not or cannot be defended on those grounds.

---

[12]   Similarly, in order to grasp the concept of a "strike" in baseball we need to understand how competent participants in that game use it as an action-guiding norm.

[13]   As he puts the point, there "is not enough discipline underpinning the use of the term 'human right' to make it a useful analytical tool." Raz, "Human Rights Without Foundations," 336.

[14]   Joseph Raz, "Human Rights in the Emerging World Order," in *Philosophical Foundations of Human Rights*, eds. Rowan Cruft, S. Matthew Liao, and Massimo Renzo (Oxford: Oxford University Press, 2015), pp. 224–5. But see Raz, "Human Rights Without Foundations," 334.

[15]   See, among others, the aforementioned proposal by Tasioulas that we characterize human rights as historically indexed. See also David Miller's response to Raz in "Joseph Raz on Human Rights: A Skeptical Appraisal," in *Philosophical Foundations of Human Rights*, eds. R. Cruft, S.M. Liao, and M. Renzo (Oxford: Oxford University Press, 2015), pp. 232–43.

Perhaps the most forceful advocate of the importance of distinguishing a theory of moral human rights from a moral or political theory of the international human rights practice is Allen Buchanan. He argues that certain philosophers of human rights appear to subscribe to the "Mirroring View," according to which "international legal human rights are simply moral human rights in legal dress."[16] Even allowing that international law may serve to specify moral human rights, or provide a valuable means for realizing them, the bulk of the work involved in identifying the content and justification for genuine human rights is an exercise in moral philosophy. The implication is that those charged with applying existing international human rights law, or enacting changes to it, should simply transcribe the conclusions of the correct (orthodox) philosophy of moral human rights into law. No attention need be paid to the various ways in which legal and political practice may introduce both facts and moral considerations that bear on the question of what the content of international human rights law ought to be.[17] While Buchanan rightly cautions against this approach to theorizing international human rights law (and, presumably, the broader international human rights practice of which it is a part), it is not clear that many or even any philosophers writing on human rights make this mistake.[18] In any case, regardless of what anyone might have claimed or implied at an earlier stage in the philosophical discourse on human rights, there is now widespread agreement that a philosophy of moral human rights is not the same as a philosophical theory of the international human rights practice. Specifically, all agree that the justification of international human rights law requires attention to facts and moral considerations besides those that figure in a moral theory of human rights.

The second point political-practice theorists press does remain a matter of dispute, however. That point, recall, is that in theorizing the constitutive norms of the international human rights practice we should not assume that they must be justified by appeal to moral human rights. Rather, we should begin by mapping how those norms function within the human rights practice. With that task complete, we can take up the task of justifying specific human rights norms, and indeed the international practice of human rights as a whole, including international human rights law. It is at this point where the most significant (and perhaps the only substantive) disagreements between political-practice and orthodox theorists of human rights arises. Before we consider these disputes, however, we must first get clear on how political-practice theorists understand the concept of a human right.

---

[16] Buchanan, *Heart of Human Rights*, p. 18. In accusing various philosophers of subscribing to the Mirroring View of human rights, Buchanan charges them with failing to recognize both of the points set out in the previous paragraph. I discuss the first point briefly here, and the second at greater length later in this section.

[17] Ibid, 51.

[18] For discussion, see John Tasioulas, "Exiting the Hall of Mirrors: Morality and Law in Human Rights," in *Political and Legal Approaches to Human Rights*, eds. Tom Campbell and Kylie Bourne (London, Routledge, 2017), pp. 77–80.

i Charles Beitz

A practical conception of human rights, Charles Beitz writes, "understands questions about the nature and content of human rights to refer to objects of the sort called 'human rights' in international practice."[19] To understand the concept of a human right is to understand the role that it plays in that practice, or what is the same, to grasp how competent participants in the practice use the concept. Since human rights are action-guiding norms, competent participants in the practice must invoke them as reasons for particular actors to take particular actions. Therefore, the questions a practical conception of human rights must answer are what kinds of action, in what kinds of circumstance, and for which agents, do human rights norms (purport to) provide reasons for action?[20]

To answer these questions, we need to construct a model of the practice, one that is consistent with those elements that are uncontroversially part of it and that offers an overarching purpose or rationale that unifies those elements and renders them individually and collectively intelligible. On Beitz's account, the elements of the practice includes major international human rights texts such as the Universal Declaration of Human Rights and the Human Rights Conventions, the activities of the reporting and monitoring bodies established by the latter, and also less formal or institutionalized activity such as "critical public discourse, particularly when it occurs in practical contexts involving justification and appraisal; evidence of the public culture of international human rights found in its history and in contemporary public expression; and prominent examples of political action justified and reasonably regarded as efforts to defend or protect human rights, such as those which are subjects of historical and ethnographic studies."[21] Reflection on the practice constituted by these elements yields the conclusion that its overarching purpose is "to protect individuals against threats to their most important interests arising from the acts and omissions of their governments (including failures to regulate the conduct of other agents) ... by bringing these aspects of the domestic conduct of governments within the scope of legitimate international concern."[22]

As this synoptic statement indicates, a proper grasp of the purpose of the international human rights practice requires attention to both its ultimate end and the specific means by which it seeks to achieve it. Beitz contends that human rights norms constitute a practice of reason giving that has as its goal the protection of "urgent individual interests against certain predictable dangers ('standard threats') to which they are vulnerable under typical circumstances of life in a modern world order composed of states."[23] Urgent interests are those that are valuable for individuals in a wide range of lives that occur in contemporary societies, but not

[19] Charles R. Beitz, *The Idea of Human Rights* (Oxford: Oxford University Press, 2009), p. 103.
[20] Ibid, p. 18.
[21] Ibid, p. 107.
[22] Ibid, p. 197.
[23] Ibid, p. 106.

necessarily every way of life that is or could be lived in contemporary societies, or every way of life that could be lived at some point in the past or future. Moreover, human rights norms only protect individuals against reasonably predictable threats they might face to their urgent interests. This constraint may reflect the fact that only such threats are amenable to, or are capable of justifying, an institutional response.

The international human rights practice adopts a two-tiered approach to achieving the goal of protecting urgent individual interests against standard threats. States bear the primary responsibility for complying with human rights norms. This requires them to "(a) respect the underlying interests in the conduct of the state's official business; (b) to protect the underlying interests against threats from non-state agents subject to the state's jurisdiction and control; and (c) to aid those who are non-voluntarily victims of deprivation."[24] States can fulfill these responsibilities through various combinations of constitutional commitment, ordinary law, and public policy. In the event that a state fails to comply with human rights norms, "appropriately placed and capable 'second level' agents outside the state" may have a reason to act.[25] Specifically, other states and certain international organizations have a *pro tanto* reason to hold that state accountable for its failure, while both state and non-state actors "with the means to act effectively" have a *pro tanto* reason assist those states whose failure to comply with a human rights norm reflects a lack of capacity to do so, and a *pro tanto* reason to intervene where the failure reflects states' unwillingness to comply with human rights norms.[26] The rights and responsibilities the international practice of human rights assigns to second level agents outside the state accounts for the description of human rights violations as a proper subject of international concern.

In sum, human rights are those norms (reasons for action) that are or should be invoked by participants in the recently emerged and still developing global political discourse that (a) aims to protect individuals' urgent interests against standard threats posed by the acts and omissions of the states that govern them, and that pursues this aim by (b) requiring states to conform to international standards in their domestic rule, and (c) treating states' failure to do so as a proper subject of international concern. Like any analysis of the concept of a human right, this one purports to clarify the justificatory burden borne by those who assert or deny the existence of a specific human right, or of any human rights at all. It does so by identifying those considerations that are relevant or irrelevant to successfully defending such claims.

---

[24] Ibid, p. 109.
[25] Ibid.
[26] Ibid. Both assistance and intervention should be understood broadly here. For example, the former may include capacity building in a failing state but also changes to international law and the domestic law of developed countries that enable developing ones to gain a larger share of the gains created by international trade. Intervention may include the use of force within another state's borders, but also (and more often) public documentation of a state's deliberate failure to comply with international human rights norms, inducements in the form of development aid or military cooperation, and targeted sanctions. For a detailed discussion, see ibid, pp. 31–42.

Consider, first, the task of justifying the existence of a specific human right, the right to freedom of religion, to emigration, or to health, say. Beitz's analysis of the concept of a human right entails that to do so a person must defend three claims:

> (1) that the interest protected has a kind of importance that it would be reasonable to recognize across a wide range of possible lives; (2) that in the absence of the protections embodied in the right, there is a significant probability that domestic-level [government] institutions will behave, by omission or commission, in ways that endanger this interest; and (3) that there are permissible means of international action such that, if they were carried out, the interest would be less likely to be endangered and that these means would not be unreasonably burdensome for those who have reason to use them.[27]

As Beitz notes, the first claim can be defended in a variety of ways. For instance, the interest a person identifies may be sufficiently generic that its urgency is immediately obvious to others despite many differences between the ways of life they lead and the one lead by the person who asserts the human right. The interest in (access to) adequate nutrition is an example. In other cases, such as the right to freedom of religion, an agent may need to characterize her interest in a way that abstracts a bit from the specifics of her own way of life in order to defend it as one it is reasonable to recognize as important or urgent across a wide range of possible lives. The essential point, Beitz maintains, is that "the importance of the interest, seen from the standpoint of a reasonable beneficiary, should be intelligible to reasonable persons who might be called upon to protect it."[28]

Satisfying this criterion does not suffice to justify a human rights norm, however. In addition, its defenders must make the case that domestic law or policy is an appropriate vehicle for protecting that interest. Is the interest even one that can be respected, protected, or advanced by the state? If so, is it morally desirable all-things-considered that the state be tasked with doing so? This is the point in the argument where specific claims regarding the content of the right, or what is the same, the specific duties it imposes on the state, must be defended. Finally, a proponent of a specific human right must establish that a state's failure to fulfill the duties correlative to that right is a proper subject of international concern. At a minimum, this requires that she show that there are forms of "interference" that are both possible and morally permissible for outside actors to perform in order to mitigate or correct a state's failure to fulfill the duties correlative to that human right. In addition, there must be outside actors who are generally capable of engaging in those forms of "interference," and for whom the burden involved is reasonable given the importance of the interests at stake. Here, too, the success of an argument for a human right depends on the specific actions it provides outside actors with a reason to perform.

---

[27] Ibid, p. 111. See also ibid, p. 137.
[28] Ibid, p. 138.

As we noted in the introduction to this chapter, skeptical challenges to human rights may take either a local or a global form. Given Beitz's political-practice account of human rights, local skeptical challenges must aim to demonstrate that an existing or proposed human right norm fails to satisfy one or more of the three conditions outlined earlier. For example, a skeptic may argue that the interest the putative right serves to protect is not (sufficiently) urgent, or that there are no feasible and morally permissible means by which outside actors can attempt to remediate any state's failure to respect or protect that interest. Global human rights skepticism, in contrast, challenges the moral justifiability of the entire international practice constituted by human rights norms, not just one or another of its constitutive norms. Here, too, a clear-eyed understanding of what human rights are serves to frame the skeptical challenge, and so what sort of argument is needed to meet it. For example, Beitz argues that we should address global skepticism vis-à-vis human rights on the assumption that the primary or central unit in the global political-legal order is the state. As he observes, for political-practice theorists the purpose of a philosophical investigation of human rights is not to defend an ideal theory of global justice. Rather, it is to describe and critically evaluate a specific historically located practice that "as it has developed so far can only be understood as a revisionist appurtenance of a world order of independent, territorial states."[29] Therefore, the global skeptical challenge to human rights must take one or both of the following two forms. Either it is the view that the development of the international human rights practice has not produced an overall moral improvement to the international legal order and the conduct of international relations.[30] Or it is the view that some alternative international political-legal practice consistent with a world of states would be morally superior to the one that the participants in the international human rights practice are trying, with some success, to create.[31] Beitz does not address the second challenge, but in response to the first he argues that the emergence of the international human rights practice is one of two developments that serve to legitimate the global political-legal order. That is, the existence of human rights norms that protect individual interests by imposing duties on states to treat their subjects in certain ways, and that make a state's failure to do so a proper subject of international concern, provide reasonable people with a weighty reason to accept and support the global political-legal order.[32] Global human rights skepticism, then, should be understood as the claim that the attempt by participants in the international human rights practice to legitimate the international legal order is doomed to fail.

[29] Ibid, p. 128.
[30] One might draw this conclusion if one views international human rights law as a form of Western imperialism.
[31] Neorealist scholars of international relations frequently defend this claim.
[32] Ibid, p. 131.

ii Joseph Raz

In many respects, Joseph Raz's answer to the question "what are human rights?" mirrors the one that Beitz defends. Perhaps most importantly, Raz also maintains that a philosophy of human rights should investigate "the use of the term in legal and political practice and advocacy."[33] The two theorists sometimes differ in matters of emphasis and detail, however, so a brief consideration of Raz's view may prove worthwhile.

Raz foregrounds the analytical relationship between human rights and state sovereignty. The actual or anticipated violation of human rights, Raz contends, "is a (defeasible) reason for taking action against the violator in the international arena, even when – in cases not involving violation of either human rights or the commission of other offences – the action would not be permissible, or normatively available, on the grounds that it would infringe the sovereignty of the state."[34] At a minimum, then, a philosophy of (the practice of) human rights should provide criteria for determining which standards of right conduct are such that their violation by a state provides a *pro tanto* justification for outside interference. These criteria can then be used to argue that the international legal order is defective either because it "recognizes as a human right something which, morally speaking, is not a right or not one whose violation might justify international actions against a state ... [or because it] fails to recognize the legitimacy of sovereignty-limiting measures when the violation of rights morally justifies them."[35]

The international human rights practice reconceives state sovereignty, and so the international legal order to which that concept is integral, in two distinct but related ways. First, it makes states accountable to outside actors for their failure to respect, protect, or advance the human rights of their subjects. Other states, international organizations, NGOs, and ordinary people everywhere have the standing to publicly criticize a state for its violations of human rights standards. Of course, the advent of the human rights practice is not a prerequisite for publicly criticizing states' treatment of those they rule. But as Raz emphasizes, its significance lies in the fact that those criticized for violating their subjects' human rights cannot respond that those actions are purely a domestic concern, ones they need not justify to outsiders. As he puts the point, "the ability of states to block interference in their internal affairs, to deny that they are responsible in certain ways to account for their conduct to outside actors and bodies, is what traditionally conceived state sovereignty consists in. But human rights, as they function in the world order, set limits to sovereignty."[36]

---

[33] Raz, "Human Rights Without Foundations," 337. See also Joseph Raz, "On Waldron's Critique of Raz on Human Rights," in *Human Rights: Moral or Political?*, ed. Adam Etinson (Oxford: Oxford University Press, 2018), p. 140.

[34] Raz, "Human Rights Without Foundations," 328.

[35] Ibid, 329.

[36] Raz, "Emerging World Order," 226–7.

Moreover, Raz maintains that the human rights practice is evolving to include more than simply holding states accountable for their violations of human rights standards. When undertaken to compel states to respect, protect, or advance their subjects' human rights, emerging norms sanction conduct that would otherwise count as impermissible interference with state sovereignty. This claim may appear hard to square with actual practice. After all, states frequently fail to do anything more than condemn other states for their failure to conform to human rights norms, if they even do that. The permanent members of the UN Security Council block any attempt at the collective enforcement of human rights norms when they believe that doing so will best advance their national interest. And recent attempts to make explicit a responsibility on all states to protect individuals against violations of certain of their human rights does not appear to add any teeth to the existing mechanisms for inducing compliance with international human rights law. But, in fact, these observations may not challenge Raz's constructive interpretation of the human rights practice. For, as he emphasizes, "the moral limits of sovereignty depend not only on the conditions within the [domestic] society ... [but] also depend on who is in a position to assert the limitations of sovereignty, and how they are likely to act as a result."[37] In the absence of impartial institutions capable of reliably applying and enforcing human rights norms, Raz maintains that we "should refrain from attempts to use any coercive measures to enforce the right ... given the common and serious harms attending the use of coercion on the international scene, and the risks that purported enforcement measures are no more than misguided presumptions."[38] In other words, at this point in the development of the international legal order other moral considerations will often defeat the *pro tanto* justification for interference in the internal affairs of a state generated by its violations of its subjects' human rights.[39] Nevertheless, because in Raz's view human rights should be enforced by supra-state law (that is, regional or global legal orders) the existence of a human right entails "a duty to establish and support impartial, efficient, and reliable institutions to oversee its implementation and protect it from violations."[40] If this is impossible in the current circumstances then the putative human right is not a genuine one.

Raz's characterization of the human rights practice as an ongoing attempt to reconceive state sovereignty explains why he maintains that we should identify as human rights only those rights that should be legally enforced. The very point of the practice is to redesign a legal entity – the state – and the legal system of which it is a part – the international legal order – so that they will better or best serve the goal of protecting or

---

[37] Raz, "Human Rights Without Foundations," 330.
[38] Raz, "Emerging World Order," 228.
[39] While Beitz makes the same claim, he also offers a much more comprehensive account of the types of actions that outside actors can and do take to contribute to the implementation of human rights. Consequently, he argues that some form of "interference" in the internal affairs of another state may be justifiable much more frequently than we may think if we focus only on compulsion or the use of force, as may be true of Raz.
[40] Ibid.

promoting individual's secure enjoyment of their moral rights. Given this understanding of the practice of human rights, a philosophy of (the practice of) human rights should aim to offer an account of the constitution of legitimate global government. Indeed, the case for conceiving of human rights as those that should be legally enforced is not only conceptual, an implication of the fact that the human rights practice concerns the construction of legal institutions, but also normative. As we saw in Chapter 6, Raz contends that law necessarily claims legitimate authority, a claim that is normally borne out when those the law addresses will do better at acting on the moral reasons that apply to them by acting as the law directs than by acting on their own judgment. In general, law ought to be designed or developed so that it normally possesses the authority it claims. Raz construes the international human rights practice as just such a development, an attempt to reconceive states' legal rights and responsibilities vis-à-vis their own subjects and the subjects of other states in ways that make it (much) more likely that international law actually enjoys the moral authority it necessarily claims.

The defining role Raz assigns to the project of reconceiving state sovereignty also explains his claim that "the distinctive element of human rights practice is its role in international relations."[41] While Raz does not deny that the human rights practice may have deepened our understanding of interpersonal morality and constitutional government, its collapse would not spell the end of either of these normative practices. The same is not true for the emerging international legal order, one that is gradually replacing a society of states that enjoy (nearly) complete freedom in the conduct of their domestic affairs with an international community in which states have specific responsibilities to their subjects that constrain their rule in various ways, and for which they can be held accountable by various outside actors. This vision of global politics would not survive a widespread loss of faith in the human rights practice, or so Raz maintains.[42]

iii Allen Buchanan

While Buchanan broadly shares Beitz's and Raz's understanding of the elements that compose the international human rights practice, he focuses his normative

---

[41] Raz, "On Waldron's Critique," 142.

[42] Raz's observation provides a response to the argument advanced by both John Tasioulas and James Nickel that human rights would have a place even in a world without international relations. See Tasioulas, "Nature of Human Rights," and James Nickel, "Human Rights," *The Stanford Encyclopedia of Philosophy* (Summer 2019 Edition), Edward N. Zalta (ed.), https://plato .stanford.edu/archives/sum2019/entries/rights-human/. If an asteroid strike killed every human being except those living in New Zealand, there would be no international human rights practice to theorize, only New Zealand's practice of constitutional government, including its recognition of individual rights. Of course, the individual interests and social conditions that call for their protection might well justify constitutional rights that closely resemble the content of human rights. But they would differ in one key respect, namely not providing a *pro tanto* justification for interference by outside actors in the event the New Zealand government fails to respect and protect its citizens' rights. On Raz's account, we should distinguish rights on the basis of the particular relationships they regulate, not the interests that ground them or any specific duties they generate.

theory on just one part of it, namely international human rights law. His reason for doing so is that international human rights law (henceforth, IHRL) "is the universally accessible *authoritative* version of the global moral lingua franca," and so "provides a uniquely salient global standard to which various parties – from international and domestic judges to NGO workers to protestors against tyrannical governments or opponents of the rapacity of global corporations – can appeal."[43] One might accept this claim while also maintaining that it is a mistake to focus too narrowly on the international legal element of the human rights practice.[44] Be that as it may, Buchanan's approach does have the virtue of avoiding disputes over the concept of a human right, at least vis-à-vis theorists who share his legal positivist conception of law. All can agree that *legal* human rights are elements of a conventional normative order that purports to constrain the exercise of government within a state's borders by according individuals rights they hold primarily against their own state.[45] This is so even if they disagree on the question of whether human rights should be understood to include only those norms that figure in the recent global movement to reconceive state sovereignty, or whether human rights should be understood as practice-independent moral norms that can and do figure in many discursive contexts besides international law and politics.

On Buchanan's account, the overarching purpose of IHRL is to "constrain sovereignty for the purposes of affirming and promoting the equal basic status of all people (the status egalitarian function) and helping to ensure that all have the opportunity to lead a minimally good or decent life by providing protections and resources that are generally needed for such a life (the well-being function)."[46] He maintains that this characterization improves on Beitz's in part because it recognizes IHRL's "robust commitment to affirming and protecting the equal basic moral status of all individuals" as an end in itself, and not merely on equal treatment serving to advance individual's well-being.[47] In fact, the difference between the two theorists is better explained in terms of how far they abstract from the practice when describing its overarching aim. On the face of it, it seems quite plausible to maintain that individuals have an urgent interest in the public recognition of their equal basic moral status, one that is subject to reasonably predictable threats from the acts and omissions of states. The same is true for the claim that states can use legal and policy instruments to protect this interest, and that their failure to do so is a proper subject of international concern. If so, then Beitz could agree with Buchanan's depiction of IHRL's overarching purpose. The reason he does not advance this claim, or for that

---

[43]   Buchanan, *Heart of Human Rights*, p. 7.

[44]   See Beitz, *Idea of Human Rights*, p. 210.

[45]   Allen Buchanan and Gopal Sreenivasan, "Taking International Legality Seriously: A Methodology for Human Rights," in *Human Rights: Moral or Political?*, ed. Adam Etinson (Oxford: Oxford University Press, 2018), p. 213.

[46]   Buchanan, *Heart of Human Rights*, p. 68. Presumably, Buchanan thinks this is also the overarching purpose of the broader international human rights practice of which IHRL is (alleged to be) the heart.

[47]   Ibid, p. 82.

matter a claim regarding what Buchanan labels IHRL's well-being function, is that he aims only to provide us with a method for critically theorizing human rights, and to illustrate how we might use it. Buchanan simply takes the process of critically theorizing the goal of the human rights practice a bit further than Beitz does.[48]

II JUSTIFYING INTERNATIONAL HUMAN RIGHTS NORMS

As should now be abundantly clear, political-practice theorists offer an analysis of the concept of a human right in terms of the role or function that human rights norms play in a distinctive and novel global political practice of relatively recent origin. At least for Beitz and Buchanan, one virtue of this approach is that it treats as an open question what sort of considerations can and do serve to justify human rights norms. In particular, we should not assume that every (or even any) norm constitutive of the international human rights practice depends for its moral justifiability on its reflecting, specifying, or indirectly advancing a moral human right.[49] In what follows, we first consider attempts by Buchanan and Beitz to demonstrate that appeal to a corresponding moral human right is not necessary to justify some of the norms that constitute the international human rights practice. We then consider the stronger claim that some political human rights *cannot* be justified by appeal to corresponding moral human rights because no such moral human rights exist.

Buchanan argues that no appeal to individual moral human rights is necessary to justify many international legal human rights. For example, he maintains that "a legal entitlement to goods, services, and conditions that are conducive to health, which include but are not limited to healthcare, can promote social utility, contribute to social solidarity, help to realize the ideal of a decent or humane society, increase productivity, and to that extent contribute to the general welfare, and provide an efficient and coordinated way for individuals to fulfill their obligations of beneficence."[50] Collectively, and perhaps in some cases individually, these

---

[48] Beitz's more abstract characterization of the overarching goal of the international human rights practice may also reflect his reticence to allow theory to get ahead of practice. He worries that "any relatively specific set of interests to be protected by human rights might be undesirably exclusive. A schema that seeks to organize our reasoning about the contents of human rights should identify the standards of judgment appropriate to the subject matter without artificially constraining the normative open-endedness we have observed in practice" (Beitz, *Idea of Human Rights*, p. 139). See also Beitz's skeptical remarks regarding the utility of conceiving of human rights norms as conditions for a minimally good life, which may mark a point of disagreement with Buchanan's claim that one of IHRL's two guiding purpose is ensuring that all have the opportunity to lead a minimally good or decent life. Ibid, pp. 141–4.

[49] On this point, Beitz and Buchanan differ from Raz, who maintains that the justification of a human right depends on three arguments, the first of which is that some individual interest, often in combination with a demonstration that social conditions require its satisfaction in certain ways, establishes an individual moral right. See Raz, "Human Rights Without Foundations," 336.

[50] Buchanan, *Heart of Human Rights*, p. 53.

considerations provide a sufficient moral justification for an international legal human right to health.

Considerations such as social utility, social solidarity, and the general welfare may seem a problematic moral basis for international legal human rights. After all, international law accords these rights to individuals, yet the aforementioned benefits do not appear to be similarly individualized. Social solidarity is a valuable feature of communities, not individuals. Of course, solidarity is typically of value to individuals insofar as they are members of a community, such as the one constituted by the state of which they are a citizen or a resident. Nevertheless, Buchanan's claim is that international legal human rights can be justified by appeal to the value of states of affairs that people can only achieve or enjoy collectively, even if the correct account of what makes those states of affairs valuable must appeal to the benefit each of the individual community members receives. Likewise, increased productivity may contribute to the general welfare without making every individual better off. It seems odd, then, to offer social solidarity or increased productivity's contribution to the general welfare to justify the claim that every individual ought to enjoy an international legal human right to health. In response, Buchanan argues that this conclusion rests on the very assumption political-practice theorists challenge. To justify international law according every human being a right to health, we do not need to demonstrate that each has an interest in health weighty enough to justify certain correlative duties on others, beginning with his or her fellow citizens. Rather, all we need to demonstrate is that according every human being an international legal right to health is a morally defensible means for advancing one or more morally desirable goals. If increasing productivity is a goal that states morally ought to pursue, and if equipping each of their citizens with an international legal right to health provides an all-things-considered morally permissible means to ensuring that they do so, then that international legal right is morally justifiable. No individual moral right to health is necessary.

Perhaps the description of increased productivity as a *morally desirable goal* pinpoints the shortcomings with any attempt to justify the norms constitutive of the international human rights practice without appealing to moral human rights. The problem is twofold. First, morally desirable goals cannot justify the sort of resistance to tradeoffs commonly associated with the concept of a right. Second, and relatedly, human rights norms play a constitutional role within the international legal order that cannot be justified on the basis of merely morally desirable goals. Let us consider each of these in turn.

Investment in health is not the only means by which a political community might pursue the goal of increased productivity or social solidarity. Why, then, should a state not be permitted to invest all of its resources in other avenues for realizing these goals, such as education or transportation infrastructure? The problem is not merely that this is unlikely to be the optimal means to promoting social solidarity or the general welfare. The problem is that states are not morally permitted to treat the protection and promotion of their subjects' health as simply one among the many morally valuable ends it can pursue. Rather, states have a moral duty to protect and promote their subjects' health. That duty is not absolute; it allows for tradeoffs in cases of conflict with the state's other duties. However, states may not choose to invest nothing in the protection of their subjects' health while, say, plowing resources into the construction of facilities to host the Olympics, even if the latter generates much social solidarity. Moreover, either the moral duty to protect and promote its subjects' health or the duty to treat its subjects as equals, or both, prohibit states from adopting laws or policies that advance social solidarity or the general welfare in ways that conflict with the equal protection and promotion of every individual subject's health. Instead, states must pursue goals like solidarity and increased productivity in a manner consistent with their duty to protect and promote all of their subjects' health.

The argument from IHRL's constitutional role proceeds in a similar manner. From the standpoint of international law, IHRL partly constitutes state sovereignty, specifying the responsibilities states have to their subjects, and the rights and responsibilities that certain outside actors (mainly other states) have to those individuals in the event that their state fails in its duties to them. Constitutional rights serve the same purpose in many domestic legal orders. Both serve to constrain the conduct of state officials, partly by delimiting the outer boundaries of their right to rule and partly by mandating that they use the rights conferred on them to pursue certain ends. In the case of IHRL, as well as most domestic constitutions, the two constraints do not perfectly coincide. Rather, state officials may exercise the powers that attach to their office for a range of ends besides those they are constitutionally required to pursue. From the standpoint of international law, the choice of whether to pursue these ends and (within certain limits) how to do so is a matter for each state's discretion, or what is the same, a matter that is *not* a proper subject of international concern. Intuitively, morally desirable goals seem to be the sort of considerations that should figure in a state's determination of how to exercise the discretion international law and its own constitution afford it. In contrast, the justification for constraints on the very constitution of the state's sovereignty seems to require an appeal to moral duties.

One response to these two arguments is to maintain that they rest on a false assumption regarding the nature of the reason for action that human rights norms provide. Careful attention to the actual workings of the international human rights practice reveals that many of the norms that constitute it do not have the properties we commonly associate with duties or rights. Rather, human rights norms often function as goals or aspirational standards that serve to orient political organization and contestation rather than as peremptory norms that individuals can invoke to demand specific conduct, as a person might do in a court or similar setting.

A second response concedes that human rights norms must be justified by appeal to moral duties, not simply morally desirable goals, but argues that these duties need not correlate to individual moral human rights. For example, Beitz appeals to a duty of beneficence to justify the international human right to health and other anti-poverty human rights.[51] Duties of beneficence are generally understood to be owed by those capable of protecting or promoting others' urgent interests to those whose urgent interests are or will be at risk without others' assistance. Crucially, none of those in need has a claim against any particular member of the set of actors able to assist them, and so none can justifiably level a complaint against a member of the latter set if he or she chooses to aid someone else. Put another way, no recipient of beneficence has a right against any particular potential benefactor that he or she help him. Furthermore, duties of beneficence are often thought to obtain only where the cost of aiding another is relatively low. Here, too, they differ from the duties correlative to a (moral) right, which generally obtain unless the cost of discharging them is quite high. If the justification for a human right to health and other anti-poverty rights rests on a duty of beneficence, then at least some human rights are grounded in moral duties that do not correlate to individual moral rights.

On closer inspection, it is not clear that Beitz's justification of an international human right avoids an appeal to an individual moral right to health. That is because his argument does not depend on the normal duty of beneficence but instead on the special case of "strong beneficence." Duties of strong beneficence arise when (1) "the threatened interest is maximally urgent, in the sense that the realization of the threat would be devastating to the life of anyone exposed to it," (2) "there is a set of 'eligible' agents with the resources, position, and capacity to act so as to alleviate the threat or mitigate its consequences," and (3) "the costs of action, if shared among these agents, and regarded from their perspectives, would be only slight or moderate, and when added to the costs previously borne by these agents for similar purposes would not be unreasonably great."[52] But then why not maintain that those whose urgent interests in health are threatened by poverty have a moral right against each and every member of the set of eligible agents that he or she contribute his or her fair share to the collective task of alleviating that risk or mitigating its consequences? Furthermore, the claim that a duty of "strong beneficence" obtains only if the cost to each of the eligible agents is slight or moderate is contestable. More importantly, most rights theorists agree that the cost to the duty bearer always figures in the specification of the duty correlative to a right. The more fundamental question is whether the value of the rightholder's interest suffices to justify *any* limit on the duty bearer's freedom. Beitz's description of the interest in health as "maximally urgent" suggests it does.

Beitz's appeal to a duty of strong beneficence to defend anti-poverty human rights purports to demonstrate the *possibility* of justifying international human rights in moral duties that do not correlate to individual moral rights. Buchanan makes

---

[51] Beitz, *Idea of Human Rights*, pp. 166–9.
[52] Ibid, p. 167.

a stronger claim, namely, that there are no moral human rights that correspond to many international legal human rights, and therefore the latter cannot be morally justified by appeal to the former. States do have moral duties to respect their subjects' equal status and to ensure they have the opportunity to lead a decent life, and specific international legal human rights may be justifiable as a means for enabling states to (better) perform their duties, or ensuring that they do so. Nevertheless, Buchanan thinks these moral duties do not correlate with individual moral human rights because, *morally speaking*, the state does not owe the required conduct to each of the individuals it governs. *Legally speaking*, the state may owe the required conduct to each of the individuals it governs, but that is because attributing a legal right to demand the conduct is morally justifiable as a means for getting the state to perform its moral duties.

Buchanan maintains that "in the case of moral rights, the corresponding duties must be justifiable by appealing solely to some morally important aspect of the individual to whom the right is ascribed, because the duties are supposed to be owed, morally speaking, to the individual to whom the right is ascribed."[53] But in many cases, the duties that IHRL imposes on a state cannot be justified solely by appeal to the moral value of protecting or promoting a single individual's interest. For example, signatories to the International Covenant on Social, Economic, and Cultural Rights "recognize the right of everyone to the highest attainable standard of physical and mental health," which, among other things, requires that they take steps to prevent, treat, and control epidemic, endemic, occupational, and other diseases.[54] Making good on this duty requires investment in public health, health-care delivery, medical education and research, and other costly institutions. Clearly these costs cannot be justified by appeal to the value of a single individual's interest in health. But it does not necessarily follow that the international legal human right to health is morally unjustifiable. Individuals' interests in health still matter morally, and their cumulative value may well suffice to justify, indeed morally require, the investments in health listed above. If so, then the moral justifiability of the individual *legal* human right to health depends essentially on the contribution the state's fulfillment of the correlative legal duties makes to protecting and promoting the interests of individuals other than the rightholder. Put another way, the reason I ought to enjoy a legal human right to health is not because my interest in health alone suffices to morally justify the legal duties correlative to that right. Rather, it is because according me a legal human right to health enables me to take actions that serve to advance many people's interest in health, and taken together our interests in health warrant these legal requirements on the state.

---

[53]   Buchanan, *Heart of Human Rights*, p. 62.
[54]   Article 12, *International Covenant on Economic, Social and Cultural Rights*, December 16, 1966, United Nations, Treaty Series, vol. 993, p. 3, available at https://treaties.un.org/doc/Publication/UNTS/Volume%20993/v993.pdf.

One concern with Buchanan's moral defense of an international legal human right to health is that it seems to leave the door open to a form of consequentialist moral reasoning that many find problematic. Absent a moral duty the state owes to each of its individual subjects, it may seem we lack any moral basis for criticizing the adoption of laws or policies that generally do quite well at protecting or promoting health but that also treat the health of some subjects as less important than that of others, or even of no concern at all. Buchanan responds that any such law or policy falls afoul of the state's moral duty to affirm and protect the equal basic moral status of all individuals.[55] Thus, the complete moral justification for an international legal human right to health invokes both of the purposes that inform this body of law, namely the status egalitarian function and the well-being function. Read in light of these two overarching aims, IHRL should be understood to accord every human being an equal right to health.[56]

A second concern, advanced by David Luban, is that absent an appeal to individual moral human rights we cannot account for the power IHRL has to mobilize shame.[57] This capacity matters not only for IHRL's utility as a means for realizing justice but for its very status as law. This is so because the existence of genuine legal rights depends on their being upheld, at least with adequate frequency, by the political community whose law it is. In the case of IHRL, however, there is often no court or adjudicatory body with the authority to hold states or other actors accountable for their violations of the law; neither is there any actor with the right, ability, or willingness to compel wayward actors to comply with it. Instead, adjudication largely takes place in the court of public opinion; various actors publicize (alleged) violations of IHRL with the hope that the resulting negative attention from other states, international organizations, multinational corporations, and so on will motivate the rights violator to alter their behavior. But Luban asks:

> [I]f legal human rights are just another bit of positive law, then why should anyone invest time and money, let alone risk their lives, to mobilize around ILHRs [International Legal Human Rights]? Why should state leaders (pretend to) feel ashamed about violating them, any more than they feel ashamed about violating technical regulations about the size and shape of cartons in international shipping?[58]

Although morally valuable, considerations such as increased economic productivity and greater social solidarity lack the qualities of necessity and urgency that moral human rights possess. It is the association of IHRL with moral norms that have these

---

[55] *Heart of Human Rights*, p. 64.
[56] Ibid, pp. 28–9.
[57] David Luban, "Human Rights Pragmatism and Human Dignity," in *Philosophical Foundations of Human Rights*, eds. Rowan Cruft, S. Matthew Liao, and Massimo Renzo (Oxford: Oxford University Press, 2015), pp. 266–70.
[58] Ibid, p. 268.

qualities that makes it possible to shame rights violators into modifying their behavior.

In response, Buchanan might agree that Luban provides a compelling reason to limit the content of IHRL to morally mandatory aims, that is, to those states of affairs that states, international organizations, and perhaps other actors have a moral duty to protect or promote. Other moral purposes, such as increasing economic productivity, would play only a supplementary role in the justification of international legal human rights norms. Nevertheless, for the reason just discussed Buchanan would deny that that every international legal human right must be morally justifiable as either a specification of, or a necessary means to, an individual moral human right. Rather, many may be justified by appeal to moral duties that states have to protect or promote certain of their subjects' interests, duties that reflect the moral importance of those interests but that not are not owed to each individual taken one by one.

Luban also worries that if we divorce IHRL from "moral claims every human being is entitled to make, where the entitlement and the content of the claim flows from our human status itself," we lack a rationale for referring to the rights this body of law creates as *human* rights.[59] Similarly, Tasioulas argues that IHRL's integrity depends on a recognition that it serves essentially to protect and promote moral human rights.[60] Absent this rationale or recognition, legal officials and other actors may develop IHRL in ways that distort or corrupt it. Christina Lafont and Jean Cohen both argue that recent conferrals of human and constitutional rights to corporations constitute just such a distortion.[61]

In response, Buchanan (and Beitz) can argue as follows. As a descriptive matter the international (legal) practice of human rights has as its overarching aim protecting or promoting the interests of individual human beings for their own sake.[62] This reading of the international human rights practice warrants rejecting attributions of human rights to corporations on the grounds that they do not fit the practice. No plausible interpretation of a body of law that has as its goal protecting and promoting the urgent interests of individual human beings can yield the conclusion that it also confers legal rights on a radically different type of agent such as a corporation. Unlike human beings, corporations have no existence apart from their recognition in law. Neither are setbacks to the interests of a corporation bad for the corporation itself, as opposed to bad for its shareholders, employees, customers, and so on; that is, bad for various individual human beings. Thus, any finding in favor of

---

[59]   Ibid, p. 269.

[60]   Tasioulas, "Exiting the Hall of Mirrors," 80–2.

[61]   Cristina Lafont, "Should We Take the 'Human' Out of Human Rights? Human Dignity in a Corporate World," *Ethics and International Affairs* 30, 2 (2016): 233–52; Jean L. Cohen, "The Uses and Limits of Legalism: On Patrick Macklem's *The Sovereignty of Human Rights*," *University of Toronto Law Journal* 67, 4 (2017): 529, 534–43.

[62]   This last clause makes explicit that the international practice of human rights treats the protection or promotion of health, religious freedom, and so on, as valuable for the individuals who enjoy them, and not merely as beneficial to others, including the state.

a corporation's claim to possess legal human rights reflects a confused and fundamentally mistaken understanding of the law. Crucially, this argument does not depend on an appeal to moral human rights to justify the norms constitutive of the international human rights practice.

Of course, political-practice theorists must acknowledge the possibility that the attribution of (legal) human rights to corporations might be morally justified on instrumental grounds. For example, doing so might result in an overall institutional order that better enables the members of the political community constituted by a given state to fulfill their moral duty to collectively promote and protect one another's urgent interests. As a matter of moral justification, this development would not accord corporations legal human rights because they are morally entitled to them in their own right. Nevertheless, it would still mark a radical change in the existing practice of IHRL, one that might be precluded if we conceive of the IHRL as necessarily concerned with protecting and promoting individual moral human rights. Political-practice theorists of human rights see it as a virtue of their approach that the question of whether to accord legal human rights to corporations must be settled on the basis of substantive moral arguments. Both Buchanan and Beitz maintain that it is a mistake to settle this question by conceptual fiat, in other words, by assuming or stipulating that international legal human rights must correspond to moral human rights. Rather, the question should be answered on the basis of empirically informed hypotheses regarding the promise and peril that conferring legal human rights on corporations poses for the protection and promotion of individual's urgent interests (and perhaps also social solidarity, increased productivity, and other morally desirable goals).

In the preceding paragraphs, we considered criticisms of Buchanan's argument that focus on one or another of the problematic consequences that allegedly follow from denying that moral human rights provide the justification for political and legal human rights. A different set of objections challenge the argument Buchanan gives to support his conclusion that many international legal human rights cannot be justified by appeal to corresponding moral human rights because the latter do not exist. For example, John Tasioulas argues that we need not demonstrate that the value of a single individual's interest in health warrants the full cost the state must bear in order to protect or promote that interest. Rather, that cost should be distributed across all of the individuals whose interest in health the state promotes when it invests in medical research, provides access to free or subsidized healthcare, enacts and enforces mandatory vaccination laws, and so on. As he writes, "what needs to be justified by the right-holder's interest is the right holder's *proportionate share of the costs* of securing his right as one among many other right-holders who also benefit in the same way from the system."[63] Crucially, because the interest in question is of great value to all human beings, the cost of protecting or promoting

---

[63] Tasioulas, "Exiting the Hall of Mirrors," 84.

a human right will always be distributed across the state's entire population. The question we need to answer, then, is "does the notional benefit to any individual right holder of securing the putative duties for all justify a proportionate share of the costs involved in doing so?"[64] Tasioulas maintains that the answer will be "yes" for many of the international legal human rights Buchanan identifies as impossible to justify solely by appeal to individual moral human rights.

Buchanan's criticism of a moral human right to health appears to entail that moral human rights are limited to those that individuals can possess even in the absence of moderately well-functioning political-legal institutions.[65] To reiterate, where the protection or promotion of an interest requires large-scale social institutions, no individual's interest alone suffices to justify the substantial costs involved in creating and maintaining those institutions. Hence there can be no moral human right that correlates to a moral duty to create and maintain these institutions, only a legal right that is justified instrumentally on the basis of the contribution it makes to advancing the interests of the many individuals who benefit from those institutions. However, philosophers such as Raz and Samantha Besson argue that the existence of moral rights may be conditional on the existence of conventional practices or institutions, including legal ones, without being reducible to legal rights.[66] Rather, we can distinguish moral from legal rights on the basis of the reason for action each provides. In the case of a legal right, the reason is "there is a positive legal norm that confers a right to X (e.g. health) on citizens or residents, to which correlates the state's duty to A, B, and C" and "this positive legal norm enjoys legitimate authority over the duty bearer (i.e. the state official), meaning that he or she has a moral duty to obey the law." In the case of a moral right, the reason is "given certain non-evaluative facts, which may be contingent and may include certain social conditions including but not limited to the existence of (or feasibility of creating) a conventional practice or institution, each individual's individual interest in X (e.g. health) is sufficiently valuable to justify a moral requirement on the state to protect or promote that interest in certain specific ways." Thus, a legally constituted practice or institution may play an essential role in providing a background or context in which the value of an individual's interest suffices to justify duties on others to advance that interest in specific ways. But it is the value of the agent's interest that grounds the moral right to which the duty correlates – a reason distinct

---

64   Ibid.

65   Or, what is not quite the same, Buchanan's argument entails that the duties correlative to a moral right are limited to those that that can be justified even in the absence of moderately well-functioning political-legal institutions.

66   Raz, "Emerging World Order," 219–20; Samantha Besson, "International Human Rights Law and Mirrors," *ESIL Reflections* 7, 2 (2018): 3–5; Besson, "In What Sense Are Economic Rights Human Rights? Departing from Their Naturalistic Reading in International Human Rights Law," in *Economic Liberties and Human Rights*, eds. Jahel Queralt and Bas van der Vossen (New York: Routledge, 2019), pp. 45–68.

from the moral duty to obey the law, which might also provide a duty to perform the same action.

III WHAT PLACE FOR MORAL ARGUMENT IN THE PRACTICE OF HUMAN RIGHTS?

The discussion in the previous section concerned the moral justification of human rights, understood as the norms constitutive of the international human rights practice (including, but not limited to, international legal human rights). Specifically, we asked whether a moral defense of these norms must invoke an individual moral human right, or whether it might depend instead on moral duties that do not correlate to individual moral rights, or even on the contribution that human rights norms make to advancing morally desirable but not mandatory goals, such as increased productivity. But what role should moral justifications of international human rights norms play in the international human rights practice? The answer may seem obvious: participants in the practice should use whichever one of these justifications is correct to defend the existing human rights it entails, to critique those it does not, and to call for the development of any new norms this justification warrants. Several theorists challenge this claim, however. Rather, as the philosopher Jacques Maritain famously said of the members of the UNESCO Committee on the Theoretical Bases of Human Rights: "[W]e agree about the rights but on condition that no one asks us why."[67] Beitz maintains that this is not a bug but a feature of the international human rights practice, a fact a philosophy of human rights ought to reflect. That is one reason why Beitz defends a concept of human rights that enables participants in the practice to agree on what it means to invoke a human right while disagreeing about the specific duties it generates or the (moral) considerations that justify it. As he observes: "[T]his does not mean that we need no reasons to care about human rights – only that it is not part of the practice that everyone who accepts and acts upon the public doctrine must share the same reasons for doing so."[68]

The norms constitutive of the international human rights practice are the product of incompletely theorized agreements or, on one understanding of that idea, norms of global public reason. For human rights to play the role Beitz maintains they do, participants in the practice they constitute must agree that those norms are morally justifiable; that is, that there exists a moral justification for norms that requires states to protect or promote certain of their subjects' interests, and that make their failure to do so a proper subject of international concern. However, it does not require that the participants agree on *why those norms are morally justifiable*. Indeed, what ultimately matters is not agreement on any justification of the norms constitutive of the international human rights practice, such as those contained in the Human Rights

[67] Cited in Beitz, *Idea of Human Rights*, p. 21.
[68] Ibid, p. 104.

Conventions. Rather, what matters is participants' *successful use* of the norms to provide other participants in the practice, especially but not only states, with reasons for action. A participant in the practice successfully deploys a human rights norm when the agent he or she addresses takes that norm as a reason for action. But again, the success of the practice does not depend on why the addressee does so, and in particular, whether she does so for the reason that the person deploying the norm thinks she should do so.

David Luban offers a similar account of the reasoning or argumentation constitutive of the international human rights practice. References to the inherent dignity possessed by all human beings (or all "members of the human family") in various human rights instruments express a commitment on the part of all participants to a particular moral ideal; in Luban's words, "that every human being should count as an object of concern" and "that no one should have to beg for their rights."[69] That commitment does not refer to some practice-independent feature of the world, one we can investigate via conceptual analysis, philosophical reflection, or empirical study, and from which we can derive specific human rights. Rather, that commitment serves as a presupposition for the international human rights practice. In arguing over the norms the practice should include, and the duties to which they correlate, participants advance claims regarding the best way to make good on a shared commitment to the abstract ideal that every human being is entitled to certain forms of treatment (by the political communities to which they belong). The success of these claims, for instance, the assertion or denial of a human right, depends on their acceptance by other participants in the international human rights practice. Acceptance, again, is exhibited in participants' actual treatment of a human rights norm as a reason for action. It is successful uptake by participants in the international human rights practice that provides the grounds for human rights norms, not their correspondence to some practice-independent fact, or to the normative practice (partly) constitutive of some other community, such as the constitutional rights recognized within a particular state's domestic legal order. As Luban puts it, "the meaning of the phrase 'human dignity' is not defined by a philosophical theory, but rather determined by its use in human rights practice."[70]

But how can the mere fact that others accept my claim that there is a human right to health, or that the human right to health generates a duty on all states to take specific steps to protect against epidemics, *morally* justify such a claim? Neither Beitz nor Luban is necessarily committed to claiming that it does so. Rather, their arguments are pragmatic, meaning they aim to give an account of how to use human rights norms to accomplish certain ends. Put blithely, they offer a theory of how to play the human rights game. But suppose a person asks

[69] Luban, "Human Rights Pragmatism," 277. See also Cohen, "Uses and Limits of Legalism," 534.
[70] Luban, "Human Rights Pragmatism," 275.

why she should accept a particular rule of this game, such as the existence of a human right to health, or indeed, why she should play the game at all. One way to answer those questions is by demonstrating that the moral principles she (perhaps implicitly) accepts in other spheres of her life also warrant her acceptance of a human right to health, or the existence of human rights in general. One need not accept those principles oneself in order to make this argument; this is the point about human rights norms functioning as the product of incompletely theorized agreement. But suppose *you* are the person entertaining local or global human rights skepticism? Presumably, you will want human rights norms to rest on moral principles that really are justified, not just on moral principles you or anyone else happens to accept or believe are justified. At this point, you may appeal to practice-independent considerations such as moral facts or the principles that suitably specified ideal agents would agree to under suitably specified ideal conditions. Or perhaps you might conclude that the justification of moral norms bottoms out in the abstract ideals of specific historically situated communities that cannot and need not be justified from an Archimedean point outside the practice itself. These justificatory accounts provide your reason to participate (or not) in the international human rights practice. But while you may also think these accounts provide all human beings with a (or the only) reason to do so, and while they may influence the sort of claims you advance or resist within the practice, they do not determine its content; that is, the specific human rights the practice accords individuals, or the duties to which they correlate. Rather, the practice itself does so via a process of uptake or the failure thereof on the part of its participants.

***

Our focus in this chapter has been on the question of how we should understand the concept of a human right, and what sort of considerations can or do serve to justify their invocation or denial in contemporary international and domestic politics. The value of this investigation lies in the clarity it brings to the task of determining which human right norms ought to be recognized by participants in this recently emerged and still evolving political practice. But an account of how to go about justifying or criticizing the international human rights practice should not be confused with actually doing so. The task of responding to the examples of skeptical challenges to human rights listed in the introduction to this chapter still remains. Moreover, as Beitz, Raz, and especially Buchanan emphasize, and as orthodox theorists such as Tasioulas agree, the justification of both the international human rights practice as a whole and the individual norms that compose it partly depends on how it is, or could be, institutionalized. The relatively primitive nature of the international legal order, the extent to which it exhibits fidelity to the rule of law, and the legitimacy of the various actors who enact, apply, and enforce human rights norms all have important implications for the moral justifiability of the international human rights practice. Nevertheless, when it comes to reflection on human rights, if philosophers enjoy any comparative advantage over theorists and practitioners steeped in other disciplines, it is with regard to formulating and answering basic theoretical questions of the sort explored in this chapter.

8

The Law of War and Its Relationship to the Morality of War

This chapter explores the moral justifiability of two core features of the contemporary law of armed conflict (LOAC), sometimes also referred to as international humanitarian law.[1] The first is the fact that its rules apply equally to those who fight irrespective of whether the state or state-like actor for whom they fight is legally (or morally) justified in going to war. From the standpoint of the law of war, combatants do nothing wrong, or at least nothing criminal, as long they adhere to the law of war. The second is the fact that the law of war categorically prohibits combatants from intentionally targeting civilians and civilian infrastructure when waging war, but prohibits attacks on combatants and military objectives only under certain conditions (for example, when soldiers are incapacitated due to injury). Following common practice, I label the first of these two features of the LOAC the equality of combatants, and the second the principle of noncombatant or civilian immunity.[2]

Are these two features of the law of war morally defensible? If so, why is that? If not, why not, and what sort of reforms should we pursue? To answer these questions, we need to elaborate and defend specific accounts of the ends or aims the law of war serves, or ought to serve, and the means whereby it can or should do so. In the first three sections of this chapter we consider the views of theorists who take the LOAC to be concerned with minimizing violations of individual rights. As we will see, some argue that the LOAC serves this goal by publicly communicating to combatants (as well as those in a position to judge their conduct) who is morally liable to defensive force. Others argue that the LOAC contributes to the minimization of individual rights violations by improving combatants' practical reasoning. The thought is that combatants do better at waging war justly, or at least at reducing the injustices they commit when waging war, if they adhere to the LOAC than if they rely on their own understanding and application of the moral norms that govern killing in war. The theorists whose views we consider section IV reject the claim that the LOAC aims, or

---

[1] For an accessible overview of the Law of Armed Conflict, see "War and Law," International Committee of the Red Cross, accessed January 10, 2020, www.icrc.org/en/war-and-law.

[2] This second principle is sometimes referred to as the principle of discrimination or distinction.

should aim, at the minimization of individual rights violations. Instead, they argue that the LOAC serves the humanitarian goal of reducing the harm war causes, and that it does so by attempting to strike an optimal balance between restrictions on how combatants may fight and their willingness to comply with those rules in their pursuit of self-preservation and victory in war.

I REVISIONIST JUST WAR THEORY AND THE INSTRUMENTAL ARGUMENT FOR THE LOAC

In his groundbreaking book, *Just and Unjust Wars*, Michael Walzer offers a moral argument for the equality of combatants and the principle of noncombatant immunity.[3] In virtue of posing a threat to one another's lives, he argues, combatants on all sides to a conflict forfeit their right not to be attacked by their opponents. They are equal, then, in the sense that no soldier, sailor, and so on, has a moral claim against opposing combatants that they not use force against him or her. Noncombatants, in contrast, retain their moral right not to be attacked, since in carrying on with their lives they do nothing to make themselves liable to defensive force. Were it successful, this line of argument might well provide a compelling moral defense for the existing law of war. The reason why international law ought to mandate the equal treatment of combatants, independent of whether they wage a just war, is that they are morally entitled to such treatment. Likewise, international law ought to categorically prohibit deliberate attacks on civilians because such attacks are morally impermissible. In short, the law of war is morally justifiable because it serves the goal of promoting moral conduct by publicly communicating to both combatants and those with the standing to hold them accountable the moral standards that ought to guide the waging of war

This defense of the law of war succeeds only if posing a threat to another's life is both necessary and sufficient to make a person morally liable to defensive force. Over the past two decades, a number of philosophers have challenged this claim. Jeff McMahan, for example, points out that if merely posing a threat to another's life suffices to justify the use of defensive force, then a bank robber who engages in a shootout with a police officer commits no wrong if he kills the officer.[4] Yet this conclusion is surely mistaken. A far more plausible view is that morality permits the police officer to use deadly force against the robber, albeit within certain constraints, while the thief enjoys no moral right to use deadly force against the officer, or anyone else. This asymmetry reflects the fact that the police officer has a just cause for the use of force, namely, the protection of his own life and that of bystanders to the crime from the actions of a culpable aggressor, while the thief enjoys no right to use force to

---

[3]   Michael Walzer, *Just and Unjust Wars*, 5th Edition (New York: Basic Books, 2015), pp. 34–41, 127–59.
[4]   Jeff McMahan, "The Ethics of Killing in War," *Philosophia* 34, 1 (2006): 25. McMahan takes this example from Walzer (*Just and Unjust Wars*, p. 128), although he argues that Walzer draws the wrong conclusion from it.

successfully advance his goal of robbing the bank and evading capture. If the possession of a just cause provides a necessary condition for the morally permissible use of force, however, then only those combatants who fight on behalf of a state or political group with a just cause for going to war enjoy a right to kill or injure enemy combatants. Unjust combatants, in contrast, have no right to do so; rather, unlike just combatants, they are morally liable to defensive force.

McMahan also denies that posing a threat to another is a necessary condition for moral liability to defensive force. Instead, he maintains "a person is morally liable to attack in war by virtue of being morally responsible for a wrong that is sufficiently serious to constitute a just cause for war, or by being morally responsible for an unjust threat in the context of war."[5] Although quite controversial, the first part of this claim might gain some initial plausibility from the thought that influential politicians, business persons, media moguls, religious leaders, and other civilians who play a key role in initiating or perpetuating unjust wars are more deserving of death or injury than are many of the men and women who actually fight them.

If true, McMahan's revisionist just war theory entails that the content of the law of war diverges significantly from that of the morality of war. Whereas the law of war holds combatants to be symmetrical in their liability to being attacked, revisionist just war theory entails asymmetric liability: just combatants may attack unjust combatants, but unjust combatants may not attack just combatants. Moreover, the criteria for liability to attack in war that McMahan defends entail conclusions at odds with the principle of noncombatant or civilian immunity. It is possible, and perhaps even likely, that some civilian members or supporters of a state or state-like actor that wages war without a just cause bear a degree of responsibility for that injustice large enough to make them liable to attack; that is, legitimate targets of defensive force. The law of war, however, categorically prohibits intentionally targeting civilians. Thus, if McMahan's revisionist account correctly describes the morality of war, the existing law of war cannot be defended on the grounds Walzer's argument suggests, namely, that it facilitates the just conduct of war by publicly communicating the correct moral standards to which combatants ought to adhere when waging war

Perhaps surprisingly, McMahan does not argue that in order to be morally defensible the law of war must be reformed so that its content mirrors that of the revisionist just war theory he defends. Rather, he maintains that the main purpose of the law of war "is to induce people to conform their behavior as closely as possible to the requirements of morality," from which it follows that the law of war ought to be morally assessed in terms of how well it serves as a tool for advancing this goal.[6] As we saw in Chapter 6, one way in which law can help agents better conform to the requirements of morality is by mediating between them and the moral reasons that

[5] Jeff McMahan, "The Morality of War and the Law of War," in *Just and Unjust Warriors*, eds. David Rodin and Henry Shue (Oxford: Oxford University Press, 2008), p. 22.

[6] Ibid, p. 33.

apply to them. If people will do better at acting as morality requires by deferring to the law's assessment of what they may, must, or must not do than if they act on their own judgment, then that is what they ought to do.[7] When it comes to waging war, McMahan maintains that in general people will commit fewer violations of the morality of war if they guide their conduct according to the existing law of war, or at least something close to it, then if they act on their own judgment of who is morally liable to attack.[8] This conclusion may seem counterintuitive. After all, the law of war does not proscribe attacks on combatants, yet at least one party to a war will fight without a just cause, and therefore its combatants will lack a moral right to use defensive force against their opponents. Compliance with the law of war does nothing to improve unjust combatants' conformity to the moral reasons that apply to them, since those reasons require that they immediately cease fighting. As McMahan points out, however, practically all those who wage war will believe that they are morally justified in doing so.[9] Moreover, given the burdens under which many combatants labor when war is imminent or ongoing, that conclusion may be a reasonable one for them to draw, even if it is often false. These burdens include limited access to the nonmoral information necessary to determine whether the considerations that morally justify resort to war have been met, attempts by various actors, oftentimes including their own government, to employ deception and propaganda to shape combatants' beliefs, and a lack of time, and/or education, and/or the maturity needed to draw a well-reasoned conclusion regarding the justifiability of resort to war. To these considerations McMahan adds "a patriotic tendency to trust in the moral rectitude of one's own society and government, deference to political and moral authority, the sense of professional obligation, and – last but not least – the pervasive assumption, promulgated by the dominant theory of the just war, that it is not a combatant's responsibility to enquire whether the war in which he or she has been commanded to fight is just."[10] Finally, even those who harbor doubts about the justice of the war they wage are likely to assert that their war is just in order to rationalize their participation in it. Insofar as we are interested in the law of war's capacity to guide the conduct of combatants, then, there is no reason for it to distinguish between those rules that apply to just combatants and those that apply to unjust combatants, since all combatants will guide their conduct according to the former. Instead, the law of war should simply consist of rules that apply equally to all combatants, and that make no reference to the justice of a combatant's resort to war.

[7]   Unless it is more important that they decide for themselves than that they get it right. Presumably that condition rarely if ever applies to the conduct of war.

[8]   Ibid, pp. 33–6. See also Adil Ahmad Haque, "Law and Morality at War," *Criminal Law and Philosophy* 8, 1 (2014): 79–97, and *Law and Morality at War* (Oxford: Oxford University Press, 2017), especially chapter 2.

[9]   McMahan, "Morality of War," 27–8.

[10] Ibid, 28.

This still leaves open the question of what the legal rules governing the conduct of all combatants ought to be, and, in particular, whether those rules ought to include a prohibition on intentionally targeting civilians. As we saw previously, if it is moral responsibility for an unjust threat that makes a person liable to attack in war, then in principle some civilians may be justly targeted, while some combatants may be immune to attack. Why not revise the law of war to reflect these moral truths? The answer, again, is that combatants will commit fewer injustices if they adhere to a rule that prohibits targeting noncombatants than if they act on their own judgments regarding specific noncombatants' moral liability to attack in war. Clearly this is true for those who lack a moral justification for resort to war; on the assumption that intentionally targeting civilians will not lead to a shorter war, and so fewer overall injustices, we ought to prefer whatever legal rule most restricts the necessarily moral rights-violating conduct of unjust combatants. McMahan maintains that it is also likely to be true for just combatants, however, who may frequently err in their assessment of enemy noncombatants moral liability to attack.[11] Moreover, the fact that a person is morally liable to attack in war does not suffice to justify an actual attack on that person; rather, doing so must also be a proportionate and necessary use of defensive force.[12] On the plausible assumption that the intentional targeting of a civilian will rarely satisfy all three conditions, the legal prohibition on targeting civilians will almost never require even just combatants to refrain from conduct permitted by the revisionist morality of war. If so, then the legal proscription on the intentional targeting of civilians generally tracks the demands of the revisionist morality of war, even if it also suggests a mistaken justification for why noncombatants ought not to be targeted, namely, that because they are civilians they have necessarily done nothing to make themselves liable to deliberate attack in war.

Adil Ahmad Haque appeals to the moral difference between killing and letting die to further buttress the kind of instrumental justification for deference to the law of war under investigation here. Suppose that the wrongness of killing someone who has done nothing to make herself morally liable to such treatment far exceeds the wrongness of letting such a person die. Haque maintains that "it is highly unlikely that by following the law [prohibiting intentional attacks on civilians] soldiers will allow substantially more harm to their fellow soldiers than they will avoid inflicting on morally immune civilians."[13] If so, then even if unfailing compliance with the law of war entails that just combatants occasionally do wrong, for instance, fail to prevent the death of a just combatant by targeting a noncombatant who is liable to such treatment, those wrongs will be examples of a lesser type of wrongdoing than the wrongs combatants will commit when they inevitably err in their identification

---

[11] Ibid, 32.
[12] Very roughly, proportionality requires that the good achieved by an act of war warrant the harm that act inflicts, while necessity requires that combatants inflict the least harm that they can compatible with the success of the particular act of war they perform.
[13] Haque, "Law and Morality at War," 88.

of civilians as liable to attack according to the revisionist morality of war.[14] Haque employs similar reasoning to defend conformity to a legal rule that permits the targeting of all combatants, regardless of whether they bear a level of responsibility for an injustice that makes a person liable to lethal defensive force:

> Soldiers who try to follow the deep morality of war and distinguish between morally liable and morally immune combatants probably will allow many more fellow soldiers to be killed as a result of constant hesitation and often misplaced restraint. At the same time, such soldiers probably will kill only somewhat fewer immune combatants, since many immune combatants will be reasonably but mistakenly identified as liable combatants.[15]

On balance, compliance with the legal rule in question leads to a morally better outcome than will occur if combatants act on their own judgment regarding liability to attack in war, since the small increase in the number of wrongful killings committed by those who follow the law will be outweighed by the large increase in the number of wrongful instances of letting die they avoid. This line of argument might be even more compelling were the law of war reformed to limit the class of legitimate targets in war to those it is reasonable to believe perform a combat function, as Haque maintains it should be.[16]

Even if in general combatants will better conform to the demands of morality if they use the law of war to guide their conduct than if they rely on their own moral judgment, McMahan acknowledges that this will not always be the case. Rather, he argues that on those exceedingly rare occasions when the morality of war requires that a just combatant violate the law of war, say by deliberately attacking noncombatants, he ought to do so.[17] However, he adds three important caveats. The first is that the combatant should be very confident in his judgment that this violation of the law of war is morally justifiable: "The presumption is against violation [of the law of war] and combatants should be reluctant to give their individual judgment priority over the law, for the law has been designed in part precisely to obviate the need for resort to individual moral judgment in conditions that are highly unconducive to rational reflection."[18] Second, the combatant must also take into account the effect

---

[14]   Note that this line of argument is distinct from the one set out in the previous paragraph, which focuses only on the frequency with which just combatants will make erroneous moral judgments, rather than the significance or seriousness of the wrong they do.

[15]   Ibid.

[16]   Ibid, 96.

[17]   McMahan, "Morality of War," 39. The requirement that such attacks satisfy the requirements of proportionality and necessity, and that they not cause a morally unacceptable amount of collateral damage, explains why these occasions will be rare.

[18]   Ibid, 41. Arguably, on the purely instrumental account of law's practical authority that both McMahan and Haque endorse, conflicts between law and morality should not be understood as conflicts between two different *reasons for action*, but instead as a conflict between two different *judgments* regarding what an actor has an undefeated reason to do. Therefore, talk of a case where the revisionist morality of war requires what the law of war forbids should be understood as one where an individual

his illegal conduct will have on others' adherence to it. If, as a consequence of his action, other combatants will engage in morally unjustifiable violations of the law of war, then even though the combatant would not morally wrong the noncombatant he proposes to attack, his conduct may not be morally justifiable all-things-considered. Finally, McMahan maintains that, in general, combatants who commit morally justifiable violations of the law of war ought to bring that fact to the attention of a court that can hold them accountable for their conduct. Moreover, that court may be morally permitted or even required to punish combatants for their illegal conduct even if it rightly judges their actions to have been morally required. McMahan defends both of these conclusions by appeal to their positive impact on overall compliance with the law of war, and so the extent to which it serves as a mechanism for reducing the injustices committed by those who fight.

II CRITICISMS OF THE INSTRUMENTAL ARGUMENT FOR THE LOAC

McMahan (and Haque's) instrumental argument for the law of war faces numerous challenges. For example, Seth Lazar contends that as long as McMahan concedes that combatants ought to violate the law of war whenever it conflicts with what the morality of war requires, he cannot defend deference to the law of war on the grounds that it will lead to greater conformity to morality's true demands.[19] Since morally astute combatants will know that under certain conditions they have a moral duty to violate the law of war, they will need to constantly consider whether these conditions are met in the situation they confront. To answer that question, they will need to determine for themselves what the morality of war requires of them in that situation; only then will they know if it requires conduct contrary to the law of war. If, in order to determine whether they should comply with the law of war, combatants must engage in the very exercise of moral judgment for which the law is supposed to substitute, then the law of war cannot serve the goal of enhancing their conformity to the reasons that apply to them by replacing their judgment with its own.

This objection misconstrues the judgment combatants must make, however. What combatants must ask themselves is not whether the morality of war requires illegal conduct, but whether they have compelling reasons to believe that, in their current situation, they are more likely to judge correctly what the morality of war requires than is the law. Insofar as all combatants have standing reasons to be suspicious of their ability to engage in sound moral reasoning regarding who among their foes is morally liable to attack, they ought to operate with a strong presumption against violating the law of war. The standards of evidence deployed in American civil and criminal law may help illustrate this point. To judge that the

---

combatant judges correctly that a prospective attack on a noncombatant is morally permissible, while the law of war communicates the mistaken judgment that it is not.

[19] Seth Lazar, "The Morality and Law of War," in *The Routledge Companion to Philosophy of Law* (New York: Routledge, 2012), p. 368.

preponderance of evidence favors X over Y is to hold that X is more likely to be true than is Y. Where one finds the evidence favoring X over Y to be clear and convincing, one maintains that X is substantially more likely to be true than is Y. In criminal trials, however, neither a preponderance of evidence nor clear and convincing evidence justifies finding a defendant guilty of the crime with which he or she has been charged. Rather, a jury (or judge) should do so only if they believe beyond a reasonable doubt that the defendant committed the crime in question. Likewise, when it comes to compliance with the law of war, combatants should treat neither a preponderance of evidence nor clear and convincing evidence that morality requires illegal conduct as justifying such action. Instead, they should violate the law of war only when they believe beyond a reasonable doubt that morality requires them to do so. Given that many of the reasons combatants have to be suspicious of the quality of their moral judgment are typical of war, the adoption of such a strong presumption in favor of compliance with the law seems eminently justifiable. Indeed, the greater challenge to McMahan (and Haque) may well be the opposite of the one Lazar levels against them, namely, that the reasons they give for a *presumption* in favor of compliance with the law of war, or at least the principle of noncombatant immunity, actually warrant the treatment of those rules as *categorical or unconditional* rules for the conduct of war.

Lazar also challenges the claim that combatants will generally do best at conforming to the demands of McMahan's revisionist morality of war if they comply with the legal rule prohibiting deliberate attacks on noncombatants.[20] His objection takes the form of a dilemma: if the threshold for moral responsibility for a wrong that makes one liable to defensive force is low, then many noncombatants will be legitimate targets of war. If so, then from the standpoint of enhancing combatants' conformity to the moral reasons that apply to them, the optimal legal rule governing targeting in war may well be less restrictive than the existing one. For example, it may prohibit only deliberate attacks on noncombatant minors. In contrast, if the threshold for moral responsibility for a wrong that makes one liable to defensive force is high, then this may well entail not only that targeting noncombatants is rarely permissible, but also that many of those who fall within the legal category of combatant are not morally liable to attack. In this case the legal rule that would best serve to enhance combatants' conformity to morality may be one that prohibits their fighting at all, even in a broad range of cases in which they rightly conclude that they have a just cause for war. Regardless of which horn of this dilemma we embrace, deference to the existing law of war cannot be justified on the grounds that it produces the optimal outcome, that is, the fewest unjust acts of war we can achieve.

In describing the first horn of the dilemma, Lazar appears to assume that the optimal legal rule ought to track only moral liability to attack in war. But this is not so; the optimal legal rule ought to track all of the considerations that figure in the

---

[20] Ibid, 368.

moral justifiability of an act of war, and this includes proportionality and necessity. If those conditions are rarely satisfied in the case of noncombatants, but combatants will be regularly tempted to think that they are, then we have compelling reasons to believe that a legal rule prohibiting the intentional targeting of civilians is optimal even if many noncombatants are morally responsible for the kind of wrong that makes a person liable to defensive force. A response to the second horn of Lazar's dilemma might begin by conceding that the law of war ought to be reformed so that it places greater restrictions on who may be deliberately attacked, perhaps along the lines Haque suggests. A compelling rebuttal to Lazar's claim that many combatants will lack responsibility for the kind of injustice that makes them liable to defensive force might then be forthcoming. Alternatively, we might argue that a legal rule prohibiting war would often be ineffective, either ignored entirely or quickly revised to contain exceptions that largely vitiated it as a tool for minimizing injustice. If so, then for all the wrongful killing of nonliable combatants it might fail to proscribe, a legal rule that prohibits only deliberate attacks on civilians but that is moderately effective at shaping the conduct of war might produce the closest conformity to the morality of war we can hope to achieve.[21]

As we saw in the previous section, McMahan contends that even when combatants are highly confident in their judgment that the morality of war requires a violation of the law of war, they should still forbear from such conduct if it will cause others to engage in morally unjustifiable illegal conduct. Substantively, Lazar contends this conclusion places excessive moral demands on (just) combatants, who are expected "to sacrifice their lives, and the opportunity to contribute to a just cause, because of speculative claims about how their conduct might connect with the voluntary wrongful actions of other combatants in the future."[22] But Lazar also adds that this argument can be framed without any reference to law: roughly, an agent ought not to perform a morally required act of war if that will cause others to commit violations of the morality of war they would not otherwise commit. Thus, he concludes that this line of argument is not really a defense of compliance with the law of war.

In one important sense Lazar's conclusion is correct: at this stage in an agent's deliberation, the mere fact that the law directs him not perform a certain act, say intentionally targeting a noncombatant, does not provide him with a reason not to perform that act. Given an instrumental account of law's authority, the law of war lacks a justifiable claim to the combatant's deference in this case. Yet the law's practical authority remains an essential consideration even for agents who rightly conclude that they are not bound by it (in the case at hand). McMahan's argument singles out one particular way in which a *pro tanto* morally required act may turn out to be morally prohibited all things considered, namely, if it makes the law of war a less effective tool for minimizing injustice. There are other paths to this conclusion, however, which do not

---

[21] In fact, this is one reason Lazar gives for rejecting David Rodin's proposal that the law of war be reformed so that its content mirrors that of revisionist just war theory. See ibid, 375.

[22] Ibid, 369.

turn on others' respect for the law. For example, it may provoke or inspire actors who are ignorant of the law of war, or who pay no heed to it, to perform immoral acts that they would not otherwise have performed. In such cases, the consequences that render a combatant's targeting of civilians morally impermissible all-things-considered make no reference to the law of war. That is not true of McMahan's example, however, in which it is *the diminution of the law of war's effectiveness* at steering actors away from the commission of certain injustices that entails the all-things-considered moral impermissibility of targeting civilians. Thus, there remains an important sense in which an argument for compliance with the law of war that rests on the effects it will have on general respect for the law appeals specifically to law's practical authority.

In a paper entitled "Do We Need a Morality of War?," Henry Shue argues that McMahan's (and, by implication, Haque's) argument for compliance with the law of war actually supports a stronger conclusion, namely, that the morally best law of war just is the morality of war.[23] Shue's argument turns on two key premises. The first is that the epistemic and motivational "defects" McMahan and Haque point to in order to justify the claim that combatants should follow the law rather than act on their own judgment are not only typical but also ineradicable features of war. Therefore, the normal state of affairs in war is one in which it is impossible for combatants to discern who among the enemy's combatants and noncombatants are liable to attack. The second is that to be plausible a putative standard of right conduct must satisfy a particular interpretation of the dictum "ought implies can," namely, that in general those who engage in the kind of activity to which that standard applies be able to use it to guide their conduct. If a necessary condition for the existence of any norm, moral or legal, is that it generally be capable of guiding the conduct of those to whom it applies, and if actual human beings engaged in war generally cannot guide their conduct according to McMahan's revisionist just war theory, then we ought to reject his account of the morality of war. This implies, of course, that the moral justifiability of the law of war cannot be grounded in the contribution it makes to enhancing combatants' adherence to the revisionist morality of war.

Haque criticizes both of the premises in Shue's argument. Whereas Shue characterizes war as "a situation in which many individuals, most of whom he or she cannot see, are routinely and relentlessly, hour after hour, day after day, trying to kill him or her," Haque argues that not all combatants currently fight in such circumstances.[24] For example, combatants such as drone pilots sometimes have access to a good deal of information regarding potential targets' moral liability to attack, as well as the time to consider that information in a setting that is fairly conducive to the exercise of sound moral judgment.[25] More generally, Haque writes, "the context of war, including its epistemic and pragmatic dimensions, may change over time, and we should have

[23] Henry Shue, "Do We Need a 'Morality of War?'" in *Just and Unjust Warriors* (Oxford: Oxford University Press, 2008), pp. 87–111.
[24] Shue, "Morality of War?" 99.
[25] Haque, "Law and Morality at War," 91.

a clear view of the moral considerations that may remain constant."[26] This claim is difficult to assess in the absence of an analysis of the concept of war. For example, it may be that the kind of technological and structural changes necessary to significantly diminish the epistemic and motivational shortcomings that typically characterize contemporary war will necessarily amount to its elimination. Whatever use of lethal force still occurs in such a world might then be best described as a form of policing, a practice that is already subject to rules governing the use of force that are distinct from, and far less permissive than, those that govern the conduct of war.

Shue's second premise, Haque argues, mistakenly treats as a necessary condition for a standard of rightness what is only a necessary condition for a decision procedure.[27] A standard of rightness specifies what makes an act permissible, prohibited, or required, whereas a decision procedure serves to guide actors' conduct in light of the evidence available to them. The revisionist morality of war provides an account of what makes killing and other acts of war right or wrong; that is, it identifies standards of rightness for the conduct of war. There is no reason to assume, however, that a standard of right or just conduct in war either provides or should provide the best decision procedure for waging war. Rather, we should adopt whatever action-guiding rules will best enable us to conform to the appropriate standards of rightness, and as we saw in the previous section, for Haque that means relying on legal rules for the conduct of war that diverge from the morality of war. As for the standards of rightness, including the moral norms governing war, their truth depends neither on what people believe nor on what people are motivated to do.[28]

Shue can concede all of the points Haque makes, however, but still maintain that revisionist just war theory ought to be rejected because it demands the impossible. It seems plausible to hold that morality does not require people to do things that are beyond our physical capacity, for instance, that require feats of strength few if any human beings can perform. Why should we not draw the same conclusion when it comes to belief formation and/or motivation? This appears to be Shue's position: among the things morality does not require people to do is to form accurate beliefs regarding others' moral responsibility for a threat that justifies the use of defensive force in circumstances in which doing so is typically impossible.[29] Haque and McMahan both take the position that nonculpable ignorance provides combatants with an excuse, but not a justification, for any infractions of the revisionist morality of war. Yet we might well wonder why the inability of combatants to adhere to the

[26] Ibid, 82.
[27] Ibid, 82–3.
[28] As McMahan writes: "[T]he morality of war is not a product of our devising. It is not manipulable; it is what it is. But the laws of war are conventions that we design for the purposes of limiting and repairing the breakdown of morality that has led to war, and of mitigating the savagery of war, seeking to bring about outcomes that are more rather than less just or morally desirable." McMahan, "Morality of War," 35.
[29] Henry Shue, "Laws of War, Morality, and International Politics: Compliance, Stringency, and Limits," *Leiden Journal of International Law* 26, 2 (2013): 275.

revisionist morality of war ought to be characterized as a moral failing, although not one for which combatants ought to be blamed, rather than as a regrettable fact about human beings. After all, we do not think a lack of superhuman strength merely excuses people, so why should we think a lack of superhuman knowledge and motivation does so? If the answer is that in the latter case we believe the actors could have done otherwise, or, in other words, that forming the right beliefs and acting on them is not inherently at odds with waging war, then we need an argument for why this is the case. Ultimately, then, the dispute between Shue and Haque and McMahan turns on different conclusions regarding human nature and the implications this has for the content of morality.

III REVISIONIST JUST WAR THEORY AND THE ARGUMENT FOR REFORMING THE LOAC

Although they draw fairly similar conclusions regarding the morality of war, David Rodin rejects McMahan's defense of the existing law of war and argues instead that it ought to be reformed so that its content closely approximates, or even mirrors, the content of revisionist just war theory.[30] Rodin begins by noting that:

> [R]ules, both legal and moral, perform many important regulatory functions beyond their role in guiding the immediate deliberations of those addressed by the norms. Most obviously they help to inform the response of others . . . [and] these reactions play an important part in the behavior regulating function of rules by creating incentives and disincentives for forming beliefs in morally appropriate ways.[31]

Therefore, a sound moral assessment of the law of war must take into account not only the negative consequence of holding unjust combatants accountable for their immoral conduct, but also "the potential benefits that may arise from providing a sanction for participation in unjust war, [which if] effective could reduce the total incidence of war with commensurate benefits of justice and security."[32]

To evaluate this argument, we must first distinguish between public and private sanctions, with criminal prosecution and punishment as an example of the former, and individual moral judgment and condemnation (including the unjust combatant's self-assessment) as an example of the latter. Suppose that the existing law of war serves to shield unjust combatants from private sanctions by creating or strengthening a widespread but, we will assume, false belief that combatants commit no wrong as long as they obey the law. Might the law of war be modified so that it no longer has this effect; for example, by explicitly characterizing the rules as applying

---

[30]   David Rodin, "Morality and Law in War," in *The Changing Character of War*, eds. Hew Strachan and Sibylle Scheipers (Oxford: Oxford University Press, 2011), pp. 446–63.

[31]   Ibid, 452.

[32]   Ibid, 452.

to *just* combatants? If so, might such a change increase the frequency with which unjust combatants are held accountable for their wrongful conduct, and so over time lead military personnel and those who care for them to take greater responsibility for discerning whether the war they have been ordered or encouraged to fight is a just one? Rodin eschews such a change to the content of the law of war, holding only that the existing, neutral, law should be given an asymmetric interpretation according to which only just combatants can comply with it. But if this interpretation is to contribute to a diminution in the occurrence of unjust war by strengthening the practice of privately sanctioning unjust combatants, it will need to be broadly disseminated and adopted. Explicitly characterizing the law of war as applying to just combatants might well provide a perspicuous means for doing so.

Public sanctions for law-abiding but unjust combatants, particularly criminal trials and punishment, appear far less likely to produce a net gain in justice and security. At present, they are likely to be administered either by the victorious party in the war, or by domestic actors in the defeated state who opposed the group that fought and lost the war. In both cases, we might well worry these actors will use the criminal law to exact revenge and/or to further their political or economic interests, rather than to hold combatants accountable for fighting an unjust war. Furthermore, there is no reason to assume that victory in war tracks the justice of a party's cause, and therefore no reason to think that a legal rule that makes law-abiding unjust combatants liable to punishment will be administered in such a way that it is (mostly) unjust combatants who are put on trial. The creation of criminal liability merely for having fought in an unjust war might also create perverse incentives that would lengthen wars while making them even more horrific. Faced with the prospect of punishment, combatants who might otherwise choose to cease fighting may instead choose to continue despite their dwindling prospects for victory. Moreover, combatants might conclude that "because *anything* they might do in war would be wrong ... they might as well abandon all restraint in order to win the war as quickly and decisively as possible, thereby affording themselves as much protection as possible, since if they win, it will be more difficult to prosecute and punish them."[33] Conversely, McMahan suggests that by not exposing combatants to criminal liability merely for fighting in an unjust war, the law may temper the righteous indignation that so often animates human beings in times of war. The goal of minimizing wrongful killing and injury may be best served if soldiers, sailors, and the like, perceive enemy combatants as simply doing their job, rather than as wrongdoers who bear personal responsibility for an unjust war.[34]

Despite suggesting that a moral assessment of the law of war should take into account the effects that its use to hold unjust combatants accountable for their wrongdoing will have on justice and security, Rodin makes no effort to explore what

[33] McMahan, "Morality of War," 30.
[34] To be clear, the claim is not that unjust combatants bear no responsibility for the war they fight, only that the law of war may contribute to mitigating the evils of war by fostering the belief that they do not.

the consequences of a change to the existing law might be. To the contrary, he asserts that we should be "highly skeptical of arguments about the likely effects of differing configurations of rules, especially when, as is almost always the case in international relations, it is difficult to support such arguments with solid empirical evidence."[35] Indeed, Rodin contends that oftentimes it is possible to formulate diametrically opposed but equally plausible hypotheses regarding the consequences of a change to the law of war. To illustrate this point, he considers the likely effects on the security of just states were the law of war reformed so as to make law-abiding combatants criminally liable for having fought in an unjust war. While the effects might be negative if it led many combatants to choose not to go to war even though they were morally justified in doing so, they might also be positive if the change in the law made it even more difficult for potential aggressors to launch unjust wars. He concludes that "speculating about the potential harmful or beneficial consequences of complex matters of rule formation is usually a futile exercise and a poor guide to ethics or to the configuration of international law."[36]

There are several reasons to think this conclusion too strong, however. The fact that we find it difficult to gather the information necessary to determine the consequences of a rule, or what the effects of some alternative rule will be, may warrant a low level of confidence in whatever conclusions we draw. However, it does not undermine the claim that the moral justifiability of adopting one legal rule rather than another depends on the former producing a morally better outcome than the latter; for example, greater conformity to the demands of revisionist just war theory. Indeed, as we will see, Rodin himself ultimately relies on an empirical claim when he maintains that the existing law of war cannot be justified as a lesser evil. Moreover, we should be careful not to move too quickly from the judgment that two contradictory hypotheses are equally plausible to the conclusion that they are equally probable. The former judgment often reflects a rough assessment of the likelihood that a hypothesis will turn out to be true, whereas the latter judgment depends on the evidence we are able to amass in support of each hypothesis, including the weight we assign to different pieces of evidence. Finally, while we often have good reason to seek additional information that confirms or conflicts with our hypothesis that one rule is superior to another, if we must choose between them then we ought to choose the one we think produces the better outcome, even if our confidence in the truth of that judgment is low.

Rodin's final objection to McMahan targets his instrumental approach to justifying the law of war. Where law regulates conduct that morality neither requires nor forbids, Rodin argues that legislators may enact the rule they believe will produce the most social utility. In such *mala prohibita* cases, the law makes it morally wrong to perform acts that it would not be wrong to perform were there no law, or perhaps,

---

[35] Rodin, "Morality and Law in War," 453.
[36] Ibid, 453.

were the content of the law different than what it is. In other cases, however, the law purports to regulate conduct that is morally wrong independent of the law forbidding it. Examples include *mala in se* criminal offenses such as murder, assault, and rape. Where "law articulates, and makes administrable an underlying moral norm," Rodin contends, it "is not free to assume any configuration that may be maximally useful; [rather] it is constrained by the content of the underlying moral norms."[37] Just as the underlying moral norms prohibiting murder, assault, rape, and so on constrain the content of (a just) criminal law, so too the underlying moral norms of revisionist just war theory place limits on the content of the law of war. In particular, if morality prohibits intentionally targeting those who have done nothing to make themselves liable to attack in war, then the law of war ought to reflect that fact by explicitly prohibiting attacks on just combatants. To defend the existing legal rule, which does not make unjust combatants criminally liable for killing just combatants, on the grounds that it will produce better consequences is to embrace a form of consequentialist moral reasoning at odds with respect for all human beings' right to life.

To drive home this conclusion, Rodin invites his reader to consider the following hypothetical example:

> Imagine a society in which an ethnic minority is despised and subject to persistent abuse and harassment. This abuse culminates in a macabre tradition on the national anniversary in which a single man from the community is captured and ritually hanged in the central square of the capital city. In the years in which the scapegoat ritual is prevented or fails, the general violence and abuse against the minority increase dramatically resulting in several dozen additional deaths. Suppose now that a proposal is put forward to formalize a set of legal rules regarding the treatment of the minority in this society. The lawmakers are humanely motivated and they have good reason to believe that the optimal law for securing the rights of the ethnic minority as a whole would be one which permitted the hanging of the ritual scapegoat under strictly controlled conditions and provided robust legal protections to members of the community outside this unique context.[38]

Rodin maintains that we ought to reject the proposed legal rules because they sanction the killing of a member of the ethnic minority as a (mere) means to minimizing the injustices committed by the majority. Likewise, because it fails to proscribe the immoral conduct of unjust combatants, "the law of war is inconsistent with morality for precisely the same reason that the scapegoat law would be inconsistent with it – it creates a legal right for certain people to violate the moral rights of others, as a means to achieving a broader desirable end."[39]

One might argue in response that Rodin mischaracterizes McMahan's and Haque's defense of the law of war, which rests not on a consequentialist account

---

[37] Ibid, 454.
[38] Ibid.
[39] Ibid, 455.

of what makes acts right or wrong, but an instrumental argument regarding the use of law to enhance conformity to a rights-based or deontological morality. Why not pick the decision procedure that best serves to minimize rights violations? Presumably Rodin's answer will be that it is not permissible to enact a law that will produce greater conformity to the demands of morality if it does so by encouraging actors to violate a person's moral rights. Rights serve as side-constraints on the pursuit of desirable states of affairs, including a range of outcomes in which those same rights are better secured or advanced. If we abandon that understanding of the nature of rights, then claims regarding rights become nothing more rules of thumb for promoting (morally) desirable consequences.

Haque contends that the instrumental approach he employs to defend the law of war does not justify the adoption of a law that permits the scapegoat ritual because "the permission does not help those subject to it conform to deontological moral norms."[40] This is not obviously true, however; Rodin's description suggests that in the absence of a law permitting the scapegoat ritual, members of the ethnic majority would violate the moral right to life of even more members of the ethnic minority. If so, then it appears that the government will enable members of the ethnic majority to do better at acting as they should if it legally permits the scapegoat ritual than it if continues to legally prohibit it. While members of the ethnic majority will still fail to fully conform to the deontological norm prohibiting unjust killing, the magnitude of their failure will be less than it would otherwise be.

The foregoing argument may misconstrue the instrumental justification for law's practical authority, however. Perhaps that justification, properly understood, requires that legislators make a good faith effort to identify what morality requires of their subjects, and to communicate that to them. The law ought to treat its subjects as responsible moral agents, actors who are capable of responding appropriately to the reasons that apply to them. In the scapegoat case, that means communicating the judgment that neither membership in the ethnic minority nor whatever rationale underlies the tradition of ritually hanging one of its members justifies the ritual killing. Were members of the ethnic majority to defer to the law rather than acting on their own moral judgment, or the moral judgment expressed by the communal norm that sanctions the scapegoat ritual, then they would do better at acting on the moral reasons that actually apply to them. Thus, the existing legal prohibition on killing, which contains no exception for the scapegoat ritual, is legitimate even if members of the ethnic majority wrongly disregard it, and so the law does not succeed at preventing the injustice of the scapegoat ritual. The question is not will subjects *actually* do better if they follow the law that if they act on their own judgment, but *would they* do better if they followed the law than if they acted on their own moral judgment. Although a law permitting but regulating the scapegoat ritual may produce a better outcome, it cannot be morally justified on the grounds

40   Haque, "Law and Morality at War," 85.

that it enhances agents' conformity to morality in the manner that makes law legitimate.

Rodin does acknowledge that the violation of individual rights, including the right to life, can sometimes be morally justifiable as a lesser evil.[41] But the evil avoided must be significantly greater than the evil committed, lest a deontological ethic like the revisionist morality of war collapse into a straightforwardly consequentialist one in which an act is right if it produces the least evil (or the most good). Given that in waging war unjust combatants typically engage in many acts of wrongful killing and assault, the law of war's failure to proscribe such conduct would have to dramatically reduce the number and seriousness of the wrongs that would otherwise occur in order for it to be justified as a lesser evil. Rodin doubts the law of war satisfies that standard. He may be right, but contrary to what he implies, this is not obviously so. For example, suppose that at present reformulating the law of war so that it explicitly condones attacks only by just combatants will make little difference to the occurrence of just wars, while permitting criminal prosecution of law abiding combatants accused of waging an unjust war will lead to many of the outcomes McMahan predicts, including longer wars, a weaker commitment to other rules that aim to limit how war is fought, and an increase in the resentment and hatred that sow the seeds for future conflict. If so, then the existing law of war may produce much less evil than would occur were it reformed so as to closely approximate the revisionist morality of war, or that would take place under any third alternative (including the absence of any law of war at all). Of course, this argument depends on the truth of the aforementioned empirical claims, but then so too does Rodin's conclusion. The key point is that it is impossible to assess the truth of the claim that a rule does, or does not, satisfy the conditions for a lesser evil justification without building an empirical argument as to what the world would be like were we to adopt an alternative rule, or no rule at all. If Rodin remains committed to the claim that at present all such arguments are only speculative, then he ought to conclude that we do not and cannot know whether the existing law of war is justifiable as a lesser evil, rather than asserting that it is not.

Two other features of Rodin's last objection to McMahan merit discussion. The first concerns how we ought to understand the law of war's failure to proscribe unjust combatants' attacks on just combatants. Rodin suggests that the law of war grants both just and unjust combatants a legal liberty or privilege to attack enemy soldiers.[42] As long as they conform to the legal rules governing how and when combatants may be targeted, soldiers do no legal wrong in attacking one another because, unlike civilians, those they attack have no legal right not to be attacked, and this is so regardless of whether they fight with a just cause. In sum, the LOAC "creates a legal

---

[41] Rodin, "Morality and Law in War," 455.
[42] Ibid, 455.

right for certain people to violate the moral rights of others, as a means to achieving a broader desirable end."[43]

Haque disagrees. He maintains that we should conceive of the LOAC as addressed to two sets of actors: combatants and the domestic and international officials who claim jurisdiction over them. With respect to the former, the LOAC does not maintain that as long as they conform to its standards combatants do no moral wrong. Rather, it maintains only that combatants will *do better* at avoiding moral wrongdoing if they act in accordance with the LOAC than if they act on the basis of their own moral judgment. The latter claim is consistent with combatants still committing moral wrongs even if they fight in accordance with the LOAC, most clearly in the case of unjust combatants. As for domestic and international legal officials who claim jurisdiction over the conduct of combatants, Haque argues that they should understand the LOAC as imparting a legal immunity to combatants who adhere to its rules when waging war, not a legal liberty.[44] When the law accords an actor a liberty to perform an act, it maintains that (at least in the eyes of the law) the actor does no wrong when she performs that act. In contrast, when the law accords a legal immunity to actors who perform a particular act, it maintains only that they have a right not to be prosecuted or punished for doing so, not that they did no wrong in acting as they did.

Consider, once again, Rodin's scapegoat example. Perhaps reform of the law that creates a liberty right for the majority to carry out its horrific ritual killing is morally problematic not only because it makes the government or the political community complicit in this injustice, but also because it expresses the view that members of the ethnic minority are of lesser moral importance than are members of the ethnic majority. After all, the state licenses the killing of the former in at least one type of case where it does not license the killing of the latter. But now suppose the reform proposal includes only the creation of a criminal defense akin to diplomatic immunity, that is, one that precludes criminal trial and punishment for a violation of the law prohibiting murder if an actor kills an innocent person as part of the scapegoat ritual. Might this reform enable the state to convey the message that, regardless of the ethnic group to which he or she belongs, no one ought to be killed if he or she has not committed an act the state declares to be one that makes a person liable to defensive force? And might the government sufficiently distance itself from the killing of the scapegoat so that it can claim not to have used him or her as a mere means to advancing a further good? After all, the government does nothing to the scapegoat; all it does is refrain from doing something to those who kill the scapegoat that it is permitted, or perhaps required, to do to those it suspects have wrongly killed

---

[43] Ibid.
[44] Haque, *Law and Morality at War*, 23–30. See also Lazar, "Morality and Law of War," 376. More precisely, the immunity concerns one state's prosecution of another state's combatants under international or domestic law. It does not preclude a state prosecuting its own combatants for violations of its own laws governing war fighting.

someone other than the scapegoat. While opinions may divide on these questions, many will likely conclude that Rodin's objection still hits home; that is, that unless a defense of "scapegoat immunity" is justifiable as a lesser evil – and he implies it is not – such a reform to the law is impermissible. Likewise, in granting immunity to criminal prosecution to all combatants, the law of war necessarily treats attacks on just combatants as a means to preventing other or more rights violations, a course of action that is justifiable only if it is necessary to prevent a far greater evil.[45]

The second feature of Rodin's objection that warrants closer examination is the conception of law on which he relies. Recall that Rodin describes as the purpose of the criminal law the articulation and administration of moral norms. One way to interpret this description is as an endorsement of the concept of law Ronald Dworkin defends. As we saw in Chapter 4, on this account of law, a practice of coercive government counts as a genuinely legal one if and only if it treats all of its subjects with equal concern and respect. Since the proposal to regulate rather than outlaw the scapegoat ritual fails to treat members of the ethnic minority with equal concern and respect, its adoption is inconsistent with government according to the rule of law. Rodin's description of the scapegoat case leaves it unclear whether the society he describes is one that satisfies to an adequate degree the conditions for the rule of law, and so what sort of moral reasoning government officials ought to use when making, applying, and enforcing the law. For the reasons described in Chapter 5, however, we may well conclude that international relations is not a context in which human interactions are subject to the rule of law. If so, then when we evaluate the law of war we ought to rely on strategic moral reasoning, not the principled moral reasoning incumbent on officials in a genuine legal order. Specifically, we should ask whether the existing rules best serve to advance the twin goals of mitigating the injustices endemic to human interaction in the absence of the rule of law, and advancing the goal of realizing the rule of law in domains of human interaction where it currently does not exist. Thus, we can agree with Rodin that genuine law ought not to be made or identified on the basis of strategic or instrumental reasoning, but deny that the law of war is genuine law, in the sense synonymous with government in accordance with the rule of law. In other words, Rodin errs when he assumes that the sort of moral reasoning appropriate for identifying permissible uses of force in conditions characterized by the rule of law ought to be employed as well to identify the rules that ought to guide actors in circumstances where those conditions are not met.[46]

---

[45] Haque's defense of a legal immunity for combatants who adhere to the law of war suggests he thinks it can be justified as a lesser evil. See ibid, 28–9.

[46] Reliance on the distinction between the form of moral reasoning appropriate to these two types of circumstance coheres with a description of war as necessarily a social practice in which participants cannot be treated with equal concern and respect. That is why we have a fundamental moral obligation to expand the rule of law, and in so doing, eliminate the occurrence of war. This line of argument coheres nicely with the one presented in the next section.

IV A HUMANITARIAN DEFENSE OF THE LOAC

Thus far, all of the theorists we have considered take the purpose of the law of war to be the advancement of respect for combatants' and noncombatants' individual moral rights.

Walzer maintains that the existing law of war serves this goal by communicating or publicizing the true moral principles governing the use of force in war, which include the *moral* equality of combatants and a moral prohibition on targeting civilians. While Rodin agrees with Walzer that the law should "articulate and make administrable" the morality of war, he embraces a revisionist morality of war and so maintains that this requires significant revisions to the content of the law of war (or at least to its interpretation). McMahan and Haque share Rodin's belief that the content of the existing law of war deviates from the true (revisionist) morality of war, but nevertheless defend compliance with it on the grounds that this will produce fewer rights violations than will occur if Rodin's demands for reform are met. Thus, they broadly concur with Walzer regarding the content of a morally defensible law of war, although they offer a different account of why a morally defensible law of war ought to have that content.

Janina Dill and Henry Shue argue for an alternative approach to morally evaluating the law of war, one that eschews a concern with individual rights and embraces instead a humanitarian concern with minimizing killing, maiming, and the destruction of property.[47] They take as the starting point for their assessment of the law of war the fact that it addresses agents who have already chosen to resort to war.[48] Given that these agents are already committed to the use of military force to achieve some goal, the most the law of war can do to affect their conduct is to channel it in ways that limit the death and destruction that are part and parcel of waging war. Dill and Shue maintain that a law of war that prohibits any conduct on the part of combatants not directly related to weakening the military forces of the enemy best serves this goal. A more restrictive set of rules will achieve less uptake among combatants, and so fail to prevent some of the harm that could have been avoided were the law less demanding but internalized to a greater degree and/or by a greater number of combatants. Of course, it might be possible to achieve even higher levels of compliance with a less restrictive set of rules. However, the more permissive content of those rules will result in the occurrence of more harm than would occur under

---

[47] Janina Dill and Henry Shue, "Limiting the Killing in War: Military Necessity and the St. Petersburg Assumption," *Ethics and International Affairs* 26, 3 (2012): 311–33. For a similar argument, see Tamar Meisels, "In Defense of the Defenseless: The Morality of the Laws of War," *Political Studies* 60, 4 (2012): 919–35.

[48] Dill and Shue do not deny that moral and legal norms also govern the decision to go to war; rather, their claim is only that the law of war addresses those who have already chosen to resort to war. The law of war should be understood to express a conditional claim: *if* you have chosen to go to war, *then* you ought to fight in accordance with these rules. See Shue, "Morality of War?" 105.

rules that limited the conduct of war to acts that directly contributed to weakening the enemy's military forces.

Dill and Shue maintain that their proposed standard for morally evaluating the law of war justifies both of the features under investigation in this chapter, namely, the fact that the law of war draws no distinctions between just and unjust combatants, and the fact that it prohibits intentional attacks on civilians but not on combatants. They emphasize, however, that their moral defense of the law of war "does not even have the pretense of providing a moral justification for wounds and deaths among combatants on the individual level."[49] Indeed, Dill and Shue's humanitarian case for the law of war pays no attention at all to justice, or to the vindication of individual rights. This conclusion may seem hard to square with their claim that the law of war serves to "protect the moral rights of many civilians to life and physical security."[50] But while the law may well have this effect, Dill and Shue do not ground the prohibition on targeting noncombatants in the fact that they have done nothing to make themselves liable to defensive force (assuming this is the case). Rather, they argue that war is not the kind of social practice that can distribute benefits and burdens in response to personal desert; it is not an activity that tracks, even roughly, moral responsibility for conduct that makes one liable or not liable to death or injury.[51] If this is an essential feature of war, as Dill and Shue maintain, then any attempt to elaborate rules for war that make its conduct just, meaning largely respectful of individual moral rights, is doomed to fail. The most we can hope to do is to make war less awful. As Dill and Shue write, "limiting the further harms and wrongs issuing from activity that ought not to be occurring at all is a morally distasteful, yet morally vital, enterprise at the heart of the laws for the conduct of war."[52]

McMahan and Haque might concede that the content of the law of war will *inevitably* diverge significantly from the content of the morality of war, and yet still maintain that the protection of individual rights, rather than the minimization of death and destruction, provides the standard we should employ to select among competing legal rules. After all, they could say, given the choice between a rule that does better at advancing the protection of individual rights but worse at minimizing overall harm, and a rule that does the opposite, we ought to choose the former (unless the latter rule is a lesser evil). Even if we assume the truth of revisionist just war theory, however, it may be that the nature of war raises insurmountable barriers to identifying the legal rules that do best at enhancing conformity to it. Instead, the kind of evidence we are able to gather regarding the effects, or likely effects, of various rules may concern only their impact on the incidence of death, injury, and

---

[49] Dill and Shue, "Limiting the Killing," 322.
[50] Ibid, 323.
[51] They point out that in this respect war is like the market, which is also a social practice ill-suited to allocating burdens and benefits in line with personal desert or moral virtue.
[52] Ibid, 326.

destruction of property. If so, then not only should individuals not rely on revisionist just war theory to guide their conduct in war, legislators ought not to rely on it when considering which reforms, if any, ought to be made to the law of war.

Rodin contends that Dill and Shue make the same error as McMahan, namely, disregarding the fact that fundamental moral rights impose constraints on the content of the law. In offering a humanitarian moral defense of the law of war, they embrace a strategy of permissive regulation, one that condones certain wrongful killing on the grounds that it leads to less overall suffering than would occur under any alternative rules. Rodin asserts that a proper respect for individual rights bars such consequentialist reasoning, however. To make his case, he asks whether it would have been permissible in 1806 to subject the slave trade to strict legal regulation rather than outright prohibition, if there had been good evidence that the former would better protect the victims of slavery than would the latter.[53] His answer is no, of course. Shue offers a twofold response.[54] First, he emphasizes that a humanitarian moral defense of the law of war does not imply that combatants act rightly as long as they comply with the (morally best) law of war. Rather, he maintains only that the most we can expect of rules that actually serve to guide the conduct of agents who have already decided to go to war is that they limit the death, damage, and destruction they cause. The humanitarian argument is premised on a claim regarding what is possible, not what is (morally) optimal. Second, and relatedly, the adoption of a policy of permissive regulation is compatible with efforts to eliminate the occurrence of war. Regarding the legality of the slave trade, then, the ex ante question is whether its prohibition *together with some further set of policies* will better advance the goal of reducing the slave trade than will some form of permissive regulation *together with some further set of policies* (which might include prohibition at a later date). To answer that question, we need to know how different legal regimes are likely to shape actors' conduct, and what supporting policies are likely to be adopted. The parallel conclusion holds vis-à-vis the regulation of war; an incremental approach along many fronts may prove a better strategy for reducing the incidence of war and the injustices endemic to it than a sweeping legal prohibition. Of course, each of these replies reflects a commitment to a form of consequentialist reasoning that Rodin rejects.

The humanitarian defense of the law of war provides one way to understand Shue's claim that the morality of war just is the morally best law of war. War is a type of social practice necessarily at odds with respect for individual dignity, or the treatment of all individuals with respect for even their basic moral rights. When it comes to the conduct of war, we must lower our moral aspirations and focus only on channeling violence in ways that make the inevitable moral toll less calamitous. What morality requires of us vis-à-vis the conduct of war is that we identify the

---

53   Rodin, "Morality and Law in War," 460.
54   Shue, "Laws of War," 282–4.

conventional codes of conduct, including the law of war, that best serve this practical goal. Once we do so, we have identified the morality of war; there are no other standards of right conduct, especially ones that are grounded in individual rights, that apply to participants in war.

This position necessitates an awkward balancing act when it comes to the moral assessment of just combatants who comply with the morally best law of war. Do they act justifiably? If a morally justified act is one that conforms to the moral rule that applies to acts of that type, then the answer would seem to be yes; by hypothesis, our combatants adhere to the morally best rules for waging war. Yet war inevitably involves terrible harm inflicted on those who do not appear to be liable to such harm. Do they really have no basis for complaint against the combatants who harm them, as the description of the combatants' conduct as morally justified implies? Perhaps, then, just combatants often only act excusably, not justifiably, even when they comply with the morally best law of war. While they still morally wrong some or even all of those they harm, they are not blameworthy for doing so.[55] But now the combatants may complain that if it is not possible for them to wage war in a way that respects individual rights, then they ought not to be charged with wrongdoing when they adhere to the morally best rules for waging war that humans can follow.

There is another way to interpret Shue's claim that the morally best law of war just is the morality of war, however, one at which he sometimes gestures but perhaps does not fully embrace. On this interpretation, the content of our moral rights is a function of the norms we can generally expect human beings to follow, which depends in turn on a number of factors, including the institutional context in which people interact. On this account, the list of acts a person has a moral right that others not perform will vary depending on the context in which she interacts with those others. Note that this does not equate the content of our moral rights with whatever existing (positive) law says it is. Rather, it holds only that the content of our moral rights is determined by the morally best law (together, perhaps, with other social norms), and that the morally best law reflects certain facts about the conditions under which norms successfully structure human interactions. What this account of moral rights does imply, however, is that the content of the moral right not to be killed or injured in the context of war may well differ significantly from the content of the moral right not to be killed or injured in "ordinary" or "peacetime" life.

When it comes to theorizing rules governing the use of force, Shue maintains that the crucial distinction is the cross-cutting one between "the standards, be they moral or legal, for ordinary life and the standards, be they moral or legal, for war."[56] This is so because "the circumstances of war are so different from the context of ordinary life

---

55   This is the position McMahan and Haque take, but as we have seen, they are both less convinced than Dill and Shue that war cannot be fought in a manner consistent with revisionist just war theory, and less concerned by the possibility that the standards of right conduct in war may turn out to be ones with which human beings will normally fail to comply.

56   Shue, "Morality of War?" 88.

that, even when the same fundamental moral touchstones are the reference, the differences in the circumstances yield different specific guidelines."[57] As we have seen, one crucial difference concerns the possibility of reliably determining which actors are liable to defensive force (and, perhaps, what type or amount of force). In addition, Shue argues that the content of the norms governing the use of force must be sensitive to the institutional setting in which they purport to govern human conduct. In domestic life, the reason "one can normally be reasonably expected and morally required to refrain from violent forms of self-help is because the background institutional context, much of it structured by further layers of laws with no analogues in the international arena, generally provides help in the form of the relatively impartial civil institutions, like police and courts, that contribute to the rule of law."[58] In contrast, "war breaks out where impartial institutions are yet to be created or any existing impartial institutions are thought by at least one party to have failed to protect their vital interests."[59] Indeed, wars are doubly anarchic. Not only do they occur in the absence of an effective impartial government that is recognized by all parties as enjoying legitimate authority to resolve disputes over the scope or content of their rights, there is also no one "available to enforce the laws of war except the participants in the war, who must then attempt to enforce the rules upon each other while attempting to defeat each other and avoid death."[60] Therefore "it would hardly be surprising if the best rules that could govern such an anarchic, violent realm as international conflict were, in various ways, disanalogous to the principles governing ordinary life."[61] Shue's reference here to "rules that could govern" reiterates the claim that discussed earlier in this chapter, namely, that a necessary condition for the existence of a norm, moral or legal, is that it be one with which human beings acting in good faith can generally be expected to comply. Taken together, these remarks by Shue point to the conclusion set out in the previous paragraph: the "fundamental moral touchstones" such as human beings' fundamental welfare and agency interests are invariable, but the content of the norms that specify appropriate responses to those "touchstones" vary depending on the social setting in which they actually serve to regulate human conduct.

This context-dependent account of moral rights entails that just combatants who abide by the morally best law of war act justifiably, and not merely excusably.[62] To see why this is so, suppose that among the set of rules regulating the conduct of war with which human beings can generally comply, the one that best reflects the

---

[57]   Ibid, 87. See also Shue, "Laws of War," 272–3.
[58]   Shue, "Laws of War," 273.
[59]   Ibid, 274. Gang wars, then, may often be genuine wars, insofar as they involve parties who rely on force to vindicate what they take to be (or at least proclaim to be) their rights in a context where the state is either ineffective or corrupt.
[60]   Shue, "Morality of War?" 104.
[61]   Ibid, 104.
[62]   Note that a fully worked out theory along the lines suggested in the text would likely characterize a just cause for war, and so just combatants, in terms of the morally best laws regulating resort to war.

fundamental moral touchstones does not prohibit deliberate attacks on those who perform combat functions. It follows that when just combatants intentionally attack individuals who perform combat functions on behalf of the party with whom they are at war, they do not violate those individuals' moral rights. If we keep in mind that on the context-dependent account the demands of justice in war differ from those in ordinary life, that is, where the rule of law provides a generally reliable mechanism for advancing or honoring the fundamental moral touchstones, then these combatants can be accurately described as waging war justly. This is so even if a world in which human beings sometimes resort to war is necessarily an unjust one because it reflects the incomplete reach of government in accordance with the rule of law. Waging war according to the morally best law of war may be the optimal means to achieving that goal, or at least to preventing it from receding even further from humanity's reach, even if it is also a social practice we should ultimately aim to eliminate. Nevertheless, we should not demand that actors comply with the norms that apply to people in a world in which all human interactions are governed according to the rule of law when they live in a world that does not satisfy that condition.

9

International Criminal Law: Crimes Against Humanity and Universal Jurisdiction

Although the phrase "crime against humanity" has a long history, the first international prosecutions for the commission of crimes against humanity took place at the Nuremberg Trials that followed the Allied victory over Nazi Germany in the Second World War. Crimes against humanity were also among the crimes for which individuals were tried by subsequent ad hoc international criminal tribunals, including the International Military Tribunal for the Far East (the Tokyo Trials), the International Criminal Tribunal for the Former Yugoslavia (ICTY), and the International Criminal Tribunal for Rwanda (ICTR). In 1998, 120 states voted in favor of the Rome Statute, an international treaty creating a permanent International Criminal Court (ICC), and following ratification of the treaty by sixty states, the ICC was formally established in 2002. The Rome Statute empowers the ICC to prosecute individuals for crimes against humanity if they are citizens of a state that is party to the treaty, or if the act took place in the territory of a state that is party to the treaty, or if prosecution is authorized by the UN Security Council under Chapter VII of the UN Convention. Importantly, the ICC is intended to complement, not replace, national criminal systems; it prosecutes cases only when states are unwilling or unable to do so.[1]

In this chapter, we will address two philosophical questions raised by the practice of subjecting those alleged to have committed crimes against humanity to international prosecution. The first is a conceptual question: what, exactly, is a crime against humanity (CAH)? In what sense, if any, are crimes against humanity wrongs done to "humanity?" What distinguishes crimes against humanity from other types of crime? Does the label "crime against humanity" identify a distinctive wrong committed by those who perform such acts? Does a proper understanding of the concept of a crime against humanity explain why legal officials charged with drafting an international criminal code have insisted that it include the crime of a crime against humanity? The second philosophical question we will consider is

---

[1] International Criminal Court, "How the Court Works," available at www.icc-cpi.int/about/how-the-court-works (last accessed December 11, 2019).

a normative one: what justifies the *international* prosecution of actors accused of committing CAH? More precisely, what entitles a court to exercise criminal jurisdiction over an individual even in the absence of any connection between it and either the alleged perpetrator or the alleged victim of the crime? In terms that may be familiar, what justifies a court's exercise of universal jurisdiction?

Each of these questions has a doctrinal answer. For example, we might look to the Rome Statute creating the International Criminal Court for a description of a crime against humanity.[2] Likewise, we might locate the justification for a particular tribunal's right to prosecute certain actors for CAH in an international legal norm granting it that jurisdiction, for instance, the fact that the state in which the alleged crime took place is a party to the Rome Statute, or the existence of a customary international legal norm granting any domestic court universal jurisdiction over crimes against humanity.

These doctrinal answers fail to fully satisfy, however. With respect to the jurisdictional question, a doctrinal answer presumes the law's legitimacy, whereas what we seek is an explicit defense of that presumption, or should it prove impossible to provide one, an alternative justification that may require and serve to guide the reform of existing legal doctrine. For instance, in light of the criticisms enumerated in Chapter 6, we may doubt that state consent provides either a necessary or sufficient condition for the ICC's right to prosecute and punish individuals accused of committing crimes against humanity. Indeed, as we will see, the exercise of extraterritorial jurisdiction over CAH may mark an important shift away from a state-centered international order and toward an individual or human-centered one. A philosophical theory of international criminal jurisdiction may serve to make explicit the new understanding of what legitimates certain international acts immanent in this evolving practice. At the same time, by defending the new practice against proponents of the old one, and critiquing rival explanations of its legitimacy, particular theories of international criminal jurisdiction may also contribute to its development.

Likewise, our interest in the concept of a crime against humanity stems primarily from the role it plays (or should play) in the identification of what the law is, and what it ought to be. For instance, how should judges on the International Criminal Court understand, and so apply, the Rome Statute's requirement that murder, rape, etc., count as CAH only if they are part of a widespread and systematic attack? Likewise, how should the ICC interpret the Rome Statute's inclusion of "other inhumane acts of a similar character" in its enumeration of the acts that can count as crimes against humanity? If Dworkin is right when he maintains that in order to identify the content of the law we must engage in constructive interpretation, then we cannot answer these questions without at least implicitly appealing to the

---

[2] Rome Statute of the International Criminal Court, Part 2, Article 7, available at www.icc-cpi.int /resource-library/Documents/RS-Eng.pdf (last accessed December 11, 2019).

concept of a crime against humanity; that is, to an understanding of the distinctive wrong done by those who commit such acts that informs or is immanent in successive attempts by international actors to make explicit and precise the kind of conduct they aim to proscribe.[3] Legal positivists may well contest Dworkin's claim that in answering these or other questions regarding the characterization of a crime against humanity judges merely identify what the law is. Rather, positivists will argue they are making new law. Nevertheless, many positivists will also maintain that when they legislate these officials draw on particular understandings of what makes an act a CAH (a descriptive claim), and that one or another characterization of a crime against humanity is the one they ought to employ when they do so (a normative claim). Indeed, incontrovertible examples of legislation clearly illustrate the crucial role played by the concept of a crime against humanity. Consider, for example, the fact that the Rome Statute eliminates the requirement contained in the earlier Nuremberg Charter and the Statute creating the ICTY that such acts be connected to an armed conflict. Does this mark a moral improvement in international criminal law, or has it instead made it worse? It is hard to see how we can answer that question without getting clear on what a CAH is, or reflecting on the purpose(s) the criminalization of CAH serves.

Since our concern is with the concept of a crime against humanity that informs or is immanent in international criminal law, we ought to begin our inquiry with a review of attempts by participants in that practice to state explicitly the features of a CAH, whether in statutes or in judicial opinions. We can then try to extract from this collection of legal materials certain core features that appear to be essential to the concept, in light of which we can offer analyses that distinguish CAH from other types of crime, and perhaps also that justify international prosecution of those who commit them. While that exercise is an invaluable one, here we will simply rely on the conclusions of several theorists who have carried it out.[4] They largely agree that these core features include:

(1) **A policy element**: CAH are committed, instigated, or at least tolerated as a matter of policy either by agents who exercise de facto (and perhaps also de jure) rule over the victims and the territory in which they reside, or by agents who are attempting to establish themselves as de facto (and perhaps also de jure) rulers over the victims and/or the territory in which they reside.

(2) **A collective element**: Victims of CAH are targeted in virtue of their membership in a group, community, or civilian population, and are therefore denied their individuality.

---

[3] See the discussion in Chapter 4, section II.
[4] See David Luban, "A Theory of Crimes Against Humanity," *Yale Journal of International Law* 29, 1 (2004): 93–108; Massimo Renzo, "Crimes Against Humanity and the Limits of International Criminal Law," *Law and Philosophy* 31, 4 (2012): 443–4.

(3) **A severity element**: CAH include, but are also limited to, the most severe evils human beings can inflict on one another, including murder, rape, torture, enslavement, forcible expulsion, and forcible sterilization. Following common practice, I will refer to these as crimes of the murder type and crimes of the persecution type.[5]

(4) **An international element**: CAH are distinctly international crimes in two respects. First, states' rights to conduct their domestic affairs free from interference by other states, acting alone or in concert, does not extend to the commission of CAH, or arguably to immunity from prosecution and punishment for former officials who committed such acts while in office.[6] Second, the standing to prosecute and punish individuals for CAH does not depend on any "traditional jurisdictional link or *nexus* with the perpetrator, the victim, or the offence."[7] In the modern era, the exercise of criminal jurisdiction across international boundaries typically requires that a state or group of states assert a tangible connection to the alleged crime; for example, that it was committed by or against one of the state's citizens. This is not the case with CAH, which are characterized instead as of interest to all members of the international community.

We will proceed on the assumption that these features characterize the core of the concept of a crime against humanity. Nevertheless, it is important to recognize that judgments regarding the core features of the concept of CAH are always open to contestation on the basis of new readings of past practice, as well as in response to the continuing evolution of contemporary international (and domestic) legal practice.

In the next section, we critically examine several attempts to elaborate a concept of crimes against humanity that fits and justifies the policy, collective, and severity elements. These features serve to distinguish crimes against humanity from other types of crime, spell out one sense in which such acts wrong humanity, and point toward a justification for their inclusion in an *international* criminal code. In the following section, we consider two approaches to answering the jurisdictional question. Each begins with the claim that CAH constitute public wrongs, and then attempts to demonstrate that the "public" in question consists of all human beings. They differ in the arguments they offer for the latter conclusion, however. While some theorists argue that the dangers CAH pose to all human beings provides the moral grounds for universal jurisdiction, others argue that it is membership in an

---

5 See Luban, "Crimes Against Humanity," 98–9.
6 On this last point, see the International Law Commission's controversial Draft Article stating that immunity *ratione materiae* does not apply in the case of CAH. International Law Commission, Report on the Work of Its Sixty-Ninth Session, UN Doc. A/72/10 (September 11, 2017), available at https://legal .un.org/ilc/reports/2017/.
7 Alejandro Chehtman, "Contemporary Approaches to the Philosophy of Crimes Against Humanity," *International Criminal Law Review* 14, 4–5 (2014): 818.

(emerging) moral or political global community that makes perpetrators of CAH answerable to courts that act on behalf of all humanity.

I THE CONCEPTUAL QUESTION

Richard Vernon, David Luban, and Larry May all offer similar explanations for the policy element of CAH; that is, the fact that legal doctrine characterizes such acts as undertaken or condoned by states or state-like actors.[8] Each begins his argument with the observation that we need government to protect us from the worst types of treatment that humans can visit on one another. In most circumstances, life under government is prudentially superior to life in the state of nature. Unfortunately, the cure for the ills of the state of nature, namely, government, can itself become a grave threat to the welfare and even the survival of (some of) the governed. As Vernon points out, this is particularly true when government takes the form of a modern state, which combines large-scale administrative capacity, local authority (or de facto legitimacy), and territorial control, meaning both de facto and often de jure control over who may enter or exit the state's territory.[9] Together these features account for the potential of the modern state to become a far greater threat to human beings than what they would face in a state of nature. The concept of a crime against humanity reflects this fact. As Vernon writes, crimes against humanity involve "a systematic inversion of the jurisdictional resources of the state."[10] Luban describes such acts as "politics gone cancerous," a metaphor that invokes the image of institutions necessary for the flourishing of the body politic metastasizing to become a threat to the security and survival of some of its constituents, and so to the flourishing of the political community as currently constituted.[11]

Now consider the collective element, the idea that victims of crimes against humanity are necessarily targeted qua members of a group, community, or civilian population. Each of the aforementioned theorists attempts to explicate this element, and to defend it as an essential component of a crime against humanity. Before we examine their arguments, however, it may be worthwhile to consider the contrary position, namely, that we ought to abandon the presumption that crimes against humanity involve essentially the targeting of individuals qua member of a group, community, or civilian population. Advocates of this view might adopt one or more of the following strategies to reconcile it with the doctrinal requirement that CAH target a civilian population. First, they might argue that this doctrinal element

[8] Richard Vernon, "What Is Crime Against Humanity?" *Journal of Political Philosophy* 10, 3 (2002): 241–6; "Crime Against Humanity: A Defense of the 'Subsidiarity' View," *Canadian Journal of Law and Jurisprudence* 26, 1 (2013): 230–3; Luban, "Crimes Against Humanity"; Larry May, *Crimes Against Humanity: A Normative Account* (Cambridge: Cambridge University Press, 2004).
[9] Vernon, "What Is Crime Against Humanity?," 243.
[10] Ibid, 242.
[11] Luban, "Crimes Against Humanity," 116–19. For May's argument that CAH constitute violations of a Hobbesian justification for state sovereignty, see May, *Crimes Against Humanity*, p. 88.

simply reflects the historically contingent fact that the category of CAH was introduced to supplement the concept of a war crime, since that concept could not be used to prohibit or prosecute acts of the murder or persecution type outside the context of a war (and, arguably, until quite recently outside the context of an international as opposed to internal armed conflict). Second, they might argue that just as the notion of "attack" in the Rome Statute's definition of a CAH as requiring "an attack on a civilian population" ought to be understood to require multiple acts of the murder and/or persecution type, so too "population" ought to be understood to require multiple victims.[12] Finally, and perhaps most importantly given the rationale for developing a philosophical theory of crimes against humanity, a person who concludes that acts of the murder or persecution type count as CAH if and only if they are examples of politics gone cancerous may argue that the doctrinal characterization ought to evolve to reflect that fact. Whether as a matter of constructive interpretation or of legislation, the "civilian population" element ought to eliminated from the legal definition of a CAH, thereby making a single murder committed as a matter of policy a CAH, collapsing the distinction between rape as a war crime and rape as a crime against humanity, and rendering moot the need for theorists to explain the sense in which CAH deny their victims individuality by targeting them qua member of a group.

Whatever the merits of this strategy, Vernon, Luban, and May do not pursue it. Instead, each offers a different interpretation of the idea that CAH necessarily target individuals qua members of a group or community. May writes that:

> [I]f an individual is treated according to group-characteristics that are out of that person's control, there is a straightforward assault on that person's humanity. It is as if the individuality of the person were being ignored, and the person were being treated as a mere representative of a group that the person has not chosen to join.[13]

On May's account, then, murder, rape, torture, and so on, appear to count as CAH only if they are individuality denying, and what makes them individuality denying is that the victim is targeted in virtue of his or her perceived membership in an ascriptive group, meaning one that it is not within her power to join or leave.

Massimo Renzo raises a number of objections to May's argument that crimes against humanity assault a person's humanity by treating him or her according to characteristics that are out of her control.[14] For example, he points out that victims may be targeted for membership in groups that they choose to join (or that they

---

[12] Note that neither interpretation need commit a defender to the claim that a state does no wrong if, as a matter of policy, it targets a single person for a single act of murder or rape. Rather, he or she may argue that at least in the current circumstances the morally best international criminal prohibition is one that generates liability to international prosecution and punishment only in the case of multiple attacks and multiple victims.

[13] May, *Crimes Against Humanity*, p. 85.

[14] Massimo Renzo, "A Criticism of the International Harm Principle," *Criminal Law and Philosophy* 4, 3 (2010): 272–3; Chehtman, "Contemporary Approaches," 826.

could choose to leave). If people are targeted in virtue of their being Jews, it makes no difference whether they are members of that community because they were born into it (and have remained part of it) or because they voluntarily chose to join it by converting to Judaism. Assuming such attacks can count as crimes against humanity, it cannot be the case that they necessarily wrong their victims by targeting them in virtue of features over which they have no control. Renzo also observes that people may be attacked in virtue of properties over which they have no control other than membership in an ascriptive group, such as a woman targeted by a rapist because she is naturally attractive. If it is being attacked because of a feature over which one has no control that defines an assault on a person's humanity, then there is no justification for limiting crimes against humanity to attacks on people qua members of a group or community.

While these objections are compelling, there are a few places in May's discussion of the individuality-denying nature of crimes against humanity that point to a different way of characterizing that harm, one that does not appeal to denials of individual choice or autonomy. This characterization comes through in May's attempt to defend the claim that CAH not only deny the individuality of those who are actually murdered, raped, and so on, but of each and every human being. Humanity, he writes, "can be harmed when its members are harmed in certain ways; that is, when the members are not treated as fellow humans but as merely members of other less inclusive communities."[15] One way to interpret this remark is as follows. Perpetrators of crimes against humanity deny their victims' dignity, by which I mean their status as creatures with moral rights, or creatures entitled in their own right to certain types of treatment. Those who commit CAH explicitly or implicitly deny that it is being human that entitles a person not to be murdered, raped, tortured, and so on, and instead assert that only humans who are, for example, Christian, or "European," enjoy that status. This is the sense in which CAH are individuality denying; those who commit such acts deny that dignity attaches to each and every human being as such, that every individual is entitled to certain forms of treatment in his or her own right, independent of his or her membership in any particular group or community. It is this expressive element of murder, rape, torture, and other such acts, committed as a CAH that distinguishes such acts from "ordinary" murder, rape, or torture. Of course, CAH are not unique in conveying this individuality-denying message; rather, that property characterizes all hate crimes (or broader still, all hate wrongs). What distinguishes CAH from other hate crimes is that they are limited to the severest evils humans can inflict on one another, committed as a matter of policy by a state or state-like actor, and are properly subject to international prosecution and punishment.

---

[15]   Larry May, "Humanity, International Crime, and the Rights of Defendants," *Ethics and International Affairs* 20, 3 (2006): 376.

The characterization of CAH as a subset of hate crimes easily accommodates the fact that victims sometimes choose to become members of the group in virtue of which they are targeted. Any attack on a Jew that targets her in virtue of her perceived membership in a group characterized as not human denies her individuality in the relevant sense, regardless of whether she or anyone else attributes her identity as a Jew to a choice she made. Likewise, the characterization of CAH as a subset of hate crimes can justify the intuition that certain attacks do not count as CAH even if the victims are targeted in virtue of some unchosen characteristic, for example, being naturally attractive. All we need claim is that the intuition reflects two assumptions: first, that the perpetrator does not intend to express the view that the characteristic in question renders the victim not human, and, second, that in the social context in which it is carried out the attack is not generally understood to express that position.

But what about May's claim that CAH harm each and every human being? How does the treatment of individual Jews as not human in virtue of their status as Jews, or of individual Tutsis as not human in virtue of their status as Tutsis, set back the interests of non-Jews or non-Tutsis in being recognized as human, as entitled in their own right to certain forms of treatment? One way of answering this question, which I discuss in the next section, looks to the effects of CAH, and in particular, the causal contribution that any particular campaign of CAH makes to the likelihood that others will become victims of a similar campaign. Apart from their effects on people's welfare, however, hate crimes also harm (or, perhaps better, wrong) people by perpetuating a lie regarding the grounds of dignity. Specifically, such acts convey the false message that it is membership in some ascriptive group or (imagined) community, one less inclusive than that of all human beings, that makes a person human in the moral sense synonymous with a creature with dignity. Even those who for any number of contingent reasons are at little risk of suffering setbacks to their welfare as a result of this lie are nevertheless wronged by those who assert it, something that on this account of the concept perpetrators of crimes against humanity necessarily do. All human beings, then, may rightly claim to be the victims of any campaign of crimes against humanity, for each and every human being may demand that he or she be recognized as an individual with dignity, entitled in his or her own right to certain forms of treatment.[16]

Both Vernon and Luban begin their analyses of the collective element of CAH with the observation that human beings are creatures who need to live in community with others. Crimes against humanity are particularly abhorrent, Vernon writes, because they are assaults on whole communities; that is, on individuals living in community with one another: "It is in communities that the primary requirements

---

[16] The claim that perpetrators of CAH wrong all human beings should not be confused with the claim that they wrong or harm them all equally. Rather, the immediate victims of CAH suffer additional wrongs, such as rape or torture. A victim of rape perpetrated as a CAH does not suffer a *greater* wrong than a victim of "ordinary" rape. Rather, she suffers the *additional* expressive wrong of being denied the status of a creature with dignity.

of human vulnerability are addressed, and so to assault communities is to heighten vulnerability to the maximum extent, by removing the principal line of defense against it."[17] Widespread or systematic crimes of the murder and/or persecution type degrade and, in some cases, destroy the fabric of the particular communities in which practically all of us must live if we are to avoid the evils of the most extreme form of a state of nature, one characterized not only by the absence of the state but by the absence of any communal relations of mutual trust and mutual reliance. Although these communities may sometimes be composed of individuals who belong to the same racial, ethnic, religious, or political group, they need not be. It is a mistake, therefore, to interpret the phrase "targeted in virtue of being a member of a group" narrowly to mean member of an ascriptive group or, to anticipate another interpretation of the collective element discussed below, member of a group organized for political agency. CAH are not attacks on individuals qua member of a group; rather, they are attacks on individuals living in groups, or more precisely, in forms of communal life that serve to mitigate the threats the natural and social world pose to every person's life and well-being. It is because living in community with others is something that practically all human beings must do to survive that attacks that severely degrade and destroy victims' ability to do so are properly labeled crimes against humanity.

Luban, too, argues that because practically all humans need to live in groups to survive and to lead flourishing lives, we all have an interest in not being subject to attack simply in virtue of being a member of a group.[18] In part, this argument is a prudential one: since, by our very nature, we cannot avoid living in groups, the possibility that we will be targeted for attack simply because we belong, or are perceived to belong, to a particular group poses a grave risk to our well-being. This risk is distinct from ones we bear in virtue of properties we have as individuals; for example, a particular interaction we have with another person, or the particular arrangement of features that figure in our unique appearance or personality. It is also distinct from the risk posed by random acts of violence, in which the property in virtue of which the victim is targeted is incidental or peripheral to that individual's identity and life. What distinguishes CAH from "ordinary" crimes are not the injuries done to the victim; a murder victim may well suffer the same setback to her interest in life regardless of whether she is targeted qua member of a group, or as an individual, or simply because she is in the wrong place at the wrong time. Rather, what distinguishes CAH murder from "ordinary" murder, and so what justifies enacting a criminal prohibition that specifically addresses such acts, is the fact that they originate in the belief that mere membership in a group can make people liable to the most horrendous treatment.

[17] Vernon, "What Is Crime Against Humanity?," 244.
[18] Luban, "Crimes Against Humanity," 111–20, 137–9.

Intertwined with this prudential rationale for criminalizing certain forms of conduct that target individuals qua members of a group is a second, moral, argument. It begins with the claim that human beings have a *right* not to be treated merely as a member of a group but also as an individual. That is, every human being can justifiably demand that he or she be recognized as an agent whose identity and life plan is not exhausted by, or reducible to, being a member of a particular group and working to advance that group's ends or flourishing. CAH wrong victims by violating this right, as well as by violating their rights to life, to bodily integrity, and so on, whereas ordinary murders do not. As Luban writes, crimes against humanity violate the victim's individuality, "respect for which requires that even my enemies must attack me because of who I am, not merely because of what group I belong to."[19] Note that this account, too, entails that individuals targeted for attack qua member of *any* group, and not merely a racial, ethnic, religious, or political one, suffer the denial of individuality that distinguishes murder, rape, and so on, as a CAH from "ordinary" murder or rape.

Luban's explanation of the distinctive wrong done to victims of CAH may appear to entail that states act unjustly whenever, as a matter of policy, they target people for certain treatment in virtue of their membership in a group. Although some might embrace this conclusion, others will argue that religious exemptions or selective hiring or admissions policies that target individuals qua members of particular groups serve to advance or realize justice. The crucial point to note here is that Luban's argument does not entail that it is always wrong to target people qua members of a group, only that doing so is wrong when it also denies their individuality. A policy of exempting individuals qua members of the Sikh religious community from a law requiring motorcycle riders to wear helmets does not deny the individuality of any Sikh man. Whether the law is nevertheless unjust is a separate question we need not explore here.

Although Luban describes the individuality-denying character of attacks that target individuals qua member of a group as an assault on the victims' nature as political animals, there does not appear to be anything specifically political about them. One way to make good on the idea that perpetrators of crimes against humanity target their victims as *political* animals is to argue that CAH are necessarily attacks on individuals qua members of a group organized for political struggle, or one perceived to be capable of becoming so organized in the future. By "political struggle," I mean any attempt to shape the terms on which members of a given community ought to live with one another. In light of the fact that human beings have different and sometimes conflicting conceptions of justice and the good life, as well as the scarcity of resources for realizing both, political struggle or contestation is

---

[19] Luban, "Crimes Against Humanity," 117. Even random attacks count as targeting me for who I am if we understand that broadly to include properties that are peripheral to my identity and life plan; for instance, being the person who happens to be walking by when a would-be gang member decides to commit the murder required for initiation into the gang.

an unavoidable feature of all human societies. One measure of the health or flourishing of a political community is its success at managing political struggle. The more members of the community view its law and legal institutions as legitimate, and, conversely, the less political order relies on prudential calculation, the healthier it is. Politics can often be unhealthy. But it turns cancerous or destructive only when actors adopt the goal of destroying the ability of certain others to engage in political struggle with them. Murder obviously serves this end, but so too can rape, torture, and so on.

In the modern world, political contestation typically takes place within or between states. CAH occur when some or all of the actors within the territory over which a state or state-like actor exercises de facto (and perhaps also de jure) control adopt the goal of severely degrading or destroying the ability of certain other actors within that territory to engage them in political struggle.[20] CAH reflect a shift in the perpetrators' conception of those with whom they are engaged in political struggle (or with whom they anticipate being so engaged) from adversaries to enemies.[21] Rather than viewing those individuals as partners in the pursuit of a common good the specifics of which are a matter of dispute, perpetrators of CAH conceive of them as an existential threat to the common good of a narrower or more exclusive political community.

The foregoing account explains the sense in which perpetrators' of CAH target their victims qua political animals. Since human beings manifest their individuality partly through political action, attacks on people qua political animals are necessarily individuality denying. But in what sense do such attacks necessarily target a person in virtue of his or her membership in a group? The answer is that politics is generally, and perhaps necessarily, a struggle between groups. This is so in two respects. First, conceptions of justice and of the good typically and perhaps necessarily reflect communal views, in other words, the views of individuals who are embedded in particular, historical, concrete communities. When individuals engage in political action, therefore, they almost always advance a conception of justice or the good they share with certain others. Second, and relatedly, in practically any human society successful political action, the actual exercise of governance, is a collective undertaking not an individual one. If the destruction of the victims' ability to engage in political action is an essential feature of CAH, and if individuals necessarily engage in political action qua members of specific groups in the two senses just specified, then it follows that those who perpetrate CAH must target their victims qua members of those groups.

---

[20]   The international crime of aggression, in contrast, characterizes cancerous political struggles that span the de facto (and perhaps also de jure) territorial jurisdiction of two or more states. Note that here, too, institutions or actors occupying certain roles that serve to protect people against threats to their survival and well-being become threats to it.

[21]   Chantal Mouffe, *The Democratic Paradox* (London: Verso, 2000), pp. 102–3; Michael Ignatieff, "Enemies vs. Adversaries," *New York Times*, October 16, 2013, available at www.nytimes.com/2013/10/17/opinion/enemies-vs-adversaries.html (last accessed December 11, 2019).

This explanation of why CAH necessarily target individuals qua members of a group may appear to be in tension with the claim that humans exercise their individuality in part by attempting to shape the terms on which they live with others in ways that reflect their individual conceptions of justice and the good. If these conceptions are those of the communities in which individuals are embedded, then would it not be more accurate to describe individual human beings as merely the mechanism whereby corporate agents engage in political struggle? Indeed, is this not the way in which perpetrators of CAH conceive of their victims, and doesn't the fact that politics is necessarily a collective undertaking warrant that conception? It does not; rather, this conception reflects a reductive, totalizing, conception of political identity that suppresses individual agency and creativity. It does so in part by ignoring the fact that political struggle takes place within groups as well as between them, from the most intimate communities of family and friends to the far larger communities of conationals, compatriots, and coreligionists. And it does so in part by ignoring the fact that human beings can and often do belong to multiple communities with cross-cutting membership. People may be members of different nations but the same religion, or belong to different racial groups but the same professional community, or participate in the same cultural community while serving in different political parties, and so on. CAH have their origin in a worldview that denies this multiplicity, one that substitutes for the diversity that actually characterizes human individuals and societies a picture not only of their opponents but also of themselves as uniform or identical. Theirs is a world of stereotypes, where there is only the Jew, the Muslim, the black, the homosexual, the communist, the intellectual, with individual Jews, blacks, communists and the rest but tokens of the type. All one needs to know about others is what *type* they are, since that is all there is to know about them. Moreover, when actors view these normative identities as exclusive, when being Jewish, black, and so on, is perceived not just as a part of an individual's identity but its entirety, they conceive of political struggle as a zero-sum game rather than one in which it is possible to work together in pursuit of a common good, the flourishing of a single community to which all belong. Of course, even when widespread in a population this mindset need not give rise to mass atrocities, since the power differentials between groups may enable one to use less heinous means to suppress the other. Yet, like a chronic disease, the lingering belief that the other group poses an existential threat to the survival of one's own community can become inflamed by demographic, economic, technological, cultural, and environmental changes, and thereby spur actors to engage in campaigns of murder, rape, torture, "cleansing," and so on as a means to political triumph.

II THE JURISDICTIONAL QUESTION

Having considered in the previous section several characterizations of the concept of a CAH, we turn now to a normative question. What, if anything, morally justifies international prosecution and punishment of actors who commit CAH, whether in the domestic criminal court of a particular state exercising universal jurisdiction, or an international criminal court created by states, such as the International Criminal Tribunal for the former Yugoslavia (ICTY) or the International Criminal Court (ICC)? Two features of extra-territorial prosecution in particular stand in need of a defense. First, the standing to prosecute and punish does not depend on any link between a particular state or international organization and the accused, such as the passive personality principle, which in a limited range of cases grants a state jurisdiction over citizens of other countries who commit crimes against its own citizens outside that state's territory. Second, an actor's liability to prosecution and punishment for the commission of CAH does not depend on the consent of the state that governed the territory where the acts were committed, either at the time the crimes were committed or at the time international prosecution is initiated.[22] These two features of so-called "pure" international criminal law, which includes CAH, constitute a momentous change in international law's doctrinal characterization of state sovereignty. A normative theory of pure international criminal jurisdiction aspires to justify, or in some cases to criticize, that change in legal doctrine.

One place to begin such a theory is with the idea that crimes constitute public wrongs, not merely private ones. If I deliberately deface your car, I commit both a tort and a crime. The former is a private wrong, and in virtue of being the victim of that wrongdoing you have the standing to seek reparation from me in a civil court. The latter is a public wrong, an act of vandalism or malicious trespass, in virtue of which the state has the standing to punish me. But in what sense does my act wrong the "public?" What is it about my defacing *your* property that gives *the state* a right to punish me? Indeed, what explains why only the state has a right to punish me, and not you, or any other third party? On what I will call the prudential account of criminal jurisdiction, the answer is that criminal acts either unjustifiably harm or pose an unjustifiable risk of harm to the "public," that is, to the people whose interests a given practice of criminal proscription, prosecution, and punishment seeks to protect. It is because criminal conduct harms them that the public is entitled to hold perpetrators accountable. In contemporary societies, this right is often exercised via the institutions of the state. In short, acting as their agent, the state has a right to punish people who unjustifiably impose harm or the risk of harm on those individuals who together constitute the public.

Who constitutes the public harmed by crimes against humanity, considered as an international crime? The very label "crimes against humanity" suggests one response, namely, that the public harmed by such acts is composed of all humanity, meaning each and every human being. But how do acts satisfying the doctrinal

The principle of complementarity contained in the Rome Statute, the treaty creating the ICC, states a presumption in favor of domestic prosecution for CAH, but the Court retains a right to initiate criminal proceedings in the event that it (or the UN Security Council) determines that a state has not made a good faith effort to investigate allegations of CAH committed in its territory, regardless of whether that state consents to its doing so.

elements of a CAH committed in Syria, Myanmar, or North Korea, set back all human beings' fundamental interests in security and subsistence? Indeed, how do they even pose a *risk* of such a setback substantial enough to justify all humanity having a right to prosecute those who perpetrate such crimes?

Perhaps they do so by undermining, or threatening to undermine, international peace and security.[23] CAH may spur or perpetuate armed conflicts that spill across state borders, or that draw into such conflicts both neighboring and more distant political communities, or that create anarchic environments in which transnational criminal gangs and political groups engaged in armed political struggle elsewhere can conduct their activities. Yet it not clear that all examples of CAH impact international peace and security, or at least not in a manner that justifies the claim that *all humanity*, acting via the political institutions of a particular state or those of the entire community of states, has the standing to prosecute those who commit them. In some cases, the commission of CAH appear to have little, or no, impact on international peace and security beyond the region in which they take place, even where the incidence of such crimes rises to the level of mass atrocities.[24] Indeed, Renzo points out a morally perverse implication of this rationale for international criminal jurisdiction, namely, that whether such acts qualify as international crimes can turn on whether they take place at a remote location deep in the interior of a state's territory, or instead occur in a region abutting the border of several other states.[25] Consider, too, that if the only reason CAH warrant international prosecution is that they (threaten to) undermine international peace and stability, then punishment for committing such acts will have to be justified on deterrence grounds, in other words, as a form of anticipatory self-defense.[26] Those who reject deterrence as a moral justification for punishment because they think it impermissibly uses convicted criminals as a mere means for promoting others' fundamental interests will need to look elsewhere to justify international prosecution of CAH perpetrators.

Both May and Luban defend an alternative account of how CAH harm all humanity, namely, by making each and every one of us more vulnerable to being murdered, tortured, and so on, simply in virtue of our membership in a particular group.[27] Call this the contagion argument for universal jurisdiction: any instance of CAH threatens to infect other actors all over the world, encouraging them to view individuals belonging to certain groups as "not human," that is, as lacking dignity, or as not entitled to recognition as individuals, or as enemies in a life or death contest between two political communities. Moreover, those who perform CAH model the

---

[23]   May, *Crimes Against Humanity*, pp. 84–8.
[24]   Andrew Altman, "The Persistent Fiction of Harm to Humanity," *Ethics and International Affairs* 20, 3 (2006): 370–2.
[25]   Renzo, "Criticism of the International Harm Principle," 276.
[26]   Chehtman, "Contemporary Approaches," 825.
[27]   May, "Humanity," 374; Luban, Crimes Against Humanity, 138–9.

kind of conduct warranted by such a worldview; as long as they go unchallenged, the very performance of such acts may well be taken as evidence of their justifiability.

The contagion argument rests on an empirical claim the veracity of which is subject to challenge. Andrew Altman, for example, writes:

> [I]f Jews or Muslims are being targeted by a genocide, then it is not humanity that is thereby harmed but rather: first, those Jews or Muslims killed or otherwise directly harmed; second, other Jews or Muslims within reach of the perpetrators; and third, possibly, but not necessarily, Jews and Muslims elsewhere in the world. Baptists in the United States, Confucians in China, and Hindus in India would not seem to be harmed.[28]

This criticism fails to address May's and Luban's central contention, however, which does not concern the harm done to all human beings that results from Jews being attacked qua Jews, but the harm or risk of harm that follows for all human beings from the spread of an individuality-denying ideology, one that causally contributes to an increase in the incidence of assaults on people simply for belonging to a group, *whatever that group may be.* As Luban observes:

> [T]oday we live in a world in which almost all nations are patchworks of ethnic, racial, religious, and cultural groups. In part, this is the result of globalization. But it is also the product of a century [or centuries] of wars and upheavals that have displaced hundreds of millions of people. ... The crimes against humanity that drenched the twentieth century in gore proved that group-on-group politics has no built-in principle of restraint. And so, just as all women share an interest in ensuring that women are not killed solely for being women, and all Jews share an interest in ensuring that Jews are not killed solely because they are Jews, all human beings share an interest in ensuring that people are not killed by their neighbors solely because of their group affiliations; for all of us have neighbors whose group is not our own.[29]

Luban's claim that group-on-group politics lacks any "built-in principle of restraint" can be read to refer both to the absence of any limits on the *kind of conduct* in which actors engaged in such politics might engage, as well as the *kind of group* that might find themselves embroiled in it. Insofar as practically all human beings live as members of a group (or many different groups), the latter reading entails that all are vulnerable to being targeted as such, while the former reading points to the horrific treatment that may follow if or when we are.

Even when properly understood, the contagion argument may remain vulnerable to empirical critique. Most obviously, the data may fail to corroborate the causal claim Luban and May assert. But the challenge may also take a slightly more sophisticated form. For example, rather than being a cause of cancerous group-on-group politics, individuality-denying ideology may simply be a symptom that societies suffer when certain other conditions are met, such as severe and rapid economic displacement. If so, then protection against CAH requires policies that address those conditions, not international criminal prosecutions. Moreover, as an attempt to make good on the prudential account of a public wrong, the contagion argument remains vulnerable to one of the moral objections raised against the argument that CAH wrong humanity by undermining international peace and stability, namely, that it appeals to deterrence in order to justify criminal punishment.

It is true that Luban explicitly embraces a forward-looking justification for prosecuting and punishing criminals against humanity. The most promising justification for international tribunals, he writes, "is their role in *norm projection*: trials are expressive acts broadcasting the news that mass atrocities are, in fact, heinous crimes and not merely politics by other means."[30] Punishment, he adds, remains essential to communicating this message, even if at present international criminal law relies less on it and more on the ceremony of a criminal trial to achieve the aim of norm projection. However, this rationale looks less like traditional deterrence, which aims to shape actors' future conduct by attaching prudential costs to engaging in certain types of conduct, than communicative or moral education theories of just punishment. The latter theories construe just trial and punishment as a form of moral address, one that aims at the perpetrator's recognition that he acted wrongly, his choice to reform his values or character, and his reconciliation with the public he harmed (or wronged) by committing a criminal act.[31] Admittedly, Luban appears to focus more on the effects that pure international criminal law may have on the moral consciousness of future potential perpetrators of crimes against humanity than on the repentance, reform, and reconciliation of the actors actually subject to trial and punishment. But note, first, that we need not choose between these two aims. Second, where defenders of moral education or communicative theories of just punishment downplay or leave out the contribution that trial and punishment make to norm projection, this likely reflects their assumption that most members of the political community in question already endorse the norm the criminal violated. There is no need, then, to discuss the contribution the practice of criminal law makes to the moral education of the wider community. That assumption, which justifies focusing exclusively on the criminal's moral development, does not yet appear to hold in the case of CAH. The upshot, then, is that even if at present the most morally consequential feature of pure international criminal law is the contribution it makes to shaping the moral consciousness of all human beings, this need

[30] David Luban, "Fairness to Rightness: Jurisdiction, Legality, and the Legitimacy of the International Criminal Court," in *The Philosophy of International Law*, eds. Samantha Besson and John Tasioulas (Oxford: Oxford University Press, 2010), p. 576.
[31] See, among others, R.A. Duff, *Punishment, Communication, and Community* (Oxford: Oxford University Press, 2001).

not entail that it fails to address actual defendants as moral agents, or that it uses them as a mere means for producing a morally better world.[32]

The fact that all human beings are "parties in interest" to the prosecution and punishment of perpetrators of crimes against humanity seems to imply the moral justifiability of vigilantism, that is, that any human being may seek to punish such actors for their misdeeds. Luban argues to the contrary that the standing to punish also depends on an agent satisfying the demands of what he calls natural justice. These include basic procedural rights such as "the right to a speedy, public trial before an impartial tribunal that bases its decisions solely on the evidence, under rules designed to reach accurate verdicts" and "the right of the accused to confront the witnesses against him."[33] It also includes certain prosecutorial duties, such as the obligation "to disclose exculpatory evidence to the accused," and executive duties, such as maintaining humane conditions of confinement.[34] Only certain states and international tribunals satisfy the demands of natural justice, Luban maintains, and therefore only they are morally justified in subjecting accused criminals against humanity to trial, and punishing them if they are found guilty. They do so, however, neither in their own name, nor in the name of the victims – and not in the name of any particular political community, either. Rather, they act on behalf of all humanity.

The most fundamental objection to both May's and Luban's defense of international prosecution for CAH contests their reliance on a prudential account of what makes an act a public wrong. On this account, recall, criminal acts are ones that unjustifiably harm, or impose an unjustifiable risk of harm, on each and every member of the public. Legal theorists such as Renzo and R.A. Duff contend instead that we ought to understand public wrongs as wrongdoings for which an actor is *answerable* to the political community.[35] In the standard case, what makes an actor answerable to the political community is his membership in it. For example, in virtue of being a citizen of a particular state, an actor has certain moral obligations to the other citizens of that state, including a duty to obey its criminal law. It is his failure to discharge that duty, one he owes to the other citizens of the state as such, that entitles them to employ the institutions of the state's criminal justice system to hold him accountable for his wrongdoing. While the infliction of harm surely plays a central role in a morally proper determination of which act types ought to be

---

[32] The argument in the text concerns the *in principle* justifiability of international prosecution as a means for norm projection. It leaves open the question of how well it has fared in practice. For concerns in this regard, see Tim Meijers and Marlies Glasius, "Trials as Messages of Justice: What Should Be Expected of International Criminal Courts?" *Ethics and International Affairs* 30, no. 4 (2016): 429–47.

[33] Luban, "Fairness to Rightness," 580.

[34] Ibid.

[35] R.A. Duff, *Answering for Crime: Responsibility and Liability in the Criminal Law* (Oxford: Hart Publishing, 2007); "Authority and Responsibility in International Criminal Law," in *The Philosophy of International Law*, eds. Samantha Besson and John Tasioulas (Oxford: Oxford University Press, 2010), pp. 594–602; Renzo, "Crimes Against Humanity," 454–60.

criminally proscribed, justifiable claims to jurisdiction flow from the fact that individuals are enmeshed in particular normative communities; that is, the fact that they occupy specific roles (citizen, for instance) in virtue of which they have specific responsibilities (to uphold the law, say).

Renzo suggests that "in the same way in which there are wrongs for which we are accountable to our fellow citizens in virtue of our membership in the polity, there are wrongs for which we are accountable to our fellow human beings in virtue of our membership in the wider community of humanity."[36] CAH constitute one such wrong. In virtue of occupying the role of member in the wider community of humanity, each of us has a duty to fulfill the responsibilities that attach to that role, including upholding those norms that govern interactions between all human beings as such.[37] Upholding the norms of a particular community requires both obedience to those norms and holding other members of the community accountable if and when they violate them. Since CAH constitute a violation of a norm that binds actors qua members of the "wider community of humanity," it follows that all human beings qua members of that same community have a right, and indeed a duty, to hold the perpetrators to account. International tribunals or, in a pinch, domestic courts exercising universal jurisdiction, provide a mechanism whereby the human community compels violators of its norms to answer for their wrongdoing.

Just as the prudential model of a public wrong is vulnerable to the objection that CAH do not harm all humanity, so too the accountability model of a public wrong is vulnerable to the objection that there is no "wider community of humanity" to whom perpetrators of CAH must answer. A description of individuals as citizens of the world is only metaphorical; there is no global state in which all humans occupy the role of citizen, only a community of states, with individuals occupying the role of citizen in a particular state (or perhaps two or three states). Neither does Renzo rely on the concept of community when arguing that human beings as such are owed certain forms of treatment. Rather, he distinguishes between "wrongs that consist in our failure to discharge duties that we have in virtue of our membership in the political community and wrongs that consist in our failure to discharge duties that all individuals have to each other independently of any social or political relationship."[38] The latter duties correlate to individuals' basic human rights, rights they possess in virtue of some *nonrelational* property or properties. There is a gap, then, between Renzo's nonrelational account of what entitles all human beings to certain forms of treatment and his role-relational account of who has the standing to hold wrongdoers accountable, or conversely, to whom wrongdoers are answerable for their wrongful conduct. Put another way, even if Renzo successfully argues that all human beings belong to the *class* or *set* of creatures who enjoy basic (moral)

---

[36] Renzo, "Crimes Against Humanity," 456.
[37] Renzo argues that these norms include many that contemporary international criminal law does not recognize, but I focus here only on the norm prohibiting CAH.
[38] Ibid, 457.

rights, the account of legitimate jurisdiction he wishes to employ requires that he show all human beings to be members of a single *community*.

One might argue, as May does, that there exists a global *moral* community to which all human beings belong, one premised on solidarity in the face of our "common vulnerability to violence and harm."[39] Yet if we understand solidarity as May does, namely, as "a sense of fellow feeling that comes from a recognition that the interests of others overlap sufficiently with one's own interests to make of the interests of others one's own interests," then we have ample reason to doubt the existence of such a global moral community.[40] Indeed, Hannah Arendt's expression of this very skepticism appears to be what motivates Luban's attempt to offer a prudential, rather than a moral, justification for the prosecution and punishment of crimes against humanity. As she puts the point, "to fall back on an unequivocal voice of conscience – or, in the even vaguer language of the jurists, on a 'general sentiment of humanity' – not only begs the question, it signifies a deliberate refusal to take notice of the central moral, legal, and political phenomena of our century," namely, the absence of any such sentiment.[41]

An alternative response to the objection that there is no global community of human beings to whom perpetrators must answer focuses on the contribution that the international prosecution of CAH can make to the construction of that community. This argument begins with the observation that communities exist in virtue of a set of agents engaging in a common or shared practice of deploying specific norms to hold one another accountable.[42] It follows that every attempt to deploy a norm to hold others accountable simultaneously presupposes the existence of a particular community and, when successful, contributes to making it the case that the community actually exists.[43] Where a particular practice of holding accountable has been fairly stable over the lifetime of most or all of those who participate in it, the existential implications of participating in that practice may go unnoticed; indeed, what are actually social facts may come to be perceived as natural ones. In contrast, challenges to a heretofore stable shared normative understanding can serve to reveal a particular social world to be one its participants collectively make via their practice of holding accountable. The treatment of CAH as an international crime illustrates this point. It directly challenges a shared understanding of the global political community as composed of individuals who exist only as citizens of particular states, an understanding central to the Westphalian ideal of international government. It asserts instead, in deed and not only words, a conception of humanity as members of

---

[39]   May, "Humanity," 376.
[40]   Ibid, 375.
[41]   Quoted in Luban, "Crimes Against Humanity," 137.
[42]   Lefkowitz, "Sources," 336.
[43]   The fact that many defenders of the accountability model of the criminal law typically focus their discussion on the legal orders of moderately well-functioning modern states may explain why they ignore the contribution that a practice of holding accountable makes to the constitution of a set of individuals as a community.

a single global political community, one composed of individuals each of whom is entitled to certain forms of treatment in his or her own right. Together with the international human rights practice that began to emerge following the Second World War, international prosecution and punishment of criminals against humanity serves to make this vision a reality by acting as if it already is – or at least it aspires to do so.

At this stage in its history, the practice of international prosecution and punishment of CAH seeks to create the conditions for its own legitimacy. In subjecting perpetrators to trial, and in punishing them if they are found guilty, a tribunal such as the ICC purports to act on behalf of all human beings who, as members of a global political community, enjoy the standing to hold accountable any member accused of committing CAH. Yet it is partly through the international practice of holding actors accountable for such conduct that such a global community comes to exist. Even those who are optimistic that this effort to bootstrap such a community into existence is making headway and will ultimately succeed may also suspect that it has not yet progressed far enough to sustain the claim to legitimacy implicit in the practice of pure ICL. Whether this is so may be a question it is presently impossible to answer; while the old international political order has clearly suffered significant disruption, it is not yet clear whether it will be restored or whether the new one that pure international criminal law presupposes will take its place. As is often true of normative change, it may only be in hindsight that we can identify with any confidence if the attempt to transform the practice of international affairs has succeeded or failed. More importantly, however, the absence of a global political community in which all human beings as such are members need not entirely undermine the ICC's standing to prosecute and punish criminals against humanity. That is because we ought to expand the task of justifying international criminal jurisdiction to include a moral defense of the attempt to create a global political community in which all human beings enjoyed unmediated membership. This is familiar ground for legal and political theorists who have long sought to justify the state, or better, to justify the exercise of coercive government whatever institutional form it takes. The argument that actors who cannot avoid interacting with one another have a duty to submit to a common juridical order may provide an attractive starting point for those who seek to justify attempts to bootstrap pure international criminal law into legitimacy.[44]

---

[44] For a thought-provoking challenge to the assumption that the justification of universal jurisdiction depends on a special relationship between the court and the alleged offender, one that makes the latter answerable to the former, see Anthony R. Reeves, "Liability to International Prosecution: The Nature of Universal Jurisdiction," *European Journal of International Law* 28, 4 (2017): 1047–67. Reeves offers an instrumental argument to justify both a court's standing to punish and the distinction between private and public wrongs.

10

International Law and Secession

Two features of the contemporary international politics make the topic of secession and its treatment by international law a morally critical one. The first is the large number of secessionist movements currently agitating for the creation of an independent state, including (but hardly limited to) those in Quebec, Scotland, Catalonia, Kashmir, the southern provinces of Thailand, the Berber regions of Morocco and Algeria, and the Kurdish regions of Turkey and Iraq. The second is the fact that the state remains the primary actor within the international legal order, the entity on which it bestows most of the rights to create, apply, and enforce law. With respect to international law, then, nothing is more important to a political community than its recognition as a state. Insofar as secession is presently the primary mechanism whereby new states may emerge, the stance international law takes regarding its permissibility ought to figure centrally in our judgment of the international legal order's moral justifiability.

Our exploration of this topic begins in section I with a brief characterization of secession and its current status in international law. We also distinguish three different questions we can pose regarding the moral justifiability of secession. In sections II and III, we examine competing answers to questions that any theory of state secession must address. First, what sort of actor enjoys a moral right to secede, and in virtue of what features or considerations does that actor do so? Second, on what particular territory is an actor with a right to secede permitted to exercise that right? As these questions indicate, state secession involves the denial of an existing state's rule over both particular people and a particular territory. Hence a moral theory of secession, and of a morally defensible international legal norm governing secession, must include both an agential component and a territorial component. In sections IV and V, we consider arguments for and against several international legal norms we might adopt to regulate secession, drawing on both moral theories of secession and empirically informed conjectures regarding the incentives those norms might create for various international and domestic actors.

I SOME PRELIMINARIES

Secession involves, essentially, a claim to sovereign equality. Necessarily, to attempt to secede is to assert both one's independence from the rule of the agent that previously enjoyed jurisdiction over one, and one's enjoyment of the same rights, liberties, powers, and immunities possessed by the agent whose jurisdiction one now contests. Our concern in this chapter is with state secession, meaning the attempt to create a new state within the existing international legal order. Consider, for example, the 2014 referendum on Scottish secession. Participants were asked whether Scotland should become an independent country; that is, whether Scotland should no longer be subject to rule by the government of the United Kingdom, and instead become its own state, one with the same international legal rights, liberties, powers, and immunities enjoyed by the UK and other states.[1]

State secession can be either consensual or unilateral. In the former case, the existing state makes no effort to prevent a portion of those it rules from creating a new state on part of its territory (and, in some cases, may even take positive steps to advance that aim). Since international law places no obligation on states to preserve their territorial integrity or their rule over particular populations, it creates no obstacles to consensual secession. That is not true when it comes to unilateral secession, that is, cases where the existing state does object to any attempt by some of those it rules to create a new state on a portion of its territory. Apart from decolonization, international law does not attribute to any group a right to unilateral secession. While it does not explicitly prohibit such conduct, international law does include norms that disfavor secession, including, most importantly, the right of existing states to use force to maintain their territorial integrity. Moreover, with the exception of Kosovo, the international community has recognized the emergence of a new state only once the original state abandoned its claim to authority over the group attempting to secede (and, more or less, the territory they claim for their new state). Perhaps the best way to characterize international law's current stance toward secession, then, is to say that it creates a presumption against it, but ultimately treats the resolution of secessionist conflicts as a matter of extra-legal politics.[2]

What morally justifies secession? Before we attempt to answer that question, we must be careful to distinguish it from two others with which it may be easily confused. The first of these is what reason(s), if any, morally justifies secession in this particular case? The second is, what reason(s) morally justify the optimal legal norm governing secession; for example, the morally best international legal norm governing secession under current conditions? Suppose, for illustrative purposes,

---

[1]   For a detailed defense of this analysis of secession in general and state secession in particular, see David Lefkowitz, "International Law, Institutional Moral Reasoning, and Secession," *Law and Philosophy* 37, 4 (2018): 387–91.

[2]   See Daniel Thurer and Thomas Burri, "Secession," in *The Max Planck Encyclopedia of Public International Law*, ed. Rudiger Wolfrum (Oxford: Oxford University Press, 2009).

that the advancement of national self-determination provides a reason that morally justifies secession. It does not follow necessarily that a particular nation's attempt to secede here and now is morally justifiable, for there may be other, more weighty, moral considerations that count against secession in this case. Indeed, as we will see it may be that in some contexts the advancement of national self-determination itself counts against secession. Neither does the fact that the advancement of national self-determination provides a reason that morally justifies secession necessarily entail that all nations ought to enjoy an international legal right to secede. Here too competing moral considerations may warrant a legal norm that is sometimes, or even never, responsive to the interest nations have in exercising political self-determination. Alternatively, or perhaps in addition, it may be that at least at present international law will best serve the goal of advancing national self-determination if it does not accord all nations a legal right to secede, but instead grants them other legal rights, or is simply silent on the question of national self-determination. Note that these last claims bear on the design of a specific institution at a particular point in human history, namely, present-day international law. A different conclusion may be warranted at other times and/or in other institutional settings.[3]

Typically, when a theorist argues that some reason R morally justifies secession, he or she describes that reason as a *pro tanto* or defeasible consideration that counts in favor of the moral permissibility of secession. Reason R entails a presumption in favor of secession in any particular case, and in favor of international law according a legal right to secede to any agent who can offer R to defend its secession. But, as we just noted, this presumption can be overridden by other moral considerations, in which case we ought to conclude that, in this particular case, secession is not permissible all things considered, or that, all things considered, international law should not accord a legal right to secede to any agent who can offer reason R to defend its secession. Ultimately, our interest in this chapter is with a particular all-things-considered judgment, namely, the content of the morally best international legal norm governing secession now or in the near future.

Nevertheless, we have several good reasons to begin our investigation by considering arguments that attempt to specify prima facie reasons that count in favor of secession by certain groups. First, absent an account of the moral reasons that favor or count against according specific groups an international legal right to secede, we have no moral basis for selecting among competing candidates for the international legal norm that ought to govern secession.[4] For example, a defense of an

---

3   For instance, in the case of a multinational state such as present-day Canada, morality may require that the domestic legal order accord those nations subject to rule by the Canadian government a suitably specified right to secede.

4   More generally, in order to conduct a moral assessment of international law, in light of which we can then argue for or against specific proposals for its reform, we need an account of the proper goals of a morally defensible international legal order, and the means by which international law may, must, or must not contribute to the realization of those goals. Furthermore, the moral standards that govern how international law should or should not seek to advance its proper goals depend on an assessment of

international legal norm governing secession might be criticized because it fails to be properly responsive to a reason that counts in favor secession. Alternatively, it may be challenged on the grounds that it relies on a mistaken understanding of the *pro tanto* moral reason(s) that certain groups may invoke to justify secession.

Second, insofar as it purports to be a moral assessment of an existing social practice, a moral account of secession ought to take seriously the arguments put forward by those who participate in that practice; that is, those who assert a moral right to engage in unilateral secession, and who sometimes attempt to exercise that purported right, and those who resist such assertions and attempts at secession. Moreover, some secessionists attempt to advance their goal of political independence by claiming that existing international law accords them a legal right to secede, or that it should do so if it is to more fully realize the self-determination of peoples, a goal to which it purports to be committed.[5] Thus, critical reflection on the nature and value of political self-determination, and what sort of group's have a claim to it, is an unavoidable concomitant of due regard for the actual practice of (global) government.

Third, if philosophy enjoys a comparative advantage over other scholarly communities and practitioners, including international lawyers, legal theorists, and social scientists, it likely takes the form of careful and systematic reflection on value and its implications for right conduct and/or a good life. Given our aim of identifying some of the ways in which philosophy can contribute to our understanding and assessment of international law, we would be remiss if we did not engage with philosophers' accounts of the moral grounds for secession.

Arguably, philosophical reflection on ideas or arguments invoked in international relations, including international legal discourse, may be valuable even if it offers little or no practical guidance for immediate or near-term reform. For example, it provides a useful check on an overly conservative approach to both theory and practice. Even if they are ultimately utopian, engagement with ideal-theoretical arguments compel us to explain exactly why that is so, an exercise that may lead us to identify prospects for moral improvement we might otherwise fail to recognize. Ideal theory can also inspire us, and in doing so propel changes that might otherwise be unattainable. This is a double-edged sword, of course; inspiration can produce morally awful outcomes when it blinds us to the various practical barriers that confront attempts to realize the ideal. Yet the kind of incrementalism, or even stasis, characteristic of approaches that eschew ideal theorizing may not only result in missed opportunities for reform but also fail to speak to many of those moved by

---

its capabilities; that is, what it can and cannot do to shape the conduct of those actors over whom it enjoys jurisdiction (and possibly other actors as well).

5   Chapter 1, Article 1, of the Charter of the United Nations identifies among that institutions purposes the development "of friendly relations among nations based on respect for the equal rights and self-determination of peoples." United Nations, *Charter of the United Nations*, October 24, 1945, 1 UNTS XVI.

(what they perceive to be) their own unjust treatment, or the unjust treatment of others. Successfully advancing a nonideal, incremental, approach to the moral reform of international law, including its stance vis-à-vis secession, may require genuine engagement with ideal theory if only to ensure that there is no void in public debate that is filled by a pernicious actor or a well-intentioned but insufficiently realistic idealist. Finally, we should be careful not to overestimate our ability to predict what will be possible in the future, or to underestimate the rapidity with which political, economic, social, and technological changes can make what was previously infeasible or too risky to pursue neither of these things. When new opportunities present themselves, we may be better prepared to seize them if we have engaged in philosophical reflection on values and norms in a manner that was relatively unconstrained by considerations of what we believed to be, at the time, practical or feasible.

II THE AGENTIAL DIMENSION OF SECESSION

Moral justifications for secession typically take the form of asserting that a particular (type of) actor enjoys a right to political self-determination. Political self-determination involves what Allen Buchanan refers to as "an independent domain of political control."[6] The actor in question has an interest in self-government that is morally important or weighty enough to ground, at a minimum, a claim against others that they not interfere with its attempt to exercise self-rule. However, the matters over which an agent with a right to political self-determination ought to enjoy political control, the extent of the control the agent ought to exercise vis-à-vis those matters, and the (institutional) form the agent's exercise of control ought to take, depend on a number of considerations. These include an account of what makes that agent's exercise of self-government valuable, due regard for other moral rights, and factors involved in operationalizing the right, such as the design of legal institutions that will function more-or-less as intended under suitably specified conditions. In some cases, these considerations may warrant only a limited form of self-government; for example, the legal right of a minority nation within a multinational state to the government's conduct of public affairs in that nation's language, as well as the language spoken by the majority. Such intrastate autonomy arrangements can take many forms, and some philosophers and international legal scholars maintain that both political philosophy and international legal reform would be better served by a focus on such arrangements than on secession. Nevertheless, since even many actors that currently enjoy a good deal of intrastate autonomy continue to press for secession, this chapter focuses on the form of political self-determination separatists demand, namely, the independent domain of political control international law accords to all states.

---

[6] Buchanan, *Justice, Legitimacy, and Self-Determination*, p. 333.

In this section, we consider three accounts of what makes the exercise of political self-determination valuable enough to ground a moral right; at a minimum, a claim to noninterference in the exercise of political control. The first points to the contribution the exercise of political self-determination makes to advancing individuals' secure enjoyment of their basic human rights. The second appeals to the flourishing of a collective agent, typically a nation, while the third argues that political self-determination constitutes a facet of the exercise of individual autonomy or self-government. While each of these accounts picks out a different type of actor with a right to secede, it is important to note that a particular group may enjoy a right to secede under two or even all three of them. For example, all three defenses of the right to political self-determination arguably entail that Iraqi Kurds enjoy a *pro tanto* moral right to secede from Iraq.

Political and legal philosophers largely agree that victims of widespread and systematic violations of their basic human rights perpetrated or tolerated by the state that rules them enjoy a moral right to secede from it. This conclusion follows from the claim that a state enjoys a moral right to rule its subjects only if it governs in a manner that exhibits a principled commitment to respect for their basic human rights. When a state fails to meet this condition, it has no claim against those it mistreats that they refrain from creating an independent state on a portion of the predecessor state's territory.[7] In short, secession is morally justifiable in this case because it provides a remedy for the grievous injustice committed or allowed by the state.

Other injustices that some theorists argue may be permissibly remedied via secession include systematic discrimination and exploitation, as well as grave threats to the survival of a group's culture.[8] Many theorists go further, however, and argue that secession can be morally permissible even in some cases where the state commits none of the aforementioned wrongs. The *pro tanto* moral right to secede, they argue, is not merely a secondary right, one that agents acquire only as a result of others' failure to respect their primary rights to bodily integrity, or to nondiscrimination, etc. Rather, it is also a primary right, a claim grounded in the interest certain groups have in the exercise of political self-determination, either because self-government is good in itself or because it is a necessary means to their successful pursuit of morally obligatory ends other than respect for basic human rights.

Arguments for a primary moral right to secede fall into two broad categories: nationalist or ascriptive accounts and plebiscitary or choice accounts. Consider, first, the argument that nations enjoy a *pro tanto* or defeasible claim to political independence; that is, to the exercise of political self-determination in their own

---

[7] Ibid, pp. 353–4; Margaret Moore, "The Ethics of Secession and a Normative Theory of Nationalism," *Canadian Journal of Law and Jurisprudence* XIII, 2 (July 2000): 227.

[8] Buchanan, *Justice, Legitimacy, and Self-Determination*, pp. 357–9; Wayne Norman, "Ethics of Secession as the Regulation of Secessionist Politics," in *National Self-Determination and Secession*, ed. Margaret Moore (Oxford: Oxford University Press, 1998), p. 41.

states. Paradigmatically, nations are composed of people who satisfy both objective and subjective conditions for a shared or common identity.[9] The objective conditions typically include a common language, history, and public culture, as well as an attachment to a national homeland. The subjective features of a national identity include members' mutual recognition of each other as co-nationals, and an acknowledgment that they have special obligations to one another in virtue of their shared nationality. Finally, nations are composed of individuals who seek to exercise collective political self-determination; that is, who aim to live under laws and a system of government that protects and promotes their own distinctive national identity. All else equal, then, nationalists maintain that we should pursue a world in which every nation is governed by its own state, and every state governs only one nation.

Philosophical defenders of nationalism offer a number of arguments to support the claim that nations enjoy a *pro tanto* moral right to political self-determination.[10] First, the relationship among co-nationals is sometimes alleged to have intrinsic value analogous to that realized in the relationship among family members. In both cases, the individual's position in the relationship constitutes a core element of his or her identity, and some argue, provides a sui generis source of moral obligations. The exercise of political self-determination provides a vehicle for the fulfillment of these obligations, as well as a means for recognizing the importance to its members of their identity as members of a particular national community.

A second argument in defense of national self-determination holds that individual human beings can only lead flourishing lives when they are embedded in a flourishing national culture. National cultures attach specific meanings or values to the various activities that constitute a life, including work, leisure, education, familial life, and, in many cases, religious practice. Individuals who find themselves living in a social world that fails to reflect their national culture will often feel alienated by it, and by the political order that protects and contributes to the (re)production of that social world. As strangers in a strange land, they will find it difficult to live a life they find meaningful or valuable, a fact that will likely encourage them to pursue a strategy of withdrawal from public life. Secession provides one such strategy, as it involves the creation of a new state that serves to protect and reproduce the national culture of (some of) those who were alienated from the social world sustained by the old state.

Third, some nationalist philosophers endorse John Stuart Mill's claim that (stable, long-term) democratic governance is only possible in a one-nation state.

---

[9] See David Miller, "Nationalism," in *The Oxford Handbook of Political Theory*, eds. John S. Dryzek, Bonnie Honig, and Anne Phillips (Oxford: Oxford University Press, 2008), p. 530; Nenad Miscevic, "Nationalism," Section 1, in *The Stanford Encyclopedia of Philosophy* (Summer 2018 Edition), Edward N. Zalta (ed.), https://plato.stanford.edu/archives/sum2018/entries/nationalism/.

[10] For summary discussions, see Miller, "Nationalism"; Miscevic, "Nationalism"; and Moore, "Ethics of Secession."

A shared nationality ensures a baseline of trust that enables losers in political contests to accept their defeat, safe in the knowledge that the winners' exercise of political power will be limited by their recognition of the losers as co-members of the community to whom they have special obligations. In contrast, where politics pits members of one nation against another, with no common overarching identity, losers are likely to be far less willing to accept their defeat, and winners far less likely to constrain their exercise of political power out of respect or concern for the interests of the losers.

Finally, some philosophers argue that a common nationality is a necessary condition for the achievement of social justice. Insofar as the achievement of social justice requires that the state redistribute resources from the advantaged to the disadvantaged, its realization depends on a substantial degree of willing support for such transfers from the former. Some nationalists maintain that this support will be forthcoming only if the advantaged conceive of the individuals who benefit from these transfers as co-nationals to whom they have special obligations, akin to members of a (very) extended family. Conversely, the more those who enjoy economic success in life conceive of the beneficiaries of redistributive policies as members of other nations, differing in their appearance, in their language, in their history, in their culture, and in their ancestral home, the less likely they will be to support these policies.

Each of these defenses of the value of national self-determination may be challenged. For example, the success of multinational states such as Canada and Switzerland at realizing both stable democratic governance and a fair degree of social justice (at least by comparison to most other states) provides a challenge to the last two arguments for a national right to political self-determination canvased above. Nationalists might respond that the challenge is only apparent, on the grounds that Canadians and Swiss constitute nations, albeit ones in which subnational identities figure more prominently than in the case of other nationalities. Arguably, this rejoinder moves nationalism in the direction of constitutional patriotism, since it appears to involve narrowing the common culture and identity that makes people members of a common nation to a shared commitment to certain political principles and practices, and to an emphasis on a community's specifically political history (as opposed to its social, cultural, or religious history). But rather than investigate further whether the arguments for a national right to political self-determination canvased above ultimately succeed, let us instead consider what follows for secession if they do.

Thoughtful nationalists recognize the impossibility of redrawing state borders so that every state encompasses only a single nation. Moreover, liberal-nationalists acknowledge that respect for basic human rights takes priority over the exercise of political self-determination. David Miller argues that these two commitments entail that nationalists should not rely on what he labels the numbers principle to determine where political boundaries ought to lie.[11] The numbers principle holds that we should seek to maximize the number of people who live in a state in which their nation forms the majority. The consequences of applying this principle will frequently be dire for the "trapped minority" in both the new state and the remnant state that secession creates. Successful secessionists frequently treat whatever national minority exists within the territory of their new state worse than they were treated by the state that previously ruled them. Moreover, the original state is less likely to make accommodations for members of the seceding nation who continue to live in its territory, since they now make up a smaller percentage of the population, and are likely to be perceived as having the option of relocating to the new state in which their nation is the majority.[12] Given the goal of promoting national flourishing for *all* of a nation's members, and not just those who reside in a state where their nation is the majority, as well as the moral importance of ensuring that all people securely enjoy their basic moral rights, liberal-nationalists themselves will sometimes argue against secession and for the preservation of a multinational state. Likewise, a commitment to the moral importance of national self-determination does not necessarily rule out support for the creation of new multinational states or super-state political orders such as the European Union. With respect to the international law, then, nationalism's concern with promoting national flourishing in a world where nations are inextricably territorially mixed cautions against too quickly inferring from the fact that nations have a *pro tanto* moral right to political self-determination that they ought to enjoy an international legal right to unilateral secession.

The noninstrumental value of self-determination also provides the foundation for choice or plebiscitary defenses of the moral right to secede. Unlike nationalists, however, choice theorists derive the right to secede from individual autonomy, and in particular, each individual's freedom to determine with whom they wish to associate for political purposes. The limiting case of a choice theory of secession treats political association itself as morally optional. Most plebiscitary theorists reject this view, however, on the grounds that membership or participation in a state is a necessary means to, or constitutive of, the minimally just treatment of others. Nevertheless, the constraint that justice imposes on individuals' exercise of their right to freedom of association appears to be consistent with the creation of far more states than exist today. Specifically, choice theorists maintain that a group has a *pro tanto* primary moral right to secede if: (a) it is willing and able to create a new state that satisfies the requirements of minimal justice domestically and internationally (for instance, its subjects secure enjoyment of their basic moral rights), and (b) what

---

[11]   David Miller, "Secession and the Principle of Nationality," in *National Self-Determination and Secession*, ed. Margaret Moore (Oxford: Oxford University Press, 1998), pp. 69–72.

[12]   Indeed, in some instances, members of a trapped minority have been forced to relocate to a state in which their nation is the majority.

remains of the original state after secession also comprises a group of people willing and able to satisfy these same requirements.

Choice theorists often eschew any attempt to defend the claim that (most) human beings have the status of autonomous agents, and that, in virtue of that status, they enjoy a right to freedom of association. Instead, they direct their arguments to those who already accept both of those claims, and then argue that the only morally justifiable grounds for limiting individuals' freedom to choose with whom to associate for political purposes are those imposed by the demands of minimal justice. In this regard, choice theories of secession often reflect a liberal approach to the justification of government, one that begins with a presumption of individual liberty and that places the burden of justification on any agent or institution that seeks to limit that liberty.

Andrew Altman and Christopher Wellman, for example, defend their version of the choice theory of secession by inviting their readers to reflect on a hypothetical case in which the United States forcibly annexes Canada.[13] Suppose the annexation causes no harm to anyone, and that the resulting enlarged United States of America does a better job at protecting the full range of all its citizens' rights. Would the actions of the United States be morally permissible in this case? Altman and Wellman think not, and believe that many (liberals) will agree with them. Just as parents who satisfy a threshold of adequacy in raising their children enjoy a *pro tanto* moral right against others that they not interfere in their performance of that task, even if that interference would be better for both the parents and for the children, so too a group of people who are willing and able to work together to satisfy the demands of minimal justice domestically and internationally have a *pro tanto* moral right against others that they not interfere with their doing so. In both of these cases, the argument takes the form of a judgment or intuition that, above a certain threshold, it is more important that agents decide for themselves what is just or good than that they decide correctly.

While choice theorists concede that oftentimes it will be nations that satisfy the conditions for a moral right to secede, they reject the claim that *only* nations can do so. Moreover, on the choice account it is not the value of national flourishing that justifies a group's right to secede, but the value of each member of the nation exercising self-determination that does so. In some cases, individuals may choose to associate with one another, and only one another, for the purpose of promoting the flourishing of the nation to which they all belong. Yet the choice theorist maintains that we ought not to confuse a moral *justification* for a right to secede with an *explanation* of why actors who possess that right commonly choose to exercise it.

[13] Andrew Altman and Christopher Heath Wellman, *A Liberal Theory of International Justice* (Oxford: Oxford University Press, 2009), p. 14.

To fully appreciate the choice theorist's defense of a moral right to secession, it may be helpful to consider noninternational secessionist movements. Consider, for example, those residents of northern California and southern Oregon who wish to secede from their respective states and create a new one, named Jefferson. Or consider the numerous cases in which portions of a more local jurisdiction, such as a city or county, seek independence from that local jurisdiction. The advantage of reflecting on cases like these is that they typically involve neither an ongoing campaign of widespread human rights violations nor a clash between members of two or more nations. If we conclude that those who wish to secede in these cases have a *pro tanto* moral right to do so, then that is most likely because we accept the choice theorist's claim that people's freedom to associate with one another for political purposes ought to be restricted only when doing so is necessary to adequately protect human rights. It is not obvious why we should not extend this judgment to the question of international political secession, even if at present nations are the only groups that satisfy the choice theorist's conditions for possession of a moral right to secession, or the only groups with such a right that wish to exercise it.

The biggest challenge for the choice theory of a moral right to secession concerns the specification of those individuals who ought to have a vote in whether or not to secede. For example, who should have a say in Scottish secession from the United Kingdom? One possibility is all those who live in Scotland, regardless of their nationality. Another possibility is all and only Scots, regardless of where they happen to reside. A third possibility is all citizens of the United Kingdom. And there are many more possibilities. Absent a morally justifiable means for identifying the people with a right to participate in a plebiscite on secession, the choice theorists' view that the people ought to decide where international borders should be drawn remains incomplete.

Choice theorists argue that a recursive process of referendums provides a satisfactory solution to the problem of identifying who should have a say on secession. This process begins with an initial referendum held in a territory specified by the would-be secessionists. If a majority of those within the territory vote in favor of secession, then the creation of a new state on that territory should move forward. However, if there is any group within the territory specified by the original secessionists who do not wish to be a part of the new state, either because they wish to remain part of the original state or because they wish to create a new state of their own, then they may call for referendum on secession, and specify the part of the territory in which it is to be held. Subject to one condition, choice theorists maintain that this recursive process of voting on where state boundaries ought to be drawn should continue until every state includes only those who choose to associate with one another for political purposes. The condition is that the process of redrawing state borders must always result in states that are willing and able to protect and respect basic human rights. Satisfying this condition will surely impose some limits on how international boundaries are drawn, and as a consequence some individuals will likely be unable to realize the ideal of associating only with those with whom they wish to share citizenship. This will not constitute a wrongful setback to these individuals' exercise of self-determination, however, since the duty to respect others' basic human rights limits the domain in which people are morally permitted to live their lives as they choose.[14]

III THE TERRITORIAL DIMENSION OF SECESSION

Secessionists aspire to create a new, independent, state on a portion of the territory ruled by the state from which they wish to secede. But where should the borders of the new state be drawn? On what particular territory should a group with a right to political independence be free to exercise that right? A moral theory of secession must identify and defend specific criteria for delimiting the boundaries between the new state and what remains of the original state. The same is true for a morally defensible international legal norm governing secession.

Consider, first, a case in which a group acquires a right to secede because its members are victims of a systematic campaign of basic human rights violations perpetrated or tolerated by the state that rules them. As we noted in the previous section, most theorists maintain that this group enjoys a remedial right to secession, a moral permission to secede as a last resort means for protecting itself against these attacks. Since it is the protection of basic human rights that grounds the right to secede in this scenario, we might conclude that the borders of the new state ought to be drawn in whatever manner will best serve to advance that aim, both at present and in the future. This answer to the territorial question is consistent with the narrow moral focus of a remedial justification for secession, in that it is responsive only to certain minimal demands of justice, namely, basic human rights, and focused solely on the forward-looking goal of better realizing those minimal demands in the future. It attributes no moral importance to individuals' or group's attachments to particular places, except insofar as they figure in a calculation regarding the borders that will best serve the goal of advancing every person's secure enjoyment of his or her basic human rights.

Yet the moral rationale for a remedial right to secession may not necessitate the adoption of this narrowly focused answer to the territorial question. Recall that on the most common account of a remedial right to secede, it is the state's failure to govern in a manner that exhibits a principled commitment to respect for their basic human rights that entitles members of a targeted group to secede. In other words, the

---

[14] A comprehensive defense of the choice theory of secession will need to address other objections as well. Consider, for example, the claim that a group can secede only if the remnant state will still be able to protect and respect basic human rights. Why should it be the secessionists who have to limit their freedom of association in order to ensure that those left behind are able to enjoy their basic human rights? Why not maintain that other actors who could bear that burden, such as a moderately well-functioning neighboring state, also have a duty to do so?

group comes to enjoy a liberty to create its own state as a result of the current state's failure to satisfy the conditions that give it a claim to rule that group. Perhaps, having lost the right to govern this group, the state also loses the right to govern whatever territory belongs to the group, or to its members. To defend this claim, we need to offer a non-statist account of attachment to territory; that is, an argument demonstrating that groups and/or individuals have certain moral claims to territory that, from a justificatory standpoint, exist prior to those of the state. That is, we need to show that a state has a right to rule a particular territory only if that territory "belongs" to (some of) the people the state has a right to rule. The rest of this section considers attempts to do just that. The crucial point here, however, is that if we can give a plausible account of what it is for a particular territory to "belong" to a particular agent, then we can use that account to help determine the borders of the territory on which a group with a remedial right to secede may create an independent state.[15]

In fact, few contemporary political and legal philosophers dispute the claim that a state enjoys a moral right to rule a particular territory T only if it serves as the legitimate representative of people, or a people, with a moral right to that territory. However, they disagree over how we ought to understand all of the key concepts in that claim. This includes the specific rights, liberties, powers, and immunities that together constitute a state's right to rule; the conditions a state must satisfy in order to count as a legitimate representative of a people; whether the moral right to territory is possessed by individuals or by a collective agent, or both; the properties in virtue of which an agent can come to possess a moral right to territory; and the content of the moral right to territory, such as whether it includes a claim to control who enters or settles in it. Since our interest in this section concerns where the borders of a new state created by an act of secession ought to be drawn, in what follows, I largely focus on competing accounts of the agents that can enjoy a right to territory, and why their bearing certain relationships to particular places give them, at a minimum, rights to occupy that territory. A right to occupy territory, as Anna Stilz characterizes it, has two components: (1) "a liberty right to reside permanently in a particular space and to make use of that area for social, cultural, and economic practices," and (2) "a claim-right against others not to move one from that area, to allow one to return to it [if one travels elsewhere], and not to interfere with one's use of that space in ways that undermine the located practices in which one is engaged."[16] While some

---

[15]   The rationale for remedial secession, namely, improved protection of basic human rights, may entail that in some cases the borders of the new state should not encompass all and only the territory that "belongs" to the group, say because an alternative set of borders will provide more defensible boundaries and so make the termination of present hostilities and the prevention of future ones more likely. However, as the following discussion will make clear, the presumption that the new state should rule the territory that "belongs" to it, or to its members, provides an intuitively superior answer to the territorial question than does one that focuses solely on advancing the secure enjoyment of basic human rights.

[16]   Anna Stilz, *Territorial Sovereignty: A Philosophical Exploration* (Oxford: Oxford University Press, 2019), p. 35.

philosophers of territorial rights defend thicker conceptions of the moral right to territory, for instance, ones that include control over the use of natural resources located within it, the thinner notion of a right of occupancy suffices to address the question of where a group with a right to secede has a *pro tanto* moral claim to create its own, independent, state.

As was the case for the moral right to political self-determination, we can distinguish between those moral theories that attribute the right of occupancy to a collective agent or group, and those that attribute it to individuals. One argument for the former, advanced by David Miller, begins with the following two claims.[17] The first we have already noted, namely, that states exercise rights over territory not on their own behalf but as the legitimate representative of an agent or agents who possess those rights. States are a particular type of institutional arrangement that can facilitate the exercise of moral rights over territory by the agent or agents who possess those rights. Second, states enjoy reasonably stable moral (and legal) rights over territory, in the sense that a state with a justifiable claim to rule territory T continues to enjoy that claim even as the individuals that compose the state's citizenry change over time. Together, these two claims entail that we must attribute moral rights over territory to a trans-historical agent other than the state, where a "trans-historical agent" is one that endures as the same agent across generations. Miller writes that "a group that fits this bill must be one whose identity is such that it can be transmitted across time, with newly arriving members being bound to the existing ones through an inherited understanding of the nature of the group."[18] Specifically, the inherited understanding of the nature of the group must treat membership in it as an essential component of its members' identity, a deep and seemingly inalterable fact about who they are, rather than a feature of their life or identity they can retain or discard more-or-less at will. Not surprisingly, Miller identifies nations (as well as indigenous peoples) as the most plausible candidate for such an agent. Margaret Moore argues along somewhat similar lines that a political people best satisfies the conditions for a non-state trans-historical agent capable of enjoying and exercising moral rights to territory.[19] A political people, as she characterizes it, is a collective agent composed of individuals who understand the nature of their group to be centered around an aspiration "to create or continue to maintain shared rules and procedures together," but who need not share a common national culture (for example, a common language) or take as a primary goal of their political self-determination the protection and promotion of a national culture.[20]

Miller argues that nations acquire a right to occupy a particular territory by interacting with it in ways that materially and symbolically transform it.[21] The

---

[17] David Miller, "Territorial Rights: Concept and Justification," *Political Studies* 60, 2 (2012): 258.
[18] Ibid.
[19] Margaret Moore, *A Political Theory of Territory* (Oxford: Oxford University Press, 2015), pp. 34–70.
[20] Ibid, p. 54.
[21] Miller, "Territorial Rights," 258–62.

cultivation of land, including farming, grazing, and forest management, and the construction of infrastructure such as roads, dams, houses, and sports facilities are examples of transformations that add material value to a particular territory. The performance of acts that become central to the nation's historical identity, or the performance of rituals and practices that make specific territorial locations sacred, exemplify the creation of symbolic value. In some cases, the symbolic value a nation attributes to a particular place may explain and justify a prohibition on materially transforming it, as in the case of battlefields that are preserved in a state that approximates their appearance at the time the nation fought on them, or sacred mountains, lakes, or forests that are protected against development for (purely) material gain. These last examples illustrate one way in which a nation can enjoy a right to some place even while doing nothing that counts as changing or "improving" it.[22]

The value a nation creates when it materially and symbolically transforms a given territory is embodied in that place, Miller maintains, and therefore the nation must occupy the territory in question if it is to enjoy that value. This claim seems straightforward in the case of symbolic value. Without access to and control over places of historical or spiritual significance, members of a nation will be hard pressed to engage in the territorially located rituals of remembrance, celebration, or worship that bind them together, both within and across generations, and that reinforce and develop their shared conception of what makes for a valuable way of life. In the case of material value, however, we may wonder whether a nation might be compensated for the full value of its investment, as suggested by the example of one state paying another for the use of the latter's military base. But while this sort of exchange may be possible at the margin, it almost certainly will not be possible for the entirety, or even a sizeable portion, of the territory a nation has transformed. That is because the conduct whereby a nation acquires a right to occupy a given territory involves a two-way interaction between people and place: while the nation shapes the territory to meet its needs and desires, and to reflect its values, the territory also shapes the nation's culture, which is to say, how its members conceive of their needs and desires, and the appropriate ways in which to satisfy them. Membership in a nation involves participation in a distinct way of life, and the distinctiveness of that way of life reflects in part the ways in which the nation's culture has developed in response to its historic homeland. It may be possible in principle to give a nation specific or all-purpose material resources that are equal in value to the material value it has created in its homeland. However, this would not fully compensate the nation in the sense of leaving it no worse off, since making use of the new material resources instead of those in its homeland would almost certainly require radical transformations to the cultural and social practices that constitute the nation as the distinct people that it is.[23]

---

[22] See also Moore, *Political Theory of Territory*, p. 119.
[23] Relocation of indigenous peoples often fails to offer their members equal material value to that which they had created in their homelands, but even leaving that aside, the changes to the environment in which they can create material value – including farming, or manufacturing goods – are often

Whereas Miller and, arguably, Moore both treat a collective agent as the primary bearer of a moral right to occupy a particular territory, and derive individuals' rights to do so from their membership in the relevant group, Anna Stilz takes the opposite tack and argues that individuals are the primary bearers of the moral right to occupancy, with groups enjoying rights to territory in virtue of their members having a joint interest in the pursuit of territorially located projects. The right to occupancy, Stilz argues, is grounded in, and serves to protect the interest individuals have in the pursuit of those life plans and projects that contribute to their living valuable lives. She notes that "most complex goals and relationships require us to form [and act on] expectations about our continued use of, and secure access to, a place of residence," one where we have "access to social practices and the physical spaces in which they unfold ... [including] the workplace, the place of worship, the leisure or recreational facility, the school, [and] the meeting-house."[24] By engaging in projects or joining in social, cultural, and economic practices located in specific workplaces, places of worship, and other areas, actors acquire a right to occupy the space in which their life plans are territorially grounded. Since most people's life plans are in this way territorially located, nonvoluntary displacement from the territory a person occupies will typically inflict a major setback to his or her pursuit of the way of life he or she finds valuable or meaningful.

Stilz adds one crucial caveat to the claim that a person acquires a right to occupy some territory T by forming and pursuing a conception of the good territorially located in it. Only those whose "connection to the territory was established without any wrongdoing on his [or her] part, involving (at a minimum) no expulsion or wrongful interference with prior occupants" may thereby acquire a right to occupy that territory.[25] Those who seize control of a particular territory without a just cause and drive those living there into exile cannot establish a moral title to live their lives in that place, no matter how long they live there and how much their life plans become tied to it. In contrast, the invaders' children who are born and raised in territory T do acquire a moral right to occupy it, because they form and pursue located life plans in T and bear no moral responsibility for the wrongful expulsion of T's prior occupants. Their moral right to occupy T is a *pro tanto* one, however, and it must be balanced against the moral right of return possessed by those wrongly displaced from T and, under certain conditions, also possessed by their descendants. How the balance should be struck will depend on a number of factors the significance of which will likely vary from case to case. These include the current plight of those unjustly driven from T, as well as their descendants; the number of the descendants of the wrongful invaders who have developed life plans territorially

devastating to their ability to sustain their historical culture. See Moore, *Political Theory of Territory*, p. 41.

[24] Stilz, *Territorial Sovereignty*, pp. 41–2.

[25] Ibid, p. 84. Wrongful interference with prior occupants or infringements of others' claims to an equitable distribution of geographical space also preclude the acquisition of an occupancy right.

grounded in T; the robustness of the relationships the descendants of the wrongful invaders have with the state that bears moral responsibility for the unjust expulsion; and the degree to which support will be forthcoming from that state to help the wrongful invaders' descendants build new lives if they are relocated to its rightful territory.

Stilz and Miller agree that those wrongly displaced from a given territory retain a right to return to it. They part ways, however, when it comes to the persistence of such a right for subsequent generations. Recall that, for Miller, it is nations who possess a right to occupy particular territories, with individuals enjoying a right to do so in virtue of their status as members of the nation. Moreover, Miller maintains that nations persist as a single agent through the changes to their membership that result from the deaths of one generation and the births of a new one. It follows from these two claims that as long as the features that entitle a nation to occupy a given territory persist, that nation retains a *pro tanto* moral right to return to the territory in question, even if none of its current (that is to say, living) members has ever lived there. Insofar as many of the material transformations wrought by a nation's inter-action with a given place are likely to persist for quite some time, and certain symbolic transformations may well persist as long as the nation does, Miller's account of occupancy rights entails that several generations of a nation wrongly expelled from its homeland enjoy a moral claim to return to it. Yet as Miller notes, those who have settled in the territory in question will also engage in activities that materially and symbolically transform it, and in doing so acquire a claim to occupy that territory. The claims of both nations (or perhaps three or more nations) will need to be balanced against each other, with "occupancy and use of land over a long period eventually [coming] to trump the territorial claims of the original [rightful] possessors."[26]

For Stilz, individuals have an interest in occupying a particular territory only if their life plans are territorially grounded in it. Since the descendants of those wrongly expelled from territory T have never lived there, and so have not developed life plans located in it, they have no right to reside there. Rather, if these individuals have developed territorially grounded life plans elsewhere, say in the territory to which their parents or grandparents fled, then that is the territory in which they enjoy a moral right of occupancy (and the state that rules that territory is the one in which they ought to enjoy legal citizenship). Contra Miller, then, on Stilz's account the children of those wrongly driven from territory T may lack any moral claim to occupancy of it. In some cases, however, the descendants of those unjustly displaced from a given territory may be unable to develop located life plans elsewhere. This is true for many of those born and raised in refugee camps, for example. These individuals have a moral claim against the state responsible for the expulsion of

---

[26]   David Miller, *National Responsibility and Global Justice* (Oxford: Oxford University Press, 2007), p. 220.

their ancestors to assistance in acquiring permanent territorial residence *somewhere*, but not necessarily in the territory their forebears once occupied. Again, since the people in question have never lived in that territory, and since Stilz treats occupancy as valuable for the contribution it makes to forming and pursuing *some* valuable way of life, but not necessarily the way of life one most desires, her account offers no principled basis for these refugees to demand that they be permanently settled where their ancestors lived. Thus, a state that bears responsibility for the resettlement of second-, third-, or fourth-generation refugees may be able to discharge it by paying another state to take them in and grant them full legal citizenship. In practice, however, such a solution may be unavailable, and in that case the state will be morally required to settle the refugees on the territory it currently rules, or perhaps a portion of it on which the refugees can establish their own independent state.

The issue of a right of return is important in its own right, of course, both as a matter of justice and as a matter of international law. I consider it here, in the context of a discussion of the territorial dimension of a right to secession, because the stark differences between Miller's and Stilz's competing accounts of the right of return clearly illustrate how much turns on whether we endorse one or the other of their accounts of the moral right of occupancy. For either one of these theories, it may be that any plausibility we attribute to it when reflecting on the question of where a group with a right to secede may create an independent state swiftly disappears when we consider what that theory implies for the possession of a moral right of return.

IV SHOULD INTERNATIONAL LAW INCLUDE A PRIMARY RIGHT TO SECESSION?

No political or legal philosopher claims that it follows straightforwardly from the fact that a group has a moral right to secede that it ought to enjoy an international legal right to do so.[27] Rather, there appears to be a widespread consensus that we ought to select among competing proposals for an international legal norm governing secession by considering how well each will contribute to advancing the proper goals of a morally defensible global political order. Of course, in spite of their agreement on this methodological point, we might expect defenders of different moral theories of secession to endorse different international legal norms governing secession, insofar as they disagree over the proper aims of a morally defensible international law. But, in fact, this is not the case. Those who argue against reforming international law to include a primary right to secession need not, and often do not, deny that advancing or respecting the exercise of political self-determination is a proper goal of a morally defensible international law.[28] Rather, they maintain only that at present modifying

[27] Much of the text in this section and the one that follows are reprinted by permission from Springer, *Law and Philosophy*, "International Law, Institutional Moral Reasoning, and Secession," David Lefkowitz, 2018.

[28] Of course, they may argue against *particular accounts* of the value of political self-determination.

international law so that it includes a primary right to secede will not actually serve this goal, or that it will it also encourage an intolerable increase in violent conflict and the violation of basic human rights.

As we will see, advocates of reforming international law to include a primary right to secede adopt one of two strategies to respond to this line of argument. First, they directly challenge the claim that the reform to international law they champion will lead to an increase in the incidence of basic human rights violations and/or a reduction in the exercise of any form of political self-determination, including not only in newly independent states but also in the form of various intrastate autonomy arrangements. Second, they maintain that we lack the data necessary to draw reliable conclusions regarding the effects that competing rules governing secession will have on the advancement of peace, respect for basic human rights, and the exercise of political self-determination. Therefore, they argue, we ought to refrain from making any claim regarding the international legal norm that, at present, ought to govern secession.[29]

Allen Buchanan contends that the morally optimal international legal norm in a nonideal world like ours permits secession only as a remedy for (a) forcible annexation by another state, or (b) as a last resort response to serious and persistent violations of basic human rights.[30] His case for a remedial right-only norm rests centrally on the claim that it gets the incentives right. For example, Buchanan alleges that such a norm will encourage state officials to respect the basic human rights of their subjects, since the failure to do so will create a legal path to the loss of some of the territory over which they currently rule. A remedial right-only legal norm may also promote greater intrastate autonomy, if its explicit restriction of a unilateral legal right to secede to victims of forcible annexation or gross violations of human rights makes states more willing to devolve political power to regional or local government. Were a remedial right-only legal norm to have such an effect, it might well serve to advance the political self-determination of territorially concentrated groups, and perhaps their secure enjoyment of basic human rights as well. In contrast, Buchanan contends that a primary legal right to secession, whether nationalist or plebiscitary, will likely fare worse at both encouraging peace and respect for basic human rights and fostering political self-determination. With respect to the former, he notes that historically attempts to unilaterally secede are nearly always accompanied by violence, and at least in the case of national or ethnic groups, frequently involve campaigns of ethnic cleansing that can become genocidal. As for

---

[29] Obviously, these two strategies are incompatible; the first relies on empirical premises the second strategy argues we cannot currently defend. All that follows, however, is that we cannot embrace both strategies.

[30] Buchanan, *Justice, Legitimacy, and Self-Determination*, pp. 353–9. See also Norman, "Ethics of Secession," 41–3; Steven R. Ratner, *The Thin Justice of International Law* (New York: Oxford University Press, 2015), pp. 160–1. Sometimes, Buchanan includes as a separate ground for secession major violations of intrastate autonomy agreements, which suggests an attribution of noninstrumental value to political self-determination.

political self-determination, Buchanan suggests that the creation of a primary legal right to unilateral secession would likely discourage states from devolving political power to regional governments and/or investing in regions' economic development, or from facilitating internal migration, immigration, or asylum, all out of fear that doing so might eventually lead to secession and so the state's loss of territory and population. In short, a more permissive legal norm governing secession would likely do a worse job of advancing those values a morally defensible international legal order should aim to advance.

Altman and Wellman challenge a number of these arguments.[31] First, they point out that even in the absence of any international legal right many states already refrain from devolving political power to regional governments and/or fostering economic development in those regions because they fear it will lead to secession. It is not obvious, therefore, that the creation of a primary international legal right to secession would lead to an increase in such conduct, and if so, how large the increase would be. Second, they note that the devolution of political power to substate regional governments has sometimes served to pacify separatist desires. It is possible, therefore, that those who aim to preserve the existing state will conclude that they are more likely to realize this end by promoting intrastate autonomy than by persisting with centralized rule. If so, then state officials may elect to devolve political power to regional governments even if international law includes a primary right to secession.[32] Finally, Altman and Wellman suggest that the creation of a primary international legal right to secession may strengthen nationalist or would-be plebiscitary groups' bargaining power vis-à-vis other groups within the state, which may enable them to negotiate domestic political and legal arrangements that better advance their secure enjoyment of basic human rights and/or political self-determination. In other words, contrary to Buchanan's claim, the legal ability to threaten secession might actually facilitate intrastate autonomy.

Elsewhere, Wellman argues that Buchanan fails to build an empirical case strong enough to overcome the presumption that law ought to track morality, and so with respect to secession, that international law ought to accord any group willing and able to perform the functions that justify the state a primary right to secede:

> Even if Buchanan is right that international laws protecting primary rights to secede could generate some perverse incentives, it is not at all clear how much weight to give to this consideration. The fact that some of these incentives will exist whether or not the international legal system protects primary rights and that there would

---

[31] Altman and Wellman, *Liberal Theory*, pp. 58–65.

[32] However, some empirical work suggests that devolution increases rebellion where there is significant economic inequality between regions, and where territorially concentrated ethnic or national groups are largely excluded from national government (Kristin M. Bakke and Erik Wibbels, "Diversity, Disparity, and Civil Conflict in Federal States," *World Politics* 59, 1 (2006): 1–50). If far more states are characterized by the presence of this kind of economic inequality and political representation than are not, then only rarely will states have good reason to pursue the devolution of political power as a means to head off secession.

also be some *positive* side effects of institutionally recognizing these moral rights makes it questionable whether Buchanan's concerns are decisive. However, because moral rights hang in the balance, there are two things about which we can be confident: that the burden of proof to establish the empirical fact of the matter lies squarely on the shoulders of those who would *restrict* these moral rights and that it would not be sufficient to show that there is merely a slight advantage in favor of restricting these rights.[33]

Consider, first, Wellman's claim that because moral rights hang in the balance, those who would restrict the moral right to political self-determination bear the burden of demonstrating that such restrictions are necessary to protect people's basic human rights. Why not adopt the opposite position, namely, that when individuals' rights not to be murdered, raped, tortured, assaulted, and forcibly displaced are at stake, the burden of proof lies with those who advocate for greater institutional protection of the moral right to political self-determination (or secession) to demonstrate that this will not increase the incidence of such morally atrocious behavior? When what is at issue is a tradeoff between individual moral rights and a socially beneficial outcome, such as greater material prosperity, it may well be justifiable to claim that those who would restrict some people's moral rights bear the burden of demonstrating that doing so will produce the socially beneficial outcome they maintain will result. Perhaps the same is true when the tradeoff is between a very weighty right and one that is considerably less important. However, where very weighty rights exist on both sides of the balance, as appears to be true in the case of secession, it is hard to see what could justify placing the evidentiary burden on either side to the dispute.

Buchanan argues that we ought to limit the legal right to secede to a remedial right because a more permissive right will lead to an increase in violent conflict and the violation of basic human rights. Therefore, I interpret Wellman's talk of the "slight advantage" resulting from a restriction on the moral primary right to secede to be an increase in peace and/or the number of people whose basic human rights go unviolated. The question, then, is how great an increase in the incidence of murder, rape, torture, and so on, we should be willing to tolerate in return for an increase in the exercise of political self-determination, either in an independent state or as a result of various types of intrastate autonomy arrangement. Our answer might well depend on how life goes for those denied political self-determination, or as much political self-determination as they desire, as a result of international law not according them a primary right to secede. For example, if all of these individuals enjoy full citizenship in moderately just liberal-democratic states, then we might well conclude that it would be unjust to expose even a few people to rape or assaults they would otherwise not suffer, just so that these individuals could enjoy greater

---

[33] Christopher Wellman, "The Morality of Secession," in *Secession as an International Phenomenon: From America's Civil War to Contemporary Separatist Movements*, ed. Dan H. Doyle (Athens, GA: University of Georgia Press, 2010), p. 34.

political self-determination. Even if we begin from the world as it is, some people may still doubt that an increase in the exercise of political self-determination, independent of the contribution it makes to advancing the secure enjoyment of basic human rights, warrants the adoption of a legal norm that will also cause even a very small increase in the violation of basic human rights. But, perhaps more importantly, it is not clear that any answer to a very abstract question regarding acceptable tradeoffs between various rights will be of much use in settling disputes over which actors should enjoy an international legal right to secede, and the conditions under which they should enjoy that right. That is because we might all agree on the answer and yet disagree about what will actually occur if we adopt a particular international legal norm governing secession. For example, we might all agree that the prevention of 100 instances of rape or torture does not suffice to justify the failure to accord to all those groups willing and able to perform the functions that morally justify the state an international legal right to do so. However, we might disagree about how many more cases of rape and torture will actually occur if we reform international law so that it includes a primary international legal right to secede, with some hypothesizing that it will be 100 or fewer, and others hypothesizing that it will be far more than100. In short, the case for a remedial or for a primary legal right to secede, or for that matter against any legal right to secede, can only be made on the basis of empirical arguments regarding the likely consequences of adopting (or keeping) such a law.

In their coauthored discussion of secession, Altman and Wellman acknowledge this point, and so offer a different response to Buchanan's claim that a remedial legal right to secession gets the incentives right, while a primary legal right does not. Both Buchanan's arguments and their own provide plausible hypotheses regarding the effects of adopting one or the other of these international legal rights, and each party can point to some empirical evidence in support of their hypotheses. However, they maintain that the overall quantity and quality of the available data does not warrant any specific conclusions regarding the incentive effects of different international legal norms governing secession.[34] Rather, Altman and Wellman contend that the only defensible view is agnosticism: "[J]udgment should be suspended on any conclusion about a right to secede under international law until those potential consequences are far less uncertain than they are at this stage in the scholarly discussion of secession."[35] Yet while the theorist can rest content with such a conclusion, the political actor cannot; his or her agnosticism does not suspend judgment but leaves intact an international legal order that strongly discourages unilateral secession. Our question then, is this: assuming, arguendo, that Altman and Wellman's agnosticism is well founded, what course of action should be taken by those political actors who could influence reform to, or the preservation of, international law's current stance vis-à-vis secession?

[34] Altman and Wellman, *Liberal Theory*, p. 64.
[35] Ibid, p. 59.

One possibility is that they should focus their limited resources elsewhere; for example, on efforts to reform international legal norms where we have data that warrants significantly greater confidence that this will lead to an increase in international law's advancement of its proper moral goals.[36] While this strategy should not be dismissed out of hand, it also seems unsatisfactory given the prevalence of secessionist movements, the number of violent conflicts to which they give rise, and the frequency with which secession is mooted as a solution to internal conflicts (regardless of whether they originated in a quest for independent statehood).[37] A second possibility, therefore, is to employ a precautionary approach when arguing for the superiority of a specific international legal norm governing secession over its rivals.

The question of how to formulate a precautionary principle so that it is both precise enough to be action guiding while also compelling as a principle of rational choice is a vexed issue. However, Stephen Gardner finds a plausible candidate for a core precautionary principle in John Rawls' characterization of the conditions under which maximin reasoning is appropriate.[38] Roughly, such reasoning involves focusing exclusively on avoiding certain evils. Gardner (and Rawls) maintain it is rational to employ maximin reasoning when an actor faces a choice under uncertainty, cares little for the potential gains he forgoes relative to the minimum he aims to secure, and views the failure to secure that minimum as unacceptable or catastrophic.[39] Arguably, these three conditions are met when it comes to the selection of a legal norm governing secession. First, if Altman and Wellman correctly maintain that we should have no confidence in predictions regarding the outcomes different legal norms governing secession will produce, then in deciding whether we should retain the existing norm or instead seek to replace it with a more permissive one we choose under uncertainty. Second, there appears to be a fairly widespread consensus (at least among liberal political and legal theorists) that peace and the secure enjoyment of basic human rights enjoy a kind of priority over the noninstrumental value of political self-determination.[40] That priority need not be

[36] The same is true for those who aim to influence the conduct of political actors, including theorists of international law and justice.

[37] A 2003 study found that about half the civil wars since the end of the Cold War involved rebels seeking to secede or gain substantial intrastate autonomy, while a 2001 study found that roughly 70 percent of civil wars since 1945 were ethno-nationalist in nature. See David S. Sirosky, "Explaining Secession," in *The Ashgate Research Companion to Secession*, eds. Aleksander Pavkovic and Peter Radan (Burlington, VT: Ashgate Publishing, 2011), pp. 45–79 for citation to these and others studies that demonstrate the centrality of secession movements to the incidence of armed conflict.

[38] Stephen Gardner, "A Core Precautionary Principle," *Journal of Political Philosophy* 14, 1 (2006): 45–9.

[39] "Uncertainty" here is a technical term denoting the impossibility of attaching probabilities to any of the possible outcomes.

[40] Altman and Wellman, for example, explicitly grant that where realizing peace and human rights is incompatible with a legal right to secession the latter right must give way (Altman and Wellman, *Liberal Theory*, p. 56). Further support for the claim that we care far more about peace and the secure enjoyment of basic human rights than we do about political self-determination can be seen in the large literature arguing for armed responses to aggression and gross violations of human rights, but

lexical, but we must care relatively little about the advancement of political self-determination in comparison to our concern for setbacks to peace and the secure enjoyment of basic human rights. Third, and finally, the gross violation of basic human rights and, typically, war (or widespread violence) constitute a catastrophic or unacceptable outcome.[41] There is some reason, then, to think that in the present circumstances we ought to adopt a precautionary approach to theorizing secession, and this requires that we exclude from our deliberations any argument for a candidate norm premised on advancing or honoring the noninstrumental value of political self-determination. In other words, the precautionary approach entails that we ought to select among competing candidates for a legal norm-governing secession solely on the basis of which one we believe will best serve to advance peace and the secure enjoyment of basic human rights.

The precautionary approach appears to favor a remedial legal right over both the nationalist and plebiscitary primary legal rights to secession. The former tracks and responds to all and only those goals on the basis of which we ought to assess candidate norms *given our current knowledge*, whereas the attractiveness of the latter rights lies in their serving to advance political self-determination even in cases where doing so is not necessary to secure peace or individuals' basic human rights. But this is precisely the consideration that the precautionary approach requires we exclude from our deliberation. Of course, primary right theorists might respond that their favored legal norm will do better at advancing peace and human rights than will a remedial right to secession. To do so, however, would be to concede that their ideal theoretical accounts of the moral right to secede, which are grounded in the value of political self-determination, contribute nothing to the moral task of evaluating and possibly reforming existing international law. More importantly, it is hard to see why an international legal norm that is not specifically designed to advance the goal of peace and the secure enjoyment of human rights would do better at achieving that end than would a legal norm that is specifically designed to do so.

V SHOULD INTERNATIONAL LAW INCLUDE A REMEDIAL RIGHT TO SECESSION?

Even if a remedial right to secession will better serve the goal of advancing peace and the secure enjoyment of basic human rights than will a primary right, it may still prove inferior in this respect to international law's current stance on unilateral secession, namely, that outside the colonial context no group enjoys a legal right to unilateral secession. Consider, for example, Buchanan's characterization of a remedial right to secession: a territorially concentrated group may unilaterally

---

hardly any arguments at all for armed intervention in support of political self-determination for groups that have been neither recently forcibly annexed nor subject to gross violations of their human rights.

[41] I say "typically" because war may sometimes be morally permissible, although, arguably, most actual wars are not.

secede only if it is the victim of (a) forcible annexation by another state, or (b) serious and persistent violations of basic human rights. With regard to the examples Buchanan offers to motivate his case for a remedial right to secession for victims of forcible annexation, there is no need to reform international law to accommodate the intuition that these political communities had a right to statehood.[42] Where one state's forcible annexation of part or all of another state's people and territory goes unrecognized as a matter of international law, the victims retain their preexisting legal right to independent statehood. This was true of the Baltic States, for instance, which were illegally occupied by the Soviet Union between 1940 and 1991. Neither do we need a remedial right to secession to account for new states produced by the dissolution of a state, as in the case of the successor states to the USSR and Yugoslavia. Rather, the original state's loss of sovereignty over people and territory as part of its dissolution creates the necessary legal space in which the new, successor, states can arise.[43] A graver concern with a legal right to unilateral secession for victims of forcible annexation is that if it applies retroactively (that is, to forcible annexations carried out prior to the incorporation of a remedial right to secession into international law), it will invite or exacerbate violent conflict. Few if any borders were established in a manner free from injustice. In theory, this cost might be outweighed by the deterrent effect the remedial right would have on potential future forcible annexations. Yet, as noted above, contemporary international law already precludes the acquisition of sovereignty over territory and people through forcible annexation, and therefore already provides whatever deterrence might be achieved by the creation of a right to unilateral secession for victims of forcible annexation.

We should also be skeptical of a deterrence argument for a remedial right to secession in the case of serious and persistent violations of basic human rights perpetrated or condoned by the state. Presumably, the territorially concentrated victims of such a campaign of human rights violations will do whatever they can to stop it, including the use of force, regardless of whether they have a legal right to secede. Whatever deterrent effect the likelihood of such resistance provides will be unaffected by international law granting the victims a legal right to secede. Third parties, or at least other states, already enjoy a legal permission – indeed, a responsibility – to aid victims of systematic and persistent violations of their basic human rights by their own state, one that some argue includes the provision of military supplies and even armed intervention.[44] Neither should we forget that

[42] See, for example, Allen Buchanan, "Secession," section 2.2, *The Stanford Encyclopedia of Philosophy* (Fall 2017 Edition), Edward N. Zalta (ed.), https://plato.stanford.edu/archives/fall2017/entries/secession/.

[43] See the discussion of the Badinter Commission's findings vis-à-vis the new states that emerged on the territory formerly ruled by Yugoslavia in Matthew Craven, "Statehood," in *International Law*, 4th Edition, ed. Malcolm D. Evans (Oxford: Oxford University Press, 2014), p. 231.

[44] On the Responsibility to Protect, see paras. 138–9 of the 2005 World Summit Outcome Document, available at www.globalr2p.org/media/files/wsod_2005.pdf (accessed December 18, 2019).

international law already sanctions a number of practices that can be used to deter states – or better, government officials – from perpetrating gross violations of (some of) their subjects' basic human rights, including economic sanctions and international criminal charges. Taking all of these considerations into account, it seems highly unlikely that the fact that their conduct would create a legal right to unilateral secession for their victims would make the difference in state officials' decision not to engage in systematic and widespread violations of some of their territorially concentrated subjects' basic human rights.

Moreover, even if we concede *arguendo* that a remedial right to secession would make a small contribution to deterring violations of basic human rights, we must also take into account any incentives for perpetrating such violations this right would create. Donald Horowitz argues that were international law to include a right to remedial secession some would-be separatists would be motivated to provoke the state that rules them into violent crackdowns against their group, in the hope of acquiring a legal right to secede.[45] There is some evidence that exactly this line of thought motivated the Kosovo Liberation Army's conduct in the late 1990s.[46] Nino Kemoklidze argues that the recognition of Kosovo as an independent state by some members of the international community created a moral hazard subsequently realized in the separatist conflict in South Ossetia.[47] Others might add attempts at secession in Abkhazia and Eastern Ukraine. Of course, we must be careful here; actual examples of such conduct will not show that recognition of a legal right to secession would increase their incidence, since they occurred in the absence of such a right. Nevertheless, they do provide evidence that some actors seeking independence are prepared to instigate great violence against the very people whose interests they claim to be seeking to advance. Therefore, we should be wary of legal reforms that might encourage these actors to pursue such a course of action, particularly if we have compelling reasons to doubt those reforms will produce much good.

Perhaps a remedial right to secession can be defended on the grounds that its successful exercise will decrease the occurrence of gross human rights violations perpetrated by states against some subset of their subjects. Where such a campaign has taken place, it might be thought that the likelihood that the perpetrators and the victims will be able to coexist as equal citizens of even a federal state is less than the likelihood that they will be able to coexist as citizens of two, independent, states. Whether this is true depends on a host of factors, however. For example, the division

---

[45] Donald Horowitz, "A Right to Secede?" in *Secession and Self-Determination*, NOMOS XLV, eds. Stephen Macedo and Allen Buchanan (New York: New York University Press, 2003), pp. 50–76.

[46] See Alan J. Kuperman, "The Moral Hazard of Humanitarian Intervention: Lessons from the Balkans," *International Studies Quarterly* 52, 1 (2008): 49–80. For a contrary view, see Alex J. Bellamy and Paul D. Williams, "On the Limits of Moral Hazard: The Responsibility to Protect, Armed Conflict, and Mass Atrocities," *European Journal of International Relations* 18, 3 (2012): 539–71.

[47] Nino Kemoklidze, "The Kosovo Precedent and the 'Moral Hazard' of Secession," *Journal of International Law and International Relations* 5, 2 (2009): 117–40.

of the original state may give rise to irredentist conflicts, or to systematic persecution of members of one group that remain "trapped" within the territory of the state in which the other group is a majority. Indeed, a recent study concludes that partition does not prevent the recurrence of civil war.[48] More importantly, whether a single- or two-state solution is most likely to reduce the likelihood of conflict in the future depends on a variety of factors that vary from case to case.[49] Perhaps, then, a morally defensible international law ought to give international actors greater flexibility to determine in each case which course of action will best serve to advance peace and the secure enjoyment of basic human rights. By this measure the existing international legal norm governing secession may be superior to one that would create a remedial right. While the current norm recognizes no right to unilateral secession it does permit consensual secession, even in cases where that takes place in conditions that could hardly be described as voluntary. The secession of South Sudan provides a contemporary example; Eritrea is a slightly older one.

Of course, this argument entails that a group whose members have been subject to gross violations of their basic human rights by the state that rules them are largely at the mercy of other states' willingness to pressure their state into holding referendum on secession. Surely, the fate of these victims should not rest on power and interest; rather, they should enjoy an entitlement, a right, to their own state. While understandable, this reaction may prove mistaken for two reasons. First, whether a group ought to enjoy an international legal right to secession depends on the contribution a norm according groups of that type such a right will make to the advancement of peace and the secure enjoyment of human rights. The mere observation that a candidate legal norm will leave certain actors dependent on politics does not suffice to show that the norm is morally indefensible. Despite that fact, the norm may still be the best means to achieving the aforementioned goals, even if, in this context, "best" means only "bad, but not as bad as the feasible alternatives." Second, it may be a mistake to oppose law and politics, and to think that the creation of a legal right to remedial secession offers an alternative to power and interest – to politics – as a means for achieving peace and the secure enjoyment of basic human rights. Law can serve to channel politics, to shape its exercise, but so too power and politics shape the form and exercise of law, as would no doubt be true were international law to incorporate a remedial right to secession. What we must aim for, therefore, is not the replacement of politics with law but the optimal mix of law and politics. The claim here is that at present it is the existing international legal norm governing secession that does so, not a remedial right.

---

[48] Nicholas Sambanis and Jonah Schulhofer-Wohl, "What's in a Line?" *International Security* 34, 2 (2009): 82–118.

[49] Among myriad factors that Sirosky identifies in his three level analysis of the causes of secession are political grievances, economic inequality, ethno-demography, ethno-geography, the state's institutional capacity and strength, state policies of repression and inclusion, and other states' strategic interests. See Sirosky, "Explaining Secession."

The foregoing considerations add up to a plausible case for the conclusion that, at least at present and for the foreseeable future, international law will better serve to advance peace and the secure enjoyment of basic human rights if it includes no right to secession than if it includes a remedial one. These arguments are conditional on empirical premises, of course. The complexity of the phenomena in question and the limits on our ability to control the many variables that are plausibly thought to contribute to the incidence of demands for secession, as well as the use of violence to advance or respond to such demands, warrants considerable modesty when drawing a conclusion based on such claims. As we noted earlier, however, we must choose some norm to govern secession, and can only do so on the basis of the best information currently available to us.

11

International Trade Law: Free Trade, Fair Trade,
and Trade in Stolen Goods

In 2018, the value of international trade in goods and services was more than 25 trillion US dollars.[1] This was a 3 percent increase over the previous year, and marked the eighth straight year in which the value of international trade had increased. While the United States, China, and several European countries remained the world's leading traders, developing economies had a 44 percent share in world merchandise trade, and a 34 percent share of world trade in commercial services. Although it contributes a smaller share to most countries' economies than does domestic exchanges of goods and services, international trade directly impacts the lives of hundreds of millions of people around the world in significant ways, and indirectly shapes the lives of billions more.

International trade is governed by international legal rules set out in hundreds of agreements between states. The most well-known of these is the Marrakesh agreement establishing the World Trade Organization (WTO), and the various Annexes to which the WTO's member states have subsequently agreed. As of 2019, only sixteen countries remain outside the WTO agreement, most of which are either small island countries or entities that are not universally recognized as states. Other important multilateral (i.e., multistate) trade agreements include the North American Free Trade Agreement (recently superseded by the US–Mexico-Canada Agreement), the European Union, the Southern Common Market (or Mercosur), the ASEAN Free Trade Area, and recently, the Comprehensive and Progressive Agreement for Trans-Pacific Partnership. Many countries are also party to multiple bilateral trade agreements, such as the Australia–United States Free Trade Agreement, the Comprehensive Economic and Trade Agreement between Canada and the EU, and the China–Peru Free Trade Agreement.

Our concern in this chapter is with the moral justifiability of the legal rules governing the exchange of goods and services across international borders set out in agreements like those listed above. We begin in section I with the economic

---

[1] The data presented in this paragraph comes from the World Trade Organization's *World Trade Statistical Review 2019*, available at www.wto.org/english/res_e/statis_e/wts2019_e/wts19_toc_e.htm (last accessed December 6, 2019).

argument for free trade, namely, that the elimination of barriers to international trade such as tariffs or import quotas facilitates the efficient use of natural and human resources. In section II, we consider three moral arguments for free trade: (1) by increasing the rate of economic growth, free trade contributes to the goal of maximizing aggregate or total human welfare; (2) free trade provides an especially effective mechanism for assisting those living in multidimensional poverty to escape it; and (3) free trade follows from our duty to respect individual freedom, and in particular, individuals' rights to property and freedom of contract. Moral arguments for constraints on cross-border trade are the subject of section III. Specifically, we examine whether either permissible partiality to compatriots or considerations of fairness require states to restrict or place conditions on international trade. We conclude in section IV by considering the claim that as citizens of states that import oil and other natural resources from countries ruled by tyrants, and as consumers of those resources, we facilitate and engage in trade in stolen goods.

I THE ECONOMIC ARGUMENT FOR TRADE

Why should states engage in trade, and so, all else equal, eliminate or forbear from erecting barriers to doing so? For example, why should a state that currently imposes a high tariff on manufactured goods such as cars and computers, or on agricultural products such as soy beans and shrimp, reduce or eliminate those tariffs, or maintain a low- or no-tariff policy if it already has one? The most common answer is that by doing so the state will achieve a higher rate of economic growth than it will if it maintains or adopts more protectionist measures, that is, laws or policies that make economic exchanges across international borders costlier. In other words, by encouraging international trade a state will make itself richer than it will become if it adopts less trade-friendly laws and policies. This is so because international trade enables a society to generate more value from its limited natural and human resources, or what is the same, to use those resources more efficiently.

Most importantly, international trade facilitates production in accordance with each society's comparative advantage. Suppose state A produces both computers and cars for consumption in its domestic market, but that it does better at building the former than the latter. Trade with other states enables state A to generate more value from its limited resources by importing those goods it produces less efficiently, while focusing on producing those goods it can manufacture more efficiently. The more state A can shift its productive resources to manufacturing computers, while still meeting domestic demand for cars, the more value it will generate from the use of those resources. This is true even if state A is better at producing both computers and cars than is any other state. The comparison in comparative advantage is not between states but between the different productive activities a single state may undertake. The point is really a simple one. As much as possible, states should seek to engage in those activities that generate the most value. Insofar as trade with other states allows them to shift some of their resources from less productive to more productive activities, trade makes them richer.

International trade spurs economic growth in myriad other ways as well. For instance, it often makes possible greater division of labor, economies of scale, and specialization than can be achieved within a single state. As a consequence, the cost of products drops and/or their quality (and so their value) increases. Moreover, the efficiency gains produced by the division of labor, economies of scale, and specialization free up resources that can be put to other uses. Oftentimes, international trade enhances competition in domestic markets, particularly in states with smaller economies where the size of the domestic market favors the emergence of monopoly or oligopoly. Finally, international trade facilitates innovation by rapidly disseminating new ideas and, through greater competition, strengthening producers' incentives to improve their existing products and to create new ones.

On its face, then, the case for free trade seems quite compelling. Trade enables a state to generate more value from its limited resources, and so grow richer. Yet resistance to lowering barriers to trade, or calls to raise them higher, comes from many quarters. Consider, first, those who argue that under the right conditions a state can actually do better at growing its economy by adopting certain protectionist measures than if it embraces free trade. For example, under certain conditions state A may be able to improve its terms of trade with state B by raising an existing tariff or imposing a new one on imports from the latter. These conditions include state B not retaliating by raising an existing tariff or imposing a new one on goods it imports from state A, the tariff not resulting in decreases in the efficiency of state A's use of its resources that exceed the income gains produced by paying for fewer imports from state B, and consumers in state A not simply substituting products imported from state C for the now more expensive goods produced in state B. Still, at least in theory, a tariff that reduces imports without too much impact on exports or the efficient use of domestic resources will make a state richer than if it goes without that tariff, and so sends more money to other states to pay for the larger amount of goods it imports from them.

Likewise, as a matter of economic theory infant industry protections serve to maximize a state's national income over the medium to long term. For instance, high tariffs on computers may allow domestic computer manufacturers the time to gain the skills and size they need to compete with computer manufacturers located in other countries. Without the protected market tariffs provide, these domestic firms would not be able to compete with foreign manufacturers, and so would not remain in business long enough to become competitive in a relatively open market. Particularly where infant industry protection serves to move more of a country's labor force from low-productivity occupations such as farming small plots of land to higher-productivity occupations such as manufacturing, they provide a superior boost to economic growth than what would be achieved in their absence. As in the terms of trade example described above, however, the income-maximizing argument for infant industry protection goes through only if certain conditions are met. Most importantly, those protections need to be removed once domestic producers have had time to grow to the point where they can compete with foreign producers.[2] If they are not, citizens of this state will lose out on the various gains from international trade described earlier. In concrete terms, the computers available to them will likely be inferior in quality and higher in price, which will result in lower productivity than would occur in the absence of those tariffs. Moreover, the production of domestic computers is likely to be less efficient, and indeed, the most efficient use of the country's resources may turn out not to involve computer manufacturing at all.

While conceding that in theory protectionist measures can sometimes be justifiable on income-maximizing grounds, advocates of free trade contend that this is rarely so in practice. Rather, attempts to impose tariffs or to use other measures to improve the terms of trade produce retaliatory measures or inefficient reallocation of domestic resources that make a state's economy smaller than it would have been in their absence. Similarly, domestic producers who have benefited from infant industry protections frequently work hard to preserve them long after the point where doing so produces a net benefit to the present and future citizens of their state.[3] From the standpoint of evaluating trade policies in terms of their impact on a state's economic growth, protectionist measures appear difficult to defend.[4]

A second, especially vocal, set of agents who advocate for protectionist measures are those individuals within a state who stand to lose from their elimination, or to gain if they are put in place. While lower barriers to trade in cars may allow state A to produce to its comparative advantage in computers, and so reap greater value in total from its limited resources, this policy will likely also produce job losses in the car-manufacturing sector (as well as financial loses for the owners of companies in this sector). Some of those workers may quickly find employment with computer-manufacturing companies, conveniently located where they currently live, and so end up no worse off. Others may end up employed by new companies, possibly in new industries, that exist only because state A is now using its limited resources more efficiently, thereby freeing up resources that can be put to other uses. And all may benefit from reductions in the price of computers and an improvement in their quality that comes from greater economies of scale in the computer manufacturing industry. Nevertheless, taking all of this into account some workers will still end up

---

[2] Indeed, the commitment to reduce or eliminate infant industry protections must be credible or domestic producers may have little incentive to take the steps necessary to become globally competitive.

[3] Some might argue that defenders of free trade are too quick to dismiss the possibility of designing rules and institutions that reduce these risks. Even if this is true, however, advocates of free trade are right to caution against too quick a move from theory to practice.

[4] Note that this conclusion does not rule out a defense of trade barriers on fairness grounds. It may be that some (risk of) reduction in economic growth is a cost we ought to bear in order to ensure that states or individuals are treated fairly. See the discussion in section III.

worse off than they would have been had the tariffs remained in place, and the same is true for some investors in the car-manufacturing sector. Even where this is not *actually* the case some workers and owners may *mistakenly believe* it is, because the benefits they receive from lower barriers to international trade are hard to identify and often realized in the future (for instance, only with the emergence of new industries) while the costs of a lost job are clear and immediate. Finally, many workers and owners view their jobs not merely as a means to satisfying material needs and desires but also as a central element of their identity and their conception of a good life. It is (almost) as much a part of their sense of who they are and what makes their life worthwhile as their familial roles as mothers, fathers, sisters, brothers, and so on, or their membership in a religious or political community. Where this is the case, many individuals may prefer the preservation of their jobs or companies over the prospect of a certain amount of material gain that will follow from reducing barriers to international trade. Taken together, these considerations provide strong incentives for people in import-competing industries to pressure political office-holders to create, maintain, or increase barriers to trade that make foreign firms less competitive in state A's domestic market. We will consider below whether these considerations ever *justify* protectionist measures. Here, our concern is simply to explain why some individuals support protectionist measures even though lower barriers to trade enable faster economic growth.

The fact that under the right conditions certain barriers to trade can make a state richer than it would otherwise be, as well as the presence of domestic interest groups that benefit from particular protectionist measures, explains why states enter into international trade agreements. Many political leaders recognize that international trade can be mutually beneficial – good for their own economy as well as for the economies of the states with whom they trade. But they also recognize that other states may be tempted to adopt protectionist measures, for either or both of the reasons noted above, and that other states have the same concern toward them. Thus, states need to provide one another with assurance that they will not adopt beggar-thy-neighbor trade policies; for example, that political leaders will not give in to demands for protection from domestic producers who fare worse in the market as a result of lowered barriers to competition. International trade agreements that create binding legal obligations on states help address this assurance problem. First, they enable political officeholders to respond to domestic pressure for protection from international competition by claiming that their hands are tied. While they may sympathize with the plight of those facing tougher competition as a result of freer trade, the law prevents them from responding with protectionist measures. But second, and perhaps more importantly, by reducing barriers to trade international agreements contribute to the growth of export industries whose workers and owners can be negatively affected by any protectionist measures other states impose in retaliation for state A raising barriers of its own. These workers and owners can, and often will, offer domestic support to political leaders who resist calls for protectionism, or withdraw support from those who do not. In short, while the initial argument for free trade is an economic one premised on efficiency, the argument for trade agreements or treaties is a political one.[5]

The discussion in this section supports two conclusions. First, in general, states benefit by lowering barriers to international trade, at least in the sense that they grow richer in material terms than they would were they to retain or adopt protectionist measures. Second, international trade law, which is primarily the product of bilateral and multilateral international trade agreements, plays a crucial role in enabling states to reap the rewards of trade. It does so by providing them with assurance that their trading partners will not give in to the temptation to pursue beggar-thy-neighbor policies, or to sacrifice long-term gains for immediate political benefits. By themselves, however, these observations provide neither a moral justification for engaging in trade nor a specific moral standard (or standards) we can use to morally assess the arrangements set out in any particular trade agreement. Rather, we still need a moral argument demonstrating that reducing barriers to trade is morally permissible or perhaps even obligatory because of its contribution to economic growth, or as we shall see, because respect for individual autonomy demands it. In addition, we need to consider whether there are any moral considerations that qualify the pursuit of economic growth; for example, certain conditions it must satisfy, or constraints on the means we may adopt to advance this goal. It is to these tasks that we turn in the next three sections.

II THE MORAL ARGUMENT FOR TRADE

Some defenders of free (or freer) trade advocate for it on the grounds that it maximizes aggregate or total human welfare.[6] Consider two versions of this argument. The first defines human welfare in terms of preference satisfaction. Individuals are presumed to have preference rankings over outcomes, and to do better (in other words, enjoy greater welfare) when one of their higher ranked preferences is satisfied than when one of their lower ranked preferences is satisfied. For example, suppose I rank getting a free piece of pizza over having to pay $1 for a slice, and I rank paying $1 for a piece of pizza over going without pizza at all (but having one more dollar in my wallet). If you give me a piece of pizza for free, you will maximize my welfare. If you do not and I buy a piece of pizza for $1 instead, I will be

---

5   The argument in the text also serves as a response to those who maintain that state A will often do best by reducing barriers to trade even when other states do not. While this may be true, the adoption of such a policy will often be political suicide, as those domestic actors harmed by such a policy will have an easy time making the case that other states are taking advantage of state A, and that state A needs leaders who will stand up for its citizens by adopting protectionist measures. International trade agreements reduce political leaders' vulnerability to losing office as a result of such arguments.

6   This view is probably most common among economists, although often neither explicitly formulated nor defended. However, it has its defenders in other disciplines (including philosophy) and some economists reject it, typically in favor of the individual liberty/autonomy argument discussed below.

less well off than I might have been, but still better off than if I have no opportunity to buy pizza and therefore go without it. Now, suppose that morally defensible laws and public policy, including those that regulate trade, ought to maximize human welfare. Given a preference satisfaction account of human welfare, trade law and policy are morally justifiable if and only if they maximally satisfy the preferences of those subject to (or affected by) it. Markets, or at least well-functioning markets, are especially well-suited to maximizing aggregate preference satisfaction; that is, to enabling many individuals to satisfy higher ranked preferences. Insofar as free trade improves the performance of markets in myriad ways as described in the previous section, it follows that international trade enhances preference satisfaction, and so better serves the goal of maximizing human welfare than does protectionism.

The second version of the aggregate welfare maximizing moral argument for free trade substitutes an objective account of human welfare for the subjective account of human welfare as preference satisfaction. On this account, human welfare is a matter of getting what is good for you and not merely what you happen to want. Put another way, it is a matter of enjoying those elements that make up a truly flourishing life for human beings, not leading whatever way of life you happen to desire.[7] Increased economic growth can promote human flourishing in many ways; for example, by enabling people to escape conditions that leave them vulnerable to disease and funding new research into cures for those illnesses people still suffer, or by expanding the available types of employment and entertainment as well as people's ability to pursue them. Given that free trade produces faster economic growth than occurs in the presence of barriers to trade, it can better serve the goal of maximizing objective human welfare than will the adoption of protectionism.[8]

Both versions of the aggregate welfare maximizing argument for free trade confront numerous objections, starting with the specific conceptions of human welfare they invoke. For example, critics of the preference satisfaction account argue that when people's preferences are the product of oppressive social practices their satisfaction does not provide a compelling account of what it is for a person's life to go well. People's preferences may also reflect false factual beliefs, in which case satisfying them may not provide people what they really want, meaning what they would desire were their preference ranking based on true factual beliefs.[9] In one sense, the objective account of human welfare fares better than the preference

---

[7] Of course, satisfying some of your desires and successfully pursuing certain projects you set for yourself may be among those elements that make up an objectively good human life. The key distinction is that on an objective account of human welfare the value of those things that contribute to a good life do not depend entirely, or in some cases at all, on whether they are valued by the person whose life it is.

[8] As we will discuss below, the success of both versions of the aggregate welfare maximizing argument for free trade may depend on the adoption of additional laws and policies that do not directly concern the international exchange of goods and services.

[9] For discussion of these and other objections to a preference satisfaction account of welfare, see Daniel M. Hausman and Michael S. McPherson, *Economic Analysis, Moral Philosophy, and Public Policy, 2nd Edition* (Cambridge: Cambridge University Press, 2006), pp. 118–29.

satisfaction account, since reflective people generally agree that wanting something does not always suffice to make it good for a person, and not wanting something does not necessarily entail that getting it adds nothing to a person's welfare. Still, there are plenty of disputes regarding the elements of an objectively good life for human beings, whether specific elements are necessary or sufficient for an objectively good life, and how important each element is in comparison to the others. These disputes make it harder to determine whether free (or freer) trade or specific protectionist measures better contribute to maximizing human welfare. Indeed, the contested nature of the good life is sometimes invoked to justify reliance on preference satisfaction when evaluating law and public policy. The argument is that these should be designed to maximize preference satisfaction not because the good life is getting what you want but because in general individuals are more likely to correctly identify what is truly good for them than are legislators or policymakers. How often and under what conditions this is true is a matter of serious debate, however, and any attempt to answer these questions may well depend on an objective account of human welfare, and so have to contend with all of the disputes that accompany it.

Many critics also reject the premise that morally defensible law and public policy should aim to maximize *total* welfare, without regard for the distribution of gains and losses in welfare among the state's citizens (or all those affected, which may include many noncitizens). In principle, the aggregate welfare maximizing argument justifies a trade policy or legal regime that produces fabulous lives for a few, while also leaving everyone else destitute, as long as the result is more welfare in total than would be achieved under any other policy or legal regime. This implication strikes many people as deeply problematic, and a sufficient reason to deny the moral relevance of gains or losses to *aggregate* welfare. Defenders of maximizing aggregate welfare counter that such a scenario is extremely unlikely. Indeed, given certain uncontroversial facts about human beings, such as the diminishing marginal utility that characterizes our consumption of any good, the goal of maximizing aggregate welfare is far more likely to justify laws and policies that produce a fairly egalitarian distribution of resources, and perhaps also opportunities. Some critics will remain unimpressed with this rejoinder, however, since it still denies that human beings enjoy a certain type of moral status that places significant *principled* limits on sacrificing the welfare of some to increase the welfare of others.

Setting aside this general dispute between consequentialists and non-consequentialists, few challenge the claim that the aggregate welfare maximizing argument for free trade depends on how the gains from trade are distributed. Rather, disagreement centers on what follows from that observation. Advocates of free trade argue that aggregate welfare maximization is best achieved via a two-step process. First, a state should adopt laws and policies, including those that reduce or eliminate barriers to trade, that maximize the size of its economy. Second, it should adopt laws and policies that distribute the resources and opportunities its economy produces so that they maximize the total welfare of its citizens (or, perhaps, all those affected by its laws and policies). In crafting the latter laws and policies, however, the state should be careful not to reduce economic growth. Put another way, a state should try to make its economic "pie" as big as possible, and then adopt policies that ensure the "pie" is distributed in such a way that it maximizes aggregate welfare. It should avoid policies that result in a smaller pie, and so leaves less to be distributed to its citizens, even if those policies ensure that some of its citizens will enjoy more pie than they would in the absence of those protectionist measures.

Thus, those who argue for free trade on aggregate welfare maximizing grounds may also defend redistributive domestic policies, including those that specifically target individuals made worse off as a result of international trade. These trade adjustment assistance (TAA) programs can include training in new skills, assistance in job searches, an extension of the duration during which workers are eligible for unemployment benefits, and supplementary payments to workers whose new jobs pay them less than their old ones. Much depends on the specifics of the program, however. Unsurprisingly, some advocates of free trade maintain that displaced workers will be far better served by reducing or eliminating domestic market-distorting practices such as occupational licensing or zoning laws that make housing in economically dynamic cities prohibitively expensive than they will be by trade adjustment assistance programs. Moreover, whatever domestic policy conclusions may be warranted as a matter of ideal theory, we still confront the question of what we ought to do in nonideal circumstances. Expanding trade adjustment assistance programs may be more politically feasible than reforming occupational licensing laws or zoning rules that severely limit residential development. Or, perhaps, if neither robust TAA measures nor domestic market-expanding measures are politically feasible, then certain protectionist measures that contribute directly or indirectly to a more egalitarian distribution of the gains from a slower growing economy could prove to be aggregate welfare maximizing. Regardless, two key points warrant emphasis. First, on the aggregate welfare-maximizing approach the justifiability of a law or policy depends on both immediate and more distant consequences, for example, on lower barriers to trade and domestic policies that shape how the gains from trade are distributed. Second, any conclusion depends heavily on empirical claims regarding how our natural and social worlds work, or could be made to work.

Even those who deny that morality requires that we attempt to maximize aggregate welfare typically accept more modest welfare-promoting duties, such as a duty to alleviate the suffering of those who live in multidimensional poverty, or who are at risk of falling into it.[10] Some defend this conclusion by appeal to basic moral rights, arguing that the weighty interests all human beings have in freedom from the

---

[10]　As the name suggests, a multidimensional account conceives of poverty in terms of a set of deprivations, some of which are components of well-being and some of which are reliable and relatively easy to measure proxies for risks to human well-being. One common multidimensional conception of poverty includes measures of health (for example, malnourishment), education (such as years of

deprivations that characterize multidimensional poverty ground claims against all other human beings to assistance in escaping or avoiding it. A duty to alleviate poverty may also be defended as an instance of Good Samaritanism; that is, a duty to rescue others from grave harm when doing so is not too costly. Finally, the duty to assist the global poor may arise as a consequence of their shared membership or participation in the global economic and/or political order (in which case, the global poor may be owed more than just assistance in escaping or avoiding multidimensional poverty). Whatever its foundation, nearly every theorist of global justice, as well as nearly every scholar or practitioner of international trade law, defends (or assumes) the existence of a duty to alleviate poverty. Contemporary debates regarding the relationship between trade and poverty alleviation center on the contribution specific trade rules make to enhancing or alleviating poverty, not on the moral relevance of these effects.

Some theorists contest the assumption that the moral justifiability of law, including trade law, turns on whether it promotes human welfare, let alone whether it maximizes it. Many of these critics maintain instead that morally justifiable law serves the goal of protecting individual freedom or autonomy. This includes freedom from assault or rape, of course, as well as freedom of speech and association. It also includes liberty of contract, however; the right to dispose of one's labor and one's property as one wishes consistent with respect for others' freedom or autonomy. No doubt the desire to improve their own lives, and that of friends and family, is what normally motivates people to engage in trade. Nevertheless, the moral case for reducing barriers to trade does not depend on its producing such improvements, on its promoting or maximizing welfare, even though it often will. Rather, the moral case for free trade rests on respect for individuals as creatures capable of choosing for themselves how to live their lives.

The success of this argument as a defense of free trade likely depends on the nature and scope of the rights to contract and to property. If those rights are natural or prepolitical, any laws that constrain their exercise beyond what is necessary to respect and protect other natural or prepolitical rights will be morally unjustifiable. Given that protectionist laws are unlikely to satisfy this condition, a liberal or libertarian natural-rights conception of the rights to contract and property likely entails the moral justifiability (indeed, necessity) of free trade. Alternatively, it may be that the rights to contract and property should be understood as derived from principles of justice that specify fair terms of cooperation for members of a political society. This may entail that individuals have no right to engage in economic exchanges, including international ones, that will produce an unfair distribution of burdens and benefits among the members of this society. Protectionist measures that preclude these sorts of exchanges will not violate

schooling), and living standards (type of cooking fuel, source of drinking water). For a helpful introduction, see the Oxford Poverty and Human Development Initiative's "Global Multidimensional Poverty Index 2019," available at https://ophi.org.uk/wp-content/uploads/G-MPI_Report_2019_PDF.pdf (last accessed December 10, 2019).

individual's right to contract (for the exchange of goods and services), since the scope of that right is set by the terms for fair cooperation. Still, the goal of protecting individual freedom or autonomy may provide a powerful argument in favor of trade, and so law that facilitates trade, even if it also justifies certain conditions or limits on it.

Consider, for example, barriers to trade in agricultural products. Both developed and developing countries currently employ a mixture of at the border measures such as tariffs and import quotas and behind the border measures such as subsidies and sanitary regulations to favor domestic farmers over foreign ones. In doing so, they interfere with, and often prevent altogether, voluntary transactions between domestic consumers and foreign producers. If foreign farmers are willing to sell their crop at a lower price than are domestic producers, and domestic consumers prefer to buy cheaper agricultural products from foreign farmers than more expensive agricultural products from domestic farmers, the state will need to offer a compelling moral justification for using coercion to prevent this exchange, or for shaping the terms on which it may be carried out. Indeed, in the case of agricultural goods, this conclusion also follows if we take the promotion of aggregate welfare to be the moral standard that norms governing international trade must meet if they are to be morally defensible. Arguably, the same is true if we evaluate norms regulating trade from the standpoint of poverty reduction. The devil is in the details, however. Incomplete trade liberalization can leave the poor worse off than they were even if full liberalization would have improved their lot and/or shrunk their number. Domestic policy choices are also crucially important, since a corrupt governing elite can deprive poor farmers of the benefits that flow from freer trade.

In short, whether we ground it in a duty to maximize aggregate welfare, a more limited duty to alleviate and ultimately eliminate poverty, or a duty to respect individual freedom or autonomy, there is a compelling moral case for facilitating and engaging in trade. In fact, few thoughtful people deny this. The debate between advocates of free trade and defenders of fair trade does not concern whether or not to engage in trade. Both acknowledge that there are weighty moral considerations that favor international exchange. Rather, the debate concerns the terms on which trade must be conducted if it is to serve the moral values listed above. The point may be put this way: while the promotion of human welfare and/or respect for individual autonomy creates a presumption in favor of eliminating barriers to trade, those same values, or perhaps some other equally important value, may qualify or override that presumption, at least under nonideal circumstances. In the next section, I consider several arguments to this effect.

III MORAL ARGUMENTS FOR CONSTRAINTS ON TRADE

A *The Argument from Permissible Partiality to Compatriots*

Many people believe that members of a political community are permitted and perhaps even required to exercise greater concern for one another's welfare than they are for the welfare of nonmembers. Citizens of the United States, for example, have a moral right and perhaps a moral duty to prioritize the flourishing of their fellow citizens over the flourishing of citizens of other countries. Under certain conditions, the moral permissibility of partiality to compatriots might be thought to justify raising or maintaining barriers to trade even though this will reduce the rate of economic growth in (some) other countries, and so lead to lower gains in welfare for (some) people living in those countries than they would otherwise enjoy. In other words, a state's right to give greater weight to the welfare of its own citizens justifies its adopting trade policies that benefit its own citizens but that also produce a lesser gain in total global welfare than would occur in the absence of those protectionist measures.

One response to this defense of restrictions on trade is to reject the claim that compatriots have a right, let alone a duty, to give greater weight to one another's welfare than they do to the welfare of those who are not members of their political community. Yet even if we grant the moral permissibility of partiality to compatriots the justifiability of restrictions on trade does not necessarily follow. Most importantly, there are limits to the morally permissible partiality people may exercise toward those to whom they stand in a special relationship. Many readers will likely agree that I may improve my daughter's chances of making the soccer team by practicing with her, even though I do not extend that same benefit to the other girls who also wish to make the team. But surely it is impermissible for me to improve my daughter's chances of being selected for the team by breaking the legs of her competitors. This suggests that our duties to respect certain rights held by all people constrain what we are morally permitted to do to benefit those to whom we bear a special relationship. Assuming this is just as true for compatriots as it is for family members, trade restrictions will only be justifiable on the basis of permissible partiality if they do not violate these rights.

If the rights that limit permissible partiality include the freedom to contract and to acquire and dispose of property then permissible partiality to compatriots will not provide a moral justification for any trade restrictions. That is because protectionist measures interfere with the exercise of the rights to contract and to property by both members and nonmembers of the political community who wish to engage in exchange with one another. This argument rests on a highly contentious notion of property, however, and perhaps also a disputable understanding of the scope of freedom of contract. Yet a similar, albeit narrower, conclusion may follow from a more widely accepted claim regarding those rights that limit permissible partiality, namely, that they include the right to adequate nutrition, to clean drinking water, to adequate shelter, and to freedom from the other deprivations that characterize multidimensional poverty. If trade restrictions prevent (some of) those suffering from multidimensional poverty from escaping these circumstances either by engaging in international trade or benefiting from others doing so, then those measures fall outside the scope of permissible partiality, and instead count as wrongs done to those whose rights they violate. As we noted in the previous section, restrictions on trade in agricultural products may frequently satisfy this condition. Two points regarding this argument are worth noting, however. First, in some cases it may be possible to contest the claim that the trade restrictions are the cause of the rights violations. Rather, the deprivations suffered by those living in multidimensional poverty may be due to the absence, incompetence, or corruption of domestic government, so that the elimination of the protective measures would make no difference to the incidence of these deprivations.[11] Second, it may be that while some protectionist measures fall afoul of rights that limit the scope of permissible partiality to compatriots, not all do. For instance, the use of import quotas on films to protect domestic filmmakers from foreign competition may not violate foreign filmmakers' rights, in the same way that my practicing soccer with my daughter may give her an advantage over her competitors for a spot on the team but not violate their rights. If so, then such quotas may be an example of morally permissible partiality to compatriots.

Many of those who believe that, within limits, states may favor their own citizens over foreigners will deny that favoritism or partiality is permissible when it comes to the state's treatment of its own citizens. Rather, the state ought to display equal concern for the welfare of each of its citizens, and/or equal respect for their autonomy. While in some cases that may involve extending certain rights or benefits to some but not others, or imposing (or enforcing) duties on some but not others, these differential forms of treatment will reflect divergences in need, ability, or circumstances, and not in the weight or importance the state attaches to the welfare or autonomy of its citizens. The problem with protectionist measures is that even if they fall within the ambit of permissible partiality between states, those same measures are likely to fall afoul of the requirement that states treat their own citizens impartially. This is so because in adopting protectionist measures that preserve some jobs, the state also prevents the creation of other jobs, namely, those that would have arisen as a result of the greater efficiency realized through international trade. While tariffs on auto imports may protect some jobs in car manufacturing, they also prevent jobs from appearing in those industries that provide the goods and services people would consume (more of) if they had the opportunity to spend less to buy a car. Consequently, some people who would have worked in those industries will go unemployed instead, or earn lower incomes than they would have received in those industries, or work jobs they find less satisfying or fulfilling. Of course, these consequences may also befall some workers employed by car manufacturers if the tariffs are eliminated. But insofar as protectionism leads to slower economic growth,

[11] One might also argue that while a state's protectionist measures do contribute to the persistence of multidimensional poverty in other states, this would not be the case if rulers in those other states fulfilled their moral obligations to their subjects, and that one state should not have to forgo what would otherwise be morally permissible partiality just because the rulers of another state are treating their subjects unjustly.

and that leads in turn to higher unemployment (and oftentimes lower wages, except for those in the protected industry), it amounts to a choice to benefit a smaller number of better off citizens at the expense of a larger number of worse-off citizens. Such a choice is incompatible with equal concern for each and every citizen. Moreover, trade restrictions that compel consumers to pay more for products so that domestic producers can keep their jobs or earn higher wages are an affront to the former's autonomy.[12] In Kantian terms, protectionist measures treat consumers as a mere means to promoting the welfare of the protected workers.

While permissible (or obligatory) partiality to compatriots is occasionally invoked to justify trade restrictions, the far more common claim is that such measures are necessary to ensure that trade is fair. A careful review of these claims reveals a number of different conceptions of fairness, or arguably, a number of distinct moral complaints only some of which can be understood as specifications or interpretations of the concept of fairness.[13] In what follows, I examine two such arguments. The first, developed by Aaron James, holds that trade is morally defensible only if the gains from trade are distributed fairly, both between states and among the citizens of a single state. The second argument, advanced by Matthias Risse and Gabriel Wollner, defends the claim that norms governing trade are unfair if they enable or facilitate exploitative exchanges of goods and services.

B *Fair Trade and Equitable Outcomes*

Aaron James contends that justice in international trade requires that the gains from trade be distributed equitably.[14] An equitable distribution, he argues, is one that satisfies the following three principles:

> *Collective due care*: Trading nations are to protect people against the harms of trade (either by temporary trade barriers or "safeguards," or, under free trade, by direct compensation or social insurance schemes). Specifically, no person's life prospects are to be worse than they would have been had his or her society been a closed society.
>
> *International relative gains*: Gains to each trading society, adjusted according to their respective national endowments (including population size, resource base, level of development) are to be distributed equally, unless unequal gains flow (say, via special trade privileges) to poor countries.

---

[12] Fernando Teson, "Why Free Trade Is Required by Justice," *Social Philosophy and Policy* 29, 1 (2012): 135.

[13] See David Miller, "Free Trade: What Does It Mean and Why Does It Matter?" *Journal of Moral Philosophy* 14, 3 (2017): 249–69. On the concept/conception distinction, see Hart, *Concept* [pp. 144–59, 1st edition] John Rawls, *A Theory of Justice* (Cambridge, MA: Harvard University Press, 1971), p. 5, Dworkin, *Law's Empire*, p. 71.

[14] Aaron James, *Fairness in Practice: A Social Contract for a Global Economy* (New York: Oxford University Press, 2012).

> *Domestic relative gains*: Gains to a given trading society are to be distributed equally among its affected members, unless special reasons justify inequality of gain as acceptable to each (as, for example, when inequality in rewards incentivizes productive activity in a way that maximizes prospects for the worst off over time).[15]

The first principle speaks to the distribution of the burdens produced by international trade, while the last two address the distribution of the benefits. As some of the parenthetical remarks in James' statement of these principles indicate, they provide the moral rationale for the adoption of a range of trade-related laws and policies. Specifically, they indicate that a just international trade regime may include both limits on free trade, such as infant industry protections that enable developing countries to reap a greater share of the gains from trade than do developed ones, and conditions on free trade, such as domestic social insurance schemes that ensure that the members of no social class end up worse off as a result of trade than they would have been had their country not engaged in it.

James begins his defense of fair trade, understood as a practice of trade that satisfies the three principles specified above, with the following observation: All states face a choice between reducing and raising barriers to trade, between engaging in international trade and pursuing autarky, meaning total economic independence or self-sufficiency.[16] Each state knows that it will achieve greater economic growth if it lowers its own barriers to trade and its trading partners reciprocate, but each is also aware that its neighbors may choose not to reciprocate, instead adopting beggar-thy-neighbor policies that favor their own economic growth at other states' expense. In short, and as was explained in the first section of this chapter, states confront an assurance problem: whether it is rational for them to pursue the greater economic growth international trade can provide depends on how confident they are that other states will cooperate by not adopting beggar-thy-neighbor policies. James argues that an international practice among states of reliance on common markets provides the necessary assurance.[17] That practice consists of norm-governed coordination on policies needed to create and maintain a common market, say, a market in automobiles that spans multiple countries. This coordination is the product of each state's expectation that other states will pursue the policies necessary for a common market, and its responsiveness to a like expectation from those other states. These expectations are set and adjusted in various ways, including multilateral treaties such as the WTO and NAFTA (or USMCA), bilateral treaties such as the United States–Korea Free Trade Agreement, informal diplomatic understandings, and advocacy by interest groups including nongovernmental organizations, multinational corporations, and unions. The goal of spurring economic growth, one shared by all states, provides the organizing aim for this process of negotiating each state's contribution

---

[15]   Ibid, pp. 17–18.
[16]   Ibid, pp. 52–6.
[17]   Ibid, pp. 56–9.

to the collective enterprise of sustaining a common market. In sum, states provide one another with the confidence necessary to overcome the assurance problem they confront by displaying a "willingness to establish a practice of mutual market reliance that will last ... confirm[ing] this over time in routine mutually beneficial commerce, and ... constructively address[ing] new sources of uncertainty as they arise with diplomatic and policy assurances."[18]

On James' account, the possibility of reaping the benefits of international trade depends on a collective undertaking among states. It is their practice of mutual reliance on common markets that creates the norm governed social space in which individuals and firms can engage in the international exchanges of goods and services. As in any case where agents cooperate to produce some good, each has a claim against the others to fair terms of cooperation, or as James puts it, to structural equity. This requires that the international social practice of mutual reliance on common markets be designed so that "it distributes the benefits and burdens it creates according to a pattern that is reasonably acceptable to every country and class affected."[19] As participants in this social practice, contributors to the collective effort to create and sustain the background conditions necessary for international exchanges of goods and services, each of us can ask: "[I]s my country, or my class, or, more specifically, am I, being given fair terms? Can we, or I, find our shared international arrangements reasonably acceptable, given the costs I am [or we are] being asked to bear?"[20] James maintains that only if the international practice of mutual reliance on common markets satisfies the principles of due care, international relative gains, and domestic relative gains can we answer these questions in the affirmative.

As a cooperative undertaking that makes economic growth possible, states' practice of mutual reliance on common markets poses two questions of fair division: first, how should the gains from trade be distributed between states, and second, how should the gains from trade be distributed among the members of each state? In both cases, James maintains that three considerations favor an equal division.[21] First, all participants in the social practice that makes international trade possible are equal in moral status. No state or individual enjoys an inherent moral superiority that entitles it, him, or her to a greater share of the value produced through international exchanges in goods and services. Second, all of the participants in the practice have a similar interest in obtaining greater rather than lesser shares of the net benefit they help to create. No state will accept as a reasonable justification for its receipt of a lesser share of the gains from trade that it simply cares less about these benefits than does a state that receives a greater share. The same is true for individuals within a single state; all else equal, each would rather be richer than poorer. Finally, no

---

[18] Ibid, p. 59.
[19] Aaron James, "A Theory of Fairness in Trade," *Moral Philosophy and Politics* 1, 2 (2014): 179.
[20] James, *Fairness in Practice*, p. 14.
[21] Ibid, pp. 168–79.

state or individual can point to any special entitlements that gives it, him, or her a claim to a greater share of the benefit made possible by the practice of mutual reliance on common markets. In particular, James rejects the claim that states or individuals may be entitled to unequal shares of the gains from trade in virtue of differences in the contributions they make to creating and sustaining a common market. This conclusion rests partly on skepticism regarding the possibility of a nonarbitrary measure of contribution to creating and sustaining a common market, and partly on skepticism regarding the moral importance of contribution in a context where the choice of whether to participate in a cooperative scheme is not fully voluntary. For these three reasons, then, equality provides the default answer to the question of how the gains from trade ought to be distributed. While inequalities in the distribution of the gains from trade are not categorically prohibited, their defense requires an appeal to considerations powerful enough to warrant deviating from equality.

The principle of due care describes one such consideration. It identifies as unfair any reduction in barriers to trade that benefit some members of a society while leaving other members worse off over the course of their entire lifetime than they would have been had their society not engaged in trade.[22] To assess this claim, it may be useful to borrow John Rawls' device of a veil of ignorance.[23] Individuals behind a veil of ignorance lack knowledge of particular facts about themselves or their society. The point is to exclude from deliberation about the rules under which we ought to interact with one another any morally arbitrary considerations, or in other words, to prevent us from selecting rules that are unjustifiably biased in our favor, such that others would rightly view those rules as unfair. Suppose that from behind the veil of ignorance we can choose from three options: R_1 prohibits trade, R_2 involves a change to those rules that opens our society to trade, thereby producing both winners and losers in our society, while R_3 involves a change to the rules that opens our society to trade but also creates a scheme to compensate those who lose out from greater international competition. Under R_3 there are no losers, but there are also fewer winners and/or smaller gains for those who benefit from the reduction of this particular barrier to trade. Since we do not know whether we are among those who stand to benefit or (absent compensation) to lose from our society becoming more open to international trade, we should adopt the standpoint of winners and losers under the three options, and consider from those vantage points the strength of any objection we might have to the pursuit of each option. If we imagine ourselves among the winners, we will object to the pursuit of R_3 over R_2 since this will leave us less well off than we would otherwise be. However, if we imagine ourselves among

---

[22] The qualifier "over the course of their entire lifetime" is crucial here, since initial setbacks may sometimes be compensated for (and then some) in the longer run. For a response to the claim that lowering barriers to trade ultimately benefits everyone, and that therefore no one has a claim to compensation or protection, see James, *Fairness in Practice*, pp. 209–12.

[23] Rawls, *Theory of Justice*, pp. 136–42.

the losers than we will object to the pursuit of R2 over R3, since that is the policy that will leave us worse off. Having imagined ourselves into both positions, we can then consider which objection is the more powerful one. Having thought about it from both perspectives, would we really think it unfair to make some members of our society accept a lesser benefit (or a lesser chance of being a beneficiary) so as to ensure that the change did not worsen the lives of other members of our society? James thinks not: "Other things being equal, the objection 'I am made worse off' is more powerful than 'I could have been better off,' in which case either market protection or compensation of the loser carries the day."[24]

The principle of due care does not protect all members of a society from the harms trade can cause, however. James asserts that the privileged "lack a reasonable objection to being disadvantaged if this provides significant benefits to people who are less well-off, especially given the substantial opportunities for adaptation afforded by their greater wealth."[25] Their ability to recover from the disruptions of trade, and indeed to take advantage of the new opportunities it creates, makes it far more likely that the well-off will receive a net benefit from moves toward a more open economy, at least over the course of their lifetime, than is true for lesser, and especially the least, advantaged people in society. The principle of domestic relative gains also figures here, however, since trade liberalization may sometime mark a significant improvement when measured against that standard even if it also leads to a reduction in the economic well-being of the more advantaged. Put another way, where domestic actors are not morally entitled to (all of) the economic advantages they enjoy, a change in law or policy that deprives them of (some of) those advantages will not be unfair, even if it leaves them worse off than they would otherwise be. For example, trade liberalization may leave a former monopolist worse off while also marking a significant advance in a society's realization of domestic justice.

The need to ensure that no member of our society will be harmed by a policy or law that reduces barriers to trade provides one moral justification for distributing the gains from trade unequally. The prospect of making all members of society better off than they otherwise would be provides a second. In a Rawlsian vein, James notes that "from a domestic point of view, the gains from trade chiefly result from a national-level choice of policy," and that "as the fruit of domestic social cooperation . . . [they] cannot be said to be owned by anyone independently of what distribution is fair."[26] A fair distribution, James suggests, is one that satisfies Rawls' difference principle, which holds that economic inequality is permissible if and only if it works to the

---

[24] James, *Fairness in Practice*, p. 207. Note, however, that because we do have a legitimate interest in growing our income, the winners in R3 have a powerful objection to the pursuit of R1 over R3, while no one has a powerful objection to the pursuit of R3 over R1 (since compensation ensures that no one is made worse off if R3 is adopted than if R1 had been pursued instead).

[25] Ibid, p. 209.

[26] Ibid, p. 219.

greatest benefit of the least advantaged members of society.[27] In general, permitting individuals to keep a greater share of the value they produce motivates them to be more productive, leading in the aggregate to greater economic growth. Even the least well-off in society will find an unequal distribution of the gains from trade reasonably acceptable if they are a necessary feature of an economic order that maximally improves their economic well-being in comparison to what it would be were the gains from trade distributed equally among all members of their society. Thus we arrive at the principle of domestic relative gains, according to which "gains to a given trading society are to be distributed equally among its affected members, unless special reasons justify inequality of gain as acceptable to each."[28]

Turning to the distribution of the gains from trade between states, the principle of international relative gains identifies two bases for deviation from the moral presumption in favor of equality. The first concerns the need to adjust for differences in each state's trade-independent endowments, such as the size of its population, its natural resource base, and cultural norms that affect its citizens' productivity: "Endowment sensitivity simply reflects the limited aim of trade practice, namely to *improve* upon endowments roughly as given (through specialization and exchange), rather than to redistribute the benefits of those endowments as such."[29] Unless we strip out those elements of economic growth that owe to each state's trade-independent endowments, an equal distribution will unfairly transfer to other states some of the income a well-endowed state would have generated even in the absence of trade.

James offers as a second justification for an unequal distribution of the gains from trade between states the fact that an equal division imposes very different opportunity costs on rich and poor states. A fair distribution, he maintains, will give some priority to those who are worse off in absolute terms, since the marginal utility they gain will far exceed the marginal disutility the richest or most developed states lose. James invokes the following analogy to support this conclusion. Suppose two friends regularly dine together, with one paying for their meal on some occasions, and another paying for their meal on others. If their wealth is roughly equal, and so too is the cost of their meal, then fairness requires that they each pay for a (roughly) equal number of meals. But if one diner is far wealthier than the other, then James maintains that she ought to pay for more of their meals together, since the opportunity cost to her of paying for their meals is far less than it is for her companion. The same conclusion holds vis-à-vis the distribution of the gains from trade between states. To insist on an equal division between rich and poor states amounts to prioritizing a relatively small gain for those who are already well off over a larger gain for those who are not.[30]

---

[27] Rawls, *Theory of Justice*, pp. 60–82.
[28] James, *Fairness in Practice*, p. 18.
[29] Ibid, p. 222.
[30] Ibid, pp. 224–5.

Even if James rightly claims that fairness requires that the wealthier diner pay for a greater share of the meals she and her companion take together, we might resist the extension of that claim to the distribution of the gains from trade between states. In particular, friends necessarily have a concern for one another's well-being that states need not (and likely do not), even if they cooperate with one another to create and sustain common markets. A rich friend who failed to pay for a larger share of the meals she shared with her companion could be rightly criticized for her lack of concern with the impact her choice had on her companion's welfare. If we alter the scenario so that the two individuals dine together only because doing so is mutually beneficial – perhaps they get a table more quickly than they would had they each dined alone – then it becomes much more difficult to see how the poorer diner could have a *fairness* claim against the wealthier one that she pay for more of the meals they eat together. That is not the only kind of claim the poorer diner could make, however. If an equal division would threaten her ability to meet her basic needs then she might well have a claim to the rich diner paying for a larger share of the meals they eat together. The same might be true if equal division would significantly lengthen the time it would take the poorer diner to improve her well-being (for instance, by paying for an education). But again, this would not be a matter of fair treatment, neither would it be a claim that could be directed only to the rich diner, since there might be other individuals for whom the opportunity cost of helping the poor diner would be the same or even lower. The same sort of reasoning might well apply in the case of rich states obligations to poor ones. If so, then we can accept James conclusion, namely, that a just international trade regime should allocate a larger share of the (nontrade endowment adjusted) benefits to poor states than to rich ones, while denying his claim that doing so is a matter of fairness, a duty that arises out of the fact that rich and poor states engage in a shared social practice of mutual reliance on common markets.

A second objection to the principle of international relative gains concerns the possibility of distinguishing that portion of a society's economic output for which it is solely responsible from that portion that owes to it engaging in trade with other societies. As Mathias Risse and Gabriel Wollner point out: "[I]n a world that has been more or less densely interconnected for several thousand years, what people are capable of is a function of their history."[31] For example, the use of land in every country on Earth reflects the history of international trade, as crops such as sugar-cane, coffee, cotton, and potatoes were spread across the world in response to market demand. The cultivation of these crops contributed in turn to the spread of new technologies, social mores, and people, including millions of Africans sold into slavery. Given our history, then, it appears to be impossible to separate the portion of a society's economic production that owes to its nontrade endowments from the

---

[31] Mathias Risse and Gabriel Wollner, "Critical Notice of Aaron James, *Fairness in Practice: A Social Contract for a Global Economy*," *Canadian Journal of Philosophy* 43, 3 (2013): 398.

portion that does not. Or as Risse and Wollner put the point: "[I]n an interconnected world we cannot identify any baseline of autarky that could plausibly identify what states can consider *theirs* and thus do not need to share."[32] If so, then the principle of international relative gains gets no purchase on reality, since its applicability depends on a condition that cannot be satisfied in our world.

James use of autarky as a baseline for calculating the effects of trade also poses a problem for the principle of due care. Trade harms a person, James contends, if his or her life goes worse than it would have had his or her society pursued autarky around the time of his or her birth. Christian Barry casts doubt on our ability to discern how well-off a person would be under autarky, pointing out that the challenge of doing so is far greater than predicting the effects of a policy change on the status quo.[33] It is one thing to predict the effects that a 10 percent increase on steel tariffs will have on a society, but a far harder and likely impossible task to predict the effects of completely closing a society to trade (let alone imagining what a society would be like had it never engaged in trade). Moreover, the effects that closing a society to trade will have on its members depends on the type of domestic institutions we postulate in our counter-factual, as well as the foreign policies other states adopt in response to a state closing itself off to trade:

> Were Mexico to have become closed to trade with the USA, for instance, it seems likely that the US posture on immigration from Mexico, and assistance provided to Mexico, would have been quite different. And of course, as the remuneration available through legal trade between Mexico and the USA would diminish, gains available through illicit trade could be expected to increase. Increased returns to engagement in illicit trade with the USA could well be a factor of no small consequence for Mexicans and Mexican state institutions.[34]

As Barry emphasizes, the challenge is not simply one of characterizing what life is like for members of a given society under autarky, but also of selecting nonarbitrarily among the various counterfactual scenarios that could serve as the baseline for identifying harm.

It appears that as a description of the terms under which trade is morally defensible, James' view faces significant challenges.[35] Yet it may be that we should accept some of his conclusions even if we reject his arguments for them, and in particular, his attempt to ground those conclusions in a conception of international trade that generates its own, freestanding, demands of fairness. For example, the moral justifiability of trade rules may depend on their not worsening or undermining

---

[32] Mathias Risse and Gabriel Wollner, "Three Images of Trade: On the Place of Trade in a Theory of Global Justice," *Moral Philosophy and Politics* 1, 2 (2014): 206.

[33] Christian Barry, "The Regulation of Harm in International Trade: A Critique of James' Collective Due Care Principle," *Canadian Journal of Philosophy* 44, 2 (2014): 257.

[34] Ibid, p. 258.

[35] For his responses to some of these challenges, see Aaron James, "Reply to Critics," *Canadian Journal of Philosophy* 44, 2 (2014): 286–304.

states' pursuit of domestic economic justice.[36] If so, then it is possible that reductions in certain trade barriers will need to be accompanied by domestic redistributive programs if they are to be morally defensible. The same may also be true for rules governing innovation, such as intellectual property law. On this approach, trade will not (and should not) be treated as morally distinctive but simply as part of a state's or society's overall economy. Principles of domestic distributive justice apply to the economy as a whole, and therefore any moral assessment of trade rules must be undertaken from a perspective that considers the distribution of all the economic goods and opportunities available, and not just those that are the product of trade.

C *Risse and Wollner on Fair Trade as Non-Exploitation*

Risse and Wollner contend that trade is morally unproblematic only if it is not exploitative, from which it follows that norms governing trade are morally unproblematic only if they do not facilitate exploitative trade.[37] Starting from a colloquial description of exploitation as one person's taking unfair advantage of another, they argue that this idea is best characterized in terms that reference both features of the transaction between the agents and the outcome or state of affairs it produces. Specifically, they define exploitation as "a transfer T or a distribution D between two parties A and B, which arise as a consequence of an interaction I, enabled by some *ex ante* feature F, violating some moral principle P such that the moral defect cannot be readily reduced to a defect of either T, D, I, or F."[38] This last clause, which distinguishes the wrong of exploitation from other types of wrongdoing, need not detain us. More important for our purposes is the fact that so defined exploitation can encompass different types of unfair advantage taking, distinguishable from one another in terms of the interaction, transfer or distribution, ex ante feature, and/or moral principle P that must be violated in order for an act to count as exploitative.

Two examples serve to illustrate this point, while also offering support for the claim that in order to be morally unproblematic trade must not be exploitative. Consider, first, exploitation as taking advantage of a wrong. Hillel Steiner maintains that a voluntary, mutually beneficial, exchange between A and B is exploitative if in virtue of a rights violation that occurred prior to the exchange B benefits less from the exchange than she would have had that rights violation not taken place.[39] While A might have been the perpetrator of the rights violation, and B the victim, neither of these conditions is necessary for the transaction between them to count as an instance of exploitation as taking advantage of a wrong. Rather, "the wrong in [this type of] exploitation is to *benefit* from an unrectified wrong, combining the

---

[36] Barry, "Regulation of Harm," 262.
[37] Risse and Wollner, "Three Images of Trade," 210–21.
[38] Ibid, p. 215.
[39] Hillel Steiner, "Exploitation: A Liberal Theory Amended, Defended, and Extended," in *Modern Theories of Exploitation*, ed. A. Reeve (London: Sage, 1987), pp. 132–48.

wrongness of the original violation with a subsequent transfer or distribution."[40] To illustrate, Risse and Wollner argue that some domestic workers in state S who earn lower wages as a result of foreign competition may be victims of this type of exploitation. This will be so if these foreign competitors drive down their production costs by violating people's rights; for instance, by treating their labor force in ways that violate those workers' rights to adequate health and safety, or by acquiring land in ways that unjustly deprive its rightful owners of their property rights. Workers in state S do not suffer these rights violations, and employers in state S do not perpetrate them. Nevertheless, the latter still wrong the former by taking advantage of the unjust treatment of foreign workers to pay their own workers less than they would need to pay them if those foreign workers or property owners were not being treated unjustly. Of course, employers in state S will likely respond that they can only remain in business if they pay these lower wages, since their products must compete with those produced by rights-violating foreign enterprises. The real culprits are the domestic consumers who choose to buy whichever goods are cheapest, or at least they are complicit in the exploitation of these domestic workers by domestic employers. The imposition of tariffs on the goods produced by rights-violating foreign enterprises that eliminate whatever price advantage they gain from their wrongdoing may be the best or only way to effectively address this particular injustice. While those tariffs may not eliminate or rectify the rights violations, they will prevent domestic employers and consumers from taking advantage of those rights violations to pay domestic workers less in return for their labor or the products they produce.

A second form of exploitation involves taking advantage of the vulnerable. Following Robert Goodin, Risse and Wollner maintain that "it is inappropriate to play for advantage when others are (a) not doing so, (b) unfit to do so or are no match to us, or (c) suffering a misfortune."[41] These conditions capture seemingly widespread intuitions regarding fair play or fair competition. Consider, for example, a sporting contest in which players forbear from taking advantage of an injury to their competitor. If pressed to defend their conduct, the players will likely respond that while the rules of the game grant them the right to press their advantage, it would not be fair or "sporting" of them to do so. Likewise, teams that demonstrate a clear superiority over their competitors often refrain from pressing their full advantage; for instance, by not attempting to score as often as they might, or by giving their less talented or experienced members more playing time than they would against better competition. These practices suggest that the propriety of distributing goods on a competitive basis is conditional on the quality of the competition. With respect to international trade, individuals who suffer the deprivations constitutive of multidimensional poverty may be unable to compete in any meaningful way in international markets. Even those who are not poor may be at a severe disadvantage vis-à-vis

---

[40]   Risse and Wollner, "Three Images of Trade," 217, emphasis added.

[41]   Ibid, p. 218. See Robert Goodin, "Exploiting a Situation and Exploiting a Person," in *Modern Theories of Exploitation*, ed. A. Reeve (London: Sage, 1987), p. 185.

foreign competitors if they lack access to relevant information or the education necessary to make use of it. Finally, the small size of some states' domestic economies together with their lack of political and legal expertise may leave them unable to effectively "compete" with richer states, both in the negotiation of trade rules and in their use of those rules to garner the benefits to which they are legally entitled. In such circumstances, individuals, firms, and states that choose to (fully) press their advantage over their much less able competitors wrong them by exploiting their vulnerability. As in the case of a sporting competition, the (full) benefits the more powerful accrue cannot be justified on the grounds that they were earned in a fair competition.

The charge that some element of contemporary international trade or international trade law is exploitative raises two questions. First, is it accurate? Second, if it is, then how should we respond? Consider the claim that trade in products manufactured in sweatshops is unjust, and that to the extent they permit or encourage such trade, so too are international trade agreements. The alleged injustice of sweatshops owes partly to the factory owners' violations of their workers' (moral, and possibly also legal) rights, partly to their exploitation of those workers, and partly to the fact that it enables other employers in that industry to pay their own workers lower wages, as explained above. If we employ the taking advantage of a wrong conception of exploitation, the claim that sweatshops involve exploitation requires demonstrating that sweatshop owners wrong their workers when they subject them to working conditions well outside those legally permitted in developed countries.[42] This may prove difficult if we concede that sweatshop workers are morally entitled to waive their rights to better working conditions, something they may well be willing to do in exchange for a greater income than they would otherwise be able to earn.[43] Indeed, where low labor costs account for a firm's competitive advantage, improved labor conditions may lead to fewer jobs, or be incompatible with the firm remaining in business at all.[44] If so, then it is hard to see why that firm's workers would not consent to lower labor standards, and arguably why they should not be free to do so. It follows that sweatshops do not necessarily wrong their employees by requiring them to work in conditions that deviate considerably from those required by law in developed countries. At least where the employees consent to work in these conditions, their employers do not engage in exploitation as taking advantage of a wrong, and therefore neither do employers in developed countries who are able to pay their workers a lower wage as a consequence of competition from foreign sweatshops.

---

[42]   I use the phrase "well outside those legally permitted in developing countries" to indicate that the argument does not turn on workers in developing countries counting as exploited unless they enjoy the same or a close approximation to the wages and working conditions enjoyed by workers in developed countries.

[43]   Teson, "Why Free Trade," 145.

[44]   Benjamin Powell and Matt Zwolinski, "The Ethical and Economic Case Against Sweatshop Labor: A Critical Assessment," *Journal of Business Ethics* 107, 4 (2012): 456–60.

Even if the labor conditions characteristic of sweatshops do not constitute the taking advantage of a wrong, they may still be an example of employers taking advantage of the vulnerable, and so qualify as a form of exploitation. The success of such an argument depends on whether it is open to the factory owners, the alleged exploiters, to forbear from pressing their advantage against their workers as much as they do. Sometimes, and perhaps even often, this may not be the case. Again, a sweatshop owner may be unable to employ as many workers or to remain in business if he or she allows labor costs to rise. If so, then the labor conditions are dictated by the market, that is, the choices of all of the producers and consumers of the good in question, rather than by the factory owner enjoying an overwhelming advantage in negotiating the terms of employment with his or her workers. Of course, that does not mean no one is taking unfair advantage of the vulnerable employed in sweatshops. Some firms may enjoy large enough profits that they can afford to drive a less hard bargain with sweatshop workers, for instance, by requiring the factories where their products are made to meet more demanding health and safety standards, and compensating the factory owners for the additional cost. Corrupt political and legal officials may also be the primary agents of exploitation if, for example, sweatshop owners' inability to provide better working conditions while staying in business owes to the bribes these officials demand, or if they actively seek to disrupt workers' efforts to organize and advocate for better treatment (to which they may already be entitled as a matter of law).[45] Finally, it may be that many individuals living in developed countries are most guilty of exploiting vulnerable workers in developing ones. As consumers, they (we) generally choose to pay less for a good rather than buy a more expensive version of the same good that is not produced in a sweatshop. As citizens, we severely limit the number of vulnerable people we allow to immigrate, a policy that deprives both would-be immigrants and those who would remain in their country of origin of many opportunities to better their lives. In short, the root cause of much exploitation may lie not with trade or the rules that regulate it, but instead with political practices and policies in both developing and developed countries that leave many workers with no better option than to labor in sweatshop conditions.

As the foregoing arguments indicate, the claim that sweatshops exploit workers in developing countries and facilitate the exploitation of workers in developed ones is debatable. Nevertheless, suppose it is true. What follows? The answer might seem obvious: since exploitation is wrong, we should at least refrain from complicity in it, and perhaps also take steps to end it. For developed countries, this might take the form of trade barriers that serve to protect domestic workers against the wage and job losses that follow from exposure to this sort of unfair competition, while lowering the payoffs to sweatshop owners of engaging in exploitation. Yet this conclusion may be premature. Higher barriers to trade in goods produced in sweatshops will cause some

---

[45]   Ibid, 467.

of those employed there to lose their jobs, or to work under even worse conditions and/or for even lower wages. If citizens in developed countries have a duty to alleviate poverty wherever it exists, then perhaps that duty outweighs or defeats our duty to refrain from exploiting our fellow citizens who work in an industry that competes with imports from sweatshops. That is, reducing or eliminating barriers to trade in goods produced in sweatshops may be the morally correct course of action all things considered, even if this enables the exploitation of those who work in them as well as domestic workers who compete with them. As Risse and Wollner observe, "exploitation might even be the right thing to do, the smaller evil all things considered."[46] Of course, this conclusion depends on the absence of any alternative policy or set of policies that achieves roughly the same reduction in poverty without permitting nearly the same level of exploitation. Arguably, the last several hundred years of human development provide compelling evidence that no such alternative is forthcoming. Nevertheless, actors in both developing and developed nations have duties to mitigate the harms exploitation causes, and to take measures that will reduce or eliminate it without requiring them to bear too high a moral cost. For example, workers in a developed country who lose their jobs or suffer reductions in their wages may well have a claim to some form of compensation from their fellow citizens. This could be the case if the losses they suffer are greater than what they are morally required to bear to alleviate global poverty, while that is not true of their compatriots. Even if this is not the case, these workers may bear more than their fair share of the cost of alleviating global poverty while their compatriots bear less, in which case the former have at least a prima facie claim to compensation from the latter.

Now consider a second allegedly exploitative feature of the legal regime that regulates international trade, the World Trade Organization's dispute settlement system. In addition to setting out rules governing international trade, the WTO treaty created a dispute settlement process to resolve disagreements among the signatories over the interpretation and application of those rules. This process, overseen by a Dispute Settlement Body (DSB) composed of representatives from all the members of the WTO, begins with consultations between the states who are party to a dispute. If these states fail to resolve their disagreement, the complainant state may submit the dispute for adjudication by a WTO Panel. After hearing from both sides to the dispute (and sometimes from third-party states who formally express an interest in it), the Panel members issue a report, or judgment, in favor of one or the other of the parties to the dispute. The state that loses before this panel may appeal its judgment to the WTO's Appellate Body, which may uphold, modify, or overturn the panel's report. The decisions of the WTO's Appellate Body are the final word on the question of whether a state's domestic law or policy violates its obligations under the WTO treaty. Barring a consensus against doing so, the WTO treaty

[46] Risse and Wollner, "Three Images of Trade," 221.

requires the DSB to formally adopt any report issued by a Panel or the Appellate Body.[47]

A state that loses its case before the Appellate Body must, within a reasonable amount of time, implement those changes to its domestic law or policy necessary to bring it into conformity with the WTO treaty. If it fails to do so, and does not settle with the complainant state, the DSB authorizes the complainant state to retaliate by suspending concessions or other obligations it has to the defaulting state under the WTO agreement that equal in value the losses it has suffered as a result of the latter's violation of its treaty obligations. To be clear, the WTO does not itself enforce the Dispute Settlement Body's judgments; rather, it authorizes the victorious party in a dispute, and only that state, to enforce its rights under the WTO treaty through a limited form of "self-help."

The design of the WTO's enforcement mechanism entails that a complainant state's ability to effectively press for the treatment to which it is legally entitled largely depends on how powerful it is relative to the state denying it that treatment. Imagine a trade dispute between a relatively poor, weak, state such as Bangladesh, Haiti, or Malawi and a rich, powerful, state such as the United States and Japan, or a supra-state polity such as the European Union. The cost to poor state P of raising tariffs or imposing quotas on imports from rich state R will often be quite significant, at least for the population of P as a whole, both immediately and in terms of its effect on future economic growth. Those costs may easily outweigh any benefit P stands to gain from R complying with the WTO agreement, particularly if R prefers to bear whatever costs follow from P raising barriers to its exports. Furthermore, P may have good reason to fear that if it adopts such measures in an attempt to enforce its rights, R may retaliate by modifying its relationship with P in domains other than trade. Suppose, as is often the case, that R provides P with development aid or training programs for P's police force and equipment for its military. In such circumstances, P may rightly worry that any tariffs it imposes on imports from R will be met with a reduction in the assistance R provides it. If poor, weak, states cannot effectively enforce their legal rights under the WTO agreement against rich, powerful, states, then the latter are free to effectively renegotiate the terms on which they actually trade so as to maximize their gains. In doing so, rich powerful states exploit poor/weak ones; they play for (maximal) advantage in the market when poor states are unfit to do so or no match for them.[48]

The process for bringing a dispute to the WTO and successfully making the case that another state is acting in breach of its legal obligations also unfairly favors rich

[47] See "Understanding the WTO: Settling Disputes," available at www.wto.org/english/thewto_e/whatis_e/tif_e/disp1_e.htm.
[48] For a recent empirical investigation of many of these issues, see Arie Reich, "The Effectiveness of the WTO Dispute Settlement System: A Statistical Analysis," *European University Institute Working Papers* (2017), available at https://cadmus.eui.eu/bitstream/handle/1814/47045/LAW_2017_11.pdf?sequence=1 (last accessed December 10, 2019).

powerful states over poor weak ones. The latter often lack lawyers and diplomats who can identify when their state is a victim of another state's violation of the WTO agreement, and who possess the expertise necessary to compete with officials from better off states when presenting their state's case before a WTO panel or the Appellate Body. Efforts undertaken since its inception to address the fact that poor states are unfit to take advantage of the opportunities the WTO Dispute Settlement Understanding formally offers them have had little impact. For instance, while the WTO has determined that poor states may employ lawyers in private practice with expertise in international trade law to argue on their behalf, the cost of doing so precludes many poor states from pursuing this option. Likewise, rich states have stymied efforts to allow poor states to recover their litigation costs if they win their case before the WTO. Finally, while organizations such as the Advisory Center for WTO Law provide poor states with legal advice, most rich states have provided few if any resources to support such efforts.[49]

While impossible to deny, these moral shortcomings with the design and operation of the WTO dispute settlement system should not be exaggerated. For instance, the foregoing argument is deliberately framed in terms of a comparison between poor weak states and rich powerful ones, rather than between developing and developed states. Developing countries are not all equally poor and weak. While the economic (and military, political, and cultural) power states such as Brazil or India exercise is still inferior to that exercised by some developed countries, especially the United States, this does not appear to prevent them from making good use of the WTO dispute settlement process, or from using tariffs and other measures to enforce DSB rulings in their favor. Moreover, in the majority of the trade disputes brought before the WTO developed countries are both the complainant and the respondent. Perhaps, then, the actual workings of the WTO's dispute settlement system frequently raise no concern regarding exploitation. Of course, that may simply reflect a prudent choice by poor states not to avail themselves of a dispute settlement system that hides their exploitation behind a veneer of legality.

The WTO's enforcement mechanism suffers from a second moral defect, in addition to permitting or facilitating rich, powerful, state's exploitation of poor, weak, ones. Suppose states have a moral obligation to reduce and ultimately eliminate barriers to trade, one grounded in a fundamental moral duty to promote human welfare, or to alleviate poverty, or to respect individual rights of contract and property. If so, then a just trade agreement ought to serve this end, not only in the legal obligations it places on states to reduce or eliminate barriers to trade, but also in the design of its mechanism for enforcing those obligations. That is, in a just trade agreement enforcement ought to serve the goal of motivating states to fulfill their legal obligations under that agreement. However, the WTO's enforcement

[49] For further discussion, see Kim Van der Borght, "Justice for All in the Dispute Settlement System of the World Trade Organization?" *Georgia Journal of International and Comparative Law* 39, 3 (2011): 787–806.

mechanism serves a different goal, namely, maintaining whatever balance of benefits and burdens the parties to the dispute negotiated on their entry into the treaty,
or in a subsequent round of trade negotiations.[50] It is true that WTO officials express
a preference for maintaining this balance through states' conformity to the terms of
the WTO agreement; that is, by fulfilling their obligations to reduce or eliminate
trade barriers. Yet the WTO's enforcement mechanism does not reflect this preference; rather, it is ambivalent between a state of affairs in which two states both
adhere to the WTO agreement and a state of affairs in which they each raise barriers
to trade against the other, so long as those barriers impose equal costs on the two
states. Appearances to the contrary, then, the WTO does not create *genuine* obligations, considerations that preclude certain sorts of legislation and policymaking.
Instead, it merely attaches prices to engaging in such legislation or policymaking.[51]
While this enables states to better pursue their interests in light of their relative
power, it contributes to the advancement of both freer and fairer trade only when
such policies coincide with what states perceive to be in their national interest. In
the terms introduced in Chapter 5, the WTO provides an example of rule by law, but
not the rule of law.

What sort of reforms to its enforcement mechanism might make the WTO
a better vehicle for promoting free trade – and so, we are assuming, advance the
realization of justice? Joost Pauwelyn suggests that enforcement become a collective
undertaking, with all members of the WTO authorized to impose countermeasures
designed to motivate a defaulting state to comply with its obligations.[52] This differs
from the current practice both in terms of who would be authorized to enforce the
law – at present, only the successful complainant state – and in terms of the costs that
could be imposed on the defaulting state, which could exceed the value of the trade
losses that state's noncompliance imposed on other states. Additionally, Pauwelyn
maintains that complainant states (and perhaps others as well) be granted a right to
reparation for any losses they have suffered as a result of a defaulting state's violation
of its obligation(s) under the WTO agreement.[53] Collectively, these reforms might
well deter states from engaging in prohibited forms of protectionism even in many
cases where it would be worthwhile for them to so under the present regime, one that
makes such illegal conduct far less costly. Furthermore, as Pauwelyn emphasizes,
these reforms would contribute to a change in how states conceive of their obligations under the WTO treaty. Instead of viewing them as products of a private
contract, instruments for their pursuit of national interest in light of their relative
power, states would come to understand those obligations as genuine constraints on

[50] Joost Pauwelyn, "Enforcement and Countermeasures in the WTO: Rules are Rules – Toward a More
     Collective Approach," *American Journal of International Law* 94, 2 (2000): 339–40.
[51] Warren F. Schwartz and Alan O. Sykes, "The Economic Structure of Renegotiation and Dispute
     Resolution in the World Trade Organization," *Journal of Legal Studies* 31, 1 – Part 2 (January 2002):
     S179–S204.
[52] Pauwelyn, "Enforcement and Countermeasures," 343.
[53] Ibid, 346.

permissible conduct, a specification of their contribution to the promotion of the shared aim of global economic growth, and conduct for which the society of states can properly hold them accountable. In other words, Pauwelyn's proposed reforms would lead states to conceive of their trade relations with one another as the pursuit of the global common good in accordance with the international rule of law.

IV TRADE IN STOLEN GOODS

For trade to be just, those who participate in it must have a right to dispose of the goods they exchange, or be authorized to do so by those who do have such a right. It follows that the justice of an international trade regime depends on the norms governing the acquisition and continued possession of rights to dispose of various goods. Thomas Pogge contends that the global institutional order suffers from a serious moral defect in this respect because it tacitly endorses the principle "might makes right."[54] By and large, international practice grants those who effectively govern a state the right to determine ownership of goods in its territory, regardless of how they came to power and, with a few exceptions, regardless of how they exercise it. Pogge focuses on the implications this practice has for the extraction and sale of natural resources located within a state's territory, including oil, diamonds, and metals such as tantalum and tungsten that are used in cellphones and laptop computers. He argues that, as far as international law is concerned, a dictator enjoys the legal authority to allocate property rights in a state's natural resources even if he came to power in a coup, regularly persecutes any of his subjects who oppose his continued rule, and governs in a corrupt and arbitrary manner that deprives many citizens or residents of the state of their basic human rights.[55] If the dictator grants a firm the legal right to extract oil from a portion of the state's territory, international law treats that oil as the firm's legal property, and permits it to sell the oil in other states, where buyers likewise obtain a legal property right in the oil.

Leif Wenar argues that international law does not require states to accord domestic property rights to natural resources extracted from states ruled by tyrants.[56] From the standpoint of international law, neither recognition of Saudi Arabia as a sovereign state nor recognition of the Saudi King (or the House of Saud) as its government requires that the United States, China, India, or any other country grant those who import Saudi oil a clear title to that oil under its domestic law, one they can transfer to domestic companies who purchase and refine it, or domestic consumers who buy the resulting gasoline. The decision to do so lies within the

---

[54] Thomas Pogge, *World Poverty and Human Rights* (Cambridge: Polity Press, 2002), pp. 112–13.
[55] The incentives it creates to launch a coup, and to use whatever means necessary to remain in power, constitutes a further moral defect of the international legal norm that empowers those who exercise effective control over a territory to create, modify, or extinguish property rights over natural resources that lie within it. See Pogge, *World Poverty*, p. 113.
[56] Leif Wenar, *Blood Oil: Tyrants, Violence, and the Rules that Run the World* (New York: Oxford University Press, 2016), pp. 111–13.

discretion of each sovereign state. Contemporary practice is the result of state's independently converging on "might makes right" as the basis for jurisdiction over natural resources, not the product of a collective determination, expressed in international law, that this should be the case.[57]

Furthermore, Wenar maintains that international law actually denies tyrannical governments an entitlement to exercise jurisdiction over the natural resources that lie within the territory of the state they rule.[58] Although they may exercise effective control over those resources, they lack the legal standing needed to alter existing property rights, or to create property rights in newly discovered oil, diamonds, cobalt, and so on. Wenar's defense of this claim begins with the observation that nearly every state in the world is party to the International Covenant on Civil and Political Rights and the International Covenant on Economic, Social, and Cultural rights, both of which begin by declaring in their first article that "all peoples may, for their own ends, freely dispose of their natural wealth and resources," and conclude by asserting "the inherent right of all peoples to enjoy and utilize fully and freely their natural wealth and resources."[59] Together, these two passages evince a commitment to popular resource sovereignty: the right of the people of each country to freely control the resources of their country.[60] In virtue of their agreement to these Human Rights Conventions, states have an international legal obligation to refrain from facilitating trade in natural resources extracted from tyrannical states; that is, states ruled by governments that deny the people sovereignty over their natural resources. It follows that in granting domestic property rights to natural resources that originate in tyrannical states, states that are party to ICCPR and/or ICESCR violate international law.

Like all of the rights contained in these Human Rights Covenants, popular resource sovereignty constrains and conditions a government's exercise of political power. Since it is the people who have a right to freely dispose of their natural wealth and resources, a government may create legally valid property rights in those resources only if the people have authorized it to do so. Furthermore, in exercising the authority granted to it by the people, the government must pursue the people's enjoyment and full utilization of their natural wealth and resources. In the language of the Natural Resources Declaration adopted by the UN General Assembly in 1962, the people's right over their natural resources must be exercised "in the interest of their national development and of the well-being of the people of the state concerned."[61] However, the fact that popular resource sovereignty is but one of the rights included in these conventions indicates that they are not the only

---

[57] Ibid, 115–17.
[58] Ibid, 190–207.
[59] Quoted in Wenar, *Blood Oil*, p. 196.
[60] Ibid, p. 197.
[61] "Permanent sovereignty over natural resources," United Nations General Assembly Seventeenth Session, Resolution No. A/RES/1803/(XVII), December 14, 1962.

constraint on the exercise of political power. Rather, Wenar maintains that "the group rights of popular sovereignty in Article 1 are limited by the human rights of individuals in the articles that follow."[62]

Government provides an institutional mechanism whereby the people of a state can exercise their sovereignty over the natural resources that lie within the state's territory. Of course, not every government plays this role. Rather, the government of a particular state acts as an agent of the people only if the latter enjoy at least bare-bones civil liberties and basic political rights.[63] The former includes rights that protect citizens' access to information regarding the management of their resources, such as the costs involved in their extraction and the distribution of the resulting revenue, as well as rights that enable them to publicly debate their state's natural resource policies without having to fear imprisonment, torture, or death. Only where the rule of law effectively protects citizens' freedom of speech, freedom of assembly, and the freedom of the press can a government plausibly claim to be authorized to act on behalf of the governed. Moreover, the people must possess those political rights necessary to hold the government accountable for the policies it pursues: "If a majority of citizens strongly disagree with what the government is doing with the country's resources, government policy must change to reflect this within a reasonable time."[64] Importantly, Wenar's concern is not with the defense of an ideal of representation or accountability but instead with the description of a minimum threshold that must be met if a government is to have any reasonable claim to act as the agent of a state's citizens. Such a strategy seems defensible given how many resource-rich states fail to cross even that threshold, and the hardly coincidental fact that many of the world's worst injustices take place in or at the hands of those states.

On Wenar's account, international law already contains morally defensible norms governing the exercise of jurisdiction over natural resources. The problem lies in states' failure to comply with those norms. The horizontal (or primitive) structure of the international legal order rules out certain strategies for addressing this problem. There are no international police available to enforce states' legal obligations to honor popular resource sovereignty, neither is it likely that the society of states will collectively perform that task. Indeed, it is not clear what sorts of measure states are legally permitted to take to enforce other states' compliance with their legal obligation to respect popular resource sovereignty. However, Wenar argues that international law does permit certain sorts of unilateral action by states that could put an end to much of the trade in stolen natural resources. He starts with the observation, noted above, that international law does not require states to grant property rights in their domestic legal order to natural resources extracted from other states. It follows

---

[62] Wenar, *Blood Oil*, p. 206.
[63] Ibid, p. 228.
[64] Leif Wenar, "Beyond Blood Oil," in *Beyond Blood Oil*, Wenar et al. (Lanham, MD: Rowman & Littlefield, 2018), p. 16.

that states can uphold their legal obligation to respect popular resource sovereignty by enacting two *domestic* laws.[65] The first is a Clean Trade Act that would make it illegal for actors within the state's jurisdiction to purchase natural resources extracted from territory ruled by governments that fail to meet minimal standards of accountability to their citizens. For example, were the United States or Japan to enact such a law companies in those countries would not be legally permitted to purchase oil from states such as Saudi Arabia, Russia, or Angola, or tantalum from the Democratic Republic of Congo. Of course, countries such as China or Vietnam might continue to purchase oil from states ruled by tyrannical governments, and use some of it to manufacture goods they export to developed liberal-democratic countries such as the United States or Japan. Therefore, Wenar urges the latter states to enact a second domestic law, which he labels the Clean Hands Trust. This law would impose tariffs on the import of goods manufactured using oil purchased from tyrannical governments. All else equal the value of those tariffs would be equivalent to the value of the oil imported from such states. The money raised by the tariff would be set aside in a trust for the people whose oil had been stolen by their tyrannical government, to be handed over to them once that government had been replaced by one that satisfied the minimum standards of accountability required by the principle of popular resource sovereignty.

These tariffs will be costly for United States and Japanese citizens, of course, but then as we saw in our earlier discussion of exploitation, no one is morally entitled to benefit from another's purchase of stolen goods. Moreover, in combination with the fact that they would likely become the primary target of attacks by the revolutionary movements tyranny inevitably spawns, these tariffs might well provide China, Vietnam, and others with an incentive to reduce or end altogether their oil imports from states ruled by tyrannical governments. Without the income necessary to buy the support of a minority and the arms necessary to oppress the majority, these governments will find it exceedingly difficult to remain in power without embarking on the reforms necessary to conform to the principle of popular resource sovereignty.

Unilateral changes in domestic law constitute the first steps in advancing states' respect for popular resource sovereignty. At this stage, international law's primary contribution consists in its presentation of a clear and nearly universally agreed on statement of who enjoys jurisdiction over natural resources. Activists can invoke international law to help make the case for the adoption of domestic Clean Trade laws. Yet a convergence by an increasing number of states on roughly similar domestic Clean Trade laws might lead in turn to changes in international law that further serve the aim of maximizing compliance with popular resource sovereignty. For example, whether through legislation (that is, a new round of treaty negotiations), administrative rulemaking, or judicial interpretation multilateral trade rules might change in ways that sanction states' collective enforcement of popular

---

[65] Wenar, *Blood Oil*, pp. 283–91.

resource sovereignty, and that make it a morally defensible and effective means for reducing trade in stolen goods. At this point, international law and institutions would begin to play an independent role in shaping the conduct of governments and other actors.

Wenar's argument has been subject to many criticisms. Some of these reflect a misunderstanding of the position he defends. For instance, while Wenar contends that the people of a state enjoy ultimate jurisdiction and original ownership rights over the natural resources located within the state's territory, that does not entail that those resources must be owned or managed by the state. Rather, popular resource sovereignty is compatible with a range of different legal regimes governing natural resources, including transferring ownership over particular resources to private companies, or licensing private companies to manage state-owned resources. The key points are that (a) the choice of a particular type of legal regime governing natural resources must be made by a government with a reasonable claim to be acting as the agent of the people, and (b) the people always retain the right to change whatever legal regime they had previously implemented (via a sufficiently responsive government).[66]

A second set of objections take issue with one or another of the empirical claims on which Wenar rests his argument. The claim that a Clean Trade Act or Clean Hands Trust will never be adopted, or that they will not make any difference to the ability of tyrannical governments to remain in power by selling (the right to extract) stolen natural resources, are two examples.[67] A third set of objections contest the moral permissibility or obligatoriness of the means Wenar proposes for advancing respect for popular resource sovereignty. The refusal to trade with a resource-rich state ruled by a tyrannical government may well impose enormous costs on the citizens of that state, perhaps even the deaths of many thousands who would otherwise not die. If so, then we have a weighty moral reason not to enact the Clean Trade policies Wenar defends. Yet if a refusal to trade makes a state responsible for these deaths, then its participation in trade with a resource-rich state ruled by a tyrannical government must also make it responsible for all the harms that follow from that choice. Perhaps both claims rest on a problematic understanding of moral responsibility for others' suffering. But if not, the question is which policy is likely to produce more rights violations, which then points us to empirical questions regarding the likely timeline for a transition to a minimally accountable government, and the number and kind of rights violations likely to occur prior to and during that transition.[68] Consider, too, that a state's adoption of a Clean Trade Act

---

[66] Ibid, p. 206.
[67] See, for example, the essays by Michael Blake and Nazrin Mehdiyeva in *Beyond Blood Oil*, Leif Wenar et al. (Lanham, MD: Rowman & Littlefield, 2018).
[68] If acts constitute graver wrongs than do omissions, as some maintain, then there is some moral reasons to favor refusing to trade over trading, apart from a concern with the number and severity of the rights violations the rival trade policies will produce.

and a Clean Hands Trust will impose significant costs on that state's citizens, who may have a moral right against bearing too great a burden in order to benefit distant others. Yet the fact that foregoing the purchase of stolen goods will be costly for me is not generally a compelling moral justification for proceeding with the purchase.

A last set of objections consist of moral challenges to popular resource sovereignty. What makes a group of individuals a people with a claim to sovereignty over resources within a given territory? Why do they (and they alone?) have a right to sovereignty over the natural resources located in some territory T, and why that particular territory? To some extent these questions were taken up in Chapter 9.[69] Wenar adopts a broadly consequentialist (or, arguably, pragmatist) method to answer these questions, one that focuses on responding to or mitigating existing injustices, evaluates rival norms in terms of which is better (or less bad) rather than trying to determine what norm would be best or ideal, and takes considerations of feasibility into account from the very start.[70] While he acknowledges that the citizenry of a given state may be composed of members of distinct peoples – for instance, in the case of the United Kingdom, the English, the Scots, the Welsh, and the Northern Irish – he nevertheless argues that international law rightly limits popular resource sovereignty to the citizens of a state while according no right to independent statehood to such "peoples within a people." That is because "the state system that allocates territories to national peoples is justified by the monumentally important human goods that this system produces: peace, prosperity, and freedom – and because we have scarcely any feasible idea of how we could reallocate power to do better."[71]

Wenar likewise dismisses as unrealistic the argument that human beings own the Earth in common, and so are all entitled to a share of the value created by the extraction of natural resources from any place on the planet. Specifically, he contends that unlike popular resource sovereignty, common ownership of the world is not a widely shared moral ideal, and so any attempt to implement a global resource tax and redistribution program that rests on that ideal will be viewed as illegitimate. If principles of justice are to guide our conduct, Wenar argues, they must be responsive to the world in which we actually live. At present, there is simply too little social cohesion and trust across borders to support a global resource tax and redistribution program.

Theorists who ground principles of global justice in common ownership of the Earth may accept this conclusion, while still defending their own view as a correct account of a fully just world. The same is true for those who advance rival accounts

---

[69] Note that the considerations that morally justify jurisdiction over human interactions with specific natural resources, and that spell out the scope of that jurisdiction, may differ in some respects from those that morally justify jurisdiction over other domains of human conduct.

[70] "The best practical reasoning is about reaching the best future we can, thinking through the likely results of our actions and how our actions will affect the balance among the many things that have real value." Wenar, *Beyond Blood Oil*, p. 155. See also Lefkowitz, "Institutional Moral Reasoning," 391–7.

[71] Wenar, "Beyond Blood Oil," 147. See also Wenar, *Blood Oil*, p. 260.

of the people entitled to sovereignty over resources. In their eyes, Wenar may offer a compelling pragmatic argument we can act on now, but even if successful the program he proposes will only mark a moral improvement in our international practices, not the realization of a just global order. Wenar finds this position unconvincing. He readily concedes that popular resource sovereignty may not always be the morally optimal norm governing the allocation of jurisdiction over natural resources. However, he expresses a deep skepticism toward ideal theoretical accounts of global justice or resource rights that make no real effort to explain how the institutions they describe will manage the stresses imposed by actual human beings, or how we can transition from our current arrangements to the ones these theorists identify as fully just. In this regard, Wenar is representative of a growing number of political and legal philosophers who take the history and current practice of international law as the starting point for their normative theorizing, and who offer modest and empirically informed proposals for its improvement.[72]

---

[72] See, for instance, Buchanan, *Justice, Legitimacy, and Self-Determination*; Ratner, *Thin Justice of International Law*; Pavel, *Divided Sovereignty*; and Lefkowitz, "Institutional Moral Reasoning."

Bibliography

BOOKS AND ARTICLES

Adams, N.P. "Institutional Legitimacy," *Journal of Political Philosophy* 26, 1 (2018): 84–102.

Alkire, Sabina, et al. "Global Multidimensional Poverty Index 2019: Illuminating Inequalities." Oxford Poverty and Human Development Initiative (2019). Last accessed December 10, 2019. https://ophi.org.uk/wp-content/uploads/G-MPI_Report_2019_PDF .pdf.

Altman, Andrew. "The Persistent Fiction of Harm to Humanity," *Ethics and International Affairs* 20, 3 (2006): 367–72.

Altman, Andrew and Christopher Heath Wellman. *A Liberal Theory of International Justice*. Oxford: Oxford University Press, 2009.

Austin, John. *The Province of Jurisprudence Determined*. London: University of London, 1832.

Bakke, Kristin M. and Erik Wibbels. "Diversity, Disparity, and Civil Conflict in Federal States," *World Politics* 59, 1 (2006): 1–50.

Barry, Christian. "The Regulation of Harm in International Trade: A Critique of James' Collective Due Care Principle," *Canadian Journal of Philosophy* 44, 2 (2014): 255–63.

Beckett, Jason A. "The Hartian Tradition in International Law," *Journal of Jurisprudence* 1 (2008): 51–83.

Beitz, Charles R. *The Idea of Human Rights*. Oxford: Oxford University Press, 2009.

Bellamy, Alex J. and Paul D. Williams. "On the Limits of Moral Hazard: The Responsibility to Protect, Armed Conflict, and Mass Atrocities," *European Journal of International Relations* 18, 3 (2012): 539–71.

Besson, Samantha. "The Authority of International Law: Lifting the State Veil," *Sydney Law Review* 31, 3 (2009): 343–80.

  "State Consent and Disagreement in International Law-Making: Dissolving the Paradox," *Leiden Journal of International Law* 29, 2 (2016): 289–316.

  "International Human Rights Law and Mirrors," *ESIL Reflections* 7, 2 (2018): 1–11.

  "In What Sense Are Economic Rights Human Rights? Departing from Their Naturalistic Reading in International Human Rights Law." In *Economic Liberties and Human Rights*, eds. Jahel Queralt and Bas van der Vossen. New York: Routledge, 2019, pp. 45–68.

Bingham, Tom. *The Rule of Law*. London: Penguin UK, 2010.

Bodansky, Daniel. "Legitimacy in International Law and International Relations." In *Interdisciplinary Perspectives on International Law and International Relations: The State of the Art*, eds. Jeffrey L. Dunoff and Mark A. Pollack. New York: Cambridge University Press, 2013, pp. 321–41.

Buchanan, Allen. *Justice, Legitimacy, and Self-Determination: Moral Foundations for International Law*. Oxford: Oxford University Press, 2004.

The Heart of Human Rights. Oxford: Oxford University Press, 2013.

"Secession." In *The Stanford Encyclopedia of Philosophy* (Fall 2017 Edition), Edward N. Zalta (ed.), https://plato.stanford.edu/archives/fall2017/entries/secession/.

"Institutional Legitimacy." In *Oxford Studies in Political Philosophy, Volume 4*, eds. David Sobel, Peter Vallentyne, and Steven Wall. Oxford: Oxford University Press, 2018, pp. 53–78.

Buchanan, Allen and Robert Keohane. "The Legitimacy of Global Governance Institutions," *Ethics and International Affairs* 20, 4 (2006): 405–37.

Buchanan, Allen and Russell Powell. "Constitutional Democracy and the Rule of International Law: Are they Compatible?" *Journal of Political Philosophy* 16, 3 (2008): 326–49.

Buchanan, Allen and Gopal Sreenivasan. "Taking International Legality Seriously: A Methodology for Human Rights." In *Human Rights: Moral or Political?*, ed. Adam Etinson. Oxford: Oxford University Press, 2018, pp. 211–29.

Capps, Patrick. "International Legal Positivism and Modern Natural Law." In *International Legal Positivism in a Post-Modern World*, eds. J. Kammerhofer and J. d'Aspremont. Cambridge: Cambridge University Press, 2014, pp. 213–40.

Chehtman, Alejandro. "Contemporary Approaches to the Philosophy of Crimes Against Humanity," *International Criminal Law Review* 14, 4–5 (2014): 813–35.

Chesterman, Simon. "I'll Take Manhattan: The International Rule of Law and the UNSC," *Hague Journal on the Rule of Law* 1 (2009): 67–73.

Christiano, Thomas. *The Constitution of Equality: Democratic Authority and Its Limits*. New York: Oxford University Press, 2008.

"Democratic Legitimacy and International Institutions." In *The Philosophy of International Law*, eds. Samantha Besson and John Tasioulas. New York: Oxford University Press, 2010, pp. 119–37.

"Is Democratic Legitimacy Possible for International Institutions?" In *Global Democracy: Normative and Empirical Perspectives*, eds. Daniele Archibugi, Mathias Koenig-Archibugi, and Rafaele Marchetti. New York: Cambridge University Press, 2011, pp. 69–95.

"Legitimacy and the International Trade Regime," *San Diego Law Review* 52, 5 (2015): 981–1012.

"Ronald Dworkin, State Consent, and Progressive Cosmopolitanism." In *The Legacy of Ronald Dworkin*, eds. Wil Waluchow and Stefan Sciaraffa. New York: Oxford University Press, 2016, pp. 49–69.

Cohen, G.A. *Self-Ownership, Freedom, and Equality*. Cambridge: Cambridge University Press, 1995.

Cohen, Jean L. "The Uses and Limits of Legalism: On Patrick Macklem's *The Sovereignty of Human Rights*," *University of Toronto Law Journal* 67, 4 (2017): 512–43.

Collins, Richard. *The Institutional Problem in Modern International Law*. Oxford: Hart Publishing, 2016.

Cotterrell, Roger. "What Is Transnational Law?," *Law and Social Inquiry* 37, 2 (2012): 500–24.

Craven, Matthew. "Statehood." In *International Law, 4th Edition*, ed. Malcolm D. Evans. Oxford: Oxford University Press, 2014, pp. 201–47.

Crawford, James. "International Law and the Rule of Law," *Adelaide Law Review* 24, 1 (2003): 3–12.

Dagger, Richard. *Civic Virtues: Rights, Citizenship, and Republican Liberalism*. New York: Oxford University Press, 1997.

Playing Fair: Political Obligation and the Problems of Punishment. New York: Oxford University Press, 2018.

d'Aspremont, Jean. *Formalism and the Sources of International Law*. New York: Oxford University Press, 2011.

Dill, Janina and Henry Shue. "Limiting the Killing in War: Military Necessity and the St. Petersburg Assumption," *Ethics and International Affairs* 26, 3 (2012): 311–33.

Duff, R.A. *Punishment, Communication, and Community*. Oxford: Oxford University Press, 2001.

    Answering for Crime: Responsibility and Liability in the Criminal Law. Oxford: Hart Publishing, 2007.

    "Authority and Responsibility in International Criminal Law." In *The Philosophy of International Law*, eds. Samantha Besson and John Tasioulas. Oxford: Oxford University Press, 2010, pp. 589–604.

Dworkin, Ronald. "Model of Rules I." In *Taking Rights Seriously*. Cambridge, MA: Harvard University Press, 1978.

    "What Is Equality? Part 1: Equality of Welfare," *Philosophy and Public Affairs* 10, 3 (1981): 185–246.

    "What Is Equality? Part 2: Equality of Resources," *Philosophy and Public Affairs* 10, 4 (1981): 283–345.

    A Matter of Principle, Cambridge, MA: Harvard University Press, 1985.

    Law's Empire. Cambridge, MA: Harvard University Press, 1986.

    Justice in Robes. Cambridge, MA: Harvard University Press, 2006.

    Justice for Hedgehogs. Cambridge, MA: Harvard University Press, 2011.

    "A New Philosophy for International Law," *Philosophy and Public Affairs* 41, 1 (2013): 2–30.

Erman, Eva. "Global Political Legitimacy Beyond Justice and Democracy," *International Theory* 8, 1 (2016): 29–62.

Estlund, David. *Democratic Authority*. Princeton: Princeton University Press, 2008.

Finnis, John. *Natural Law and Natural Rights*. Oxford: Clarendon Press, 1980.

Fuller, Lon L. "Positivism and Fidelity to Law: A Reply to Professor Hart," *Harvard Law Review* 71, 4 (1958): 630–72.

    The Morality of Law, rev. ed. New Haven: Yale University Press, 1969.

    The Principles of Social Order: Selected Essays of Lon L. Fuller, ed. Kenneth I. Winston. Durham, NC: Duke University Press, 1981.

Garcia, Frank J. *Global Justice and International Economic Law: Three Takes*. New York: Cambridge University Press, 2013.

Gardner, Stephen. "A Core Precautionary Principle," *Journal of Political Philosophy* 14, no. 1 (2006): 33–60.

Ghoshal, Neela and Kyle Knight, "Rights in Transition: Making Legal Recognition for Transgender People a Global Priority," last modified 2016, available at www.hrw.org /world-report/2016/rights-in-transition.

Goodin, Robert. "Exploiting a Situation and Exploiting a Person," in *Modern Theories of Exploitation*, ed. A. Reeve (London: Sage, 1987), pp. 166–200.

    Reflective Democracy. New York: Oxford University Press, 2003.

Hart, H.L.A. "Are There Any Natural Rights?" *Philosophical Review* 64, 2 (1955): 175–91.

    The Concept of Law, 3rd Edition. New York: Oxford University Press, 2012.

Haque, Adil Ahman. "Law and Morality at War," *Criminal Law and Philosophy* 8, 1 (2014): 79–97.

    Law and Morality at War. Oxford: Oxford University Press, 2017.

Hathaway, Oona and Scott J. Shapiro. "Outcasting: Enforcement in Domestic and International Law," *Yale L.J.* 121 (2011): 252–349.

Hausman, Daniel M. and Michael S. McPherson. *Economic Analysis, Moral Philosophy, and Public Policy, 2nd Edition.* Cambridge: Cambridge University Press, 2006.

Henkin, Louis. *How Nations Behave: Law and Foreign Policy, 2nd Edition.* New York: Columbia University Press, 1979.

Higgins, Rosalyn. "The ICJ and the Rule of Law," speech delivered at the United Nations University, April 11, 2007, http://archive.unu.edu/events/files/2007/20070411_Higgins_speech .pdf (last visited October 25, 2019).

Horowitz, Donald. "A Right to Secede?" In *Secession and Self-Determination, NOMOS XLV,* eds. Stephen Macedo and Allen Buchanan. New York: New York University Press, 2003, pp. 50–76.

Ignatieff, Michael. "Enemies vs. Adversaries." *New York Times,* October 16, 2013, www .nytimes.com/2013/10/17/opinion/enemies-vs-adversaries.html (last accessed December 11, 2019).

International Committee of the Red Cross. "Law and War." www.icrc.org/en/war-and-law (last accessed January 10, 2020).

James, Aaron. *Fairness in Practice: A Social Contract for a Global Economy.* New York: Oxford University Press, 2012.

"Reply to Critics," *Canadian Journal of Philosophy* 44, 2 (2014): 286–304.

"A Theory of Fairness in Trade," *Moral Philosophy and Politics* 1, 2 (2014): 177–200.

Kemoklidze, Nino. "The Kosovo Precedent and the 'Moral Hazard' of Secession," *Journal of International Law and International Relations* 5, 2 (2009): 117–40.

Kleinfeld, Joshua. "Skeptical Internationalism: A Study of Whether International Law Is Law," *Fordham Law Review* 78 5 (2010): 2452–530.

Klosko, George. *The Principle of Fairness and Political Obligation.* Lanham, MD: Rowman & Littlefield, 1992.

Kumm, Mattias. "The Legitimacy of International Law: A Constitutionalist Framework of Analysis," *European Journal of International Law* 15, 5 (2004): 907–31.

Kuperman, Alan J. "The Moral Hazard of Humanitarian Intervention: Lessons from the Balkans," *International Studies Quarterly* 52, 1 (2008): 49–80.

Lafont, Cristina. "Should We Take the 'Human' Out of Human Rights? Human Dignity in a Corporate World," *Ethics and International Affairs* 30, 2 (2016): 233–52.

Lamond, Grant. "The Rule of Law." In *The Routledge Companion to Philosophy of Law,* ed. Andrei Marmor. New York: Routledge, 2012, pp. 495–507.

Lazar, Seth. "The Morality and Law of War." In *The Routledge Companion to Philosophy of Law,* ed. Andrei Marmor. New York: Routledge, 2012, pp. 364–79.

Lee, Win-Chiat. "The Judgeship of All Citizens: Dworkin's Protestantism About Law," *Law and Philosophy* 34, 1 (January 2015): 23–53.

Lefkowitz, David. "The Principle of Fairness and States' Duty to Obey International Law," *Canadian Journal of Law and Jurisprudence* 24, no. 2 (2011): 327–46.

"Sources in Legal Positivist Theories: Law as Necessarily Posited and the Challenge of Customary Law Formation." In *The Oxford Handbook of the Sources of International Law,* eds. Samantha Besson and Jean d'Aspremont. Oxford: Oxford University Press, 2017, pp. 323–42.

"International Law, Institutional Moral Reasoning, and Secession," *Law and Philosophy* 37, 4 (2018): 385–413.

"A New Philosophy for International Legal Skepticism?" Draft on file with author.

Leiter, Brian. "Explaining Theoretical Disagreement," 76 U. Chi. L. Rev. 1215 (2009).

Lister, Matthew. "The Legitimating Role of Consent in International Law," *Chicago Journal of International Law* 11, 2 (2011): 664–91.

Luban, David. "Natural Law as Professional Ethics: A Reading of Fuller," *Social Philosophy and Policy* 18, 1 (Winter 2001): 176–205.

"A Theory of Crimes Against Humanity," *Yale Journal of International Law* 29, 1 (2004): 85–167.

Luban, David. "Fairness to Rightness: Jurisdiction, Legality, and the Legitimacy of the International Criminal Court." In *The Philosophy of International Law*, eds. Samantha Besson and John Tasioulas. Oxford: Oxford University Press, 2010, pp. 569–88.

"Human Rights Pragmatism and Human Dignity." In *Philosophical Foundations of Human Rights*, eds. Rowan Cruft, S. Matthew Liao, and Massimo Renzo. Oxford: Oxford University Press, 2015, pp. 263–78.

Ma, Xuechan and Shaui Guo. "An Empirical Study of the Voting Patterns of Judges of the International Court of Justice (2005–2016)," *Erasmus Law Review* 10, 3. (2017): 163–74.

Marmor, Andrei. *Philosophy of Law*. Princeton: Princeton University Press, 2011.

May, Larry. *Crimes Against Humanity: A Normative Account*. Cambridge: Cambridge University Press, 2004.

"Humanity, International Crime, and the Rights of Defendants," *Ethics and International Affairs* 20, 3 (2006): 373–82.

McMahan, Jeff. "The Ethics of Killing in War," *Philosophia* 34, 1 (2006): 23–41.

"The Morality of War and the Law of War." In *Just and Unjust Warriors*, eds. David Rodin and Henry Shue. Oxford: Oxford University Press, 2008, pp. 19–43.

Meisels, Tamar. "In Defense of the Defenseless: The Morality of the Laws of War," *Political Studies* 60, 4 (2012): 919–35.

Miller, David. "Secession and the Principle of Nationality." In *National Self-Determination and Secession*, ed. Margaret Moore. Oxford: Oxford University Press, 1998, pp. 62–78.

National Responsibility and Global Justice. Oxford: Oxford University Press, 2007.

"Nationalism." In *The Oxford Handbook of Political Theory*, eds. John S. Dryzek, Bonnie Honig, and Anne Phillips. Oxford: Oxford University Press, 2008, 529–45.

"Territorial Rights: Concept and Justification," *Political Studies* 60, 2 (2012): 252–68.

"Joseph Raz on Human Rights: A Skeptical Appraisal." In *Philosophical Foundations of Human Rights*, eds. Rowan Cruft, S. Matthew Liao, and Massimo Renzo. Oxford: Oxford University Press, 2015, pp. 232–43.

Miscevic, Nenad. "Nationalism." In *The Stanford Encyclopedia of Philosophy* (Summer 2018 Edition), Edward N. Zalta (ed.), https://plato.stanford.edu/archives/sum2018/entries/nationalism/.

Moore, Margaret. "The Ethics of Secession and a Normative Theory of Nationalism," *Canadian Journal of Law and Jurisprudence* XIII, 2 (July 2000): 225–50.

A Political Theory of Territory. Oxford: Oxford University Press, 2015.

Mouffe, Chantal. *The Democratic Paradox*. London: Verso, 2000.

Murphy, Liam. *What Makes Law*. Cambridge: Cambridge University Press, 2014.

Nickel, James. "Human Rights." *The Stanford Encyclopedia of Philosophy* (Summer 2019 Edition), Edward N. Zalta (ed.), https://plato.stanford.edu/archives/sum2019/entries/rights-human/.

Nollkaemper, André. *National Courts and the International Rule of Law*. Oxford: Oxford University Press, 2011.

Norman, Wayne. "Ethics of Secession as the Regulation of Secessionist Politics." In *National Self-Determination and Secession*, ed. Margaret Moore. Oxford: Oxford University Press, 1998, pp. 34–61.

Nozick, Robert. *Anarchy, State, and Utopia*. New York: Basic Books, 1974.

Owens, David. "In Loco Civitatis: On the Normative Basis of the Institution of Refugeehood and Responsibilities for Refugees." In *Migration in Political Theory: The Ethics of Movement and Membership*, eds. Sarah Fine and Lea Ypi. New York: Oxford University Press, 2016, pp. 269–90.

Pauwelyn, Joost. "Enforcement and Countermeasures in the WTO: Rules Are Rules – Toward a More Collective Approach," *American Journal of International Law* 94, 2 (2000): 335–47.

Pavel, Carmen. *Divided Sovereignty: International Institutions and the Limits of State Authority*. Oxford: Oxford University Press, 2015.

"Is International Law a Hartian Legal System?" *Ratio Juris* 31, 3 (2018): 307–25.

Pavel, Carmen and David Lefkowitz. "International Legal Skepticism," *Philosophy Compass*, 13, 8 (2018): 1–14.

Payandeh, Mehrdad. "The Concept of International Law in the Jurisprudence of H.L.A. Hart," *European Journal of International Law* 21, 4 (2011): 967–95.

Pogge, Thomas. *World Poverty and Human Rights*. Cambridge: Polity Press, 2002.

Posner, Eric A. and John C. Yoo, "Judicial Independence in International Tribunals," *California Law Review* 93, 1 (January 2005): 3–74.

Postema, Gerald. "Custom, Normative Practice, and the Law," *Duke Law Journal* 62, 3 (2012): 707–38.

Ratner, Steven R. *The Thin Justice of International Law: A Moral Reckoning of the Law of Nations*. Oxford: Oxford University Press, 2015.

Rawls, John. *A Theory of Justice*. Cambridge, MA: Harvard University Press, 1971.

Raz, Joseph. *The Authority of Law*. Oxford: Clarendon Press, 1979.

"The Problem of Authority: Revisiting the Service Conception," *Minnesota Law Review* 90, 4 (2006): 1003–1044.

"Human Rights Without Foundations." In *The Philosophy of International Law*, eds. Samantha Besson and John Tasioulas. Oxford: Oxford University Press, 2010, pp. 321–37.

"Human Rights in the Emerging World Order." In *Philosophical Foundations of Human Rights*, eds. Rowan Cruft, S. Matthew Liao, and Massimo Renzo. Oxford: Oxford University Press, 2015, pp. 217–31.

"On Waldron's Critique of Raz on Human Rights." In *Human Rights: Moral or Political?*, ed. Adam Etinson. Oxford: Oxford University Press, 2018, pp. 139–43.

Reeves, Anthony R. "Liability to International Prosecution: The Nature of Universal Jurisdiction," *European Journal of International Law* 28, 4 (2017): 1047–67.

Regan, Donald. *Utilitarianism and Cooperation*. Oxford: Oxford University Press, 1980.

Reich, Arie. "The Effectiveness of the WTO Dispute Settlement System: A Statistical Analysis," *European University Institute Working Papers*, 2017, https://cadmus.eui.eu/bitstream/handle/1814/47045/LAW_2017_11.pdf?sequence=1 (last accessed December 10, 2019).

Renzo, Massimo. "A Criticism of the International Harm Principle," *Criminal Law and Philosophy* 4, 3 (2010): 267–82.

"Crimes Against Humanity and the Limits of International Criminal Law," *Law and Philosophy* 31, 4 (2012): 443–76.

Risse, Mathias and Gabriel Wollner. "Critical Notice of Aaron James, *Fairness in Practice: A Social Contract for a Global Economy*," *Canadian Journal of Philosophy* 43, 3 (2013): 382–401.

"Three Images of Trade: On the Place of Trade in a Theory of Global Justice," *Moral Philosophy and Politics* 1, 2 (2014): 201–25.

Rodin, David. "Morality and Law in War." In *The Changing Character of War*, eds. Hew Strachan and Sibylle Scheipers. Oxford: Oxford University Press, 2011, pp. 446–63.

Sambanis, Nicholas and Jonah Schulhofer-Wohl, "What's in a Line?" *International Security* 34, 2 (2009): 82–118.

Schwartz, Warren F. and Alan O. Sykes. "The Economic Structure of Renegotiation and Dispute Resolution in the World Trade Organization," *Journal of Legal Studies* 31, 1 – Part 2 (January 2002): S179–S204.

Shue, Henry. "Do We Need a 'Morality of War?'" In *Just and Unjust Warriors*, eds. David Rodin and Henry Shue. Oxford: Oxford University Press, 2008, pp. 87–111.

"Laws of War, Morality, and International Politics: Compliance, Stringency, and Limits," *Leiden Journal of International Law* 26, 2 (2013): 271–92.

Simmons, A. John. *Justification and Legitimacy: Essays on Rights and Obligations*. New York: Cambridge University Press, 2001.

Sirosky, David S. "Explaining Secession." In *The Ashgate Research Companion to Secession*, eds. Aleksander Pavkovic and Peter Radan. Burlington, VT: Ashgate Publishing, 2011, pp. 45–79.

Sloss, David L. and Michael P. Van Alstine. "International Law in Domestic Courts." In *Research Handbook on the Politics of International Law*, eds. Wayne Sandholtz and Christopher A. Whytock. Northampton, MA: Edward Elgar Publishers, 2017, pp. 79–115.

Steiner, Hillel. "Exploitation: A Liberal Theory Amended, Defended, and Extended." In *Modern Theories of Exploitation*, ed. A. Reeve. London: Sage, 1987, pp. 132–48.

Stilz, Anna. *Territorial Sovereignty: A Philosophical Exploration*. Oxford: Oxford University Press, 2019.

Tamanaha, Brian. "A Concise Guide to the Rule of Law." In *Relocating the Rule of Law*, eds. Gianluigi Palombella and Neil Walker. Portland, OR: Hart Publishing, 2009, pp. 3–16.

"The History and Elements of the Rule of Law," *Singapore Journal of Legal Studies* (December 2012): 232–47.

Tasioulas, John. "The Legitimacy of International Law." In *The Philosophy of International Law*, eds. Samantha Besson and John Tasioulas. New York: Oxford University Press, 2010, pp. 97–116.

"On the Nature of Human Rights." In *The Philosophy of Human Rights: Contemporary Controversies*, eds. Gerhard Ernst and Jan-Christoph Heilinger. Berlin: Walter de Gruyter, 2011, pp. 17–59.

"Exiting the Hall of Mirrors: Morality and Law in Human Rights." In *Political and Legal Approaches to Human Rights*, eds. Tom Campbell and Kylie Bourne. London, Routledge, 2017, pp. 73–89.

Teson, Fernando R. "Why Free Trade Is Required by Justice," *Social Philosophy and Policy* 29, 1 (2012): 126–53.

Thurer, Daniel and Thomas Burri. "Secession." In *The Max Planck Encyclopedia of Public International Law*, ed. Rudiger Wolfrum. Oxford: Oxford University Press, 2009.

Van der Borght, Kim. "Justice for All in the Dispute Settlement System of the World Trade Organization?" *Georgia Journal of International and Comparative Law* 39, 3 (2011): 787–806.

Vernon, Richard. "What Is Crime Against Humanity?" *Journal of Political Philosophy* 10, 3 (2002): 231–49.

"Crime Against Humanity: A Defense of the 'Subsidiarity' View," *Canadian Journal of Law and Jurisprudence* 26, 1 (2013): 229–41.

Waldron, Jeremy. "The Core of the Case Against Judicial Review," *Yale Law Journal* 115, 6 (April 2006): 1346–406.

"The Rule of International Law," *Harvard Journal of Law and Public Policy* 30, 1 (Fall 2006): 15–30.

"The Concept and the Rule of Law," *Georgia Law Review* 43, 1 (Fall 2008): 3–61.

"International Law: 'A Relatively Small and Unimportant' Part of Jurisprudence?" In *Reading HLA Hart's "The Concept of Law,"* eds. L. Duarte d'Almeida, J. Edwards, and A. Dolcetti. Oxford: Hart Publishing, 2013, pp. 209–26.

"The Rule of Law." In *The Stanford Encyclopedia of Philosophy* (Fall 2016 Edition), Edward N. Zalta (ed.), https://plato.stanford.edu/archives/fall2016/entries/rule-of-law/.

Walzer, Michael. *Just and Unjust Wars,* 5th Edition. New York: Basic Books, 2015.

Watts, Arthur. "The International Rule of Law," *German Yearbook of International Law* 36 (1993): 15–45.

Weber, Max. "Politics as Vocation." In *Max Weber: Essays in Sociology,* eds. H.H. Gerth and C. Wright Mills. New York: Oxford University Press, 1946, pp. 2–48.

Wellman, Christopher. "The Morality of Secession." In *Secession as an International Phenomenon: From America's Civil War to Contemporary Separatist Movements,* ed. Dan H. Doyle. Athens, GA: University of Georgia Press, 2010, pp. 19–36.

Wenar, Leif. *Blood Oil: Tyrants, Violence, and the Rules that Run the World.* New York: Oxford University Press, 2016.

World Trade Organization. "Understanding the WTO: Settling Disputes." Last accessed December 10, 2019, www.wto.org/english/thewto_e/whatis_e/tif_e/disp1_e.htm.

Zimmermann, Andreas. "Times Are Changing – and What About the International Rule of Law Then?" www.ejiltalk.org/times-are-changing-and-what-about-the-international-rule -of-law-then/ (published March 5, 2018; last accessed October 25, 2019).

CASES

Factory at Chorzow (Germ. v. Pol.), 1927 P.C.I.J. (ser. A) No. 9 (July 26).
Riggs v. Palmer, 115 NY 506, 22 N.E. 188 (1889).

LEGAL DOCUMENTS

International Covenant on Civil and Political Rights, December 16, 1966, United Nations, Treaty Series, vol. 999, p. 171, available at https://treaties.un.org/doc/publication/unts/ volume%20999/volume-999-i-14668-english.pdf.

International Covenant on Economic, Social and Cultural Rights, December 16, 1966, United Nations, Treaty Series, vol. 993, p. 3, available at https://treaties.un.org/doc/Publication/ UNTS/Volume%20993/v993.pdf.

International Law Commission, Report on the Work of Its Sixty-Ninth Session, UN Doc. A/ 72/10 (September 11, 2017), available at https://legal.un.org/ilc/reports/2017/.

United Nations Human Rights Council, *Protection Against Violence and Discrimination Based on Sexual Orientation and Gender Identity: Resolution/Adopted by the Human*

Rights Council, July 15, 2016, A/HRC/RES/32/2, available at https://digitallibrary.un.org /record/845552?ln=en.

United Nations Office of the High Commissioner for Human Rights (OHCHR), *Born Free and Equal: Sexual Orientation and Gender Identity in International Human Rights Law*, September 2012, HR/PUB/12/06, available at www.ohchr.org/Documents/Publications/ BornFreeAndEqualLowRes.pdf.

United Nations, *Charter of the United Nations*, October 24, 1945, 1 UNTS XVI.

United Nations General Assembly, *Convention Relating to the Status of Refugees*, July 28, 1951, United Nations Treaty Series, vol. 189, p. 137.

United Nations General Assembly Seventeenth Session, Resolution No. A/RES/1803/(XVII), December 14, 1962.

United Nations General Assembly, Protocol Relating to the Status of Refugees, January 31, 1967, United Nations Treaty Series, vol. 606, p. 267.

United Nations General Assembly, 2005 World Summit Outcome Document, "A Responsibility to Protect," A/RES/60/1, available at www.globalr2p.org/media/files/ wsod_2005.pdf (accessed December 18, 2019).

United Nations General Assembly resolution 67/97, *The Rule of Law at the National and International Levels*, A/RES/67/97 (December 14, 2012).

United Nations Security Council, *The Rule of Law and Transitional Justice in Conflict and Post-Conflict Societies: Report of the Secretary-General*, August 23, 2004, UN Doc. S/ 2004/616.

Universal Declaration of Human Rights, December 10, 1948, 217 A (III), available at www .un.org/en/universal-declaration-human-rights/.

Index

Lightning Source UK Ltd.
Milton Keynes UK
UKHW020138190521
383969UK00019B/411

9 781316 503584